So, you want to fish?

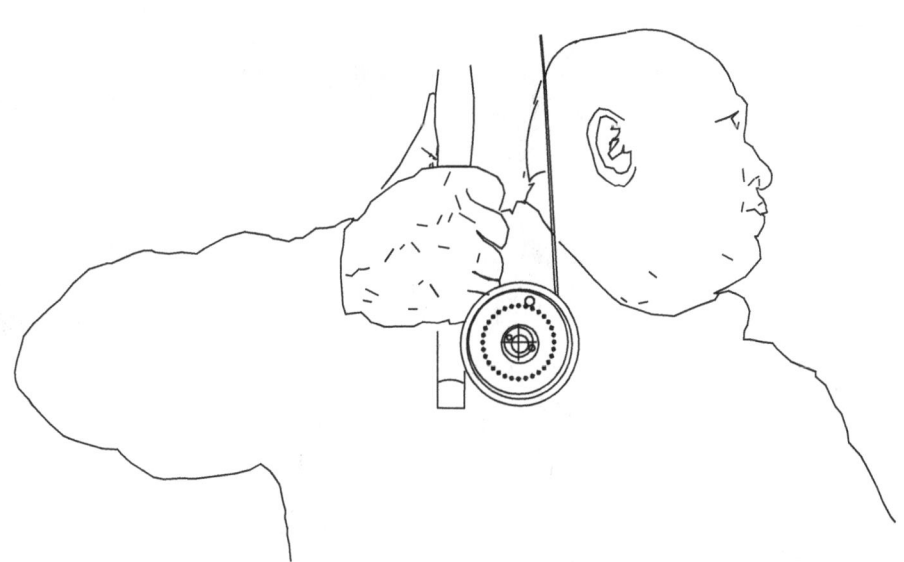

Self-portrait of the author as a sketch

First edition completed in June 2016. The book was conceptualized in 1999 with notes being filed and developed through the years.
Work began on the manuscript in earnest in May 2013.
All illustrations done personally by the author.

The author and his great-nephew Jibrael.

Photograph by Wendy Duncan Chundra

So, you want to fish?
Farhad Manjoo

Edited by experience

Publisher: Farhad Manjoo
2016

Copyright © 2017 by Farhad Manjoo

All rights reserved. This book or any portion thereof may not be reproduced or used in any manner whatsoever without the express written permission of the publisher except for the use of brief quotations in a book review or scholarly journal.

First printing by lulu.com.

ISBN: 978-0-620-72086-1

Farhad Manjoo – Author, publisher.
553 Jabu Ndlovu Street
Pietermaritzburg, KwaZulu Natal, South Africa, 3201

www.farhadmanjoo1818@gmail.com

Dedication

My brother Baboo [Feizal Manjoo] for introducing me to my two passions: fishing and snooker when I was just 5 years old. Mr Shaick and his sons Hansa and Hanief who lived on our property. Mr Rajah Moodley and Pulen with their Valiant 100, blue Mercedes and later the Chevrolet Record – so many trips.... My friend Moosa from Noorani Mansions. Mr Asmall from George Street. Shunny Naicker [Vasen Naicker's father who stopped me from walking from Loop Street in Pietermaritzburg to Peatties' Lake [now Albert Falls Dam]]. 'Whitee' [Arthur Major], now in Cape Town. My besties Semigan [Thumbee] Padayachee, Kooben Chetty, Shaun Padayachee, Deenadayalan Vather, Jayaseelan David, Sandy Moodley, Sunil Maharaj, Riekie, Jabolani, Sipho, Mayashviran Chetty, Dushi Chetty, Kammy Chetty, Boeres, Ilan Lax, Alwyn Volsum [Windy], Christopher Brice [also the best chef I know], Michael Brice, Angus Burns [of 'Crapulets' fame] Vassie [from **Logie Govender & Associates]**. *Sean Pillay [another damn good chef]and Sujata, Nush, Shannon Naicker, Karthigesan Padayachee, Vinodh Singh. My cousin Ajith Khanaye and his son, Tashen. Preggie Govender from Estcourt [now in Richards Bay / Empangeni/Port Shepstone - his boat is called "charou"]. Daniel Paul, Bhai Beharie and Abed Yousuf. Rishalin Naidoo [Winterton].*

Adv Yoga Moodley and Deshaine, his son. Adv Ravi Padayachee, Mark Mungal and his son Kiano. Jameel "James" [ex **Telkom]**, *Tony [**SAPS**], Mike [**Telkom**], Collin [Howick] and his brother Hitraj Vidhyshagar, Farouk [Shakil's, now Allandale drive selling fresh fish], Fareed and Cappo [Vinay Sewpersadh]. Gonnie [**SD Pathers**]. Peter Wickham. Kim Moodley [**Southern Carpets**]. Daya Gounden. Jasvinder Singh Sandhu [**USA**]. Dai Hughes [Wales, United Kingdom]. Deolin and Dershan Chetty and their dad, Vicky. Kevin Randall of the "Royal Salute". Lionel Peters. Jan van Heerden from Golden Lays farm in Cramond, now working somewhere in Mpumalanga. Yuri Singh from Durbz. Jayesh Mahabir from Winterton and his brother, Sanjay Mahabir now in Vereeniging / Vanderbijlpark. Friedel Kaiser from Rosewood Farms. Garreth Olivier now in* **UKZN**. *Guru Roopai. Vernon Naidoo. Trevor G Sweeney & Mike Fitzsimons. John Chetty [Port Shepstone]. Sergie and Kiashen Bremiah. Pranil Bookhan. Raj, Anita and Reva Gopie. Arthur Govender and Dalonkee from Dundee. Ramakrishna Moodley. Reagan Govender. Shiraz Manjoo. Siva Chetty. Thashen Naidoo [Twin]. Derrick Peters. Tyrone Harris. Varma Parag. Vaughn and Kenneth John. Dr Rajendra Moodley [**AUSTRALIA**]. Kapilar, Santanu and Dr Krishna Moodley. Renugaye Padayachee. Sergie and Babes [Santosh Balram]. Mahendra Gokul. Hamlook who caught iguana with his bare hands...*

*Kevin, Premla, little Abigail and Basil [Kyle] from Mossel Bay. Ahmed, Essop, Chico and Bilal Haffejee [**Atlas Sports**]. Mark, Ian and Robbie from* **Rochester Tackle**. *My cousins Kresen Manicum [Umhlanga] and Krissie who owns* **SPORTFISHER** *in Pietermaritzburg.* **Basil Manning Tackle**. **FRIENDS** *fishing club whose constitution I wrote all those years ago...* **FOSAF** *[Federation of South African Flyfishers] of which I remain a committee member. Erhard Fourie, Johnny, Hans and Dion Sookdaw [Ex* **Trotech**], *Martin Tollman and Paul Meintjies [**Trotech**]. My cousins Pravesh, Thosh, Radhi and Dees, Anusuyah and Larry, Gitanjali and Daniel and my Uncles Yeshwanth and Arthmanand. Bapoo, 'Milee from Cape Town. Keagan Naicker and his beautiful family; Shailum Moodley from Newcastle. Sunil Mungaroo [**SASOL**] and his brother-in-law Sanjeev Bikramjith from Newcastle. Shahir and Shahan Chundra. Siyalan Padayachee. Mrs Eric Narainsamy from Standerton who would encourage me to catch fish and Vanita Narainsamy who never got to go fishing with me ☺. Daya Gounden and Anil Dhanooklal. Ian Reeves. Ragu and Rishen Naidoo from Tongaat. Preggie Moodley. Yureshan Cooper who never got to go fishing with me; Tahir and Raj Ramchundra. Bojan from Macedonia. Jean-Paul from Mauritius. Bart Schmidt from Namibia. George from Poenskop. Ajay from Mezeppa Bay. Donald from Coffee Bay, Jantjies from Steenbras dam on the Brede river in the Western Cape. Dhenesh Garib from Howick. George Harripersad. Eugene, Aroosha and Tristan. And those so many other people who contributed in one way or another to my passion. And MaGic Baits a product that gives bait fishing an edge!*

My Mum and Dad, authors by their own right; and family, and friends, and Thashni, Cappo [Vinay Sewpersadh], Vasen and Thash Naicker, Russel Aldrin Naidoo, and Reva, Anita and Raj Gopie [Dundee] for the encouragement and for believing in me. My Granny who loved eels and Semigan's mother, Rajimbal Padayachee who would prepare delicious meals for me from my fishing and hunting exploits.

And for you, my amazing forever children: Davita and Adushan Pillay, Shailum Moodley, Siyalin Padayachee, Davina Maya Chetty, Dershan & Deolin Chetty, Liam Parag, Olivia Celine Pillay, Jehan and Ariel Sandhu, Talia John, Ravi Kumaran Chetty, Mikka Parag, my Godson Keanan Pillay, Prayanka Devi Chetty, Jehaan Govender, Ryshan [Vasen's nephew], Nikhil & Talin Padayachee, Liash, Neha and little Shahaan Pillay, Theshlan, Yureshan and Sayuran Chetty, delightful Jibrael Duncan-Chundra and especially you, my beautiful, Thashni.

Contents

Acknowledgements xiii

Foreword 2

Chapter 1: The rod 3
    The rod butt and the reel seat 4
    Hook eyelet 4
    Competitions 4
    Choices and rod care 5
    Line guides 5
    More on rod care 6
    Price 6

Chapter 2: The reel 7
    The Centre Pin Reel 7
    The multiplier reel [also referred to as 'baitcaster' / "Penn" reel] 9
    The 'coffee grinder' [fixed spool reel] 11
    Pushbutton / 'spincast' reel and underspin reel 13

Chapter 3: Lines 14
    Ordinary monofilament line ["mono"] 14
    Fluorocarbon line ["fluoro"] 15
    Braid 15
    Fly lines 16
    Leader materials 16
    Disposal of line 16

Chapter 4: Hooks 17
    Some notes on hook design 17
    The eye 18
    Testing hooks 19
    The barb 20
    Sharpness 20
    Circle hooks 20
    Speciality hooks 21
    Drop shot hooks 22
    How to modify a hook to render it *weedless* 22
    Trebles 22

Chapter 5: Sinkers 23
    Split shot. 23
    Grapnel sinkers. 23
    Pear-shaped sinkers. 24
    Cone-shaped 'bullet' sinkers. 24
    Pyramid sinkers 24
    Bullet sinkers. 24
    Barrel sinkers. 25

Spoon sinker	25
Tear drop sinker	25

Chapter 6: Floats 26
- Porcupine quills 26
- Cork floats 27
- Balsa-wood floats 27
- Styrofoam strips 27
- Plastic floats 27
- Shapes and uses 27
- Bung floats 28
- Necessity is the mother of invention 28

Chapter 7: Swivels 29
- The normal two-way swivel 29
- The power swivel 29
- The three-way swivel 29
- The 'clip-on' swivel 30

Chapter 8: Landing aids 31
- Drop nets 31
- Using the tackle 31
- Beaching 31
- 'Tailing' by hand or with 'tailing' device 32
- The landing net 32
- Lip-landing 33
- Gaffs 33

Chapter 9: The tackle box and accessories 35

Chapter 10: Balancing your tackle, and knots 39
- <u>SUPERGLUE ON KNOTS</u> [yes, it IS underlined!] 39
- Tying my favourite knot [let's call it the FAV knot]: 41
- Joining lines 41
- Using the FAV knot: 41
- The nail knot 42
- Tandem hook trace 43
- Tying a gamefish trace 44
- Tying on a hook using multiple strand steel wire [coated / uncoated] 44
- Tying on a hook / swivel using single strand steel wire 44
- Tying the 'bowline' knot 45
- Trace for catching pan-fries and live bait 45

Chapter 11: Choosing a spot 47

Chapter 12: Bite indicators 51
- Watching your line 51
- Using your fingers 51
- Using floats 51
- Using dough 51
- Using an audible alarm 52

- Using thread / wool 52
- After dark bite indicators 52
- Being creative 52

Chapter 13: Artificial baits 53
- Spinner blades 53
- Spinners 54
- Spinner baits 54
- Drop shot hook [aka 'jig', 'jig head'] 54
- 'Dressed' drop shot hooks [aka 'Jigs'] 55
- Spoons 55
- Plugs 55
- Crankbaits 56
- Surface fish imitation lures 56
- Surface Creature imitation lures 56
- Sub-surface [diving lures] 56
- Plastic fish and creature imitations 57
- Flies 57

Chapter 14: Natural baits 58
- Bread 58
- Flour dough 59
- Crab bait 59
- Nymphs 59
- Tadpoles and frogs 60
- Fish baits 60
- Fruit 61
- The gecko 61
- Mealie Meal [corn flour] dough 63
- Seeds [mealies (corn), beans, lentils, wheat, peas], boilies, pips, wheat 63
- Shrimp [freshwater] 64
- Snails, slugs 64
- Worms 64
- SALTWATER NATURAL BAITS - Making your bait tougher 65
- Alikreukel [periwinkle] 65
- Armadillo 65
- Cheese 66
- Crab 66
- Cracker shrimp, mud prawns and sand prawns 67
- Crayfish [rock lobster] 68
- Fish bait 68
- Marine worms 69
- Mussels [Black] 70
- Octopus 70
- Perlemoen [Abalone] 71
- Prawn 71
- Razor clams / pencil bait 71
- Red bait / rock bait 72

- Saltwater shrimp 72
- Sand mussels / clams / white mussels 72
- Sea Cucumber 72
- Sea lice [mole crab] 73
- Squid [chokka] 73
- Venus Ears 73

Chapter 15: Casting 74
- Notes: 74
- Using a centre pin reel 74
- Using a multiplier reel 76
- Using a fixed spool reel 'coffee grinder' 78
- Press button reel / push button reel 78
- Casting beneath overhanging branches / ledges / casting at wary fish 79

Chapter 16: Fishing using natural bait in freshwater 80
- Some notes: 80
- Fishing for Carp [and tilapia and yellowfish and sometimes barbel] 80
- Bread bait / flour dough / mealie meal 82
- Crab 83
- Nymphs 83
- Tadpoles 83
- Fish bait 84
- Striped frogs and *platanas* 85
- Fruit 85
- Insects and spiders 85
- Maggots 86
- Shrimp 86
- Snails and slugs 87
- Worms 87

Chapter 17: Fishing using natural bait in salt water 88
- Alikreukel [periwinkle] 88
- Armadillo / Chiton 88
- Cheese 88
- CRAB 89
- Cracker shrimp, mud prawns and sand prawns 90
- Crayfish [rock lobster] 91
- Fish bait 92
- Marine worms 96
- Black mussels 97
- White mussels [clams] 97
- Octopus 98
- Perlemoen [abalone] 98
- Prawn 98
- Razor clams / pencil bait 99
- Rock bait [red bait] 99
- Sea Cucumber 100
- Sea lice [mole crabs] 100

  Squid [*chokka*] 101
  Venus ears 102
  THE FISH [Note that *superbaits* will work for almost all species] 103

Chapter 18: Fishing using artificial bait in freshwater 109
  Spinner blades 110
  Spinners 111
  Spinner baits 111
  Drop shot hook [aka 'jig', 'jig head'] 111
  'Dressed' drop shot hooks [aka 'Jigs'] 113
  Spoons 113
  Crankbaits 113
  Surface fish imitation lures 114
  Surface Creature imitation lures 114
  Sub-surface [diving lures] 115
  Plastic fish and creature imitations 115
  Flies 117

Chapter 19: Fishing using artificial bait in salt water 118
  Spinner blades 119
  Spinners 120
  Spinner baits 120
  Drop shot hook [aka 'jig', 'jig head'] 120
  Dressed' drop shot hooks [aka 'Jigs'] 122
  Spoons 122
  Garrick plugs 123
  Crankbaits 124
  Surface fish imitation lures 124
  Surface Creature imitation lures 124
  Sub-surface [diving lures] 125
  Plastic fish and creature imitations 125
  Flies 127

Chapter 20: Offshore fishing 136
  Top and mid-water fishing 136
  Bottom fishing [Note that superbaits will work for all species] 139

Chapter 21: The fight 145

Chapter 22: Fly fishing 148
  Your Tackle 'Box' 148
  The rod 149
  The reel 150
  The Line 151
  Strike Indicators 152
  How to cast…. My way 152
  Roll-casting 154
  What species are you targeting? 155
  ANTS 156
  ATTRACTOR PATTERNS [see General Attractor patterns below] 157

BEETLES	157
BLOODWORM [BUZZER LARVAE]	157
BUTTERFLIES AND MOTHS	157
BUZZER [see midge below]	158
CADDIS FLY	158
CADDIS LARVA	158
CADDIS NYMPH	158
CADDIS PUPA	158
CORYXID [see water boatman]	159
CRABS	159
CRICKETS	159
DRAGONFLIES AND DAMSELFLIES	159
DRAGONFLY AND DAMSELFLY NYMPHS	160
FISH	160
FISH EGGS	161
FLIES [TWO-WINGED]	161
FLYING ANTS	162
FROGS	162
GENERAL ATTRACTOR PATTERNS	162
GRASSHOPPERS	163
HOPPER [see 'grasshopper' above]	163
LEECHES	163
LIZARDS	163
MAYFLIES	163
NYMPHS	164
MIDGE LARVA. [see 'bloodworm' above]	164
MIDGE PUPA. [Buzzer]	164
MOLLUSCS	165
MOUSE	165
MOTHS [see butterflies above]	165
SEDGE [see caddis above]	165
SHRIMP	165
SNAILS. [refer MOLLUSCS] above	166
SPIDERS	166
STONEFLY NYMPHS	166
TADPOLES	166
WATER BOATMAN [Coryxids]	166
WORMS	167
Tigerfish and African pike	167
SALTWATER FLY FISHING	167
Crabs	167
Fish & Fry imitations	167
General attractor patterns [all saltwater]	168
Molluscs	168
Squid & Cuttlefish	168
Prawn	168
Worm flies	168

Chapter 23: Fishing from a float tube / kick boat 169

Chapter 24: Boat fishing 171

Chapter 25: Hand line 174

Chapter 26: Crabbing 175
    Cleaning the crab 175

Chapter 27: Cleaning your catch 177
    Eels. 177
    Barbel [catfish] 177
    Scaled species 177
    Removing the fins 178
    Filleting 179
    Cleaning prawns 179

Chapter 28: Why fish are lost or not caught 181
    OH NO! YOU FORGOT SOMETHING... 181
    RELATED TO THE FISHING ROD: 181
    RELATED TO FISHING REELS: 183
    RELATED TO FISHING LINE: 184
    RELATED TO THE FISH: 191
    RELATED TO *FISHERFOLK*: 192
    RELATED TO LANDING FISH: 196
    RELATED TO HOOKS 198
    RELATED TO SINKERS: 205
    RELATED TO BEING CHASED/POISONED/STUNG/BITTEN 207

Annexures 212

Index 215

Acknowledgements

Thank you to all who fished with me, believed in me and supported me in this, my quest.

And thanks to me for believing in myself and for loving fishing as much as I do.
Learn to love yourselves --- if you don't, there is no hope for those you do love.

So, You Want to Fish?

Foreword

Whilst I relate many tactics, tricks and experiences I have learnt over the years, I do this in good faith. I love my fishing world and seek to share with you what gave and continues to give me joy in the hope that you too, will also derive as much pleasure from it. I don't believe that there is anyone out there who loves fishing who won't learn anything from this book – even *I* am learning every day.

Should you choose to go fishing, I ask just one thing in return – whether you are a novice or a pro – please always take care of our environment – it's the best gift we can give to the next generation. Don't leave fishing / picnic spots in a mess – even if you found it that way. If you can't remove all the mess some ignorant inconsiderate ass has left behind, take some of it away and dispose of it appropriately. It **will** make a difference. Every little bit counts. ☺

And yes, if you follow my recommendations and put them into practice, your chances of catching fish will be greater and the environment will endure. Note that although this book refers to fishing in South Africa, the principles can be applied just about anywhere in the world.

When I was younger, I thirstily read books and articles about fishing and most of them were well-written. But too few of them tell the reader enough about how fish are lost or simply not caught, along with associated risks. By this I refer to assignable causes attributable to either losing fish, not catching fish or both. I know that by understanding these, you will undoubtedly become more successful at this beautiful sport. Chapter 28 has been dedicated to this theme. The logic is sound: Focus on controlling what you can and immediately you have greater chances of being successful at fishing.

One important reality for you to come to terms with before going fishing is that sometimes despite your bait/offering being taken and taken, and taken [or simply not taken], you catch no fish. If this is too difficult to come to terms with – don't go fishing. But, hey, if you can come to terms with it, good! Sometimes the fish must win!

Fish populations need time to recover. If we keep on taking too many out, our chances of catching on subsequent visits grow infinitely smaller. Conservation therefore is key. And don't pay too much attention to those purists out there who swear that fly-fishing is the only way to go. And that trout is the only fish to fish for – bah - humbug! You should always have freedom of choice – if you like using bait – go for it – after all it is *your* choice, and *your* hobby. Whatever you decide to do, whether you're fishing for the pan and/or for sport, just make sure that you always respect the rules applicable to the water/s you are fishing [for the record, I do *not* fish *just* for the sport of it].

And **learn** to practice *catch*-and-*return*. If you want to be able to *return* to the waters again *and catch* fish, you must learn to *catch* and *release* some of your catch– please remember this if, like me, you also enjoy eating fish.

And contrary to public opinion, return the *bigger* fish, keeping the smaller ones. Bigger fish are prime breeding stock.

Although this book is about fishing please never forget that fishing is about the outing and experiencing the wonderful whimsical magical healing power of water, so whether you catch or not, you score because being near water is indeed magical. Enjoy every outing like it's your first or last, and there you have it:

the recipe for success and good health.

Remember this:
"One of the few fights you will walk into willingly is one with a fish. Do you want to lose that fight because you neglected to do something that was well within your control?

... I didn't think so."
Farhad Manjoo

Chapter 1: The rod

You will need to acquire a rod. Choose the right tool for the job. When making this choice, consider the following:

Firstly, the rod is an extension of your arm, providing a means to deliver the bait / lure into the feeding zone of the species you are targeting, thereby enabling you to reach the fish. This is the primary requirement a rod must be able to deliver on. For example, a boat rod is short [5 – 6foot; 1.5 – 1.83m] for obvious practical reasons and relatively slow-actioned whereas a trolling boat rod is the same length but a faster- actioned rod, an ice fishing rod is shorter [2 – 3feet long; 0.6 – 0.9m] and a surf rod can be up to 16foot [4.9m], the additional length allowing you to eliminate much of the wave [false bite] interference.

The rod should help in clearing any obstacles on the shoreline, including rocks, sandbars, structures, reeds, bushes, shrubs and trees both on the bank and in the water. For normal surf conditions, a surf rod that is 12feet [3.6m] long is more than adequate, but if there are large waves, a longer rod will help because the additional length will help keep your line clear of the waves thereby helping to eliminate / reduce wave interference. The additional length may also be necessary to help keep line away from rocks / reef. At this point you will need to consider the power that will be required for the rod you will need. The power rating, most simply put, describes the lifting power of a rod. This power also describes the load that a rod can safely carry when casting. The power rating is usually described as 'heavy', 'medium', 'light', etc. Power is directly related to the line strength the rod can support. "Power" also describes the maximum mass of a fish that can safely be lifted clear of the water.

Secondly, pertaining to the effective use of lures, the action of the rod is important as it assists you in making the movement of lures more realistic and therefore naturally more appealing to the fish being targeted. You may need three different action rods for example for bass when drop-shotting, fishing light surface lures and crank-baiting. Now for most of us it is not practical to have five or six bass rods, for example; so, we try and strike a happy medium. Find a rod that will give you the best combination of sensitivity for the fish you are targeting. You will also mostly need to be accurate in your placement of the bait or lure. This might mean distance casting or it may mean casting an offering so that it lands on, say, a targeted lily pad so that you can make it 'fall off' and therefore much more desirable as a meal to the fish lying in wait.

Thirdly, and when a bite occurs, the rod must be an effective tool in setting the hook upon striking. You will need a rod with a soft action [whippy] for soft-mouthed fish like carp, yellowfish and grunter; and a rod with stiffer action for fish with stronger mouths [bass, catfish, barracuda, tiger fish]. The 'faster action' rods are capable of setting a hook faster and being sensitive at the same time. Your choice of rod therefore must always first take into consideration the type of fish you are targeting and the nature of the fishing grounds. You would, for example use a faster action rod when fishing near structure, to power the fish away, and a slower action rod in open water. Remember that the action of a rod is best described by how much of the rod bends when strained – consider the sketch below:

Illustration of "super-fast" action rod where just the tip section bends under load. Note that the 'action' is only truly known when the tip is at 90° to the butt.

Now also bear in mind that within the category of "fast action" rods the following must also be considered:

A fast action rod for largemouth bass would in principle perform as well as a fast action rod for deep sea fishing. But these rods are not interchangeable – you cannot use a deep-sea rod for catching largemouth bass because the rod would be far too heavy for this purpose – this is why you now get rods rated for different groups and / or species of fish.

In the same way, a slow action rod for largemouth yellowfish would be different from a slow action rod for a river where the yellowfish do not grow larger than 250mm in length. 'Fast action' describes how much of the rod bends when loaded. If just the last quarter / fifth of the length of the rod bends when loaded, the rod has a very fast action. If the whole rod bends and resembles a parabola when loaded, it is a slow action rod. With this is one simple rule: the softer the mouth of the fish, the slower the action required. The stronger the flesh in the mouth of the fish, the faster the action of the rod. Also, with this, the faster the action of the rod, the heavier the weight of the sinker that can be used for casting. You will have a problem casting out a heavy sinker and bait combination with a slow-action rod. A slow action rod would be suitable for fish like mullet and yellowfish where the rod itself removes much of the fighting load of the fish to the rod so that the mouth parts of the fish do not tear. Bass and catfish, on the other hand have stronger mouth parts and therefore require a rod with a 'faster action. Typically, most glass fibre rods tend to be slow action rods.

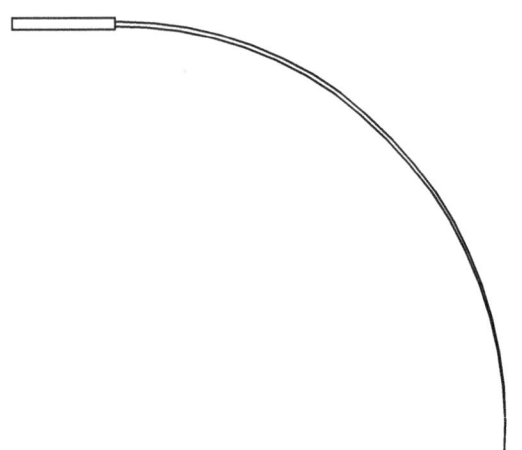

Illustration of a slow action rod – note that the entire rod is curved when under load. Note again that the action of a rod is only fully determined when the tip is at 90°to the butt. You can get a slow action rod for deep sea and a slow action rod for stream fishing – both these are not interchangeable.

So never force a rod to perform outside of its parameters… If you over load a fast action rod by using a weight that is too heavy – it becomes slow-action and the rod will under-perform. If you use a weight that is outside of the rated weight [power] the rod will support, the rod will also under-perform.

Rod categories range from ultra-light … light to medium … heavy to extra-heavy and … ultra-heavy.

Fourthly, *the rod must contribute positively to the only fight you will always walk willingly into*. It must be able to support the strain created during the fight and must be a shock-absorber when sudden dashes are made by the fish during the fight, preventing the mouth from tearing. Remember that some of the strain may also be amplified by water movement.

The rod butt and the reel seat

Many of the cheaper, mass-manufactured rods have polyurethane grips. Nothing comes close to a cork butt – the non-slip grip, the lightness and its ability to communicate the bite to you hand by means of vibrations…. Heavier rods tend to have wooden butts. The butt should end in a cap that in all cases finishes off the handle, but that is important, for most rods, to your comfort when fighting a fish. You will require padding to protect your abdomen and groin when fighting big fish - this comes in the form of a rod bucket which is worn around the waist or hips and has a receptacle to accommodate the butt of the rod, protecting you from injury. Do not think you are too man enough to do without one. Some rod butts are specialized for big game fishing – these may be banana-shaped and have a slot to prevent heavy rods from twisting. And some rod butts are designed to be used with a fighting chair and harness so that you do not end up water-skiing and diving. Line guides are covered later in this Chapter.

The reel seat should hold the reel to the rod *as close to the blank as possible*. Metal seats can also seize [jam] and stain the reel when they corrode. Graphite reel seats have become very popular and can be as strong as their metal counterparts. Some rods do not have reel seats – these are meant to have the reel clamped to them and attached to a harness for big game fishing.

Hook eyelet

Certain rods have an eyelet attached to the base of the blank, just above the butt. This eyelet is for passing your hook through so that it does not swing about madly. If you have a double hook trace, pass the hook with the longer snoot through and engage it to the other hook. If you have more than two hooks – what can I say – you are a cowboy!

Competitions

If you are going to be in a fishing competition – you will need to know what type of fish are present in the competition waters so that you can decide the selection of rods to take with. The competition may restrict you to, say two rods. This does not mean that you cannot carry more rods with different power and action combinations - you will need a range of rods that support different combinations of power and action particularly when fishing artificial lures, in order to maximize the individual action of the type of lure being used / the type of fish being targeted.

Choices and rod care

When I started fishing, the rod of choice was heavy and solid and made from glass fibre [having just shifted over from bamboo and split cane rods]. Times have changed. There is a multitude of different types of rods available. Rods are now mostly hollow tubes made from materials like Boron and Graphite. These rods have exceptional strength along the length but zero strength across the diameter. This means that exceptional care must be exercised when handling them as they are easily crushed. The glass fibre is essentially more flexible and the carbon fibre stiffer

All rods should be transported in a cloth bag and encased in a rigid container. If the rod does not come with a bag or case, acquire one with the rod. It doesn't matter if it's a 'cheapie' or expensive – it's **YOUR** rod.

Each section of the rod should be individually wrapped - If sections are placed together [directly against each other] in a cloth bag, the vibration generated during travelling will cause them to rattle against each other, creating weak points / flaws and thereby reducing the strength of the rod over time.

Graphite rods have a staggering advantage over other rods as they return to their original shape much quicker when casting. This is important - rods that take longer to straighten out during the cast create more resistance to the line that is being discharged, effectively reducing casting distance. The action also becomes an advantage when fighting a fish as it assists in eliminating slack line and keeping a constant load on the fish, tiring it quicker.

Graphite - boron, and graphite - titanium rods are also much lighter than their predecessors – this allows greater sensitivity when detecting a bite. It is therefore clear, until something else comes up, that I am advocating the use of these rods.

Just remember again that the cross-sectional strength [resistance to crushing] of the graphite and other tubular rods is low – this means that if you knock the rod against a hard surface, you are creating a potential fracture / failure point where failure will occur when the rod is placed under load. These rods therefore must be handled carefully. Do not place them directly on rocks, and if you are using rod stands, these should be lined with a buffering layer of cushioning material so the rod does not make contact with bare metal. Do not lay them on the ground because they can [and will] be stepped on and they crush easily. Rods should never be stacked so that they touch each other. Remember that Graphite is an excellent conductor of electricity.

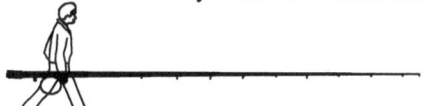
Do not use them during a thunderstorm and **hold them flat [horizontal] when walking under naked power lines.**

If you hold the rod upright when passing below power lines, you are shortening the arcing distance [the distance between the overhead conductors and the ground – 'Earth'] and you run the risk of being electrocuted – yes, ***not only lightning can do this*** *– there is a reason why overhead power cables are not low. The warning label is on the rod:* ***It is for real.***

Graphite rods can be quite expensive. If you find them too expensive, the graphite composite rods work just as well and generally cost less. If you are buying a second-hand graphite rod, scrutinize the length of the rod for damage. Any damage will compromise the strength of the rod, and will almost certainly cause the rod to break, especially when under load. Most of the more expensive rods are costly because processing is conducted at higher temperatures thereby producing a better quality raw material and rod. Save up ... it will be worth the investment. A decent rod won't make a better fisherman of you neither will it improve your casting, but if you picture playing tennis with the old heavy wooden tennis racquet and then with the lighter graphite versions, you will understand what I mean. Work at your game and you will improve – work at your game with the lighter, equipment, and you will excel in all aspects. It can be tiring holding a road all day long...

Oh yes, and if you decide to build your own rod, bear in mind that the manufacturing process for carbon fibre blanks results in imperfections and being able to make a rod from a blank means that the builder has to know where these imperfections are and mount the line guides on the face with the imperfections. Personally – I won't be in the market for a carbon fibre blank....

Line guides

The condition of line guides, [commonly referred to as "eyes"] is very important. These should be smooth [duh...] and must be regularly inspected for cracks and grooves caused by the fishing line.

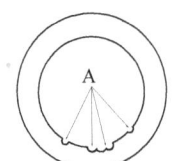
Yes, **BELIEVE IT** – line is capable of eventually cutting grooves in line guides [see sketch– the line guide has become grooved ("A") and **will** damage line!].

The more expensive branded rods *generally* have better quality line guides and are well worth the cost – this does not mean that they won't become 'grooved' – it means that they are more resistant but will eventually get grooved. It is also important not to compromise on these when repairing rods. The best quality line guides are generally manufactured from Silicon Carbide or Aluminium Oxide. Some line guides are made from stainless steel / titanium wire – the advantage in these is that they are lighter. The number of line guides is important, as a rod with less guides will not cast as effectively with one that has more. The number of eyes help to distribute the load of casting / fighting much more evenly throughout the rod. The spacing of the guides is very important as this distributes the load evenly – do not try to build your own rod without first understanding this.

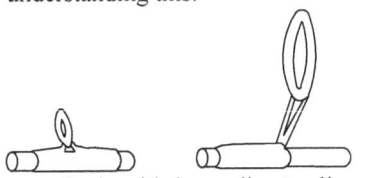
Remember: Smaller line guides ['eyes'] – bait caster and fly fishing; Larger line guides are for use with fixed spool [coffee grinder] reels.

Rods with large dimeter line guides have been made for use with fixed spool reels – this is important – when you cast with these reels, line is discharged in coils which require a larger clearance to pass through the line guides. Rods with small line guides are designed to be used with multiplier reels as the line is discharged from a spinning, moving spool and not in the form of coils as is typical from a fixed spool reel.

More on rod care

Corrosion can and will silently attack the metal parts of the line guides. You can protect these by using a suitable polish / lacquer. Inspect line guides for corrosion.

Do not leave rods assembled after fishing. Take them apart by pulling with a twisting motion and clean the joints. Use candlewax / beeswax on the mating sections by first cleaning them then by rubbing the wax on the mating surfaces. Make sure that your rod sections are dry before wrapping them and storing in tubes – trapped moisture can cause damage in the form of corrosion and moisture [and salt] can also cause deterioration of the cork / wooden bits in the form of fungi and rot.

After fishing, wipe rods down with warm soapy water and use a polish like '**Mr Min**' to sustain the life [and appearance] of the rod.

You will notice that not much is said about two-piece [and more] rods. This is because new generation carbon fibre rods perform just about as well as though they were one-piece rods. Telescopic rods also perform well. It is essential that you open and close these rods without flicking them open as this can result in it being difficult to collapse the extended rod and will almost certainly cause damage to the mating sections.

Price

So now that you have all this in mind, now you're ready to consider price…. Unfortunately, and generally, when a rod is 'cheap' *it's probably not worth buying*. Having said this, some of the top level, really good quality rods are actually overpriced. How much you can afford to spend is the limiting factor – just don't go spending so much on the rod that you end up hardly using it because it was so costly! Consider that you are now better equipped when selecting and obtaining a rod, and remember that a good quality rod is a *helluva* credit to your fishing arsenal whilst a poor-quality rod is not….

Please bear in mind that broken rods, once repaired, seldom perform as well as they did before the repair.

Replace. Replace. Replace.

Chapter 2: The reel

A fishing reel is a piece of equipment used to store and retrieve fishing line. There are various basic designs, the more common of which are discussed below.

Most reels can be adapted for left – or right-handed fishing. When reeling line in with any type of reel, tension should always be maintained on the incoming line – failure to do this means that loose line will be released from the reel and this places you at high risk for tangles, especially if there is 'twist' present in your line. When there is loose line on a reel, it allows line reeled in under tension to bite and seat itself below the loose line and this is a highly undesirable situation, increasing the risk of tangles tenfold.

Casting techniques are covered in Chapter 15. Take note that the line on the reel is for casting and **NOT** for traces. Always carry separate line for tracing-up.

Most reels are equipped with adjustable drag systems. These, when properly set and engaged:
- Assist you by applying resistance to the fighting fish;
- save your line from breaking as they release line when the pressure gets close to breaking strain when fighting a fish or if stuck;
- Allows you to catch fish whose weight exceeds your line breaking strength; and,
- Saves your line as they will release line if you miscast.

Resistance is created mechanically by drag washers or a disk braking system or by cam action using a lever connected to a cam which applies pressure, slowing the reel down or magnetically by eddy current using magnets set into the reel. Mechanical resistance is introduced by tightening a star nut or drag nut or by sliding a lever – this resistance **must** be smooth when introduced.

Drag mechanisms are adjusted while you fish and before you cast.

Be sure to loosen any drag mechanism when you are done with fishing – as sustained pressure with a tightened drag can damage brakes or drag washers.

Avoid lubricating drag washers and brakes. Get your reel serviced by professionals – in some designs putting a drag washer in in the wrong sequence or the wrong way around could be disastrous. In Pietermaritzburg I use *Rochester Tackle* or *Atlas Sports*.

Do **NOT** compromise your fishing by using a reel with too little line on it – you may well regret it. Over-filled reels are also a problem. This is addressed in greater detail below.

And remember that you can replace part of the line on a spool – you seldom have to replace all the line. Write down the date on which you filled the spool on your tackle box or on the spool where it won't easily get erased. And remember that braid – whether a backing or not – must be wound onto the reel with more tension than normal monofilament line.

The Centre Pin Reel

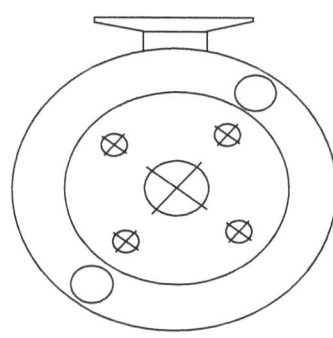

This is the most basic type of reel but it presents the greatest challenge and is sadly underrated for its casting ability. The common varieties normally have a small arbor and consequently have a poor retrieval rate, requiring great dexterity for fast reeling in due to the 1:1 retrieval rate. For casting you will need clear space to de-spool line in preparation for casting. I generally carry a straw mat/piece of tarp onto which the line is de-spooled, taking care that the coils of line do not get entangled. I mark one meter of line once it has settled with a black permanent marker so I can achieve the same distance each time. I have not experienced any line deterioration caused by markers and I have been doing this for years.

One will be amazed at the distance one can achieve with a minimal use of sinkers. Yes, there must be little or no cross-wind blowing or your line will be tossed all over the place, creating a high-risk tangle situation! This is an excellent fresh water reel when fishing for 'shy biters' as fishing can be done with just a baited hook, no swivel and no sinker. Very few people use this type of reel for conventional fishing. This is a real pity as the reel has great potential.

The reel sometimes has a ratchet mechanism and anti-reverse lever. The ratchet mechanism is normally used as an alarm when fish takes the bait. The anti-reverse lever allows you to reel in but prevents line from being stripped off the reel. Some types come with a drag mechanism that applies resistance to the spool when line is stripped off the reel. Drag mechanisms can be mechanical or magnetic. This facility is normally used to assist to apply resistance when fighting a fish and to prevent related or accidental overruns. With the design of most centre pin reels, it is easy to 'palm' the reel. This involves slowing down the reel with the edge of your palm when a fish is making a run. Just be wary that you do not get your knuckles rapped by the reel handles when the reel is spinning!!!

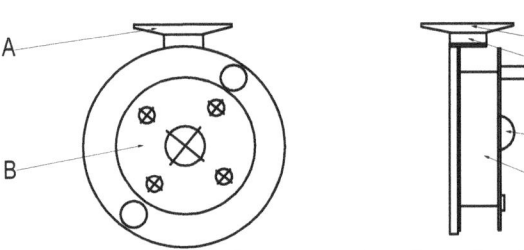

Legend: A: Reel seat; B: Spool in normal fishing position on the reel; C: Reel seat; D: Pivot; E: Spindle; F: Spool in normal casting position.

Some varieties allow you to pivot the reel so that you can cast without having to de-spool line. Alongside is the side – cast version.

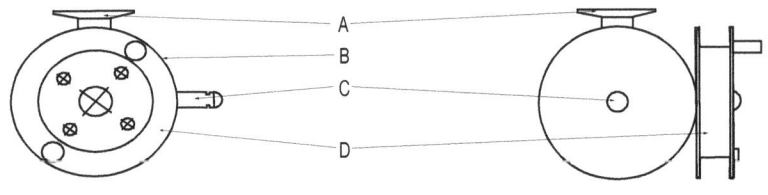

Legend: A: Reel seat; B: Spool in normal fishing position; C: Casting spindle on the left, normal fishing position spindle on the right; D: Spool in casting position. ALWAYS MAKE CERTAIN THAT THE SPOOL IS HELD CAPTIVE – in casting or normal position.

The "PHOENIX Mk 2" type of reel, for example, is actually a geared reel and should be classed as a multiplier, allowing you to remove the spool and place it on a separate spindle for casting.

Just make sure that the reel is engaged properly on the spindle or it will fall off during the cast!

I have not used this reel but it has a formidable casting potential, especially when loaded with 10lb [4.5kg] (or lighter) line.

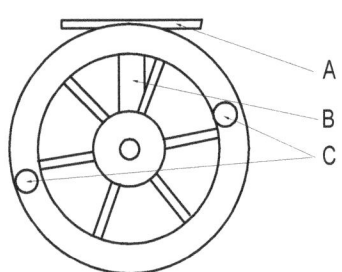

Legend: Scarborough reel. A: Reel seat; B: Spindle mounting frame; C: Reel knobs on free-spinning spool.

The "Scarborough" is also a centre pin reel with a smooth free spinning action that allows for distance casting, mainly in the surf. This reel requires great skill for casting, and once accomplished, people using it are very successful, particularly using light tackle. Normal spool diameter ranges from 4" [100mm] to 8"] 200mm]..

Deep sea centre pin reel

A larger, bulkier reel is used for bottom fishing when deep sea fishing. This is not a casting reel by any means – line is allowed to de-spool by allowing the weight [around 1kg] to gravitate to the seabed. The reel diameter is between 8" and 12" [200 – 300mm].

Centre pin reels are also the only type of reel used for fly fishing where the reel is simply a reservoir for the fly line and backing. The construction of the reel also forces one to make conventional false casts before getting one's line into the water.

Saltwater fly fishing reels tend to have a larger arbor because they can hold more backing and the retrieval rate is increased by the larger diameter which also greatly reduces line memory.

When considering saltwater fly fishing reels, resistance to corrosion must also be considered along with whether the spool bearings are sealed or not. Fly fishing is covered in Chapter 22.

Filling a centre pin reel with line

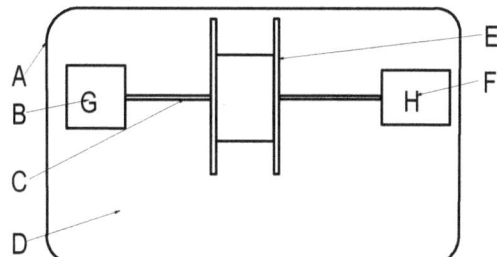

Legend: *A: 2litre ice cream [or other suitable] container; B: Cork / polystyrene float "G"; C: Skewer / pencil / suitable support; D: filled with water, enough to support rig; E: Factory spool of line; F: Cork / polystyrene float "H".*

When filling line, remember that all the line on the spool is never really used. Remember that it is generally the last 100 – 150m on the spool that is commonly used. The remaining line on the reel eventually gets damaged by the pressure of the line above it. It is therefore advisable to use a suitable backing line. In my experience, braided backing line is King. When feeding line off a factory spool onto a fishing reel, drop the spool into a container of water [set up as per sketch, the spool must touch the bottom of the container – this acts as a brake] then thread the line through the line guides and tie to the reel spool using my 'FAV' knot [refer Chapter 10] – you will not have the problem of having to hold the factory spool neither will you experience overwinds.

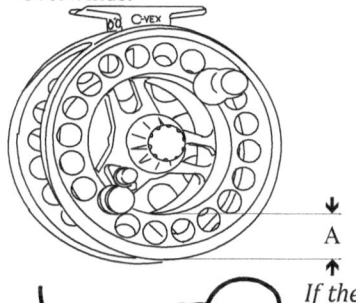

For backing, load 25% to 30% of the reel capacity [if you do not know the reel capacity, measure the depth of the spool [see "A" alongside] minus 3 - 8mm and divide the result by 3, mark on side of the spool and fill braid to this level]. If "A" measures 26mm, for example, you would load 6 – 8mm of backing. When reeling maintain line tension by pinching the line between thumb and forefinger whilst reeling. Be sure to stop at intervals to check if the line is not getting twisted. You do this by lowering the rod and allowing the line to droop.

If the line is getting twisted, it will form a series of tight coils like the sketch below. If this happens, simply turn the rig around so that line feeds out from the opposite side so that "G" and "H" on the sketch at the beginning of this subsection are on opposite sides. Continue reeling whilst checking for twist.

Once you have filled backing to the mark, join backing to the main line using a suitable knot [refer to my 'favourite' knot for joining lines in Chapter 10] and fill the reel to capacity using the procedure for filling backing [within, say not less than 3 - 8mm of the reel rim. Please remember not to take line off the reel for traces – carry a spare spool of line for this purpose. After every fishing trip always inspect [feel] the last bit of line and remove the affected line if you feel any damage.

The multiplier reel [also referred to as 'baitcaster' / "Penn" reel]

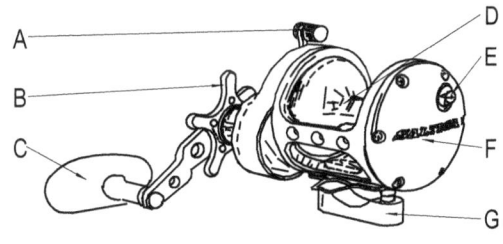

Legend*: A: This is the free-spool lever. Engages the winding mechanism after casting and disengages the winding mechanism when casting; B: Star drag. Tightening increases drag tension; C: Reel handle / crank; D: Line spool. Do not fill to less than 3 mm from spool edge; E: Ratchet; F: On the centre of the opposite side of the reel is the spool tension adjustment nut – used to adjust the extent of free-spooling for casting; G: Reel mounting block [for mounting reel to rod].*

Sometimes referred to as a 'spin caster', 'bait caster', 'bait casting' reel or a 'Penn' reel [Penn is the name of a reel manufacturer]. This is a geared centre pin reel; one revolution of the reel handle results in several turns of the spool.

The reel is mounted and used above the rod. There are various brands and types available on the market. It is essential that you buy the best reel within your price range. Good reels are more expensive for good reason. You should consider the retrieval rate, the spool should be made from low-corrosion metal, and the drag should be reliable, lubrication ports should be sealed / sealable. Serviceability is crucial. Spares must be available or you may have to scrap the reel when something goes wrong because parts are either not available or too expensive.

This would be the reel of choice for most of you fishing the surf. Contrary to public opinion, it is an easy reel to master. You must, with most models of this reel, ensure that you spread the line, distributing it evenly across the spool whilst retrieving, smaller varieties of this reel, commonly used for bass and other game fish have an automatic level-wind facility.

Most models have a ratchet mechanism which acts as an audible warning if line is stripped from the reel; a drag mechanism [lever / star nut operated] which helps in tiring the fish out by placing resistance on the spool when under tension [some reel types also have a magnetic drag system that helps slow the spool down when casting, helping to reduce the prospect of 'overwinds'.

Reels also have a spool tension nut. This nut can be adjusted to apply tension to the spool when casting so that the reel does not spin too freely and cause tangles [bird's nests]. This tension is also adjusted each time the weight of the object being cast is changed.

The best feature of this reel is the geared retrieval rate – each time you rotate the crank [reel handle], the spool spins up to 7 times, greatly increasing the rate of retrieval.

The reel also has a 'frees pool' lever which is engaged manually when casting and must be disengaged after casting. The 'frees pool' setting is also used in conjunction with the ratchet for fishing with live bait.

Filling line on a multiplier reel

Follow the same procedure as detailed for the centre pin reel above for this type of reel. Remember to check for twist. Take note of the schematic below whenever filling line on a multiplier reel.

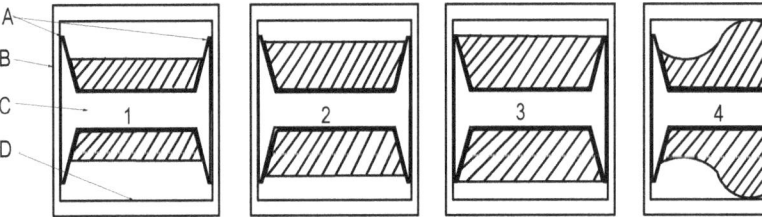

Legend: *Schematic of multiplier-type reel showing section through frame, spool and line. A: Rim of spool, where spool 'meets' spool cage; B: Side of spool cage; C: Spool; D: Spool cage, horizontal member.*

1: Line not filled to capacity. Retrieval rate will be slower because the 'effective' working diameter is smaller because there is less line on the reel. Spool will have to spin faster to discharge line. **Undesirable**.

2: Line filled to within approximately 3mm of spool rim. **Desirable**.

3: spool over-filled – line will almost certainly rub against the spool cage and get caught between the spool and the cage. High risk of line being cut by the reel. **Undesirable**.

4: Line not wound level on the spool. In extreme cases line will rub against the spool cage. When casting, this can create a hot spot when braking by hand. **Undesirable**.

The junior 'Baitcaster' reel [normally used for artificial lure casting]

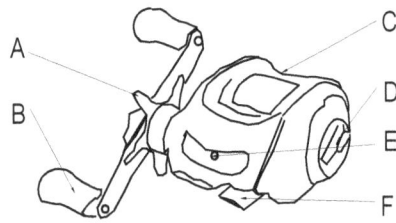

Legend: A: Star Drag. For drag tension adjustment; B: Reel handle – double handle for balance; C: Thumb - operated 'freespool' switch for casting; D: Spool tension adjustment screw; E: Level – winding guide hole; F: Reel foot for mounting rod to reel.

This is actually a multiplier reel but scaled down, allowing you to deliver relatively light lures accurately and with ease.

It requires practice to master, and once mastered, is the reel of choice for fisher folk using lightweight artificial lures, especially those targeting bass. The reel generally has a dual drag system comprising a star drag nut which puts pressure on the spool using friction washers [drag washers]. I have heard of some models with a disk drag but have not physically seen these.

In *freespool* mode, most spools have an eddy current braking [magnetic] system. Spool tension has to be adjusted whenever a lure / cast weight is changed so that you do not experience overwinds.

This reel should be serviced annually. Refer to the section above when filling line.

The 'coffee grinder' [fixed spool reel]

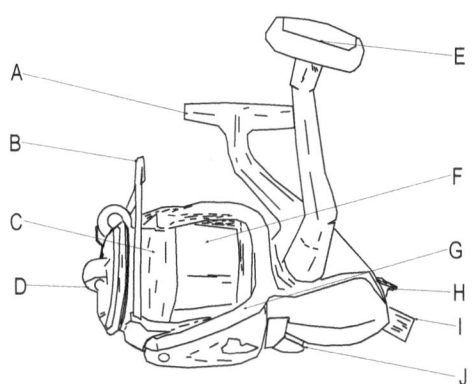

Legend: A: Reel foot. Used to mount reel to rod; B: Bail arm. This wire loop has a line roller which is used to feed the line evenly along the spool. In the open position, the bail arm is ready for casting; C: Line spool – stores line; D: Drag adjustment nut – used to generate / reduce drag tension exerted on the spool. This is sometimes located at the back of the reel [refer "I" above]; E: Reel handle / crank; F: Spool skirt – stops line from fouling below the spool; G: Bail arm support yoke; H: Bait-runner switch – not available on all reels. This allows fish to pick up bait and run. Automatically disengaged when you start reeling; J: Reverse / anti-reverse lever.

This is the reel of choice for most fisher folk. It is a simple, deadly tool as it is seldom prone to tangling [bird's nests]. Its main failing is that it will eventually twist your line so it is in your best interest to load the reel with limp, soft lines as the harder lines twist easily. 'Twist" can also be caused by a faulty lure or by a spinning bait. The roller guide on the bail arm can also cause this if it is jammed and does not spin freely.

The rod you use with this reel must have large diameter line guides. This is because of the manner in which line is de-spooled when casting – smaller guides will cause excessive resistance in the cast and compromise your casting distance.

The reel is mounted below the rod and is easy to cast with. The reel is geared – this means that one revolution of the handle will give you several turns of the bail mechanism – thereby increasing the retrieval rate markedly.

The turning action of the bail arm can easily become ensnared when fishing in long grass – soft branches / leaves / long hair / loose clothing.

Most reels of this design have the following standard features:

* To cast, the bail arm must be flipped to the casting position. [Casting is covered in Chapter 15].
* When a cast is complete, the reel handle has only to be turned and the bail arm closes automatically.
* The line spool has a drag that is mounted on the spool [D] or at the back of the reel [I]. This is generally very soft and cannot be relied on as audible bite indicator. This facility has saved many a rod from doing the 'bye bye' dance. I would recommend the design that incorporates the drag in front of the spool as the mechanism is simple and effective. The drag control screw mounted and operated from the back of the reel is essentially a complex mechanism and I would not recommend reels incorporating this design – they work well, but once the problems start....
* The anti-reverse lever is used in conjunction with the drag or if you want to wind backwards.
* The bait runner facility allows fish to pick up the bait and run. You can disable this function by simply turning the reel handle before you strike.
* It is easy to slow down or stop a cast by simply applying finger resistance to the spool, slowing down the feed of coils of line.

Filling line on a fixed spool reel

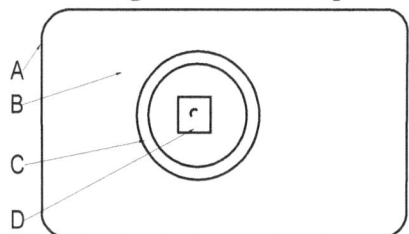

Legend: A: Container [2liter ice cream]; B: Filled with water ¾ full [doesn't have to cover the spool]; C: Factory spool of line; D: Large pyramid / cone 'sinker' with cone placed in centre hole of factory spool, weighing it down.

Filling line for this reel is easily accomplished. Check the capacity rating on the reel relative to the line diameter / strength you are filling [if the line size is not listed on the spool, it's very likely that the line is too heavy / light for the spool]. It is always advisable to load a braided backing which at its best should occupy a third to a quarter of the physical space on the reel. I personally have no problems with completely filling a fixed spool reel with braid.

Mark 30% of the depth of the spool from the inside so that you know where to stop filling the backing line. If you are completely filling the reel with braid – you don't have to mark the spool.

To fill the backing on the reel, you will need a bucket / container [not smaller than, for example, a 2litre ice cream container [refer to the sketch above].

Place the spool you have purchased on its side in the water.

Take a large pyramid / cone / bottle sinker and insert the small end into the small hole on the spool. This is to prevent the spool from lifting.

Take the free end of the line and thread it through the line guides. Open the bail arm and tie the line to the reel spool using my FAV knot [refer Chapter 10].

Wind in some line and set the drag to just release under light pressure [so that if you inadvertently apply too much pressure when you are reeling the new line in, the drag will activate and slip]. Close the bail arm.

When reeling maintain line tension by pinching the line between thumb and forefinger whilst reeling. Be sure to stop at intervals to check if the line is not getting twisted. You do this by lowering the rod and allowing the line to droop. If the line is getting twisted, it will form a series of tight coils. If this happens, simply turn the factory spool over, feeding line from the opposite side.

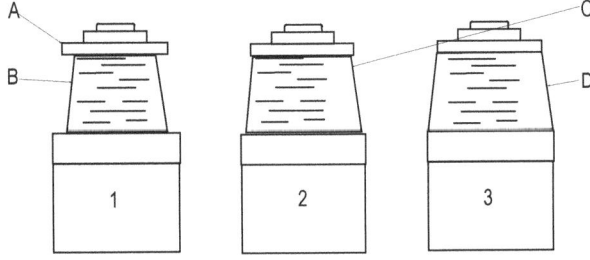

Continue reeling whilst checking for twist [refer picture alongside]. If you want to check for twist, allow the line to dangle freely and check.

For backing, load 25% to 30% of the reel capacity with the braid [if you do not know the reel capacity, measure the depth of the spool minus 3 mm and divide the result by 3, mark on side of the spool and fill braid to this level].

Legend: Spools 1,2 & 3 are identical, but filled to different levels. A: This is the leading edge of the spool.; B: This line represents the line level in spool 1. The line level is far below the leading edge of the spool; C: The line has been filled to just less than 3mm from the leading edge of the spool; D: The line has been filled in line with the leading edge of the spool. 1: In this spool, there is inadequate line on the spool. This will compromise casting distance. It also means that there is less line on the reel to play a fish. 2: The level is adequate for optimum casting. This is the most desirable of the three. 3: You may be able to cast a little further with this spool but you will experience miss-feeds, and as a result, you will almost certainly end up with too little line on the spool after having to deal with these miss-feeds.

Once you have filled backing to the mark, join backing to the main line using a suitable knot [refer to my 'FAV' knot for joining lines in Chapter 10] and fill the reel to capacity using the above procedure for filling backing [within, say not less than 3mm of the reel rim]. Don't forget to stop and check for twist. Please remember not to take line off the reel for any reason unless the line is damaged – carry a spare spool of line for tying traces. After every fishing trip always inspect [feel] the last bit of line and remove the affected line if you feel any damage.

Pushbutton / 'spincast' reel and underspin reel

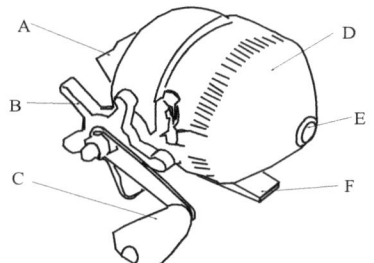

Legend: A: Push button for casting; B: Star drag; C: Reel handle; D: Nose cone; E: Line feed hole – line is fed through hole when casting or reeling in; F: Reel foot for mounting reel.

This is in fact, also a fixed spool reel. It incorporates a design where one or two 'pick up pins' are rotated below the cone shaped nose – these guide the line onto the spool when you are reeling in. the pins are not as bulky as the bail arms nor are they visible without removing the nose cone. The reel is mounted above the rod and used above the rod. When fishing a normal fixed spool reel, one has the problem with vegetation being picked up by the bail arm rotation [includes loose clothes or hair] – this will not happen with a pushbutton reel. This is an excellent reel with light lures. It will not twist line [limp line] nor does it have the potential to cause 'bird's nests' like the multiplier reels. Line coming into the reel is automatically 'level – wound'. The reel also has an anti-reverse lever. The line spool is protected by the cone shaped nose but the reel should only be used for close-fishing only as you are restricted by the reel's low line capacity. This reel should not be used for fish that make long dashing runs.

When casting, you push the button conveniently located for your thumb to activate. The button is released when you cast, and with timing, fairly decent casts can be made. The reel handle is manipulated and automatically disengages casting mode.

These reels are not popular.

When filling line on these reels, follow the manufacturer's recommendations regarding line size and capacity to the letter. These reels should not be filled with braid.

Electric reels are available and work on mounted rods for deep sea bottom fishing – these take out the joy of actually fighting fish and are best used by people who do not [for whatever reason] have the power to reel in a fish from the deep.

Chapter 3: Lines

You will find that information is repeated from time to time [in this Chapter and the book in general]. This is intentional and proportionate to just how important the information is. Having said this, remember that normal monofilament line will take no less than 20 years to break down [decompose]; fluorocarbon ten years longer, and braid more than double that. What does this mean?

It means that the line people throw away will be there for a long time, whether submerged, buried or on the surface. Have you or anyone else ever almost fallen or fallen because feet got caught up in discarded nylon? And every day, for whatever reason, there is more and more nylon discarded.

Worse – I have seen animals that must have suffered agonizing deaths because they were trapped by discarded line…

Please!!!!!!!!! – whenever you encounter nylon / line that is waste for whatever reason, please wrap it around your hand then cut through all the line on one side [or both] and you have many pieces of line that are too short to cause a problem. There is so much line in our waters – do you realize what this means? It means that if you or anyone else is in the water, it could cause you or anyone else to become ensnared or even drown. This includes all forms of animals and anything else in the water. Please, cut up that line – thereafter you can dispose of it using normal channels or you could, at the very worst, leave the pieces of line right where you found it…

When filling line onto a reel – it is good practice to ensure that the reel specification includes the breaking strain / diameter you intend loading onto the reel.

This is what twisted line looks like. Highly undesirable as it causes slack line and will tangle with anything it comes into contact with and even compromise your cast – and the worst-case scenario is that it could result in you breaking your rod.

Any fishing line can become twisted – here are the main causes:
- Incorrect transfer of line from purchased spool to fishing reel spool. Refer to Chapter 2 for instructions on loading line based on the type of reel you are using.
- Your lure is spinning, thereby twisting the line. This generally happens if the speed at which the lure is trolled or retrieved is too fast. The lure could be damaged or the swivel could be jamming.
- Your bait is spinning as it goes down – this generally happens with 'flat' baits. – This will happen even if you have a swivel.
- Your bait was taken by an eel. Eels have the habit of toying with your bait and spinning their bodies with the bait in their mouths. *Remember – once you catch an eel, it is advisable to change your trace as a slimy residue is left on your trace – this residue scares off fish. So theoretically, if you catch an eel without changing your trace, chances are you're 'gonna catch more eels.*
- Spinning spool on a fixed spool / push button reel. If this is the case, simply tighten your drag.
- You can develop twisted line on a centre pin reel by repetitive side casting.

If there is too little line on a reel, ***DO NOT USE IT***.

I believe that brightly coloured line may spook fish. This is my personal opinion.

Ordinary monofilament line ["mono"]

What a challenge it must have been before mono was invented. Horse hair, twine and silk!

Fishing line is a wonderful thing. It is also a wicked thing. I cannot describe enough the damage it can do to our flora and fauna – yes plants too! As a matter of fact – there is so much waste around that it becomes a threat to you and your companions. Wherever you find line, wrap it across your palm and roll it up – cut through it and you are left with short pieces that will not do any harm.

Raw product is only manufactured by a select **few** companies worldwide – it is then sold as raw material and processed to the different brands you see today. Different breaking strains, different processes to create and enhance physical properties like colouration, stretch, limpness, resistance to abrasion….

All from the same extruded raw material. And there you have your favourite finished product!

Ordinary mono is naturally buoyant – this means that the line is less dense than water and therefore will have a tendency to float and eventually be suspended in the water [because it is permeable to water, it will eventually absorb water]. This is a mostly undesirable characteristic as it will more than often contribute to *slack line* which is one of the principal reasons for not hooking / losing fish. This characteristic will also impact on the time it takes for line / bait to reach the bottom.

Ordinary mono can stretch by a little more than 30%. Let us say that you have made a cast of 80m [87 yards] from the reel to wherever your 4oz [about 114 g, 0.114 kg] grapnel sinker. If we are looking at a stretch factor of 30%, this means that your line can stretch up to as much as 102m before you move the 4oz sinker! This is an obvious disadvantage over distance. The only real advantage of this ability to stretch is when fighting a fish and sudden turns are made – the load of the fish pulling is **shared** by the rod and the line with the line acting as an additional shock absorber. With low stretch lines like braid, the load of the fighting fish is taken up mainly by the rod.

I for one believe that brightly coloured lines can scare fish off as they are unnatural. When I am forced to use a coloured line on a reel, I use neutral-coloured trace line. This, however is my opinion based on my experience.

Normal mono is also not naturally abrasion resistant – it has to be specially processed to become abrasion resistant.

Mono is relatively inexpensive.

Fluorocarbon line ["fluoro"]

Fluoro is also a monofilament line. It differs greatly from mono.

This group of lines is neutrally coloured and almost impossible to see in the water. Its composition is such that it will out-last normal monofilament line [in terms of decomposition over time], meaning that it will still be there many years after normal mono has started biodegrading. In short, the line has tremendous ultraviolet radiation resistance, greatly prolonging its physical abilities.

It is not as limp as normal monofilament line and therefore has limited 'memory' after being de-spooled. This makes it a great leader line for all forms of fishing, particularly in the form of stepped leaders for fly-fishing, ensuring that the line mostly lands beyond the end of the fly line.

It is a tough line and resistant to damage by abrasion. Unlike mono, it has a much lower elasticity – it does not stretch as much as mono. You have to be a better fisherman to use it as almost all the load of the fight is on the rod and you. You have to respond to every dart and dash a fighting fish can make – and you can do it.

It is very expensive and filling a reel with it can be very costly. This line is therefore used mainly for shock leaders and hook trace line.

Another property is that it has a density greater than that of water. This enables it to sink quickly, much faster than ordinary line, getting your line down more efficiently. You do not necessarily need a heavy sinker to get to the bottom with this line.

It does not absorb water readily. It is also not easily harmed by petrochemicals. This also means that its strength remains unaffected by water and oil-based substances where mono is and will be affected negatively.

Braid

Braid is expensive. There is no doubt about this. But it will outlast normal monofilament line, rendering it cheaper in the longer run. That braid is a *super line* is absolutely true. It displays little or no stretch and this helps to set a hook at a distance. You will feel that it is much more sensitive to bites – remember it does not stretch. *You therefore do not need to strike hard, generally speaking, pick up the rod and start reeling in – if you strike, the rod should never be drawn back to where it goes behind you.* It is also extremely limber and limp in that it does not have a 'memory' just like ordinary cotton thread. A quality I love!

It is very tough and you need to be careful when your hands are wet because it can cut through your skin and flesh easily. So this means that you need protection when reeling in [fortunately it is generally reeled in wet – this helps; and when you cast – there are casting clips that you engage the line in when using a fixed spool reel, and special gloves to protect your fingers. Be careful when you get stuck using braid.

Unlike its monofilament counterparts, *braid is like a good wine – it actually improves with age.* After using your reel, immerse the spool in water and shake it out. *It is a good idea to always try and keep braid damp.*

Braid is basically buoyant and needs special coatings to make it sink fast. This is not a problem due to its low elasticity [does not stretch much at all]. It communicates bites very well and when you strike almost all the energy of the strike goes towards setting the hook – so you really do not need to strike – pick up the rod and start reeling.

You will find that the new generation braids feel more like normal monofilament. But is still braid, with the power and zero stretch property of braid.

I have read recommendations not to use braid on fixed spool reels but I discard this because there are obvious advantages to using braid on a fixed spool reel – I myself have been using it on my deep sea "coffee grinder" [fixed spool reels] for years now.

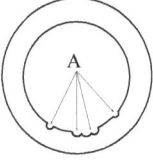

No matter what line you are using, inspect your line guides and rollers and any part that comes into contact with moving line for grooving caused by your line. If you come across these, replace the part immediately. If you go to remote areas, you should be carrying spare rods and reels and line guides. Refer to the sketch. "A" shows grooving of a line guide. Some braids contain Kevlar – used to make bullet-proof vests. It is super strong but also abrasive. Inspect your line guides on and after every outing.

Fly lines

Fly lines are special, heavy and layered lines with weight built into them to facilitate casting. These are discussed in more detail in Chapter 22.

Leader materials

Steel wire, single strand. Gone are the days when steel wire was the bomb. If you are still using steel wire, don't try to straighten out kinks – rather replace the wire with a multiple strand wire. Stainless steel is superior to normal steel wire and is quite corrosion resistant.

But we are now looking at titanium and titanium nickel single and multiple strand wire. These can be coated with a nylon polymer or exposed metal. Spend the money on the titanium wire. It lasts forever, is almost kink-proof, can be knotted, has limited stretch properties [a good property], can withstand the razor tooth clan and rubbing against reef…. Check Chapter 10 for knots with braided wire.

Fluorocarbon monofilament shock leaders are tied at the end of your line to allow you to use the additional pressure required to cast heavy sinkers. If you need to put on the power and/or use a heavy sinker, then you *have to* tie in a shock leader. Remember that fluorocarbon is denser than water – it will sink. Use ordinary monofilament leader if you do not want the sinking properties. I would recommend a minimum shock leader of 40lb [18 kg approximately] for medium tackle upwards.

Fly fishing leaders can be bought in mini rolls. These can be expensive – rather pay for the 100m roll – it will be worth it and you do not run the risk of running out of leader as often as you would with a mini roll.

There are special lead, titanium metal cored and other high density lines that are used when trolling. This is almost always a 'must have' when trolling and you want the lure to work at a certain depth.

Disposal of line

Discarded fishing line will take more than 20 years before it bio-degrades, braid even longer. On each outing, there is a good chance that you will need to discard line. Please do this with a care for the environment. Small animals, birds, crabs and reptiles can get hopelessly entangled and mutilate themselves, more than often suffering a painful and lingering death. People can also become entangled and trip and injure themselves. It is much worse when hooks are also attached to the discarded line.

Please ensure that any discarded line is cut into small pieces and then disposed of. You can do this by rolling the line over your hand and then cutting through the wraps using a scissors or sharp knife, rendering the line into short pieces.

Remember - if you encounter discarded line, please do this. And try and avoid throwing the line away – first prize would be to put the short pieces into a recycling bin. Avoid burning the line.

Go fish!

Chapter 4: Hooks

You need to understand that barbless is the best way to go. What matters is avoiding slack line and you will have the same success rate as you would with barbed hooks. It is unfortunate that most hooks that are commonly available are barbed. You will truly appreciate barbless if you are unlucky enough to get a hook stuck in any part of your anatomy. Barbless hooks are easy to extract. A barbed hook can be rendered barbless either by filing away the barb or by squeezing it using a pair of pliers – this may weaken the hook.

I also advocate that you avoid stainless steel hooks as these last much longer, especially when the fish gets away with a hook stuck in its mouth. Normal steel hooks will corrode much quicker.

Some notes on hook design

Schematic

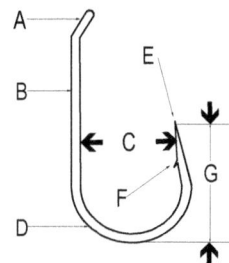

Legend: Schematic of a hook. A: Eye – the eye in this case is offset towards the point of the hook. It can also be offset away from the hook, straight in line with the shank, oriented perpendicular to the present lain [in this case, we would be able to see the ring], and spade end. There are other eye designs which have not been included here; B: Shank. May be straight, curved or in a custom form [like bass hooks] – certain hooks also have barbs on the shank – this is to hold artificial / natural baits in place [for artificial baits, the barbs / slits face downward, away from the eye]; C: Gape [the shortest gap between the point and the shank]; D: Bend; E: Point – sometimes straight in line with the shank, sometimes skew and for circle hooks, the point is perpendicular to the shank; F: Barb; G: Throat [from point to bottom of bend – see arrows above and below "G"].

The next factor is the length of the shank. Hooks with longer shanks [like in the picture above] are generally designed for use for toothed fish, particularly the 'razor tooth' clan. If the shank is more than twice the length of the gape "C", excessive leverage can be exerted on the hook during a fight and the hook could easily dislodge and … "bye-bye *fishie!*"

The shape of the hook is also important. Circle hooks are taking over the market as they mainly naturally engage in the corner of the mouth of the fish – as a matter of fact, several countries have outlawed ordinary hooks and have declared the use of circle hooks as mandatory.

The round bend hook is used for larger species. The distance between the tip of the hook and the bend is described as the "throat" of the hook ["G" above]. I prefer hooks with deeper throats.

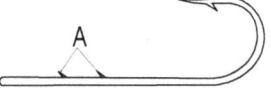 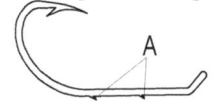

Split shank hooks have barbs on the shank "A". ['split shanks']

These are designed to hold baits in place and are ideally designed for the use of worms and meaty baits with the barbs assisting in holding the bait in position.

If the barbs [slits] are on the same side as the point of the hook, they are for holding artificial baits like plastic worms and frogs – if the barb is on the back of the shank, away from the hook tip, the hook is designed for holding bait like worm and meat in place.

An indication that a hook has been forged is noticeable by examining the hook bend. Under normal circumstances, round wire is used to shape a hook. Hooks that have been forged [impacted whilst hot or cold] will have a different profile to the normal round wire visible on the shank, looking almost square and not round.

If you look carefully, you will easily tell the difference between a hook that has been forged and one that has just be formed. Forging increased the strength of a hook.

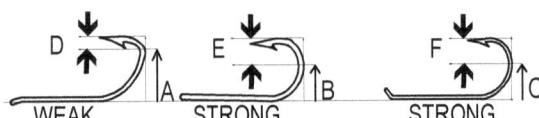

Legend: Place the hook on a square, with the shank sitting against one reference face and the bend of the hook touching the other reference face; A, B & C are dimensions taken from where the bend touches the square and D, E & F from the point of contact to the end of the hook. A: Weak design, not recommended for use for large fish because D is much smaller than A; B: Strong design, suitable because E is closer in size to B but not bigger; C: Strong design, suitable because F is closer in size to C but not bigger. These recommendations are based on my experience.

The eye

The eye of the tiger …. oops! I mean the eye of the hook: Sadly, not much is said about this 'blunt' end of the hook. Firstly, there is the spade-end hook. This type of hook is designed to be attached to your line by means of a nail knot which is tied directly to the shank of the hook. The 'spade-end' stops the knot from sliding off. This hook has no 'eye' as we know it, but the end has been flattened, resembling a 'spade' in profile, hence the name.

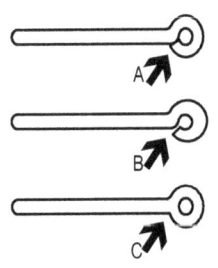

Legend: 'Eye' detail. A: This eye shows that the end of the wire used to make the hook is touching or is almost touching the shank, generally a sign of hooks that have been heat treated and tempered – strong hook feature; B: There is a noticeable gap between the wire end and the shank. This is generally a sign of an inferior hook; C: This is what a braised-end eye detail looks like. The end of the wire has been joined to the shank. This is generally done to ultra-strong hooks used for game fishing – this is generally only done to very strong hooks. Smaller hooks are available with braised eyes. Offset hooks play an important role when simulating living creature movements when retrieving flies in fly fishing.

All other hooks [except needle hooks] are terminated in a ring to which we tie the fishing line. Note that the eye on needle hooks resembles the threading end of a needle – these hooks are used for small live baits where a normal eye would damage the bait. Poor quality hooks have a gap between the end of the wire and the shank "B" above – avoid these. The stronger hooks have been braised and you cannot see where the wire ends "C" above.

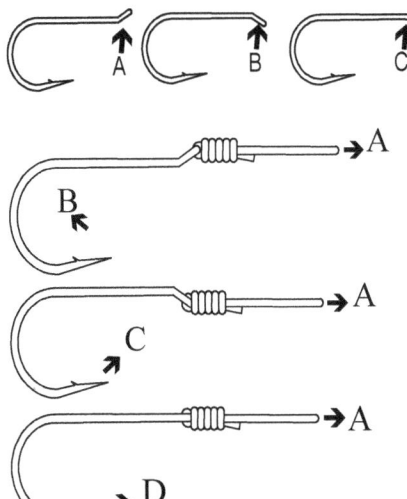

Legend: Normal 'J' hook designs. A: Hook eye offset away from point; B: Hook eye offset towards hook point; C: Eye not offset

Legend: Eye offset away from hook point. When the line is pulled in direction "A", the hook point actually moves backwards in the direction of arrow "B" as the hook tries to centre itself in the direction of the pulling action.

Legend: Eye offset towards hook point. When the line is pulled in direction "A", the hook point is actually accelerated in the direction of the pulling action, as indicated by arrow "C" in the sketch alongside.

Legend: Eye not offset. When the line is pulled in direction "A", the hook point moves in the direction of the pulling action, as indicated by arrow "D" alongside.

Looking at the above sketches, it is obvious that the offset hooks are so designed to create additional action over and above just moving when the line is moved. This should be planned when considering what bait to use. If action is not important, you will be better off using the hook without an offset eye.

Testing hooks

Generally speaking, most hooks are made from wire with most of them forged into shape. They are then fettled where necessary and heat-treated in two stages. In the first stage, they are fully hardened and can break quite easily. The second stage is tempering. In this stage, they are heat treated [tempered] down at a lower temperature and generally air-cooled. Sometimes the heat treatment can go wrong and these hooks may inadvertently [or otherwise] be released for use. Test the strength of the hook by feeling the extent of "give" in the degree of flexion [ability to bend without losing shape] you experience [hold the shank just at the eye with one hand and the tip just below the sharpened point with the other hand. Pull and release. Refer to the sketch alongside] – if this changes the shape of the hook, it is not suitably hardened, if it does not flex at all, indications are that the hook is possibly too hard [possibly 'brittle']. There should just be a little 'give' and the hook returns to its original shape. Do not use pliers or a vice to conduct this test as you can easily apply too much force than is necessary. The rule of thumb is that hooks that flex excessively should only be used when fishing ultra-light. [Note that the degree of flexion is determined by the movement between the tip of the hook and the eye. Trebles should also be tested using this method. But be careful! Also remember that you will experience no flexion with extra strong hooks.

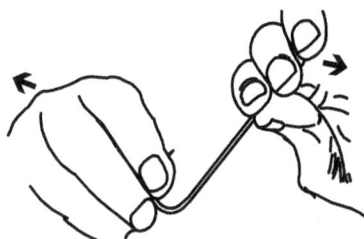

Test the strength of the hook by feeling the extent of "give" in the degree of flexion [ability to bend without losing shape] you experience [hold the shank just at the eye with one hand and the tip just below the sharpened point with the other hand. Pull and release. Refer to the sketch alongside] – if this changes the shape of the hook, it is not suitably hardened, if it does not flex at all, indications are that the hook is possibly too hard [possibly 'brittle']. There should just be a little 'give' and the hook returns to its original shape.

So, a good hook will pass the bend test described above; must conform to B & C above; should not have a barb that is too big [better to have no barb]; and should pass the sharpness test. Generally, smaller hooks are made of thinner wire – thinner means easier penetration.

You should carry a good selection of hooks and spares. Hook sizes are counted in multiples of two for normal hooks, starting [I think] as small as size 32 with size 1 being the only odd number and the largest hook in the series – although I have, upon occasion seen hooks marked 'size 5' and 'size 3'. Larger hooks than a size one are identified as a '*number*' /0, the smallest in the oversize group is size1/0 to 19/0 hook. Larger hooks are available. *I cannot believe that there are no specifications [that I know of] to standardize hook quality levels –* this is sad because people out there who do not have much money will more than often go for the lower-priced hooks to their own detriment.

Fatigue

Your choice of hook can be the next biggest cause of lost fish [the biggest being incompetence on the part of the person holding the rod!]. Why do people insist on using the same hook over and over again? Grrrrr!!! This really never fails to surprise me. I remember so many different scenarios where we are busy tracing up and the other person smiles and tells me that they are using their favourite trace…. This is a really bad practice.

How do you break a piece of wire without using some sort of cutting device? Well – you keep on bending it until it breaks, right? What you are actually doing by repeatedly bending the wire is called 'work hardening'. This means that as the wire is worked, it gets progressively harder until it becomes so brittle that it snaps. Once used a few times, hooks have been exposed to stresses in the form of oxidation with air and water, mechanical stresses from being stuck and stresses from fighting fish – in other words, the hook becomes weaker. And knots can over-tighten and cause your line to break.

Now hooks undergo the same process [as bending a piece of wire repeatedly to break it]. The bigger the fish you hook, the harder it pulls with the hook flexing each time it is under load [each time the fish makes a run and each time it turns]. And what happens next? You invariably hook into something big using an old hook, and it snaps…. or straightens or the line breaks… And you end up looking stupidly at the broken / straightened hook saying "*Aaaaaw…*" You replace it using the same trace and the knots on the swivel are still the same with the same trace line. This means that the existing knots on the swivel have been subjected to load during previous fights - a knot is only effective if all the wraps are uniformly tight. When a knot is subjected to load, it sometimes results in further, uneven tightening of the wraps comprising the knot. This tightening effect squeezes the main line, reducing the diameter, creating a weak spot. … "a chain is only as strong as its weakest link"?

If a trace has been subjected to strain [strain can be as a result of fighting a fish or from a hook that was caught on some overhead or submerged object], it should be changed using all new components. Swivels can be re-used within reason. Line can and does get damaged. Check. Replace. Check.

The barb

The next thing to consider is the size of the barb. You have to be aware that the bigger the barb, the greater the effort required to achieve full penetration – remember that for the barb to be effective, it has to penetrate fully when you strike, and only then does it assist you because it retards extraction of the hook during the fight.

If you are using monofilament line, much of the energy you use in striking is taken up by both the line and rod and only a little of that effort pulls the hook home [due to the line stretching and the rod bending].

If you are using braid or fluorocarbon, you are ok – but remember, in these cases, all the load in your strike is communicated to your hook because there is no stretch, so don't strike too hard…

Remember, your success rate is higher with hooks having smaller barbs or with hooks having no barbs. Some barbs are knife shaped to facilitate the barb 'cutting in' upon striking [generally for big game fishing].

Sharpness

The next factor is the degree of sharpness of the hook.

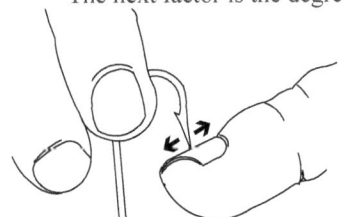

*To test the sharpness, carefully and **LIGHTLY** drag the point across your thumbnail. If it is adequately sharp, it will try to dig in and **not** slide – if not sharp enough, it will slide across the nail. If the hook slides across your nail, you will need to sharpen it or select another hook.* **PLEASE BE CAREFUL!!!!**

To sharpen your hook, you will need a *fine-grained* whet stone [made from a material trademarked as '*carborandum*', available from the average tackle shop and hardware store – NO – don't go to a tackle store – I haven't seen one that sells fine stones - go to an industrial hardware supply store and ask for a 'polishing' stone you will have a super-fine-grained stone - as in the picture to the left – they are approximately 12mm square and about 125mm long].

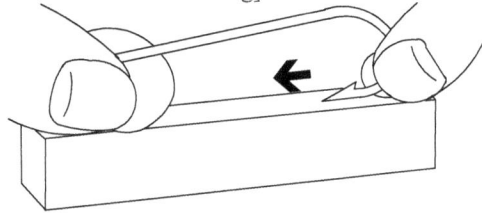

*Holding the shank of the hook, **drag** the point on the stone repetitively until adequately sharp. Always drag the hook into the stone [in the direction of the arrow, then lift and repeat until point is sharp], do not drag the hook in the opposite direction! And remember a coarse stone will never sharpen a small surface area effectively – get the polishing stone from industrial hardware supplier!*

And while we are on the subject of sharpness – remember this simple logical fact – the thinner the wire, the easier it is to penetrate – what am I saying? WHEREVER POSSIBLE, USE THE SMALLER HOOK! Especially in fresh water.

When you see 'chemically-sharpened' and laser-sharpened hooks, they are worth investing in.

Circle hooks

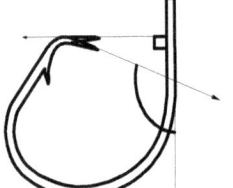

What is so special about circle hooks? To the average person, they look rather incapable of hooking anything because the point of the hook looks totally IMPOTENT!
Well, paradoxically, the design is intended to render the hook impotent whilst the hook is in the fish's stomach or mouth cavity – too many fish are injured by the normal "J" shaped hooks.
No real striking with a circle hook to engage the barb – just tight line and the fight is on!!

But are "J" – shaped hooks great? They will indiscriminately catch on any part of the fish from gut to lip, and also cause fish to become foul-hooked. This particularly with the "J" hooks where the points are angled to the extent that they are not parallel to the shank.

A circle hook on the other hand can also easily fit into the fish's mouth. When a fish takes the bait, the hook is impotent until the fish swims away or turns [the point of the hook is roughly 90° or greater to the shank – see illustration – the illustration depicts two points – the average circle hook point is anywhere on or in the range described by the two points].

At this point, the line and hook are directed to the corner of the mouth where the hook will turn and engage automatically.

You do not need to strike when fishing circle hooks!!! You just need a tight line – pick up the rod, raise the tip and reel rapidly until you feel the fish.

The information in this paragraph is not going to be repeated later in this book – perhaps it will be mentioned once or twice, but these is a way to bait these hooks in such a way that it almost guarantees a hook-up. The following sketches illustrate how a circle hook should be baited – please don't exploit our waters!!"

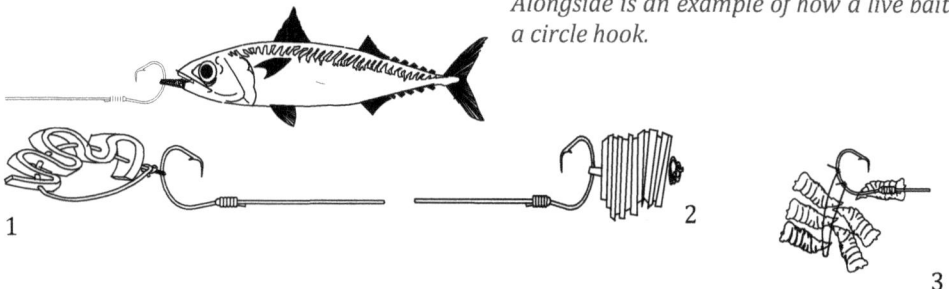

Alongside is an example of how a live bait is rigged with a circle hook.

The above three drawings illustrate how dead bait is rigged. Item 1 is using a strip of bait, item 2, a series of pieces stacked together, and item 3 is using very small independent baits in a cluster. In all cases, the bait is arttached to a loop of cotton and the cotton is attached to the bend of the hook.
You're welcome!! **Please take only what you need, and DO practice catch-and-release.**

Speciality hooks

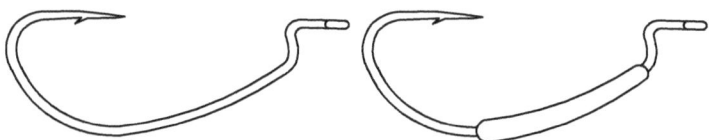

There is a large variety of speciality hooks used to catch bass, I only use 1 design – weighted or ordinary.

On the left is the ordinary bass hook which is suitable for all plastic worms and designs long enough to be pinned using this hook. On the right is the weighted hook – this design allows the hook to be bounced or dragged along the bottom. It can also be raised and allowed to fall back to the bottom creating very realistic enticing movements when used properly. The best feature of this hook is that it allows the bait to be presented in an upright position if not retrieved at too great a speed.

There are hook designs that utilize a spiral wire / pin attached to the eye section of the hook – this is for anchoring plastic worms '/ frogs. I have found that they do more damage to the plastic lure and am happy to use hooks without the spiral / pin.

Remember that you have to select the correct hook for the purpose – some hooks are made to minimize weight – these are mostly used to tie dry flies so make them as light as possible. When you are fishing for strong jawed fish like musselcracker – they will make short work of a normal hook and will crush and distort the hook – this means that you will lose them.

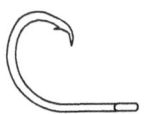
*For the stronger species, you must use the extra strong hooks made by reputable companies like **Daiichi, Gamagatsu and Mustad.** Pay the extra money– they are well worth it.*

Drop shot hooks

Alongside are four examples of what I call 'drop-shot- hooks. These are designed to sit [almost all the time] on the bottom with the hook safely up and away from snags on the bottom.

This type of hook is designed for use with plastic baits – some resembling some type of submarine creature and some just a general attractor pattern. The hook has several design variants, each designed for use with a specific type of plastic lure.

The head of the lure is fed onto the hook for 10 – 15mm and the hook is allowed to emerge with it being pushed over the side of the sinker where it is held by a spike or the shape at the end of the lead head. The hook can also be used with real live / dead bait.

How to modify a hook to render it *weedless*

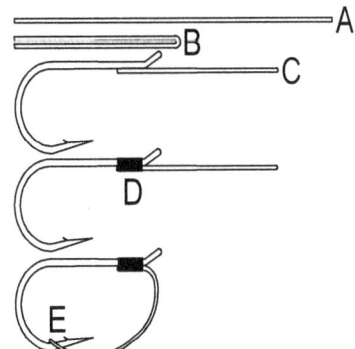

Cut a length of heavier line [not braid], "A" about 2½ times the length of the hook you intend using.

Fold it back on itself tightly, creating a loop at "B".

Overlap about 4mm of line using the two loose ends on the hook, just behind the eye "C". [Put a few wraps of cotton on the hook first!]

Using cotton, attach the two ends of line to the hook by whipping, glue the cotton in place "D". Locate the loop around the hook at "E".

You know that fish love reeds and that you will have to fish in and around reeds and high-potential snag areas.

Trebles

Treble hooks are designed for hooking and holding. I prefer not to use them except when fishing for larger salt water game fish with live bait. When buying lures, these should always be tested and replaced when found to flex too much. They should also be inspected and changed when necessary, if they are used.

Note that the type of treble illustrated here has a full radius on the bend and that the hooks are welded together along with a welded eye

Now having said all this, go barbless! You can file away the barb on larger hooks or, with smaller hooks, displace it [by squeezing] using a pair of pliers.

Chapter 5: Sinkers

Sinkers are commonly made from lead which is a *toxic* substance. Sinkers lost to the sea and other fishing waters eventually break down, increasing lead levels in the water. Lead can be ingested [by swallowing] but needs to be chemically broken down for it to be absorbed and is commonly absorbed in the body by inhalation and touching the white, powdery lead oxide film. Avoid contact with lead in its organic form – yes – that white powdery residue you see when you find a sinker- beware of that. Fumes containing lead compounds are released when lead is melted [like making sinkers]. So please refrain from making sinkers from lead. **Try and find alternate forms of sinker materials – old steel nuts, spark plugs, washers, and ferrules are examples of items made from steel / copper / brass that you can use.**

The obvious function of a sinker is to assist in getting your bait out when casting and to take your line to the bottom, and anchor it there. There is a large variety of sinkers. These are broken up into three main categories: pinch-on sinkers, terminal sinkers and running sinkers.

Pinch-on sinkers [split shot] come in a variety of sizes. These are generally in the form of shot and are mainly used in conjunction with floats although they may also be used for relatively short-distance casting. Some of you may elect to use strip lead cut into the size / sizes you prefer.

Terminal sinkers are located at the end of traces, allowing your line to reach the bottom.

Almost any sinker can be used as a running sinker, this is dependent on the structure and type of submarine terrain.

The following types of sinkers are commonly available:

Split shot.

Legend: *No – it's NOT* ***Pacman!!!*** *Lead balls of variable sizes [normally up to 6mm with a slit in the middle to accommodate your line]. Some shot has two 'ears' – these, when squeezed together, open the slit.*

Shot should be doctored using a knife before use if the slit is too narrow. This is done by inserting the sharp end of a knife into the slit to open up the shot to a *'vee'* before you go fishing. This makes application so much easier.

How many times have you tried to put on shot only watch helplessly as it slips from your fingers, plopping into the water or into cover? ... [*Buhuhuhuuuhahahahaaaaa!!!* :D]

Shot is used to assist in casting, therefore enabling you to fish as light as possible. It is normally used for float fishing, to set the float at the correct height, making it extra-sensitive to bites, but I find it especially useful when using just a hook to lure shy fish into biting. Little or no resistance is felt by fish taking the bait. Shot is put onto the line by slotting it into the *vee* shape on the sinker and then pinching the lead using your hands [some people bite it but this is an *unhealthy* practice].

It is not advisable to bite the shot closed as this could contribute to lead poisoning by degrees [the effects of lead poisoning are cumulative]. It is always advisable to use several small shot instead of larger shot. When float fishing in a river with shot, the shot is generally placed at the depth you are targeting – it keeps the bait at the depth you require despite the current.

Shot is also used to set 'stick' floats at the optimum depth so that just the tip of the float is visible, allowing you to identify a bite with ease.

Grapnel sinkers.

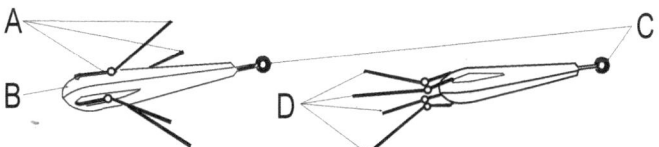

Legend: *A: There are two sets of wire grapnels on each sinker. Each wire runs through the body of the sinker. These wire grapnels are engaged in grooves on the sinker body. Each wire has a plastic bead threaded on it which helps the wire locate securely in the groove; B: Main sinker body, normally lead; C: Wire ring to which the fishing line is secured to the sinker; D: Wire grapnels*

disengaged from grooves in sinker body.
There are other designs, but these all work on the same principle.

Grapnel sinkers are normally used to try and anchor live / dead baits where there are water currents that can move normal sinkers out of the bite zone, and to prevent the live bait from dragging the sinker. These sinkers have either wire or nylon inserts that jut out like an anchor. Some wire grapnels need to be set by snapping them into the grooves on the sinker before casting [see sketch above]; you may also need to bend the wire so that it is angled towards your line, resembling a grapnel. Normally used in salt water.

They are best used when fishing live bait, and are cast out with the bait being clipped on after the cast has settled.

Pear-shaped sinkers.

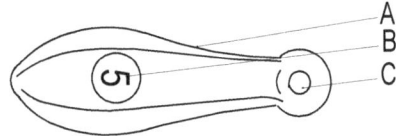

Legend: *A: Sinker body, normally cast using molten lead; B: Ring in which there is normally a number. This number describes the approximate mass of the sinker in ounces [1 oz = approximately 28.35g; C: Ring by which the sinker is attached to the fishing line. Use in high-risk snag conditions.*

These are normally used for bottom fishing using live / dead bait. These are normally used in zero or low-current fishing where the underwater current will not roll / drag the sinker.

Cone-shaped 'bullet' sinkers.

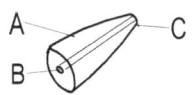

Legend: *A: Bullet-shaped conical sinker normally cast in lead; B: Hole running through sinker through which line passes, rendering the sinker a 'running' sinker as it freely allows line to pass through it; C: Apex of cone. This end always is closer to the rod.*

Normally used when fishing artificial lures, like plastic worms. The pointed end is always away from the hook with the blunt end sitting on the swivel or directly on the hook. This type of sinker is used when fishing an area with structure. It is also used on flat, bottoms where there is little or no apparent structure.

Pyramid sinkers

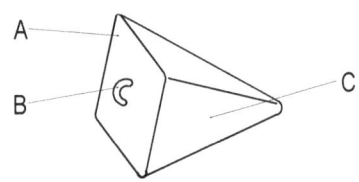

Legend: *A: Sinker body, normally cast in lead; B: Wire loop cast into sinker. Fishing line is normally secured to this; C: There normally is a number on one or more of these faces. This number represents the approximate mass of the sinker in ounces. [1oz is approximately 28.35g]. The shape of this sinker may also be conical. Do not use in high-risk snag conditions.*

These are designed to stay on the bottom when there are currents dragging your line. Normally only used in saltwater on a sandy bottom.

Bullet sinkers.

These are normally used in fresh water and lagoons.

Legend: *Egg-shaped / spherical bullet-shaped sinker, normally made from lead; These sinkers have a hole running through for fishing line to be passed through rendering them 'running' sinkers;*

Suited best for running traces in areas where the current will not cause the sinker to roll. Also used to keep artificial lures on and close to the bottom, and to keep live / drift bait below the surface.

Barrel sinkers.

Legend: *Barrel – shaped sinker, normally made of lead. It has a h through the length, along the centre. Fishing line is threaded through this hole, rendering it a 'running' sinker.*

These are also best suited for use as running sinkers. They are also used with drift baits from a boat.

Spoon sinker

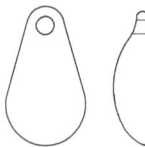

Legend: *Two views of this type of sinker showing its basic shape. These have a hole through which fishing line is attached. In most instances, the mass of the sinker is identified by an impression on the curved face of the sinker. Use in high-risk snag conditions.*

Tear drop sinker

Legend: *This sinker has a wire ring built into the moulded product. Fishing line is tied to this loop. Use in high-risk snag conditions.*

And remember – lead metal is ***toxic***. All those lost sinkers sitting on the bottom, slowly and inexorably being broken down by the elements, increasing the soluble lead levels in the water…

Chapter 6: Floats

Floats are primarily used as bite indicators, and are used to set your baited offering at a predetermined depth presenting it close to the surface, at mid-water or even on the bottom. They can also assist in preventing your hook from becoming snagged.

Floats also add weight to your rig, improving your casting range.

The colour of the float is generally immaterial as the fish see them as dark objects silhouetted against the sky.

Floats should normally offer minimal resistance when taking the bait. It is important to leave as little of the float showing as possible – this way a bite is instantly detected; the part of the float that remains visible should be brightly coloured so that you do not lose sight of it.

You should always keep the line between the rod tip and the float as straight as possible so as to avoid slack line – slack line will contribute to fish being lost.

When fishing in saltwater, floats are used during bottom fishing to lend buoyancy to your bait – this enhances your presentation by making your baited offering move with the water current thereby making it more attractive – it also keeps your bait off the bottom, away from flatfish like sand shark, skate and rays.

For freshwater applications, all floats are used, in principle, as illustrated for the porcupine quill-type float. Long floats are seldom allowed to float flat on the water – these must almost always be fished with only part of the tip showing – this enhances the sensitivity of the float. Floats with larger bodies are generally used when fishing live-bait.

You always want to use the lightest weight possible for the job.

Porcupine quills

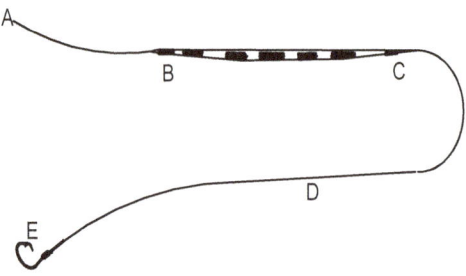

Legend: Porcupine quill rig. A: Fishing line leading to reel; B: Insulation tape attaching line to 'blunt' end of quill, as close to end as possible. Place one wrap of tape around the dry quill before trapping the line to this end; C: Tape wrapping line to sharp end of quill as close to end as possible. Be sure to apply one wrap of tape directly to dry end of quill first; D: 'Pinch on' lead ball [split shot] positioned on line.

The lead weight should not be closer than 300mm to the hook. Use as many weights as necessary to cause the float to just stand erect in the water; E: snoot or line leading to hook. In rapids, this line should be long enough to allow the bait to run as close to the bottom as possible. In still water you need to set it to the depth you want to fish at.

Nothing beats a quill for bite sensitivity when using a float. These are excellent but can only be used for small baits. I normally use a piece of insulation tape attaching it to the line at each end of the quill. Do not allow the quill points to protrude at either end as this will cause problems when casting with the line fouling on the exposed ends, or worse, the baited hook. Under normal circumstances use black tape, but you can change the colour accordingly to enhance visibility.

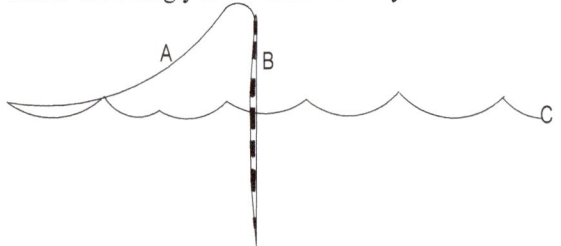

Legend: Correctly set quill rig. A: Line leading to rod – avoid slack line so you can tighten up at any point; B: Quill standing up at 90°, being set by the addition of split shot; C: water level. Any movement of the float now is translated as a bite.

Cork floats

These floats are easily obtainable and can be used for all types of fishing. They should be painted to seal the outer surface, preventing them from becoming waterlogged. The main disadvantage with these floats is that fish feel resistance when taking the bait as the shape of the float offers resistance when they bite – most fish are likely to abandon the bait when this happens.

The float can be attached to your line by cutting a slit in them, inserting your line into the slit and wrapping a section of insulation tape or a rubber band around the float to help prevent it from being lost if your line works out of the slit. You can also drill a hole in the float and pass your line through the hole

Cork floats are best used to keep your bait off the bottom if you want to avoid hooking bottom feeders like rays, skates and sand sharks. But this is not the only reason for using a float on submerged bait – using a float on submerged baits makes the bait more susceptible to underwater currents, causing it to flit and drift enticingly whilst it is anchored on the bottom by the sinker. *Bait movement is a bonus feature that **will** attract fish*. You will do well to remember and apply this concept.

Balsa-wood floats

These 'stick' floats are commonly available and are worth investing in. When using this type of float, remember that only the brightly coloured-tip should be visible – to achieve this, you will need to test the float on a baited rig.

Along with the weight of the bait, you will have to attach split shot to your line so that just the tip is showing as illustrated for the quill float. The bulkier floats are designed for heavier baits.

Unlike cork and plastic floats, these long-bodied floats when properly set, are not greatly affected by wind – the slimmer the exposed tip of the float, the less the wind resistance it offers – wind can make your bait move unnaturally.

Heavier and bulkier floats allow you to cast further, should the need arise.

Styrofoam strips

These must be tailored to be used to keep bait off the bottom whilst at the same time lending buoyancy to the bait, making it more sensitive to water currents – bait movement can and will attract fish. [the bait is wrapped around the strip and held in place by latex bait cotton].

Plastic floats

These are traditionally red and white and generally come in spheres of varying diameters. These are really only suitable for smaller fish like bluegills. The wire attachment rings are generally spring-loaded for easy application and removal from line.

These floats offer high resistance when fish take the bait – this can cause the larger fish and shy fish to abandon your baited offering. I do not use them, nor do I recommend them.

Shapes and uses

Floats having this shape and design are generally used to present live bait. These are generally red topped and white bottomed with a tapered rod in the middle. When using, pull out the rod, pass your line through the middle and then replace the rod after selecting the depth you want to fish at [when you re-insert the tapered rod, it locks the line in position. Note that the line from your reel goes through the larger end of the tapered hole with the smaller end of the taper facing the hook.

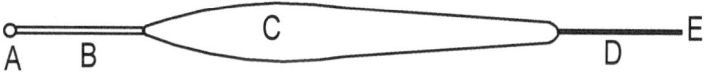

Legend: *Schematic pencil-shaped float design [aka 'stick' floats]. A: line ring – I normally disable the ring. Your line is supposed to go through the ring in order to keep the float captive. I use a section of insulation tape wrapped around here to hold the line captive; B: Immersed shank – this, being the bottom of the float, is normally submerged and can vary in length – I normally use insulation tape here, as close to the end as possible to hold the line captive; C: float body – this may be made up of any material [either naturally buoyant or trapping air]. This is the buoyant body of the float; D: Top shank – this is the only part of the float that should be visible when the float is in use – it is normally brightly coloured to enhance visibility. Any movement here signifies a bite; E: top end of the float shank – this is sometimes terminated by a ball. I use insulation tape just below this section to attach the rod end of the line here. Floats sometimes have plastic / rubber sleeves here – these are supposed to have your line passed through them and fit over the shank, giving the float adjustability in use in terms of set depth. With insulation tape, you can just pull the line through either way – it remains captive. Note that you can use different coloured insulation tape until you find the type that is most visible over the distance you are casting. A champagne or wine cork can be attached in the same way.*

Bung floats

These are really weighted floats, around 75 – 100mm in length and around 40mm in diameter. Made from wood / cork / plastic and very buoyant.

Designed for use in the surf zone. They are weighted to facilitate casting and can support a whole sardine [or just a fillet]. Normally used for shad but can quite easily be used for larger game fish, including shark. They are generally supplied with a wire running through, terminated at both ends by a ring where the trace and main line can be attached to the wire rings at opposite ends.

Necessity is the mother of invention

Should you need a float and do not have any of the above, a straw / papyrus stalk / bamboo / stick can be used. A straw can also be used by sealing the ends.

Use your imagination.

Chapter 7: Swivels

Before you even go any further, know this: your swivel [in good working condition] is only going to do what it is meant to do if your knots are well-tied.

Don't rush that knotting process.

The purpose of a swivel is to protect your line from becoming twisted. Twisted line bunches up and can create all sorts of nightmares for you. Swivels are is designed to allow line to untwist while it is out, and whilst reeling in. There are various designs out there, most of which are covered below. If you are going for biggies, especially in the salt, you will need to use power swivels. You also need to remember that as swivels increase in size, so too does the diameter of the wire. The smallest swivel [I think] in the standard swivel is a size 20. This is made from a very small diameter wire and should only be used for ultra-light applications. Choose your size based on the line strength. For line 8pounds and less, you can use sizes 20 – 12. For line strengths of 10pounds to 15pounds, you can use sizes 10 – 8. And the larger swivels size 7 – 5 up to 20 pounds... From 25pound line upwards – you should be using power swivels. For big game fishing, you should be using ball bearing or heavy-duty type swivels.

Many think that the next benefit of using a swivel is that it can be used to stop a sliding hook trace or a sinker. In theory, this is true, but any sliding trace or sinker is going to hit the swivel at high impact quite often [see top and bottom pictures on inset sketch]. This is even worse when your line is caught on the reef / structure. Wait a minute... before the line impacts with the swivel, what happens??? Whatever is sliding on your line will almost certainly more than often impact with the knot connecting the swivel to your line before it is finally stopped by the swivel – this is not a benefit.

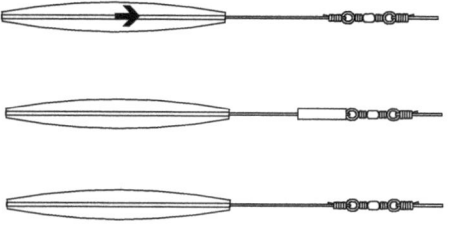

What I do to protect the knot from impact-damage is illustrated alongside in the centre inset sketch. I remove the tube from ball point pens with depleted ink, cut them to a convenient size, and thread the line through after the sinker and before I tie the knot. I then slide the tube over the knot. The sinker in the illustration now harmlessly impacts the tube, and not the knot.

The further one casts, the more essential a swivel becomes. They are generally made of rust-resistant material and will outlast most hooks in your tackle box. There are four main types:

The normal two-way swivel

 *This is used when fishing with a running sinker or a single hook, or when using a lure.*

Note that you only use the ring on the left to attach line from the reel, and the ring on the right to attach the snoot line [the line to your hook].

Buhuhuhuuuhahahaaa!!! ***Any*** side can be used!

The power swivel

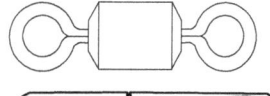 *These are more expensive but much more reliable and are generally used when going for bigger / stronger fish, especially in the salt and especially when fights are prolonged.*

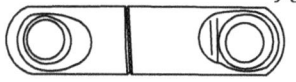 *The swivel to the left is also a power swivel but HEAVY duty. It is cylindrical in shape and very nice to have. It costa plenty.*

The three-way swivel

 *This is generally used when fishing with a sinker. The sinker is ALWAYS attached to the swivel leg that is perpendicular ["C" in sketch] Never attach your hook to this leg of the swivel as it will eventually weaken it, causing failure when under load. You should also tie in a weaker line for your sinker.*

The 'clip-on' swivel

These devices are very handy for a quick changeover of baits / traces / lures.

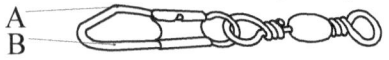

*The design alongside is sometimes called a 'snapper' swivel and should **NOT** be used to attach hooks to the mainline because they are designed to release under load.*

Make sure the clip is fully engaged. Use these to attached to sinkers in high snag-risk situations – if you get caught up, the wire clip will eventually release, saving your trace but losing a sinker. Leg "A" is unclipped for a quick changeover of sinkers and "B" is the fixed leg of the clip.

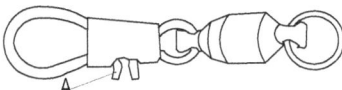

Refer to the sketch alongside. As you can see, with the design of the clip "A", it will not release if properly secured. If you are attaching a lure, hook or trace to a clip-on swivel, be sure to use this design.

There are several alternate designs that can be as secure – all of them have positive legs that hold the clip closed, even when under load.

I saw an article on the internet that claimed that adding swivels to your line will compromise your casting accuracy and even your line strength. *Well done, Captain Obvious!* There is no doubt that this is true – but until we figure out some other way to reduce / eliminate twist, continue using swivels where necessary. All you have to do is be aware that not only swivels, but every knot one ties on a line, potentially reduces your line breaking strain. Although I still have to figure out how a swivel compromises casting accuracy...

When not to use a swivel:
- When fishing for tigerfish – they will attack the swivel.
- When using a drop-shot hook – there is no need as this hook does not spin and twist the line.

Chapter 8: Landing aids

If you are going to return a fish to the water, always avoid handling it by the soft underbelly area as this can easily cause injury to the creature's organs. It is not a good idea to attempt to land a fish unless it has been played to the extent that it is swimming on its side. If you are fishing in an area, it is necessary to know where and how you can land a fish safely. If you do not have such a plan, you are wasting your time.

Drop nets

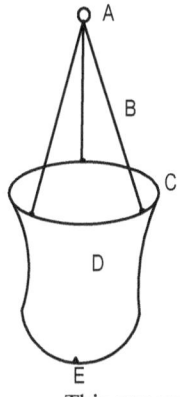

Legend: Long drop net ☺. A: Galvanized steel suspension ring to hold tie lines and to tie suspension rope to. Rope and lines should be fine woven and capable of lifting at least 40kg; B: Tie lines attached to suspension ring and net ring; C: Net ring [about 750mm diameter] made from steel with three eyes welded to it at 120° intervals for attaching tie lines. Steel ring should be galvanized. The net is attached to the steel ring by strong bindings; D: Net at least 1m deep; E: Weight tied to bottom of net so that it sinks [depicted as a little triangle].

This apparatus is used when fishing from a high point into deep water. It is lowered into the water when the fish has been suitably played and is tired. It is held in position with the rim submerged enough to clear the body of the fish whilst the person fighting the fish leads the fish over the rim of the net and the net is lifted clear off the water.

Be sure to watch waves that may drive the net onto rocks or the pillions of the pier or whatever structure you are fishing from or the net will surely get caught up. The person manipulating the net must act fast and pull the net up immediately the fish passes over the hoop. If the fish swims over it and between the suspension lines of the net....

Using the tackle

I avoid fishing for shad because of two reasons: The first is that you can't really fight a shad because the object [for everyone else] is to take the fish out as quickly as possible so that the next cast can be back in the water before the shoal moves on. Consequently, the fish, once hooked, ends up being towed out by heavy tackle without fear of breaking rod, tackle or line – if you try and 'play' the fish, you will create high risk tangle situations as the fish will cross over the 1001 lines in the water – There are almost always too many lines in the water – as I said before, I have always been a loner.

Call me selfish, but I like fishing waters where I and the people with me are the only ones on the beach.

And there are no cries of: *"Coming over!"*

Beaching

This is a technique where the fish is brought into the shallows and then dragged out of the water. This is fairly easily accomplished in most fresh water venues. Where there is flowing water, use the flow to your advantage. Don't fight the current *AND* the fish. Try and get downstream and work the fish to the side, out of the current in progressive moves, and into the shallows where it can be beached. It is always a good idea to place a rag over its eyes as this calms the fish.

In the sea, use the waves to bring the fish closer. When waves recede, do not force the fish out of the receding water. Use each wave to bring it progressively closer, and once the fish is lying on its side you should be able to drag it away from the water. If there is a side-wash [current flowing to one side], use it as much as you can to progressively bring the fish closer.

Never fight the fish **AND** the current! Beaching a fish is always a last option.

'Tailing' by hand or with 'tailing' device

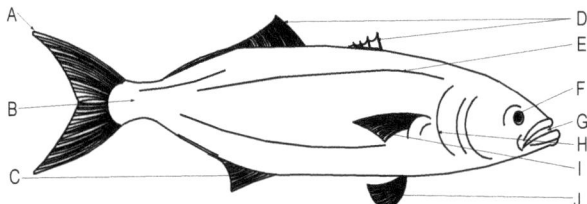

Legend: *Pictured is a shad. A: Tail fin, aka Caudal fin; B: Caudal peduncle [base of the tail]; C: Anal fin; D: Dorsal fin [this bugger has two]; E: Lateral line [any damage on or near this line will almost certainly kill the fish]; F: Eye; G: Mouth [this particular fish has razor sharp teeth – be warned!]; H: Gill slit [fish hooked in the gills are not likely to survive]; I: Pectoral fin; J: Pelvic fin. The heart of the fish is generally situated in a straight line between the pelvic fin and the eye, in front of the gill slit.*

Tailing involves grabbing the fish by the tail [refer "B" in the sketch above] and hauling it out, this requires skill and experience and is only accomplished with fish that have tails firm enough to grab.

Remember, or you will not have a tail to tell – you will have a 'tale' to tell.

It is preferable that you wear a suitable glove to do this – the first reason is that you may get injured as some fish have appendages like 'scalpels' that can cut you; the second is if you intend returning the fish, **you may injure it by removing protective slime thereby exposing the fish to disease**.

If your hand cannot fit around the tail, there are tailing devices available that have a nylon coated loop and a long handle – the loop needs simply to be passed over the tail and a simple 'pull' on the handle will engage the loop and hold the fish captive.

Such a piece of equipment should only be used if you have no intention of returning the fish [fish are not designed to be held up by their tails].

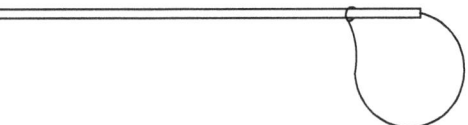

Legend: *Tailing device. Comprising a handle and nylon-sheathed cord. One end of the cord is securely fitted to the end of the handle and the other has a loop. Slide the loop over the handle and it is ready for action! It is best to make certain that the fish is tired and with a little practice you can slip the device over the fish's tail without touching it –* **touching will spook the fish!** *Make your own tailing device!*

The landing net

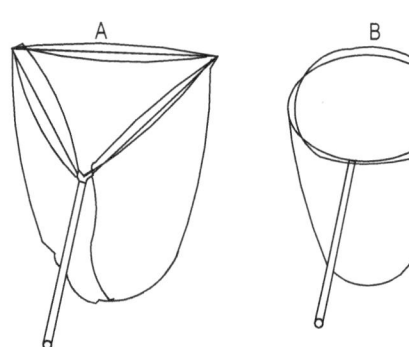

The perfect net has a flat lip that allows room for error and sudden movements of the fish from side-to-side.

The lip "A" has a wider mouth whereas the mouth "B" is curved, increasing the risk of accidental contact with the fish. This is why you see fewer circular nets around.

Avoid collapsible landing net designs – some of them will try to collapse if you inadvertently use them the wrong way around [an easy thing to do in the moment!].

Avoid netting members of the *razortooth* brigade [shad, walla walla, snoek, barracuda, couta and wahoo – to name a few] – they are capable of biting through the net fabric, creating holes.

Always inspect nets before and after an outing and make repairs whenever necessary – if a fish escapes through a hole in the net, you will be faced with fighting it with your line running through the net… you do not *ever* want to experience this.

Netting should *never* be performed by an inexperienced person.

Always bring the fish to the net, **NEVER** bring the net to the fish – this will almost always spook fish. Once the fish has entered the net, lift until the fish goes into the body of the net, then pull the net towards you.

Do **NOT** try and lift a net horizontally.

Carry the net with the handle in a vertical position as this will not strain the net or its handle.

Lip-landing

This tool [below] is used by positioning the caliper over the lower lip of a fish and clamps on the lower jaw, enabling the fish to be lifted clear of the water. Some of them, like the sample alongside, have a scale built-in to make it convenient for the mass to be read off. Some of these are in the form of a spring balance, and some are digital. I do not like these devices – if a fish is to be returned to the water, take note of my comment below [in bold]:

I don't believe that a fish's weight should ever be supported by its jaws. If the fish is to be landed using some form of lip grip, <u>the body should also be supported.</u>

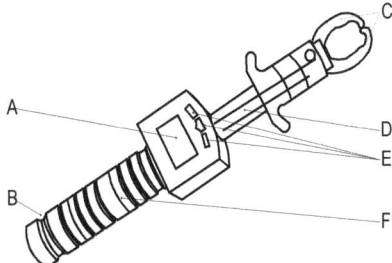

Legend*: Lip Grip. A: Digital readout display for weight; B: Groove for attaching wrist-band; C: Jaws / caliper for grabbing fish lips; D: Shaft; E: Buttons for zeroing scale and converting from lbs to kg and to switch device on/off; F: Handle.*

Lip -landing by hand: This technique only works with selected fish like bass and barbel [catfish]. Once the fish has been played out, bass are lip-landed by inserting your thumb into the fish's mouth and grabbing it by the lower jaw in one quick firm movement. This practice can be quite risky when treble hooks are involved. Barbel [catfish] can be lip landed by firmly grabbing the upper and lower lips together firmly.

And once you have a grip – don't let go! Just be careful of the hook. Get away from the water quickly and safely if you will be keeping the fish. Any extended time the fish is held over water increases the risk of losing it.

Always support the body of the fish when holding it by the lip/s.

Gaffs

Gaffs are best used only when you intend keeping a fish. Always be careful when gaffing a fish. Gaffing must be done in one smooth stroke without first touching the fish – a spooked fish can and will take off like an express train, and the longer the fight, the greater the chance of losing the fish. Ideally, the gaff should stab the fish so that the hook goes around the centre bone. I aim for the heart – this means gaffing the fish below the head, just in front of the gill slit. The advantage of this is that the fish bleeds out fast. Having said this, remember that once the gaff has been driven home, you should simultaneously pull the fish out. Ever heard the expression 'tiger by the tail'? If you aim for the head like I do, the tail is still in the water, and if you delay, one flick of the tail and the fish is literally in your face – you do NOT want to experience this, particularly if you have a barracuda on the line. Avoid gaffing the centre or the tail – apart from ruining the meat, natural panic movements by the fish can easily dislodge the gaff.

Note that big fish that are going to be returned to the water can be gaffed by the jaw.

If you are on a boat, make sure the deck is clear or that someone can open the stowaway door so that the fish can go straight into the fish hold if there is no place on deck. Someone has to be quick with a club to kill the fish by striking it just behind the eyes.

Do not attempt to gaff large shark with a hand-held gaff – if gaffing is going to happen, it can only be done with a flying gaff handled by an experienced person. It would be prudent to cut the trace and release the shark with the hook still in its mouth.

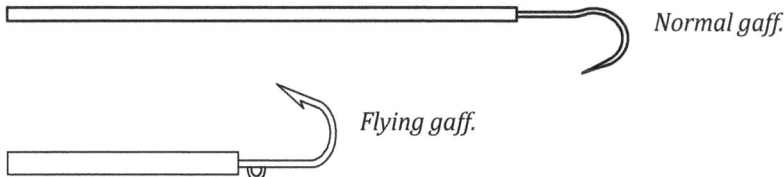

Normal gaff.

Flying gaff.

The barbed hook is held captive in the handle by a fusible link and a rope is attached to the eyelet on the back of the hook with the other end normally fastened to a bracket on the transom. When a fish is gaffed, the fusible link breaks and the hook is released. The rope holds the gaffed fish. Remember: When a flying gaff is used, the rope comes alive – *all the rope should be clear of hands / feet because if you get tangled, you may well be injured and/or end up in the water.*

Once landed, be wary of teeth, spines and tails. Use a hook disgorger if it is a toothy fish. Use gloves if it is a spiny fish. And for flatfish like rays and skates be wary of their tails.

I once watched a young man take a netted fish his mate caught to store it away from the water. I was pleased to see that he did not attempt to carry the fish without the net, but the fatal error that he made whilst carrying the netted fish [a salmon of around 8-10 kg] was to hold it against his body while he walked proudly. As he negotiated the rocks the fish wriggled in the net, knocking his knee just as he was stepping from rock to rock. The blow threw him off balance and he fell between the rocks, breaking his leg very badly. It was the remote spot called Poenskop just North of Port St Johns. End of fishing trip and hours of pain as there was no medical treatment nearby.

So be careful at all times!

Chapter 9: The tackle box and accessories

A well-kitted tackle box will generally be large and bulky. You therefore should also have smaller tackle box/boxes for carrying when you will be some distance from your vehicle. It is also a good idea to have separate boxes for salt water and fresh water and also for fly fishing. A good fishing vest can easily be converted into a tackle box – just make sure that all the pointed items are in rigid unbreakable containers.

Make sure that when you handle hooks kept in a container or packet that your hands are dry – hooks are made of metal and metal *will* corrode based on the amount of salt / moisture / air exposed to and the duration of storage. When hooks have been stored for a while, be sure to inspect them from time to time so that you can check for corrosion. Keeping hooks stored in oil would be ideal but unfortunately oil has an odour to it and this odour will be foreign to the fish and will scare them away. Remember to clean containers thoroughly before you use them for storage – residue from the previous contents could accelerate corrosion. Go to your local pharmacy and get packs of silica gel. This is a relatively harmless substance that adsorbs [not absorbs] moisture. Good for metallic components like hooks etc.

Hook disgorger [my design]

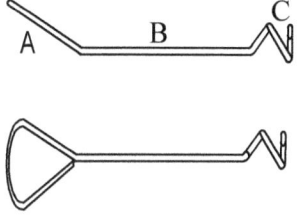

Legend: Hook disgorger – first sketch = side view- second sketch = view from above. A: Handle – must be shaped to allow a non-slip grip; B: Shank – 250mm should suffice; C: 1 turn spiral ending in a flat, open ring. The line is introduced into the spiral via the open ring. With the line held rigid [and with the fish subdued], slide the disgorger down the fish's throat until it engages in the bend of the hook. Push to disgorge the hook and holding the line rigid, still engaged in the bend of the hook, remove the hook. You will need a longer disgorger for fish like barracuda and wahoo. With shark and razor toothed fish, you are better off cutting the trace and removing the hook later. A screwdriver can be modified to perform this function.

When we plan fishing trips, we allocate responsibility to various members of the group for the different requirements. I have compiled a list to help you with planning. Use it well – there are little squares for you to mark whatever applies to your trip. There are blank lines as well to add stuff for your 4x4 and/ trailer and/or boat.

Photocopy the list and use for each trip – where you make additions, amend the list in the book and post it on my website so others can learn. A copy of the list is also included as an annexure for your convenience.

	PRE-TRIP LIST
1.	☐ A copy of my book [essential] ☺
2.	☐ Fishing license, ID book, passport, cash, proof of booking if you are going to a resort. Border documents – always check for compliance requirements if you are leaving the country
3.	☐ Hat/cap and polarised glasses, reading glasses, magnifying glass
4.	☐ Rags to wipe hands
5.	☐ Spare line for emergency topping up of a reel, tracing up, leaders and shock-leaders
6.	☐ Wire for steel traces. Ferrules for the steel wire, crimping tool
7.	☐ A selection of hooks for the species you are targeting. Treble hooks for live baiting and lures
8.	☐ A selection of swivels and snapper swivels
9.	☐ Split rings and clips to attach lures, hooks and traces
10.	☐ A selection of floats
11.	☐ Fishing lures and flies
12.	☐ Pre-tied traces
13.	☐ Superglue for knots [buy the long-life type]
14.	☐ Bite indicator / policeman / fluorescent / other
15.	☐ A selection of weights ['sinkers'] including split shot and strip lead
16.	☐ Landing net / gaff. Will the handle be long enough to permit you to safely land your fish?
17.	☐ Is there need for a 'drop net"? refer to Chapter 8 for this item
18.	☐ Hook disgorger. See my design above. Make your own
19.	☐ Lip landing device [if you must use one]
20.	☐ Spring / electronic balance
21.	☐ Keep net
22.	☐ Cast net
23.	☐ Rod bucket [the kind you buckle around your waist to protect your midsection when fighting fish]. This will protect you from injury.
24.	☐ Bucket / container for live bait, aerator [battery operated / 12volt] and/or oxygen tablets for aerating water
25.	☐ Priest [a club used to administer the 'coup de grace' knocking a fish senseless = is there any other way to describe it?]
26.	☐ Kick boat, flippers, hand pump / electric pump
27.	☐ Net for catching bait / checking life forms prevalent in the area
28.	☐ Prawn / worm pump and floating sieve
29.	☐ Rod stands and a spare rod stand for the baiting area so you do not have to set your rod on the ground or against rocks or other structures
30.	☐ Fine cotton for whipping + sewing and bait needle
31.	☐ Bait cotton [latex]
32.	☐ Spare reel and other reels
33.	☐ Rods and spare fishing rod
34.	☐ Gaff
35.	☐ Maps [the area you access may not have reception for your phone]
36.	☐ Bomb mixture for carp ground baiting
37.	☐ Dips, *'boilees'* and pips
38.	☐ Bait knife and scissors and bait cutting boards. Sharpener / whetstone/sandpaper
39.	☐ Towel and spare clothes
40.	☐ Warm hooded top
41.	☐ Gloves
42.	☐ Raincoat, gumboots, umbrella
43.	☐ Waders. Wetsuit
44.	☐ Life jacket, pool noodle to make bungs and floats for bait

45.	☐ Tent and groundsheet. Don't forget the anchoring spikes for the tent
46.	☐ Sleeping bag
47.	☐ Gas lamp / lantern and stove. Candles, two litre bottles to render candles wind-proof
48.	☐ Gas lamp mantle
49.	☐ Spare batteries
50.	☐ Ski rope coz you never know what you will need to tie down
51.	☐ Refuse bags and plastic packets. Ground sheets to protect upholstery.
52.	☐ A roll of insulation tape. This is great for taping on floats without having to tie them in. many other uses
53.	☐ Headlight & / or torch [flashlight]
54.	☐ Matches / lighter + [emergency matches or a lighter kept in a waterproof bag along with your licence and other important documentation]
55.	☐ Toilet paper, paper towel
56.	☐ Toilet spade [shovel]
57.	☐ A bottle of water as emergency water
58.	☐ Cooler boxes for food and bait, spare containers
59.	☐ Pegs. Great for keeping plastic or other bags closed. Can also be taped to a stick and making a makeshift rod stand
60.	☐ Spices
61.	☐ Food and fruit [plan daily menus so you can buy only what you need to carry and generate shopping lists]
62.	☐ Knife and spoons for cooking, can and bottle openers
63.	☐ Cutlery
64.	☐ Pots, pans, three-legged / cast iron pot, stand for pot
65.	☐ Salt tablets for electrolyte replacement / isotonic
66.	☐ Aluminium foil
67.	☐ Firewood, charcoal, firelighters
68.	☐ Axe / bush knife / machete
69.	☐ Generator / inverter and fuel in proper containers, 2-stroke oil if required, necessary cables and extensions, spare globes and fittings, stands for lights
70.	☐ Phone charger, phone, spare sim if you are going out of the country
71.	☐ Tools including screwdrivers, long-nosed pliers
72.	☐ Small first aid kit [*panado*, gauze, antibacterial crème, anti-diarrhoea meds, malaria meds, deep heat, insect repellent, *allergex* …]
73.	☐ if any member of your group is on medication, make sure that they carry what is needed for the duration of the trip
74.	☐ Ice
75.	☐ milk powder/long life milk
76.	☐ juice concentrate
77.	☐ alcoholic beverages
78.	☐ water
79.	☐ Cool drinks
80.	☐ 12volt air pump / manual pump
81.	☐ And … Don't forget the bait! Check what you will need to take with and what can be obtained at the spot.
82.	☐ Soap, toothpaste and toiletries. Carry unscented soap for when you are fishing.
83.	☐ If you are going to watch TV, carry your satellite card and DVD's
84.	☐ playing cards and games
85.	☐ Tow-rope, spade [shovel]
86.	☐ a list of all persons coming on the trip and an account of monies paid
87.	☐

88.	☐
89.	☐
90.	☐
91.	☐
92.	☐
93.	☐
94.	☐
95.	☐
96.	☐
97.	☐
98.	☐
99.	☐
100.	☐

Include a list of all joining the fray here:

Chapter 10: Balancing your tackle, and knots

This Chapter simply provides guidelines on balancing rod-line-reel combinations and describes how to tie the various knots I recommend. Subsequent Chapters tell you where to use them. My illustrations, unless specifically otherwise-stated, are for the right-handed. Simply switch if you are left-handed.

Most rods available nowadays have ratings displayed on them. The rating [***POWER** (a description of the load and lifting capability the rod is capable of handling)* and ***ACTION** (a description of how much of the rod bends when the tip is perpendicular to the butt)* - refer Chapter 1 for rods, and Chapter 2 for reels] gives you an idea of the line you should be using, along with the size / type of fish you are targeting. Use the ratings to match the rod to a reel. For example, a rod with a power rating of 7.5kg and with a fast action tip should never be used with a reel holding 8pound line.

When you look at the reel specification, it describes the range of lines that can be filled onto the spool. For example, a fixed spool reel that gives a specification of 8pounds [3.6kg] to 12pounds [5.44kg] should be used on a rod that matches the line strength range. For example, such a reel loaded with 12pound line can be used on a fast action bass rod, but the same reel loaded with 8pound line cannot.

Please bear in mind that you can easily hook fish outside of the rating and that's where skill comes in! Remember that rods with large line guides ['eyes'] are designed to be used with fixed spool reels and centre pin reels [excludes fly-fishing rods – DUH!].

Centre pin reels are best used with rods having a slow action [this excludes fly fishing where the reel is used for fast / slow action rods although it is not a good idea to use weak tippets with a fast action rod]. If you are fishing specifically for fish with strong, hard mouths, it can be used with a fast action rod.

Take your selection of rod and reel, attach the reel to the rod and hold the rod with a finger on either side of the reel. If it is balanced, the assembly will be horizontal – if not, the heavier part will show up quite easily. It is best, from my experience for the butt section to be heavier – I have come to realize by experimentation, that the heavier the butt, the further you will cast. Some people put weights inside the blank – I don't believe a blank is designed to support weight on the inside so please don't do this. Add weight to the butt section by wrapping strip lead or weighted line to the butt or by added a weighted end-cap. Remember that the rod needs to be housed in a bucket when you are holding it or fighting a fish so do not make the end too bulky! If you use strip lead, make sure you cover it as lead can be absorbed by extended contact, and lead is toxic.

You **must** carry spare line for tying traces. *Never* compromise your reel capacity by taking line off the reel to tie on traces. *Never* 'wrench' on a knot to set it. If the loops are unevenly snugged down, you have rushed the process. ***Clip and re-tie***. Traces are illustrated in the various Chapters for the various types of fishing. Your reel should also, for distance casting with heavy sinkers, have a shock leader of at least three times the rod length on it. Every time you tie your shock leader to a particular rig/trace you will be using up at least 100mm of line which you should really discard when you tie on another rig.

If you are going to be fishing lures, make sure that they are attached to your mainline using a suitable split ring, snapper swivel or a line clip – this assures that the performance of the lure is enhanced and that changeover of lures is efficient and effective. The oval split rings are used for lures [generally spoons] where the attachment hole does not support the diameter of a split ring.

You **do** know what a tangle is – well, ask yourself what the difference is between a tangle and a knot. A tangle is mostly a random event and it can only sometimes be unraveled [given time constraints] – **a knot, on the other hand, is a desired, planned, organized and repeatable tangle.** If you have knots that you are familiar with and choose to continue using them – it is *your* choice. The knots I recommend in this Chapter have been tried and tested literally thousands of times – try them.

There you have it.

SUPERGLUE ON KNOTS [yes, it **IS** underlined!]

Okay – personally I use superglue on high impact and high-performance knots – especially shock leader-to-main line joints [including fly line-to-leader joints]. Many of you out there may think that superglue is used to strengthen the knot – au contraire – it is mainly to **PROTECT** the line, knot and rod [line guides].

Legend: *Superglue. You should invest in the more expensive, long life superglue – the cheap stuff lasts for up to three weeks after opening before you have to replace it. The long-life glue lasts longer than 12*

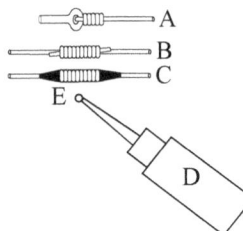

Once this has been done squeeze the superglue container until a droplet is formed at the nozzle and touch this to the bottom of the knot. Superglue has a very low viscosity [it flows easily] and applying it from above will discharge too much to the knot. If there is too little glue in the container, place a droplet on a clean surface and introduce the knot to it. Allow to dry thoroughly or you will come to a sticky end. ☺

There are certainly many knots out there. You don't need to know them all. Being a Magnus boy scout when I was little helped a lot in giving me an understanding of knots. I learnt the best knot I use quite by accident. I was taught what is now called the blood knot by old man *Shaick* at home and my brother *Baboo* from *Isipingo Beach*. I found that sometimes when fish bit shyly I would battle to catch and I attributed this to the tag-end of the knot sticking vertically outwards. I experimented with knots, toying with the hangman's noose and other barrel-type knots until I stumbled upon a double wrapped knot in 1970 when I was just 10 years old and have used it ever since. I have not seen this knot used anywhere else and have tried and tested it extensively [*when I was 10, I had my own laboratory at home. It was better equipped than my high school lab – I load-tested the knot using simple mechanics and the line always failed before the knot did!*] and have taught it to *many* people along the way since then. Numerous people dismissed the knot as being too complex but it really is quite easy to tie if you follow my simple instructions.

This is my favourite knot to use and I use it all the time *and I have fished a **LOT***. I remember talking excitedly about it to my friend Guy King [of **King's Sports"** sports and tackle. He mentioned that the knot was called a *grinner knot* – but when he brought out a sketch, we both saw that it was not the same. But with so many people sharing my passion, I realize that there might be many out there using the exact same knot and swearing by it as vehemently as I do – what I am saying here is that I am not claiming ownership to this knot unless, of course, it did not exist before 1970.

It is the strongest knot I know and can be used for almost *all* applications:
- Tying to the spool when filling line,
- Joining backing to braid,
- Joining backing to mono / fluorocarbon,
- Joining backing to main line,
- Joining main line to leader,
- Joining line to a swivel,
- Tying hooks, lures and flies,
- Securing sinkers for terminal traces, and,
- Various other applications. I have NEVER used a doubled line. **But if you are one of those who likes a DOUBLED line, just go and try my FAV knot using TWO strands of line together and tying the knot – you will [K]NOT be disappointed!**

And some pointers for tying knots:
- Don't waste valuable fishing time learning these knots when you are out there fishing. Become proficient at tying them at home. Twists mean that both pieces of line are twisted. Wraps mean that **ONE** of the lines is turned about the other. This is important.
- When tying a knot – do not use the line that is all squiggly from previous tying – use fresh line. Feel the line for damage by running it repeatedly through your fingers. Always use fresh line for tracing up or leaders.
- A good knot will have all loops comprising the knot evenly tightened – this is achieved by simply lubricating the wraps **BEFORE** it is pulled tight and snugged down. Tightening is achieved by even pulling and not by jerking it tight. Look at the knot after you tie it and after a fight or if your line was stuck. The loops of the knot should all be the same diameter – if they are not, it means that the line inside the tighter coil is being squeezed – this reduces the diameter of the line at that point and acts like a guillotine under load – it will cause failure at that point.
- For all lines [excluding single strand steel wire] you can have a tag end that is 4mm long without any bother.
- If you are rigging a running sinker / trace, use a section of ball point pen ink tube that slides over the knot, protecting the knot from impact damage.

Do not use it to tie multi-strand or single stranded steel / titanium wire.

Do not use it to moor a boat / kick boat / float tube – one end of the line attached to the floatation device can be secured using this knot, for the other end, use the bowline knot.

I use other knots as well, for various other special applications - these are described below.

Tying my favourite knot [let's call it the FAV knot]:

Tie this knot once and you will be convinced.

Thread the line through the eye of the hook/swivel/sinker/lure, and pull through about 100-150mm [keep it longer while you are learning to tie this knot] and wrap it around the main line 5 times for mono; 8-10 times for braid. **DO NOT TWIST.**

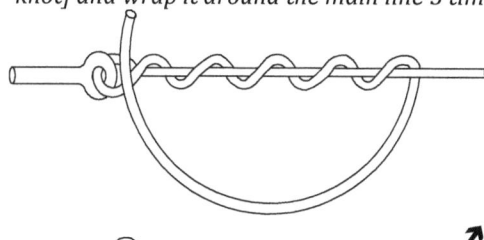

Place the line **OVER** *the first loop alongside the eye. Do* **NOT** *thread the line through the loop!*

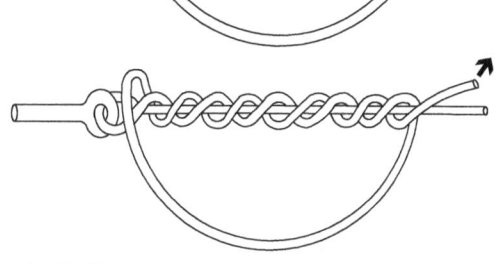

Now pass the line over the existing wraps making the same number of wraps. Lubricate and pull the end of the line in the direction shown by the arrow [Note that it is not a good idea to use saliva – dip your finger in the water and use this to lubricate the line]. Then pull the main line until the knot settles as shown in the next sketch. Trim the tag-end about 3-4mm from the first coil in the knot.

The reason for not using saliva is that you can infect yourself with microbes present from the water or on your line. Use a clean damp rag.

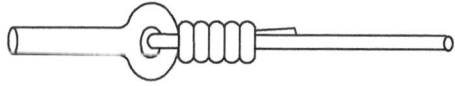

Once the coils in the knot are nicely 'snugged' down, it should look like this. Notice that the tag-end sits back **AGAINST** *the main line and does not stick out like a sore thumb.*

The FAV knot is indeed the best knot ever for me. I have caught fish well over 50kg using it and it ties well on the lower diameter lines as well as lines of different diameters too. Again – should you be one of those who likes to use a doubled line, try the FAV knot with two pieces of line. In other words, use two pieces of line held together and follow the steps as described above for the FAV knot. ***TRY IT!!***

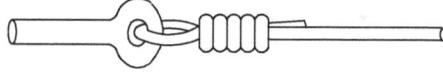

Once the knot has been snugged down, it can be pushed away from the eye of the hook / fly / lure to lend additional movement to it. Try it!

Joining lines

[shock leaders, fly-fishing leaders, adding line to your reel…]

Using the FAV knot:

This knot works for braid – mono as well – just remember the additional wraps for braid! Hold the two lines side-by-side with a 100mm-150mm overlap [keep it longer while you are learning to tie this knot]. Take the end of the one line and wrap it around the other line 5 times for mono; 8-10 times for braid. **DO NOT TWIST.**

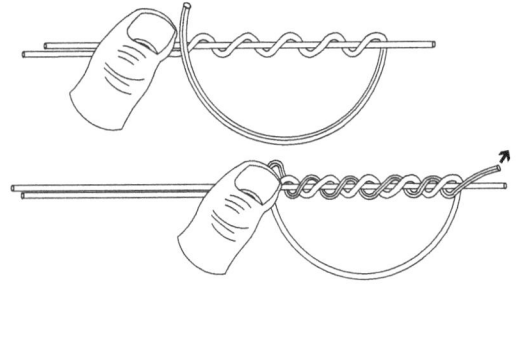

*Place the line **OVER** the first loop alongside the eye. Do **NOT** thread the line through the loop!*

Now pass the line over the existing wraps making the same number of wraps. Lubricate and pull the end of the line in the direction shown by the arrow [Note that it is not a good idea to use saliva – dip your finger in the water and use this to lubricate the line]. Then pull the main line until the knot settles as shown in the next sketch. Trim the tag-end about 3-4mm from the first coil in the knot.

Now repeat the entire process on the other side.

*Once the coils in the knot are nicely 'snugged' down, snip the ends 3-4mm from the knot on either side and it should look like the sketch above. Notice that the tag-ends sit **AGAINST** the main line and do not stick out like a sore thumb.*

The nail knot

I sometimes use the nail knot to tie on any hook having an offset eye. If I need to create an articulated action with an offset hook, I use the FAV knot with the knot moved away from the shank of the hook [see inset sketch]. I also use the nail knot when tying on a leader to fly line. It is not necessary to thread the leader through the end of the fly line when tying this knot.

The nail knot can also be used directly, for attaching multiple-strand steel / titanium wire to hooks / lures / flies / swivels.

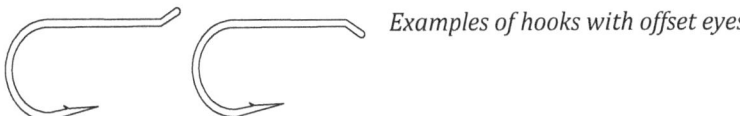

Examples of hooks with offset eyes.

Do not use this knot on hooks with split shanks *[barbs on the shank as the barbs may nick the line]. The shank of the hook has been 'split' creating barbs.*

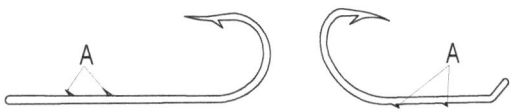

Split shank hooks have barbs on the shank "A". ['split shanks']. Far left is for use with plastic worms and immediate left for real worms.

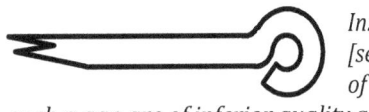

Inspect the eye detail – if there is a gap between the eye and the shank, [see sketch alongside], do not use the hook for this knot as the wire end of the hook may dig into the line and cause failure. Besides –hooks with such a gap are of inferior quality and should not be used.

To tie a leader to fly line, simply replace the hook [in the illustrations below] with the end of the fly line.

This knot should only really be tied to spade-end hooks or normal hooks having offset eyes. If the hook you would like to tie on is not offset, you can create the offset required by clamping the hook in a pliers and gently bending it to create the offset. Some hooks are hardened and will resist the bending process- leave these as they are. Please note that a straight eye hook can be used but don't thread the line through the eye – simply bypass the eye as though it were a spade end hook. The knot will hold. Believe it.

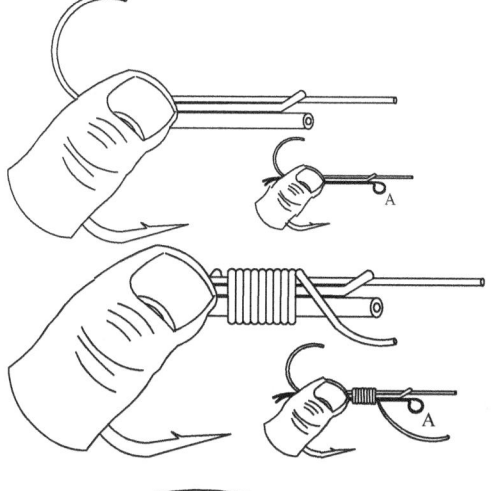

Remove the tube from an ink-depleted ball point pen and cut off a section about 30mm in length. Thread your line through the eye of the hook with about 200mm beyond the eye [you can use shorter lines as you get accustomed to tying this knot]. Position the tube as illustrated alongside. In the inset picture alongside, a loop of line "A" is depicted instead of a ball point pen tube

Make 8 to 10 wraps against each other whilst firmly holding the line against the hook. Hold it firm but not too tight as you will need to remove the tube later.
If you are using a loop of line instead of the tube, make the wraps as illustrated with the loop protruding at "A".

Move your thumb over the wraps and clamp down tightly. Pass the line through the tube as illustrated below. Whilst still holding the wraps together, and with the other hand, ease the tube out, keeping the tag under tension. As the end of the tube releases the wraps, pull the tag end so the coils sit against the hook. Repeat until the tube is completely removed. Pull the tag end and main line.
If you are using a loop of line instead of a tube, insert the tag end through the loop and gently pull the tails of the loop until the tag end comes out with the loop at "B".

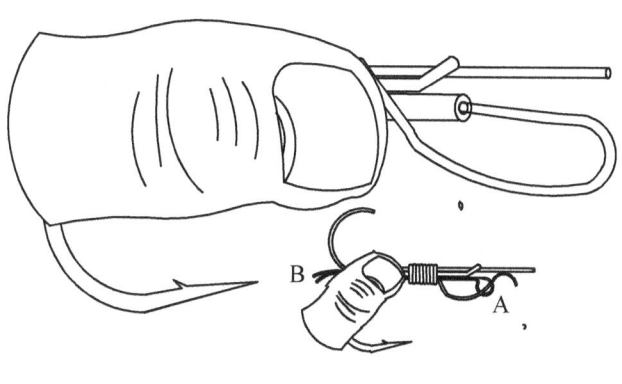

Slide the coils until the leading coil is sitting against the eye.
Finished knot should look like illustration immediately alongside.
Pull the tag end and main line to snug down. Snip.
Now you can go fish!

Tandem hook trace

When tying a tandem trace, you will need to allow for 300mm to 350mm of line when tying on the first hook. Repeat the process described above and when tying on the second hook the spacing is critical and dependent on the bait being used.

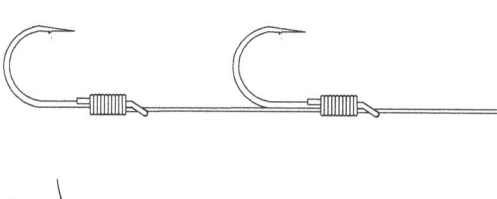

Schematic. The hook on the immediate left is tied on first with the one on the far left being tied on last [after spacing it to meet the requirements of the bait you intend using].

For example, if using a swimming prawn bait, the spacing is dependent on the size of the swimming prawn.
In the example alongside, the prawn is about 4inches long and the hooks are spaced 1½ inches apart.
I can hear big grunter and salmon [kob] calling....!!!

Tying a gamefish trace

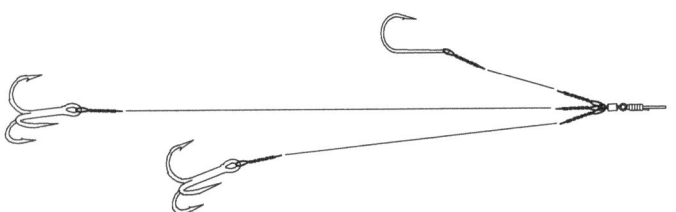

Follow the instructions below, depending on whether it is single strand or multi-strand wire to create a rig that looks like the illustration alongside.

Tying on a hook using multiple strand steel wire [coated / uncoated]

Now for the good news – tie the hook on using the same nail knot. Use two pairs of pliers to snug the coils down once the knot has been completed [use one plier to hold the hook and the other on the end of the wire]. If you can get hold of the titanium multi-strand wire – GREAT!!!! Avoid re-using wire unless you are using titanium. If the wire is kinked – DON'T use it. You can also tie a tandem trace as described above using this type of trace wire, **OR**

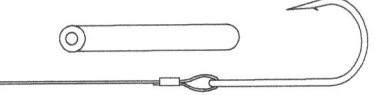

Legend: Steel wire [single / multiple strand] terminated by means of crimping. Note that the line is looped TWICE through the eye of the hook. The Ferrule [inset above the hook alongside] is made of soft material. It is a hollow tube that is slid over the main line and the end of the line is passed through the eye of a hook [twice] and then back through the ferrule. The wires are held captive by crimping the ferrule, thereby locking it in place. If the wires are not kinked during this process, they will pull out under load. Keep the loop small. You will need a special crimping tool and ferrules of various sizes. The inside diameter of the ferrule is critical as is the outside diameter of the strand/s being crimped.

Tying on a hook / swivel using single strand steel wire

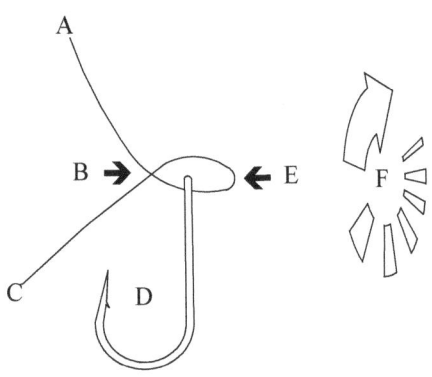

*Legend: Creating the haywire loop. **Do NOT attempt this method using multi-strand wire.** Pass wire through hook with about 150mm of wire beyond the hook. Bend wire trapping hook in a loop with a crossover at roughly 90°. A: 150mm of wire through eye of hook; B: Hold firmly here between thumb and forefinger; C: Wire leading to coil – do not cut until complete with entire procedure; D: Hook dangling from loop; E: Clamp across the end of the loop with pliers; F: Make 4 – 6 full rotations with pliers whilst holding firmly with thumb and forefinger at "B". Note that the first rotation determines the size of the loop holding the hook captive. You can control this – it is advisable to keep this loop as small as possible. You should end up with 4-6 twists on the wire [refer "C" in the next sketch].*

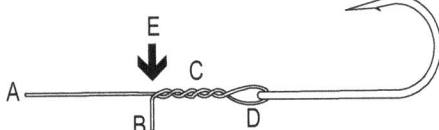

Legend: Haywire loop – in progress. A: Main wire leading to coil; B: Free leg bent at 90° to main wire. Supporting the main wire at "E", force "B" into tight coils around the main wire; C: Winds made in previous step; D: Loop holding hook – this loop not be too tight on hook and should not be too big. Aim for an oval about 8 – 10mm long and about 5mm wide; E: Support at this point and bring your thumb to bear on "B", forcing it into tight coils. You want 4 – 6 tight wraps sitting side-by-side.

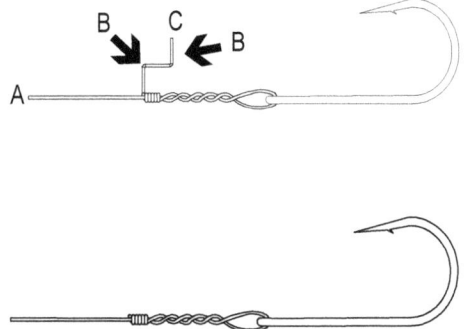

Legend: Safely breaking off waste wire. A: Main line, leading to coil of wire; B: Hold firmly across these two points and rotate in any one direction as though you are operating the 'crank'; C: Waste wire bent into the shape of a 'crank' to facilitate twisting. Rotate "B" in any ONE direction and the wire will break at the last wrap on the main line without leaving a sharp edge to snag on or cut you.

You **HAVE TO** learn this properly – wire ends snipped with a pliers or broken by bending repeatedly can leave a sharp end that will almost certainly injure you, especially when there is a fish on the line.

Once the tag-end breaks off the complete haywire loop should look like this. Practice until you have no kinks in the rig.

Tying the 'bowline' knot

This is normally done when securing a boat / other floatation device / horse to a mooring / tethering point, as applicable. I also use it to secure a rod to a suitable anchor point.

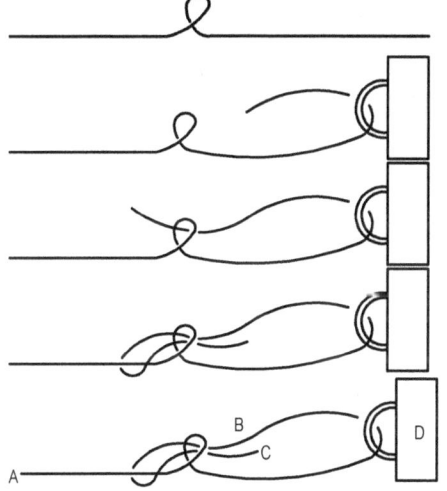

Make a one-wrap loop as shown alongside, about half a meter up the line.
Pass the end through the mooring / tethering point.

Now pass the end through the loop you initially formed.

Pass the line around the main line above the loop and back through the starting loop.

Legend: Bowline knot. A: This end already attached to the mooring / tethering point; B: Reference point; C: Hold this end and "B" in one hand. Also hold the line at "A" with other hand and pull apart until a knot forms, looking like a skew figure-of-eight; D: Anchor / mooring / tethering point.

Trace for catching pan-fries and live bait

This trace is generally tied without swivels, but because I nag you so much about not using line from the reel to tie traces, always terminate the mainline with a swivel.

This trace is sometimes called a banana-bunch trace.

Take a length of 8 – 14pound trace line. Double it leaving enough room at the crossover for connecting to mainline and connecting to the sinker to the left of the crossover. The length of the loop to the right of the crossover should be about 100mm.

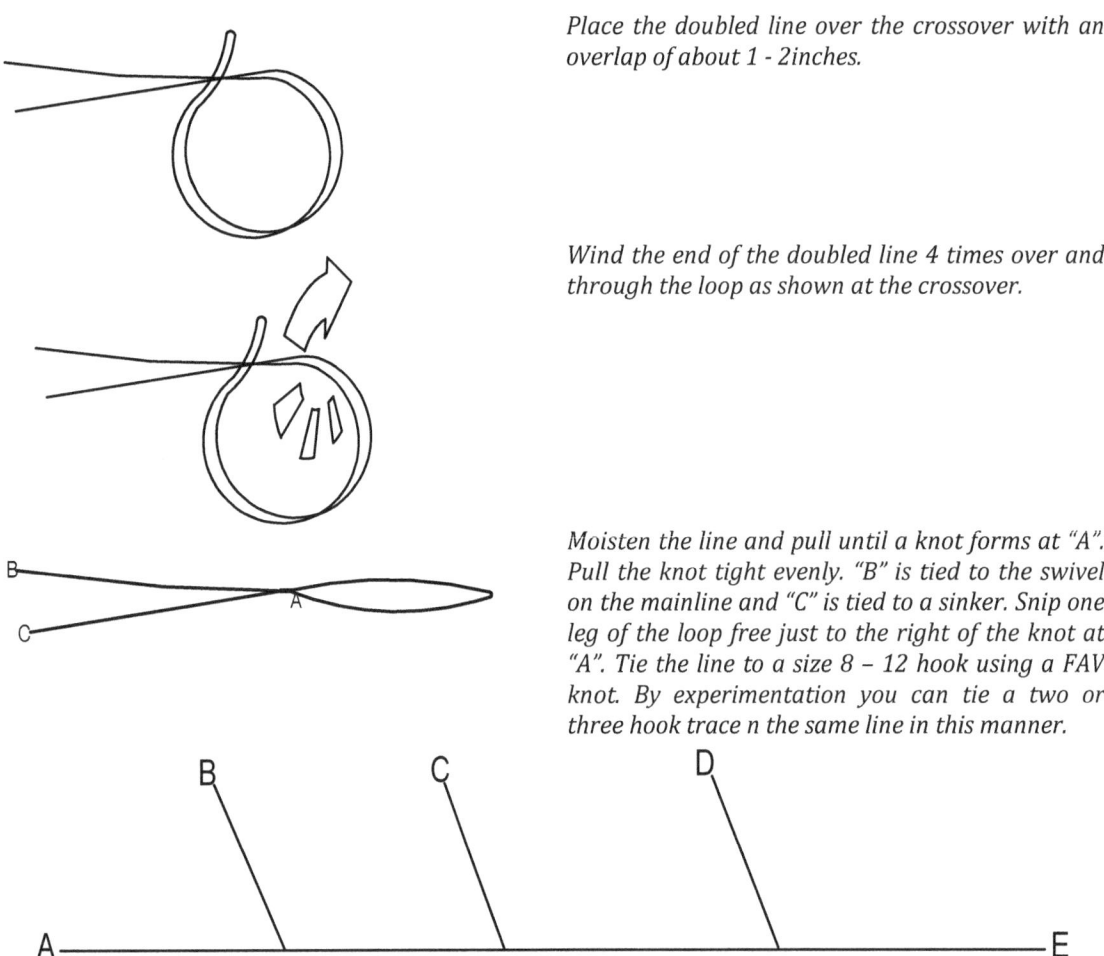

Place the doubled line over the crossover with an overlap of about 1 - 2 inches.

Wind the end of the doubled line 4 times over and through the loop as shown at the crossover.

Moisten the line and pull until a knot forms at "A". Pull the knot tight evenly. "B" is tied to the swivel on the mainline and "C" is tied to a sinker. Snip one leg of the loop free just to the right of the knot at "A". Tie the line to a size 8 – 12 hook using a FAV knot. By experimentation you can tie a two or three hook trace n the same line in this manner.

Legend: Banana bunch trace. A: tie sinker here; B, C, D: tie hooks here – size 8-12 "J" or circle hooks; E: tie to swivel on mainline.

And these are the knots I more than survive on.
You can too.

Chapter 11: Choosing a spot

Look for evidence of previous fishing

It's not too difficult to find evidence of someone having fished an area – some people are pigs and leave everything they came with behind; some even bring filth from their homes to dump. Try and take some of the filth away with you and dispose of it in an acceptable, conservation-smart way. Please.

Meanwhile, on the flipside: *If you have a favourite spot, keep it clean – people will think that no-one catches fish there!!*

What is the weather like? What was the weather like?

Fishing is generally bad after extreme changes in weather, Floods don't help – you have more water to cover to find fish. It can take more than two days for fish to go back on the bite.

What do you know about the fish you are targeting?

Do you know the type of fish you are targeting? Is it primarily - a carnivore, a herbivore or an omnivore? Based on this, you will be able to identify areas where you will not expect to find the species you are targeting, and the converse of this is also true. Herbivores need to be near vegetation that they feed on, carnivores will need to feed in areas where their favourite foods will be found – in freshwater, the bass is a carnivore – a predator constantly searching for food. It will not easily find food in the depths and can only feed on creatures that can fit into its mouth and swallow. So, when feeding, bass are found in the shallows where it can find and consume MEAT. If you get to a place where small fish normally abound, and you see none, it means that something has scared them off – so ask yourself – was it you that scared them off, or was it the presence of a predator? Be vigilant. [although sometimes the predator may be an otter or a cormorant! ☺ :-D]

Carp and yellowfish are examples of omnivores. When these are feeding selectively – the only chance you have of catching them is by using / imitating what they are feeding on. Yellowfish will sometimes elect to feed on the green spirogyra [fine haired, green weed] that grows on rocks. I remember seeing the fish in the rapids yet they were not taking any fly – I resorted to bait and still no fish… I then waded up to the rocks and scooped up some of the slimy weed and drifted some of it entangled on a hook and – *WHAM*!! – every drift was a fish!

Fish have a line running down the sides of their bodies. This is a tube-like structure that is loaded with sensory organs that relay information like vibration, scent, temperature. This is the lateral line and is probably capable of sensing more than our five senses and it even works in murky water. So – approach the water with stealth [lagoons and freshwater]. Avoid walking noisily through the water and banging rocks together.

Look at the fish – what type of mouth and teeth does it have? The tigerfish has sharp pointy teeth that it uses to capture [not bite] small prey before it swallows. Tilapia have fine teeth for capturing or taking small bites. Carp and yellowfish have no teeth … what? Don't you believe it. They have bony plates in the back of the throat – these are used to crush anything needing crushing like snails, crabs, insects, seeds, reeds…. Mud suckers have mouths facing downwards – bottom-feeder! The size of the mouth tells you how big a hook to use. A size 5 hook would be useless for bluegill. The salmon [kob] has fine teeth - but the bony plates in the back of its throat can render a treble hook useless! If you are after Musselcracker – make sure your hooks are up to it – it will crush an inferior hook all too easily! Shad, barracuda, 'couta, wahoo, snoek are members of the razor tooth gang – their mouths are equipped to bite and tear…so you know you need steel wire. And if a fish loses teeth, it grows new ones.

How big is the mouth? Bass, rock cod, salmon, trout = large mouths = meat eaters. Generally small mouthed fish are vegans. Some fish with large, protrusile [the lips can extend outwards] mouths feed on microscopic creatures like plankton.

If the mouth is angled upwards, the fish feeds on or near the surface. If the mouth is central, the fish feeds mid-water, and if the mouth faces downwards…. But some fish like to ambush their prey. Bass will wait motionless for small fish to come by… Rock cod and scorpionfish and stonefish all ambush their prey and are bottom feeders and have mouths angled upwards. Just the act of opening their mouths rapidly cause the prey to be 'sucked' in.

Fish like the barbel, yellowfish and the goatfish have appendages around the mouths called barbels – these can sense food by touch and smell. Fish also have a 'nose' – referred to as a 'nare' which is used to smell. They can also smell through their skin, mouth and lateral lines. This means that you can attract or repel them by using items that emit scents – smokers leave residue of tobacco when handling their lines, if you use aftershave or lotion, you are transferring the scent to your line. Wash your hands with natural unscented soap. This is why I suggest that you keep the 'essence' of whatever bait you use to attract the fish and increase your chances of catching – e.g. when you use crab bait, pulverize whatever portions you are going to discard – add water and dip your crab in it every time you cast – you can do this with most baits – worms, prawns, shrimp, mussels, ... but be sure to keep the 'dip' on ice.

Rays, skates and sand sharks have mouths below the head and body. This is why you use a float / polyurethane foam attached to your bait – to keep it off the floor! These fish have to swim over their food to eat.

You need to know if the species you are targeting are seasonal or nocturnal. Some species become herbivores in winter and this will impact on the taste of their flesh, generally compromising the taste. Always remember that most fish do not have eyelids – this means that in the hours between 10:00 and 16:00 when the sun is at its highest, you will not catch many when the sun is at its highest unless you are fishing water deeper than 2.5m.

If the area that you are looking at holds fish, will you be able to cast and strike? Overhead obstacles and trees dangling branches in the water may restrict your ability to cast – but think out of the box: You don't need to swing your rod to cast. Use a catapult [slingshot] to get your bait in the water – just make sure that the hook is securely placed in the cradle of the catapult. You can cast quite well and accurately using this method.

'... I remember Mezeppa Bay – what a beautiful place! Just about 400m from the suspension bridge, heading south, I found a beautiful little lagoon.

I singled it out as the perfect place to catch some mud crab. The lagoon was bordered by marsh grass but the approach from the beach was clear. I also noted that the clean sand was dotted profusely with holes showing evidence of sand prawn and tubeworm. Thinking I might be in the running for some river snapper / rock salmon / bream / steenbras, I put in two rods, targeting the above species. I waited for Kooben and Leshanthan to come with some supplies and when they arrived, I set the crab lines. I sent Leshanthan up the beach for a prawn pump.

*Funny thing – no sign of fish – no mullet milling about – no isolated splashing – no birds... I stupidly pushed the thought out of my head, saying to myself that my suspicions were wrong – this place was far from sources of pollution - there **had** to be life in this lagoon!*

After four hours there was no movement on the crab lines – the bait was untouched – not even little fish picking at it... Leshanthan arrived with the pump [having taken a beer detour] and my worst fears were realized.... I pumped some 50 square meters of sand. Not even a dead sand prawn – no worm either. The water was definitely toxic.

We packed up and got out of there... And this is the lesson that you need to learn: Pay attention to the environment – look for signs of life – all waters should have crab – if they are not around, THAT's a bad sign. All lagoons [including the mini lagoons] will have swimming prawn and these are easy to catch with a fine mesh net. Study the sand prawn burrows – you will notice signs of life – they keep the water flowing – you will see this in some of the holes. You will see bird life. You will see splashes from juvenile fish being chased by young game fish. If you bait up and cast – your bait should never come out untouched in a lagoon – it is supposed to be a breeding ground – it is supposed to have those nibblers. Like I said – PAY attention. When we got back to the beach, I encountered some Rangers and reported the lagoon – they didn't seem too interested. That water although crystal clear and cool, was TOXIC.'

If it is the first time you are fishing an area, the presence of cormorants, pelicans, fish eagles and otters mean that there are fish in the area. Look for nests and perches overhanging the water – fish will be waiting below these sites waiting for the birds to drop something or for their droppings...

Remember that fish have eyes with no eyelids. This is one of the reasons why best times to catch are early morning and late afternoon, and, at night. The higher the sun, the deeper the fish. Unless there is cover in the form of lily pads, overhangs and structure in the shallows. Fish will be lurking there when the sun is high. All fish need cover.

Find out about the animals one would expect to encounter at the venue at as early a stage as possible. You need to know about baboons and monkeys, seals, hippos, crocs, other animals. You need to know about robberies and associated risks – speak to local authorities and not the people you may be hiring premises from.

If there has been a drought, you generally have more odds of being successful as there is less water to go through to encounter fish.

In rivers, look for channels. Slow moving. Fast moving. Look for rocks breaking the flow. Look for signs of holes in the river bed [detectable by watching the turbulence]. Fish will be out of the current, lying in wait, behind the rocks / obstacles / in the holes waiting for food to drift by [in the form of terrestrial creatures that have fallen into the water, larvae of water-borne animals, worms, and anything else that might be edible]. If there is a lot of activity on the river bank you do not have to be too cautious [about scaring fish] when approaching the water, in areas not frequented by man, be cautious.

Look for banks that have been undercut – perfect cover for game fish and other fish.

Fallen trees. These are a magnet for insects, bait and fish. Use shallow treble hooked lures or better, go *weedless* so you don't catch the fallen tree! Game fish prefer structure so that they have shelter from the light and camouflage. Other fish also find the structure as a means of protection.

Freshly sprouting water reeds and plants. Somehow there are always fish around these. Cast to the area closest to you then the sides and lastly, the far side of the growth. There are also always fish near and in reed banks.

Shallow inlets and bays. Best for early mornings and late afternoons. These are the areas that warm up first. Fish are cold-blooded and will feed readily in the shallows. Remain still and watch for tell-tale signs of cruising fish. Never cast into the group or directly at the fish once you spot them. Intercept by casting a distance ahead of their projected path. Remember – if you can see the fish, it can probably see you too – don't spook the fish. Don't make sudden movements. The smaller the water – the greater the need for stealth. Use the surroundings to blend in. Always be aware of your shadow. Line-flash can also be a problem.

Inlets. Fish will always congregate and find cover at inlets. This is the source of highly oxygenated water and yes… food. They will generally always face into the current, waiting on tasty morsels drifting in. Look for areas where oxygen rich water will be entering the main body of water [turbulence]. Look for green algae and plants in the water.

Outlets. [Weirs, deep run ends….] these are ideal spawning sites. You will also generally catch eel at outlets, in the shallows at the foot of pools, just where the water exits a deep run or pool.

Mudflats. Bloodworms and insect larvae inhabit these areas. Fish will approach these areas and it will then be up to you to either scare them off or stalk them.

Weed beds. Look for dead weed beds. This is where fish expect to find food – insects and invertebrates need the oxygen from weeds. When the weeds die, there is a lack of oxygen and the insects, larvae and shrimp die or get weakened – easy game for feeding fish. If there has been recent flooding, fishing is going to be tough because there will be no shortage of drowned terrestrials.

Deep runs and deep pools. Look for surface activity resulting from a hatch [insect pupa to insects]. The emerging insects more than often get trapped in the surface film of the water and fish will rise and feed on these creatures. Sometimes the fish will be specific in their feeding and ignore anything else tossed at them. This would be the time for fly fishing.

Fish rising to a fly / lure / bait but not taking it. You can either keep casting to the same spot until you trigger an aggressive response. Fish not taking bait in this way may actually be breeding – especially mouth brooders like tilapia and other *Chiclids*.

If you are fishing in winter – remember that they are cold blooded and will not expend energy chasing a fast-moving lure – slow down your retrieval in winter – and strike anything that feels like a bite.

If you are fishing an area that the sardines have just visited or exited, you have very little chance of catching any decent game fish. You are better off targeting pan fish.

Fish need the protection of the reef so fishing on a sandy bottom is not a good idea unless the sandy bottom is near prawn beds or rich in tubeworms / ghost crab / mole crabs 'sea lice'. You will confirm the presence of sea lice by studying the waterline. Watch the wave as it recedes and you will soon see tell-tale evidence of sea lice, tube worm or shellfish. You also need to focus on a wave front just before the wave breaks – you will see fish silhouetted in the wave if they are there. You may not see the fish but the flash of sunlight reflecting off their sides – particularly in gullies and around reef. Use your eyes.

Study the high-water line – the witness left by high tide. You will see various animal remains washed up. Look out for crab and crayfish remains. Watch out for pollution – some effluents cause colour changes to the water, foam, oxygen deficient water, dead fish…

When fishing deep sea or even lagoons, the presence of gulls, fish eagles, pelicans and kingfishers indicate the presence of baitfish. Don't complain about catching small fish in lagoons – after all, it is a breeding ground. In lagoons, it is best to target drop-offs and deep channels, preferably in the time range from 3hours before and up to 3hours after high tide.

If someone has caught a fish species that you are targeting, take a clean rag and wipe slime off onto the rag. Wipe your trace line down with this – your line will not smell foreign to the fish.

And people, once you have decided on the spot – make sure that you have a plan for landing…. The spot you choose may not be practical or safe to allow you to do this. It may be holding fish, but at the same time, may be too high from the water level – or may be reeded up… whatever the reason, if the fish are there, then you have to fish there. ***But you have to have a plan of how you are going to land a fish.*** You have to take the time to visualize how you will land fish. You may say that you can use the rod to lift the fish out of the water, but what if it is a big fish? Will you need a net / gaff or other means? Will the net/gaff handle be long enough to safely reach a fish? Will you need someone to help you? If you were coming out of the water, where would you be able to do this as safely as possible? You should not have to expose yourself to unnecessary risks like having to lean over an overhang or negotiate slippery rocks, or be swamped by waves… It *ain't* worth it.

And if you don't have a plan, you are almost certainly doomed.

I have seen people who say that they only came for shad, so its ok to be fishing from a cliff 5m above water level. And every time they fish its ok. But just once a Garrick comes by and takes a hooked shad and they have to watch helplessly as the Garrick breaks free because it simply cannot be landed...

I have seen people who say that they were only after pan fish which could easily be lifted to the safety of the pier when the bass of dreams hit one of those fish and could not be landed because of restricted access to the waters...

I have seen people fishing off the cliffs for yellowtail when a GT [Caranx Ignobilis, aka Kingfish] of dreams hits the spoon and the 6m gaff was useless because there was not enough leverage to lift the gaffed fish out and both gaff and fish were lost...

So many tragic stories because people failed to realize that planning is important because that day might be the day on which they hook the fish of your dreams!

*You **have** to have a plan.*

Chapter 12: Bite indicators

Watching your line

Wherever possible, I fish without a weight, mostly with just a swivel and a hook. This means I am fishing close to the edge so movements I make to try and put on a bite indicator may more than likely result in scaring fish off. Now sometimes it is hard to see your line, especially since I try and avoid coloured lines. So how do I succeed? Knowing how far I will cast, I mark my line with a permanent black marker with short strokes. Now I can see the line! Use this method and you will hardly ever miss a bite, especially in fly fishing.

What to look for? Your line follows a natural arc from the tip to the water. If it is windy, shorten the distance between the rod tip and the water. Take up slack line slowly without [hopefully] disturbing the bait. Any movement away from you is a potential bite. Pick up and strike lightly when the tip moves [unless you are using live bait. If this is the case, once the line moves, count off 10 seconds and then strike. But at the same time, remember that live bait will become agitated when something is nosing around looking for it. This produces a flurry of activity from the scared baitfish as it sees / senses danger and tries to escape. Don't interpret this flurry of activity as a bite – it is really a warning that something has spooked the baitfish.]

Using your fingers

This method is best used mainly in salt water and other applications when the rod is held in your hands. Get rid of slack line until you feel the weight, then hold the line against your finger tip. You will feel the bite. Rods with cork grips transmit bite and other vibrations more effectively.

Note that if you are using braid, bites are amplified because the line has close to zero stretch – this means that you will feel just about ANY contact with the bait...

Using floats

In still water or running water – great to use particularly when there are numerous snags on the bottom. I always prefer a quill but sometimes the situation calls for a heavier float designed to support a heavier trace or to achieve more distance in a cast.

Most people advocate waiting for the float to be pulled underwater.

My viewpoint is a little different – unless you are using live bait. As soon as the float moves, start tightening your line and reel in slowly. If the fish is there, you will feel it. Just raise your rod whilst reeling in fast and you will almost certainly hook the fish.

If not re-cast to the same location and when the float moves, start reeling slowly until you feel the fish....

Using dough

There's nothing like a ball of dough on your line. In South Africa this bite indicator is referred to as a '*policeman*'.

Legend: *The circle is the 'policeman'. A: Policeman set at optimum – movements up or down can readily be seen; B: Policemen set too high; C: policeman set too low.*

This concept is best used in dams, rivers and lagoons where the current is not strong. It is best to first wait until your line has settled. If there is a cross-wind, keep your cast low so that the wind does not cause too much of a bow in your line. It is best for this type of fishing that you use a fluorocarbon line which will sink quickly. If you are using ordinary line or normal braid, it will take a while for your line to settle. Make sure that your line has settled without dragging your bait. A bite where the fish swims directly away from you or to the left or right will cause the policeman to rise. The secret with this type of bite is not to strike too early. Strike when the policeman is straight in line and you have tip movement on your rod.

Sometimes, the fish will swim towards you or disturb the bait. Resist the temptation to strike when this happens and do not make an adjustment to the policeman or your line. Wait for a few minutes then reel in the slack line and readjust the policeman. If this happens again, strike. There is very little chance of hooking a fish like this, but I have been lucky on several occasions.

Using an audible alarm

I remember fishing with Kenny and Vaughn John on a farm in Camperdown – I set up an audible alarm I had made up and set it up much to the amazement of Kenny.

Nothing much to say here except for you to make sure there is no slack line before setting the alarm. ***Always test the alarm before you use it.*** Carry spare batteries for this gadget. It is a nice to have.

Using thread / wool

I do not advocate tied on bite indicators – clearly – I have faith with my black marker.

Note that tied-on bite indicators are only normally used in fly fishing but these end up putting a kink in your line…

After dark bite indicators

Fluorescing light emitting sticks can be incorporated to be used as bite indicators. Stick them to some dough or press stick and attach it to a paperclip that clips on your line. Light sticks also have come with a lifeline to your rod stand [attach to your rod stand so when you strike it doesn't go flying into the water or elsewhere.

Being creative

Newspaper / toilet paper / tissue can be we made into balls when wet. Makes a good policeman. Balls of clay / mud….

Some people use automatic strike devices – these are triggered by a bite and a spring-loaded mechanism 'strikes'… Don't like these as they remove the fun and sport aspect. But some people need them!

When there is wind in freshwater / lagoons, keep the rod tip low. As soon as you cast, take up the slack before the wind grabs a hold of it. Keep your cast trajectory low and the wind will not take as much line as it would for a high-trajectory cast.

Chapter 13: Artificial baits

Yup. You can trick a fish into believing that an artificial bait is the real thing. Sometimes, a general attractor pattern [artificial bait that resembles no living creature] can be used to trigger an aggressive response from fish, particularly when the fish are territorial.

The advantages of using artificial baits are obvious:
- They are easily switched.
- Apart from the convenience of not having to handle bait that sometimes can be a combination of messy and difficult to get hold of, you can cover much more water than you would if bait fishing, and covering more water means more chances of encountering fish.
- Using artificial baits also allows you [mostly] to target specific species.
- In areas where natural bait fishing presents you with a high-snag potential, artificial bait can be rendered 'snag-less'.
- Also – apart from the occasional risk of foul-hooking fish – you hook most fish in and around the mouth and not in the throat and stomach, so if you are practicing catch-and-release, survival statistics are higher because you virtually eliminate injuring the fish anywhere but in the mouth.
- You control the action of the artificial bait.

Obviously, artificial baits can be quite costly to acquire [and to replace!] – this means that you have to exercise caution in their use. Compounding this is the fact that you generally are forced to use artificial baits in areas that present a high-risk snag potential, like around serious structure. If you over- or under-cast, it could mean losing the artificial bait! You can control this mostly by practicing until you become adept at reaching a target [aim for a target on a field]. Further compounding the risk of losing artificial baits, most gamefish [excluding Garrick] will head for structure and try and break you off.

Try and make your own lures and learn to tie …. *I think I have found the subject matter for my next book!*

Just remember that most fish will take artificial bait if properly presented. Gamefish are always on the lookout for injured or weak fish or they will have to expend far too much energy hunting and chasing down healthy fish. You must keep this in mind when presenting your artificial bait. Except for fly fishing, all lures should have a split ring on for tying the line to – this allows the artificial bait to move more realistically.

To successfully use an artificial bait, you must ensure that you use all features of the bait, you must appeal to all the fish's senses, sight and sound being the most important. This is why some lures are segmented – the moving segments emphasize natural movement. This is why lures have little frilly aspects that 'come alive' when in the water. This is why they are shiny and bright, reflecting light as though it was reflecting off the sides of a real creature. This is why they must be used maximizing sounds that the predator will interpret as though they are injured, panicked or perhaps just moving naturally. This is why there are 'rattles' available for inserting into lures.

Any movement will disturb the water and disturbance is sound – perhaps not loud enough for our senses to pick up, but to a fish movement can be picked up by sight or by their lateral lines. Fish will be able to attack a lure even in murky conditions… use this information along with any other feature that the lure may offer and you will be successful.

The performance of any lure can be increased tenfold not only by the manner in which you present it, but by also dipping them in chum that you make from bait, or by being coated with the slime of fish that you have caught.

This Chapter merely describes the types of artificial baits there are, Presentation and use are covered in Chapter 18 for freshwater fishing and Chapter 19 for saltwater fishing.

Spinner blades

Spinner blades are a ***must-have*** for all of you who use artificial lures ***and*** natural bait. They can be added on to spinners, put in front of any lure, can be used in place of a skirt that you would normally use in deep sea, can be used instead of *yo-zuris*, and can be used in front of any bait.

Whether they are moving – Yes, they will spin and gyrate! - or static, they will reflect light and create vibrations in the water and will attract fish.

 They are available in many sizes from little 18mm blades to 75mm blades [in length].

If you are fishing for razor-toothed fish, you will need to place them on the wire, above the hook – once you have put your bait on, they are supposed to sit just above the bait.

More than one can be used, but if you do, they should be placed back-to-back [note that the blades are concave both to facilitate spinning and the emission of vibrations (sound)].

I have also used them to great advantage in saltwater fly fishing. Purists out there may not like this – but I consider it as an enhancement to the attractive element of the saltwater fly.

Spinners

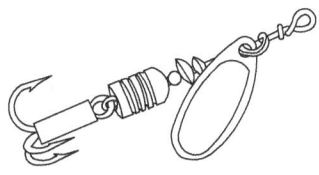 *Alongside is the famous and effective **MEPPS** spinner design – the best spinners I have ever used.*

Spinners are activated by drawing them through the water – this causes the blade / blades to rotate. This rotation reflects light just as light is reflected off the sides of a baitfish.

The colour of the blades is also important - for example, salmon prefer gold/bronze/yellow whilst shad prefer silver.

Combined with this, the blade creates vibrations in the water [sound]. This vibration [sound] is picked up by the fish's lateral line as a baitfish that is injured, just swimming or trying to escape.

Spinners are very successful lures. They are available in a large range of sizes and colours, allowing you to target predators of any size. Unfortunately, spinners are limited in that they can only be used in open water as they will foul easily in reeded / grassy / structure-rich areas, and, if allowed to sink to the bottom [as can happen during a miss-cast], they can be easily lost.

Spinners are operated by repeated casting and retrieving at various speeds.

Some spinner designs have feathers and / or fibres attached to the hook to make them more attractive to predators *and* cause the spinner to seem more like a live creature. It is important to ensure that spinner blades are well polished so that they reflect light well.

Spinners should always be tested to make sure that the blade rotates smoothly when they are dragged through water before you start fishing.

Spinner baits

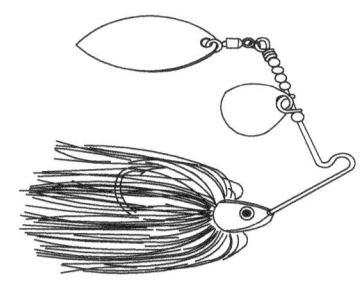 The advantage that this lure has over normal spinners is that it is '*weedless*' and can easily be dragged through reeds and grass. It should be cast and retrieved at various depths.

These lures do not spiral like conventional spinners but swim upright. Consequently, they do not require swivels when used.

Refer to the section on "Spinners" above – this lure is really also a spinner. Great lure for bass. I have also caught shad and dorado using this lure.

Drop shot hook [aka 'jig', 'jig head']

These hooks come in a full range of sizes and are used in conjunction with plastic imitations of various aquatic and/or terrestrial creatures.

The design is such that they are meant to be fished off the bottom, but they can be successfully used in mid-water as well and in keeping with the terrain found on the bottom, these hooks are also available '*weedless*' or can easily be rendered '*weedless*' by using a loop of heavy fishing line.

Some of the heads are streamlined and coloured and have eyes fixed to them. These generally 'complete' the look of the lure they are used in conjunction with.

'Dressed' drop shot hooks [aka 'Jigs']

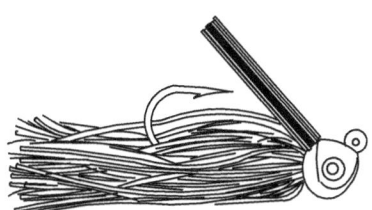

Dressed drop shot hooks are bought with various fibres permanently fixed behind the weighted head. They can be acquired in a huge assortment of colours and combinations of plastic and/or feathers and/or fibre strips. They can also be used with plastic baits attached to the hook.

I don't think I have encountered a single one that was unsuccessful although I have a preference to the combinations of white and other fibres/plastic strips. The pattern included alongside is *'weedless'* by fixing a group of straight fibres that are rigid enough to render the hook *'weedless'*, but soft enough to collapse when there is a 'take'.

Spoons

Spoons should be fished in a manner that imitate panicked, escaping baitfish / squid.

S-bend spoon

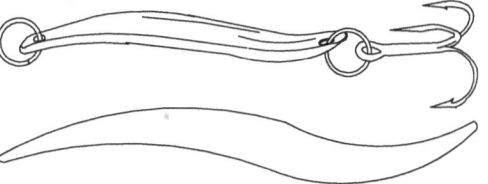

Alongside is the typical shape of the 's-bend' spoon. A killer pattern. As this pattern is dragged through the water, it gyrates and twists much like an escaping baitfish when retrieved.

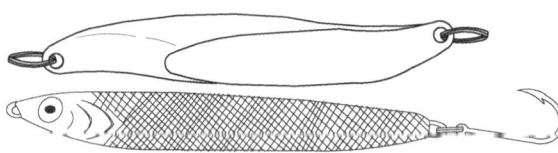

A variation of the s-bend spoon design.

This metal spoon looks like a baitfish.

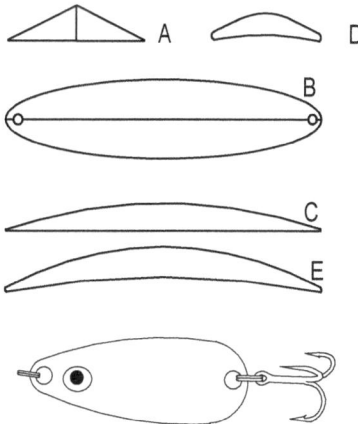

Legend: *'Flat" spoons. "A", "B" and "C" are different views of the 'knife-edged' flat spoon, designed for high speed retrieval. "A" = end view, "B" = top view and "C" = side profile. Use oval split rings on these lures to attach line and hooks. Whilst most people use trebles on these lures, I prefer single 'J' hooks [obviously extra strong designs only]. I have not tried circle hooks on spoons although I am certain that they will work.*

"D" and "E" are views of the 'curved' flat spoon. This type of spoon is curved along its length [refer view "E"], and sometime features a curvature across the width [refer view "D"]. This type of spoon is retrieved at a much slower rate than the 'knife edge' spoon

This spoon is made from metal strip [it is actually a modified spinner blade] and is concave, forcing it to spiral and gyrate in the water.

Plugs

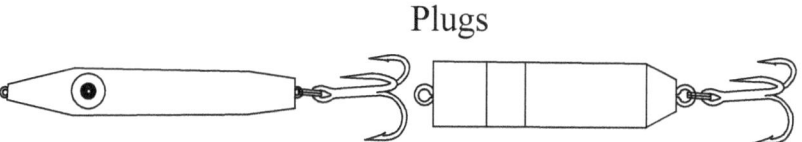

These normally solid-polyurethane lures are designed for top-water fishing although they will sink like a stone if static.

They are normally available in two colours, red and white and can be totally red, totally white or combinations of red and white. They can be round [cylindrical] or square shaped in profile.

Crankbaits

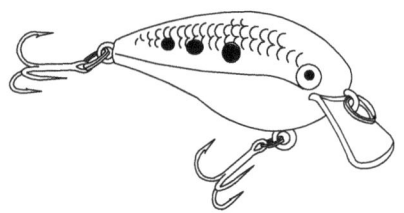

These floating little beauties are designed to 'nose' the bottom when retrieved, kicking up little clouds of dirt as they are retrieved, making them resemble a feeding baitfish.

This lure should never be fished without the split ring attached to the eyelet on the nose. If there is no split ring, put in one.

The action of this lure will be compromised if it is not allowed to articulate freely, without the restraint of a knot.

They come in a myriad of colours and in many sizes. Be aware of the baitfish in the area – this will empower you to select a colour combination that is certain to work!

Surface fish imitation lures

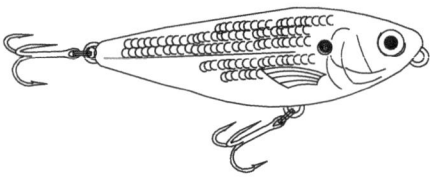

This floating lure imitates an escaping baitfish and is excellent when there is surface activity [evidence of feeding on the surface]. It is a valuable addition to your arsenal and the best imitation is **Heddon's "spitting image"**. Note that this lure needs a split ring attached to the nose. Fish will strike at surface lures so violently that you may develop a heart condition!

Surface Creature imitation lures

Mouse imitation lure – this is a GREAT lure – can't remember where I bought it and who makes it... ☹ Perhaps one of you readers will let me know?!

When retrieved, it 'swims' nose-up, much like a mouse does and should be retrieved slowly to imitate a swimming mouse.

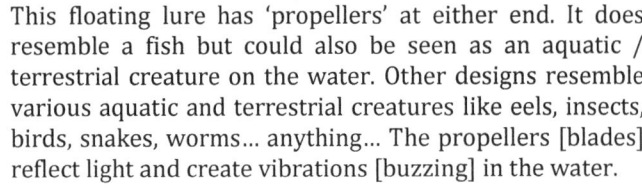

This floating lure has 'propellers' at either end. It does resemble a fish but could also be seen as an aquatic / terrestrial creature on the water. Other designs resemble various aquatic and terrestrial creatures like eels, insects, birds, snakes, worms... anything... The propellers [blades] reflect light and create vibrations [buzzing] in the water.

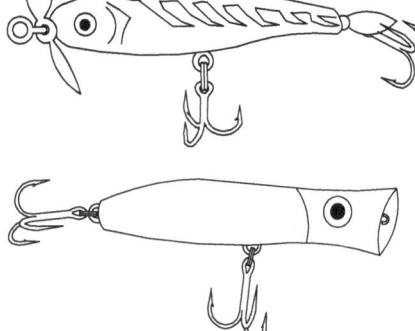

Popper-type lure [left]. This lure has a concave face designed to scoop and forced the water forward and upwards, creating a 'popping' sound when suitably retrieved.

Depending on the retrieval, this lure may resemble a frantically feeding [or frantically escaping!] baitfish. It is retrieved starting with a jerk of the rod [producing the popping sound], and can be left to stand for a while.

Most strikes actually come when this type of lure is static. So, take advantage of this and punctuate your retrieval with occasional pauses.

Sub-surface [diving lures]

These lures may be heavier than water or buoyant and are induced to dive whenever dragged through the water [by YOU, of course!].

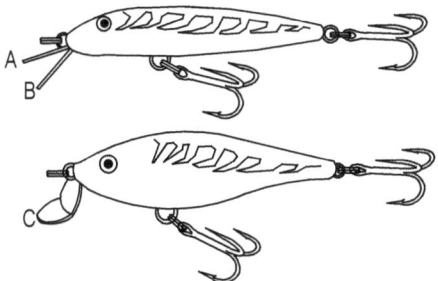

The lure patterns alongside are fish representations. They are made from various materials. They normally float well and have a little blade at the front called a diving vane. The size, angle and design of this vane determines how deeply the lure dives. Vane "A" is a shallow diving lure, vane "B" is a deep-diving lure and vane "C" is a shallow running lure. These lures will float and only dive when you retrieve line.

When the retrieval is paused, they will float back to the surface. Some of these lures are heavier than water and will sink whilst some lures have the same density as water and will remain in position whenever the retrieve is stopped. Use these characteristics to your advantage when working these lures.

Good lures come packaged with performance specifications that describe how to retrieve them and the depth the lure will dive to.

You will generally regret buying 'cheapies'.

Plastic fish and creature imitations

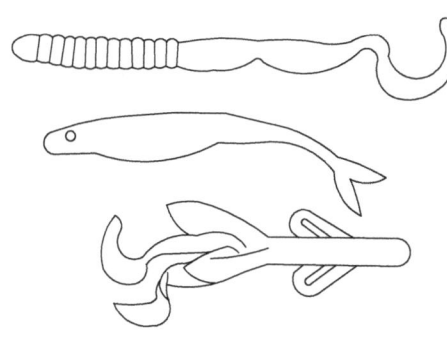

There are hundreds of variations of plastic lures designed to resemble various creatures. These are used with hooks concealed and manipulated to make them seem alive and thus attractive to fish as food, enabling you to catch them. These lures are used in conjunction with special hooks.

They have soft bodies – this gives you that extra bit of time to strike as the fish, by feel, thinks it has caught a living creature. The additional advantage is that some of the are scented.

Flies

These are used to resemble and imitate existing life forms or, as general attractor patterns, to induce takes simply because it appears *foreign* to the fish. There are literally thousands of fly patterns. The key is to find out what creatures abound at the waters you are fishing. Once you do this, you can use the pattern that most closely resembles the life-form you are imitating – correspondingly, you can then fish the pattern on the surface, in mid-water or off the bottom, as required. And don't think for one moment that you only use fly fishing equipment to cast a fly out. You can fish successfully using flies with conventional tackle – use a float to get the fly out.

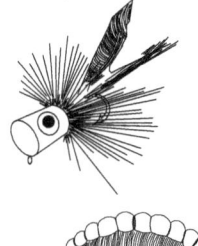

This is a popper, a surface fly. It is a general attractor fly that resembles several creatures like fry feeding and grasshoppers, to name a few. It makes popping sounds when retrieved properly and should be allowed to stand static after each mini retrieve. The fibres and feathers move in the water and give it signs of being alive. It can be taken violently or vanish leaving a tiny whirlpool...

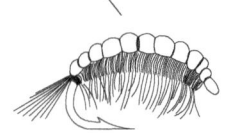

This is a wet fly, designed to be fished at the bottom. It resembles a caddis pupa / larva.

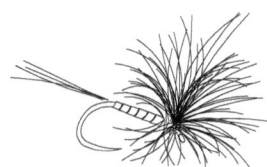

Dry fly. Designed to float on the water. Must have floatant applied. The entire fly must float on water.

Dry flies are generally made with modified hooks that are physically lighter in weight than conventional hooks.

Chapter 14: Natural baits

Please note that this Chapter only describes natural bait, how to get it and conditions for storing it where practical. Keep natural baits out of the sun.

You should always avoid introducing animal / plant matter to waters where they do not exist naturally – even if they do exist naturally, you may be introducing pathogens / algae / fungi unknowingly. You may also be contaminating the water or there may be much more complicated ecological implications.

Remember to check the regulations applicable to the areas you fish. I have excluded bag limits and legal sizes deliberately as these can and will change from time to time and, where regulated, will be strictly enforced. Please abide by these regulations as they are in place to protect our natural resources. Even in the absence of regulations / restrictions please be reasonable in what you choose to remove. If you are on private property, the rules of the owner apply over and above any other regulations – please respect them.

You will also notice that my sketches generally use a circle hook – they work! You do know that you don't need to strike!! By the way and just so you know, ordinary hooks are illegal in many countries.

When using a bait needle, fishing line needs to be doubled – this additional thickness may damage the bait as it passes through. Try and use as supple a line as possible, and as low a breaking strain as well. I would recommend braid as nothing is as supple.

You will have the remains of the various baits you clean [for example, crayfish peelings and the carapace, guts and antennae]. Break these up and liquidize them – keep it cool [freeze when storing] and dip your prepared baits into this mix before casting. Keep the dip cool – it will go off quickly at room temperature! The same for crab. If you cannot liquefy the remains, crush them using water from the area you are fishing and keep in a container on ice / in a cooler box. Every time you reel the bait out, you can dip it and the bait is perceived by the fish as being fresh!

If you need cutting boards for bait, make sure they have holes in them through which a lifeline can be attached so they don't blow away or get washed away. If there is nothing to tether the cutting board to, use a heavy sinker.

And, if the idea of handling bait is too much for you, use artificial lures!

Bread

Bread is included as natural bait because it is made from wheat. It is a simple, versatile bait and works both in fresh and saline waters. It can be used in three forms: slurry, dough and crust and is always easily available. Slurry is comprised of bread and water and is used to attract fish – throwing a handful in the water will attract fish like mullet for cast-netting.

- It is essential that you use water from the location you are fishing. Do not make the dough at home as it may present an alien scent to the fish. You may well catch fish like this but the fish will generally circle something that smells foreign to them for much longer before they actually engage in eating it.
- If you are a smoker or if you have handled anything foreign like cigarettes, cologne, lotion, sunblock etc., wash your hands using water and grit, not soap.
- Wet 2/3 slices and add dry bread to it, kneading continuously, ensuring that bits of crust are blended well. Flavouring should be added at this stage, but do not mix them into all the bait. Keep some natural and wash your hands between flavours.
- Any flavourings may be added to the dough. My personal favourite for saltwater is cheese, and for freshwater, I use spearmint. Other common flavourings are onion, garlic, custard, honey and sugar. One of the best additives I have found is coarsely-crushed wheat flour.
- Egg yellow is an excellent flavouring. Don't use the albumin [the 'white' of the egg]. Remove only the yolk by squeezing the air out of a 2l plastic bottle then hold the nozzle to the egg while you release the bottle. It will suck up the yolk. Use the yolk.
- You know the dried spices and herbs you have in the kitchen? You can use most of them to flavour dough, pap and bread baits.
- The consistency of the dough should be such that it is soft enough to pull free from the hook, yet must withstand the stress of casting.
- My recommendation is that only a swivel be used with no other weight when using this bait. A float may also be used.

- Wash hands thoroughly and keep a wet rag handy for wiping your hands clean. Dough stuck to your hands is removed by rubbing them together as it dries. This does not work well when egg is in the mixture – wash and use a rag.

Bread crust is used when there is surface activity close to you. For this you will need hard-crust bread [like the French loaf and 'special' loaf. Pass the hook through the crust from the underside of the crust so that the hook hangs straight down. There should be enough bread attached to the crust to allow you to press it into dough around a short section of the shank. Do not use a sinker or swivel. A stick float or quill may be used with a short line to the hook [about 15cm] to ensure that once the bait is waterlogged, it will be just sub-surface. Fish caught like this generally hook themselves, but if you see the take, just tighten your line and start reeling.

Flour dough

Mix dry flour with egg white – initially very sticky – use a stick to mix. Keep the yolk as a flavouring for some of the bait. Add dry flour until the consistency is enough for the dough to stay on a hook. Keep the bait in a plastic bag. Bait stores well and can be frozen. To test, make up a ball of dough around a hook and pull gently. The ball should not flatten as you pull. Rinse hands thoroughly – you do not want the sticky residue on your rod and/or reel.

Keep a wet rag handy just in case you get a bite whilst making up bait. The bait stores well if refrigerated. Ball the bait into spheres not bigger than the bend of the hook then add bait to cover the shank. Dough is best used without a sinker.

Dough can also have egg yolk mixed into it. Great bait – to remove the yolk, use a plastic bottle to suck just the yolk up and mix it into the bait.

Crab bait

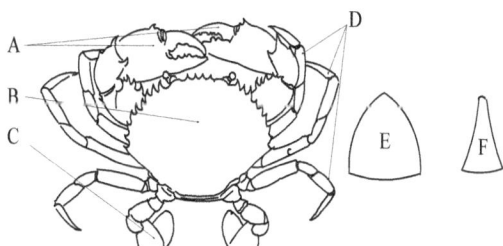

Legend: A: Claw – be careful this appendage is capable of inflicting serious damage; B: Carapace; C: flattened swimming leg of mud crab; D: Legs; E: Broad flap on opposite side of carapace = female crab.
If you see what looks like small eggs, the crab is 'in berry' and must be released; F: narrow 'vee'-shaped flap = male crab.

Small crabs can be captured quite easily by hand. With the larger crabs, watch out for the pincers!

You can remove the pincers of the larger crabs as they can damage other creatures being held as bait. Crabs should be kept wet in a container.

Small crabs up to 20mm across the carapace can be used whole by passing a hook through the carapace [main body], at one side, between the four legs. Larger crab can be cut into pieces. Pass the hook through and fish with a running trace. Do not leave rods unattended. Takes are generally very violent. Check your bait after at least 45 minutes as some fish can pick up the bait and suck the meat out quite easily without you detecting the bite.

Crab is a favourite of barbel [catfish], yellowfish and carp although other species will also feed opportunistically.

Nymphs

Legend: A: Damselfly; B: Dragonfly; C: Stonefly; D: Mayfly

This group of insect nymphs constitute much of the diet of any fish big enough to eat them. Consequently, these creatures live under water and close to aquatic vegetation [including grasses]. They are also found hidden in the gravel and/or mud.

They are easily captured and keep well as long as they are kept wet. If you are going to store them in a container, change the water frequently as the oxygen level will drop. They can only be used alive. They are best used pinned on small hooks [size 14 – 10 – hook should not be bigger than the creature, on the bottom using a terminal or sliding trace. Excellent bait. A porcupine quill float can be used on the margins, near drop-offs.

Tadpoles and frogs

Perfect for bass, barbel [catfish], bluegill and tilapia. This is the tadpole of the striped frog.

Tadpoles in excess of 35mm [1.4 inches]. It may be used whilst it has a tail and before it develops into a *"froggie"* when it is a little too small to be used as bait. It should be pinned by a hook just above the centre of the tail, as close to the body as possible. Hook size should be 6 – 10. Use with a small float with the hook just above the bottom or the tadpole will find a crevice to swim into. It may be used in conjunction with a running sinker between rocks and near structure. These tadpoles are captured on shallow gravel bottoms and between water and normal grasses. Keep in water from the location you catch and will need oxygenated water. Keep some grass and gravel at the bottom of the container.

The very small black tadpoles are offspring of the toad family and are NOT suitable as bait. Do not attempt to capture or touch tree frogs as these are mostly dangerous to touch.

The striped frog

This is the striped frog and lives all of its life in and near water.
It is best used for barbel or bass when it is pinned in the meat of the leg as close to the body as possible using a size 6 hook. Use from when it is 2.5cm to a fully-grown adult. This frog drives bass crazy and is excellent bait.

Capture using a fine meshed net. Keep the net handy whilst turning over rocks – it sometimes stays motionless beneath or between rocks. It also can be found in and around aquatic plants and grasses. Once you have it in the net, get a firm grip on it and keep it in a container with a lid. Change water as and when oxygen depletes but note that it can also breathe air.

The platana

The platana is a flat-water dwelling frog also known as the clawed African frog. Excellent bait for barbel. I haven't caught bass with it but I am sure that it will work, pinned by the leg.
You will increase your chances of catching with these if you use a float to keep them from going into hiding when in the water.
These can be caught by dredging or with a large diameter, fine-mesh net and using worm on a size 14 or 12 hook. You will spot them in still pools where they stick their snouts up for a quick gulp of air.

Fish baits

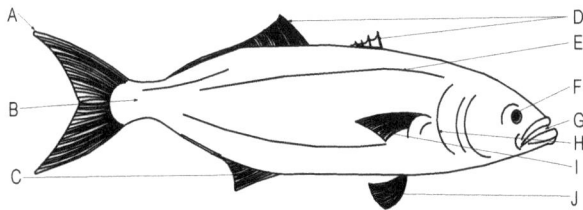

Legend: *Pictured is a shad. A: Tail fin, aka Caudal fin; B: Caudal peduncle [base of the tail]; C: Anal fin; D: Dorsal fin [this bugger has two]; E: Lateral line [any damage on or near this line will almost certainly kill the fish]; F: Eye; G: Mouth [this particular fish has razor sharp teeth – be warned!]; H: Gill slit [fish hooked in the gills are not likely to survive]; I: Pectoral fin; J: Pelvic fin. The heart of the fish is generally situated in a straight line between the pelvic fin and the eye, in front of the gill slit.*

Small fish make good bait even in freshwater. Any freshwater fish will take live small fish [up to 30mm long] for bass, anything up to 100mm [4 inches] and sometimes a little bigger. Dead fish will be taken by barbel and/or eel.

In saltwater, you are allowed to use a cast net to catch bait fish – just remember that some areas are restricted – make enquiries before you go to any spot. And make sure you have a license.

A cast net is a circular net with weights fixed to the circumference, the outer extremes of the net. It is correctly thrown by using centrifugal motion to spread the net. This means, that when correctly thrown, it will land in a perfect [well, perfect enough!] circle.

I have been using a cast net for a long time and I started using the over the shoulder method but I didn't like the idea of having to use a raincoat to throw the net. I experimented and experimented until I found a way that ensures that the net opens and lands correctly *every* time.

Secure the loop to your right wrist. The drawstring ends with a loop – pull the drawstring through the loop and pass your hand through this, pulling it tight.

Hold up the net and check that all the strands of line attached to the perimeter ring are intact and are not tangled. Do this by pulling at the net with the weights just on the ground.

Drop the net to the ground and gather up the rope, starting from your wrist, gather up loops in your right hand, each about a foot long until you reach the swivel. Hold all the loops together so that when you throw the net, the rope will unravel without tangling.

Pick up the guide ring with your left hand. Again, make sure the net is not tangled.

Pass the guide ring to your right hand, holding it along with the rope. Hold the guide ring by grasping the net immediately below it.

Hold the ring high with your right hand and grab the net with your left hand, fingers around the entire part of the net that is hanging down.

Grab the net at the point where there is just about 1 - 1.5m between where your left hand is holding the net and the weights.

Whilst holding this tightly, pass what you're holding in your left hand to your right hand. Your right hand is now holding the coils of rope, the part of the net immediately below the ring, and the section of net that leaves about 1 - 1.5m of net dangling.

With your left hand, fan out the net lightly and roughly split the suspended net into half. Start by reaching down and grasping the edge of the net closest to your body, and then progressively gathering the net, using your fingers, until you are holding roughly half in your left hand and the other half is dangling freely.

Now pass this to your right hand, holding it firmly along with the coils of rope, the part of the net immediately below the ring, and the section of net that leaves about 1.5m of the remaining half of the net dangling.

With your left hand, pick up and hold the section of weighted line that is closest to your body.

Swing the net out and throw in an arc with your right hand.

Keep a hold on the section of weighted line with your left hand until all of the net passes your body.

Let go whilst pushing your left hand to the right, spinning the net in the throw.

Work on the timing of letting go until the net spreads out completely and lands in a circle.

Fruit

Mulberries work – but only fully ripe and in season and at areas where the trees overhang the water. They are buoyant and normally float, so when you use them, fish light, using only a hook – no swivel or sinker.

I haven't had much luck with other fruit – but fruit juice and concentrate can be used to mix and flavour dough. A personal favourite is **Tropika**'s pineapple flavoured dairy drink for carp. You can buy just about any kind of fruit juice – just mix your bait with the juice of your choice!

The gecko

A superbait for bass! Although they do a good job eating mosquitos and other insects, they can become a little troublesome at times - this is one way to control populations!

Not easily caught using a butterfly net or sticky tape – but it will be worth the effort.

Just hook it in the skin behind the neck using a size 5 or 6 hook. No weight, just the hook. You have to sight fish or respond to surface activity by bass.

Allow the gecko to run madly on the water.

Oh, and I hope you have a strong heart – when a bass/pike takes one of these critters, it can give you the shock of your life with the savagery of the take! It can induce a take by any fish large enough to mouth the gecko.

Insects and spiders [ants, crickets, grasshoppers…]

Generally, all insects with the exception of the brightly coloured [the touch me not's] are good bait. The hook can be attached using a few wraps of ghost cotton or better still, latex cotton [without piercing the insect], keeping the insect alive for longer.

Leave caterpillars and hairy worms alone – but use moth worms [these look like silkworms]. When hooking these up, the hook must only just pass through the skin and immediately out again.

Grasshoppers make excellent bait, for bass, the bigger the better. Do not use the brightly coloured ones – they exude stinky stuff on you and in the water – use the green / brown coloured ones.

Carry a light net [butterfly net] to catch insects or you may injure yourself with the gymnastic skills required.

Crickets can be caught by finding their burrows on a lawn [yes, they can wreck a lawn!]. Pour water into the hole until the cricket tries to escape the water by emerging from the water-filled hole.

Catch and keep in a bottle with holes punched in the lid and some grass in the bottle – most insects can be stored this way.

When using them, do not pierce with a hook – rather use a few wraps of latex bait cotton to attach them to the hook – not too tightly.

A wriggling cricket is more enticing than a dead one!

Flying ants

Flying ants. There are two main large varieties to this creature which is actually a termite.

One species is honey brown and yellowish and the other, depicted alongside is a very dark brown / black and white / tan. Easy to catch but why bother when you can trap them?

These critters are eaten by many people. I have tasted them and found them to be quite palatable – a little 'buttery' perhaps!! ☺

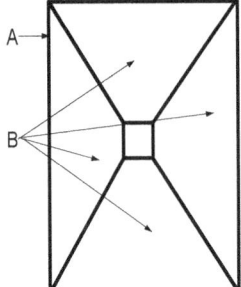 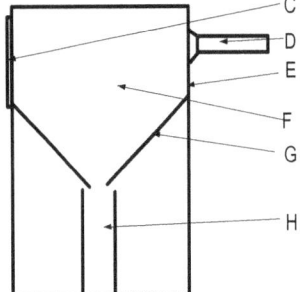

Legend: A: View of funnel from above; B: Four pieces of cardboard cut and stuck in the shape of a funnel; C: Opening at the front of the box opening starts at the top of the box and ends where the funnel begins; D: Light source battery or from electricity supply – the brighter the better.; E: rear wall of the box covered on inside with foil; F: Both sides of the box above the funnel coated with foil on the inside. The foil is to reflect light; G: Funnel; H: bottle / bucket. Note that the top of the box is covered with a lid.

Clearly the trap can only be used at night [duh!] Termites generally come out on hot summer nights. When you see them congregating around street lights, try and find where they are emerging – this will not be hard to do. Place the box facing the hole with the light on. Watch the bottle / bucket collect flying ants!

Using your trap just a few times and you will have plenty. Use some of the flying ants as bait – the balance will need to be stored. Freeze the flying ants [make sure that the bottle is sealed properly].

You can either elect to use frozen flying ants. I prefer to dry them [after freezing] using a biltong machine and then crush them into powder using any means possible and store the dry powder in an airtight container. When you are fishing, take a small quantity of dough and work some of the powder in until well mixed. You are now fishing with the essence of flying ant. You can do this with just about any bait.

Maggots

You will need to breed these. Don't poo-poo the thought of touching them. It will be worth it.

Maggots are a *superbait* and when used, are more desirable to fish than worms.

They will attract any fish, particularly bottom feeders and are good presented on the bottom, or suspended by a float near structure. Once the scent is in the water, fish will eventually go off the bite and feed selectively on maggots [in other words, fishing will be gone to maggots☺].

Maggots can't bite you. Don't be a '*scaredy* cat'. They only feed on dead and decaying matter.

Breeding them is easy. You will need some processed chicken or red meat *vienna* sausages and a container to breed the maggots in. Grate the meat and place it in the container – use at least two of the normal 6inch long [150mm] *vienna* sausages. Leave the container out in on a hot day in the shade for flies to lay their eggs on. Inspect the container – if your eyesight is keen, you will actually see the eggs [small whitish dots] on the meat. At this point you will need to cover the container to stop more eggs from being laid. Cover the container with some plastic cling film and punch fine holes in the plastic only to admit air and not flies – *make sure that the holes do not admit flies*. Maggots will hatch in a few hours – you will need to add more food on a daily basis – the maggots will take about 7 days to develop to full size. You will then need to remove most of the fully developed maggots, wash them in clean water **[NO SOAP! NO DETERGENT!]** These little critters can move – so do the following quickly! Dry them by placing them on some paper towel. Sort them into quantities of say 50 and place in small plastic bags, seal and freeze.

How to use them? The first couple of times will be with you gingerly and repulsively touching the maggots with a shudder of disgust… This won't last long. You will need to use size 10 – 14 hooks. I have pulled out carp in excess of 9.5kg with hooks this size – so never fear! Just don't put too much of pressure on the fish… but we're jumping the gun here…

Remember that maggots are almost entirely fluid. This means that if you try passing a blunt hook through one, you are wasting it as it will just become a strip of skin devoid of shape and form. When you pass a hook through a maggot, aim just to go into the skin and out, just hooking the maggot by a tiny strip of skin. When you slide a maggot down the thread [described below] make certain that you do it very carefully or the movement will sever the strip of skin.

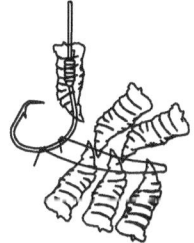
If you are using live maggots [and there's no better way to use them!], thread one onto the hook, slide it carefully over the knot. Take a fine gauge sewing needle with fine cotton threaded. Tie the end of the cotton to the shank of the hook. Pass the needle through just the skin of the pointed end of a maggot and carefully slide it down the thread. Hooking a live maggot like this will cause it to gyrate and this alone will make it irresistible to any fish. Repeat this for 4 or 5 maggots. Slide them one at a time so that they are about 10mm from the hook, on the thread. Wrap the free end of the cotton around the hook shank below the first knot. Now knot the thread and snip the needle end off. Cast the line in and have fun!

So – how many of you are going to thank me for identifying a great niche market for you. Not many of you will be able to breed maggots – so who is going to start a maggot farm?

Mealie Meal [corn flour] dough

The time has come when you no longer need to mix this bait as it is easily available from fast food outlets. If you do have to make it, use an old pot. I normally use 3 cups of mealie meal with 2 tsp salt. Bring 500ml of water to boil, add the mealie meal, stirring continuously. Add a pinch of salt and, if available, one tablespoon [15ml] of oil / margarine. Allow to cook for 4-5 minutes and turn of the heat, allowing it to stand. Do not try to knead until it has cooled down for at least 15 minutes after being removed from the stove.

You may knead it by touching it directly, using your fingers but I recommend that you keep an old pillowcase handy. Empty the cooked mealie meal in this and then knead. Keep some uncooked mealie meal handy. When you bait up, sprinkle some over your bait. This is released on impact and around where your bait lands, being carried away by the current, providing the fish with accurate directions of where to find your bait.

But hey!! You don't have to make mealie *pap [putu / phuthu]* anymore – just head on to your local fast foods franchise – you can buy it over the counter! Excess water can be removed by wrapping it in sheets of newsprint.

This bait is also great when mixed with egg yolk. You do know how to remove an egg yolk? Just break the egg into a bowl and squeeze the air out of a plastic bottle [2litre bottle is ideal], hold the mouth of the bottle to the yolk and release the pressure on the bottle – the yolk will be sucked up neatly, leaving the albumen [egg white] behind.

Seeds [mealies (corn), beans, lentils, wheat, peas], boilies, pips, wheat…

Allow to germinate [keep soaked in water until roots form and keep wet until use. [stop further growth by boiling for 5 minutes then wrap in newspaper and freeze. Examples are *biryani* dhal [lentils], pea dhal [lentils], beans, peas, corn. Works well for all bottom feeders. Use a fine gauge needle and thread as you would for maggots – same procedure. *Excellent bait*. If materials get too soft to stay on a hook or with items like peanuts and other nuts, crush and mix into unflavoured bread dough.

Shrimp [freshwater]

Freshwater shrimp occur naturally in most waters. Use a fine-mesh net to dredge **grassy** verges of the waters you intend fishing. If there are shrimp present, it is a natural food and can be successfully used as bait [note that you will also catch damselfly and sometimes dragonfly nymphs this way].

Although the common way of using this bait is by threading it onto a hook, it is best used alive. Thread it onto a hook if you are after pan fish. If your target is bigger than just pan fish, pass the hook [number 10 or 12] through the last segment the tail is attached to. Cast carefully – a 'whiplash' type cast will leave you with no bait on the hook.

If you are fishing a river, use a porcupine quill, cast upstream with at least a meter of line between the float and hook. Ideally, the bait should be just above the bottom. Allow to drift downstream. At the end of the run, repeat the process. Strike on *any* movement of the quill.

Do not use fresh chlorinated water to keep these and any other creatures alive as the chlorine will kill them.

Use the water they were found in and make sure that the water is oxygenated using an air pump or oxygen tablets. They will keep indefinitely in oxygenated water with some grass and gravel.

Snails, slugs

These can be fished in running water by passing a hook through the flesh and drifting into the current with just a hook and no sinker – not even a swivel. I don't like touching them unless its escargot I am eating. I tried slugs but caught nothing.

I didn't want to touch the aquatic snails because they carry the bilharzia parasite. The aquatic snail will work well as bait. Pass the hook through the shell and try it.

Worms

Earthworms. All earthworms make good bait – from the 1m + monsters to the Kariba worm…

Great bait for *all* fish. Now to the average person, an earthworm is an earthworm. True enough. But there are different species. I am not going to go into descriptions like *Phylum annelida…* this is useless to the average person. This is what to look for in worms. Forget about those small worms that can barely move. You are looking for worms with a bluish and/or purplish tinge to them. These are the 'jumpers'. Worms that are reddish in colour are also good bait. Take only worms that are active.

If you are fishing for pan fish, you can thread the worm onto the hook. If it's bigger fish you are after, don't thread the worm onto the hook. Just pass the hook through the centre of the worm. Big fish just open their mouths and the entire worm is sucked in, and when they turn and swim away, the circle hook engages in the corner of the mouth and…

There are two methods I use to catch earthworms.

- My grandmother saved the '*dishwater*' to water the vegetable garden in our yard. I noticed that the soapy water would cause the worms to come up, out of the ground, so whenever I wanted worms, I would pour soapy water onto the ground and the worms would come up to the surface, out of the ground. It's easier nowadays… Just mix some dishwashing liquid with water in a bucket. Go to the garden and pour this onto the ground. Wait and after a few minutes, you can just pick up the worms from the ground!
- I was busy digging for worms [no soapy water available], using a garden fork. The fork got stuck into some roots and I was levering it to get it loose and I noticed that worms came up out of the ground in the soft soil. I tried it and it worked! Just stick the fork into the ground and work it back and forth and you will see the worms come out of the ground! I think the vibrations make them believe that there is a mole in the vicinity, and moles *LOVE* earthworms! Try it!

If you must dig for worms, be sure to turn the soil over to how it was when you are done.

To breed earthworms, follow the instructions for the Kariba worms *and you can add shredded leafy veggies and grass*. Excludes melons chillies and citrus.

Kariba worms – those red short worms from *Zimbabwe*. They don't die easily when immersed in water… Better bait than normal earthworms. You can easily breed them. You will need a container and, to start, you will need some sifted soil [you sift the soil because you are going to be, from time to time, running your fingers through the soil and you really don't want any sharp objects in it, do you? You will also need a supply of shredded newspaper [not the glossy paper!].

These worms only thrive on yellow fruit and vegetables. This includes the following, in order of preference: Avocado, peaches, apricot, nectarines, pumpkin, butternut, carrot, gem squash, pears. I normally grate the hard veggies. Place the food on the soil and cover it with a layer of the shredded newspaper. Keep a clean trigger spray bottle filled with water. Spray the shredded paper until it is wet. And the magic has begun – you will need to feed once a week. The newspaper will be converted to soil by the worms. Keep out of direct sunlight and away from serious cold and protected from rain. You can change to a larger container as soon as you see fit.

No grass, no leafy veggies, no potato, no onion, no chillies, no melons, no citrus, no apples, no grains, no beans.

Note that you should make pinholes on the base of the container – trap the watery runoff – *you have a super-fertilizer for your garden!*

SALTWATER NATURAL BAITS - Making your bait tougher

Most fleshy baits [sardine and mackerel in particular] soften up when exposed to the sea and elements-if you salt your bait, the salt draws out moisture, toughening the meat – *tough meat will last longer on the hook.*

Keep a few bags of salt handy [normally used for saltwater pools, not table salt]. Defrost your bait in your own time. Once defrosted, you will need a container [normally a tub or trough] large enough to accommodate the amount of bait you wish to process. Avoid mixing baits. Squid will need to be cleaned [it is tough enough, so I rarely salt squid], sardines can be processed whole or in fillets. Prawns will need to be de-headed and de-shelled. If you plan on using whole prawn, butterfly them.

Lay down about two inches of salt on the base of the container. Cover with a layer of bait. No overlapping. Cover with at least an inch of salt. Do not cover container with a lid or cloth and make sure that there are no cats or other animals around.

Prawn will be ready in 24 hours, squid, shellfish meat and red bait in 48 hours, fillets in 72 hours and whole fish in 6-7 days.

Wrap in cling film, bag [plastic], place in a plastic container and freeze. Take out the night before and keep cool and out of the sun.

Bait processed in this manner is tougher and lasts longer, resists nibblers and will not get mushy.
Try it!

Marker buoys spend a lot of time in the water. What does this mean?

It means that entire colonies of marine creatures develop and grow below the waterline on the buoy body over the years that it has been in use.

If you see the authorities servicing a buoy, get in there and offer to help clean it – marine worms, rock bait, crab, prawns … and marine worms, *and also, marine worms*!! – if they are servicing a buoy, they will need to clean the surface to work on it. Trust me, I know. Having worked at almost all the petrochemical plants situated on the coast, I would always enquire about the service schedule… In *Mossel Bay*, I got just about 1kg of mussel worm and a few tapeworms and loads of rock bait… all off a single marker buoy….

Alikreukel [periwinkle]

This is a snail [mollusc]. It is a regulated bait [as are all sea creatures].

The white meat is used as bait and the green parts are the guts. Great bait and doesn't need cotton to hold it onto the hook. Great eating – warms the cockles of my heart ☺.

Armadillo

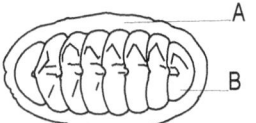 This segmented mollusc [it is actually known as a *"CHITON"*. "A" in the sketch alongside is the muscular foot which extends from the body when feeding and/or travelling. "B" refers to the body shell, actually comprised of several independent shell segments.] is found in the intertidal zone.

An excellent bait for Rock cod and musselcracker. And #AnyOtherBigFish.com

It is found hidden in crevices and under rocks during the day as it is a nocturnal feeder.

When collecting, **make certain** that you waste no time harvesting it as it can clamp down on rock and reef so soundly that you will *not* be able to remove it.

Cheese

This is an excellent bait in lagoons from two hours before and after high tide. Normally cheddar/gouda can be used. Mix into bread dough or attach some cotton wool fluff to your hook and press the cheese into this.

Be prepared to be frustrated with the lightning 'takes' you'll get. I haven't tried blue cheese – maybe you will? Let me know about it. It is a killer bait for steenbras and perch.

Crab

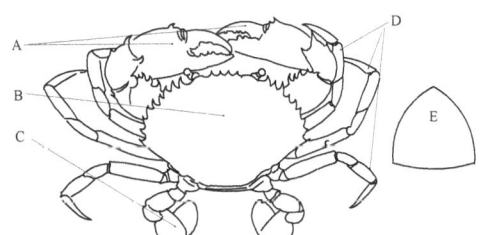 *Legend: The illustration alongside depicts a South African mud crab, a species of swimming crab [note the flattened small legs]. A: Claw – be careful this appendage is capable of inflicting serious damage; B: Carapace; C: flattened swimming leg of mud crab; D: Legs; E: Broad flap on opposite side of carapace = female crab. If you see what looks like small eggs under the flap, the crab is 'in berry' and must be released; F: Small, narrow 'vee'-shaped flap = male crab*

 *The ghost crab [illustrated alongside]. In my opinion the* **best crab bait** *ever. This decapod has caught me many pompano ['permit'] and grunter and the odd salmon [kob].*

Most crab species can be used as bait. The sand swimming crab and the ghost crab are found buried in the sand, coastal reasons, in the tidal zone and deeper waters.

You don't have to dig them up – take a 5litre bucket and bury it in the sand up to the rim. Put a piece of sardine in the bucket and cover with a stone so the gulls can't get it. Leave overnight and check in the morning.

Please note that you only need a few crabs for bait – return the balance to the sands please.

If you find crab that is moulting, it is better as bait than normal crab.

The octopus is a natural enemy of marine crabs. You can use this to your advantage to assist you in catching crabs. Rubber strips tied together to resemble an octopus can be used to scare crabs out of hiding where you can capture them easily – and carefully!!

 *The red hairy crab that scampers around on the rocks along the shoreline is also excellent bait and will be readily eaten by all larger reef fish.*

Can be captured by putting sardine bait in a bucket on the rocks where they have been seen. Don't be catching gulls!

Put some sand in the bucket so the wind doesn't blow it over and make sure that the rim of the bucket is in line with the rocks so that they can scamper into the bucket.

Cracker shrimp, mud prawns and sand prawns

These are excellent. The cracker is normally found in mud and / or below and between rocks in lagoons.

You can detect the presence of crackers where you will hear them 'snap' their claws, making a sound much like you snapping your fingers.

These creatures can be detected by the tell-tale holes leading into their burrows.

Study the burrows and you will see where the shrimp are – water is forcibly ejected from the active burrows!

Always remember that the cracker shrimp is the best bait from this shrimp family. It's a pain in the butt to get, but well worth the effort.

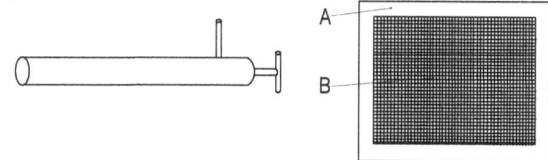

Pump for sand and mud prawns, cracker shrimp, marine worms. Sometimes crab and white mussel and other surprises you!! Alongside is a rectangular floating sieve. Floatation is provided by a frame made from a pool noodle "A" with a mesh "B" fine enough to allow mud / sand to pass through but not the creatures we are hunting.... Make your own. Superglue holds the frame together and the netting is held in place by binding.

Both can be caught using a pump which is obtainable from tackle shops. There are two techniques to using the pump – one is by blowing into the burrow using the pump, and the other is by sucking them out of the burrow.

To blow them out of the burrow, place the pump over the surface hole with the pump handle extended and push the pump handle in 3-4 seconds. You will see water forced out of the connected surface holes – keep an eye on these and you will see the shrimp emerge. Catch and place in a container. With sand on the bottom – do not store submerged in water, but keep moist.

To suck them out of the burrow you will need a floating sieve if you are pumping in water. These can be ridiculously priced – make your own!

- You will need an inner tube [car/trailer] and a length of 25% shade cloth that covers one side of the tube. The shade cloth should be square in shape and should easily allow sand to go through the mesh. Tie knots at each corner and secure a piece of string above each knot. Place the shade cloth on the ground with the tube above it and tie the pieces of string together so that the tube is sandwiched. Voila!
- You can also use a pool noodle. Paste contact adhesive onto the flat faces on the ends, wait for the contact to become tacky, bend the noodle into a circle and press together. Splice and clamp with tape until dry and process as above for the inner tube design.
- Remember to carry a rod stand or stake with you and secure the floating sieve to this – both tide and wind can surreptitiously steal your sieve if you do not do this! I generally use a lifeline connecting the sieve to my thigh.

You will need to scout the water's edge for evidence of these creatures. Once you find their burrows, place the pump over the burrow and draw in water and sand. Eject whatever you draw onto the shade cloth – the sand and water should drain out, Repeat the process on the hole you are working on until you are at the full depth the pump will allow. Collect shrimp as they become exposed on the shade cloth. Please release the ones you find in berry [with eggs]. They should be stored in a bucket with wetted strips of newspaper [do not cover with water – as the oxygen in the water will be rapidly depleted and once these shrimp die, they cause the remaining shrimp to die – you do not want dead shrimp – they become slimy and degenerate and are not easily hooked]. The bucket should be secured to the stake / rod stand anchoring the sieve. Only take the amount your permit allows. Be vigilant for tubeworm, bloodworm and tapeworm which are also found in similar burrows – make sure you are licensed to use these as these invertebrates are considered to be *SUPERBAIT*.

Crayfish [rock lobster]

This creature is found in up to 5m of water. It is great bait, especially for larger reef fish and is wasted where there are 'peckers'. The bait of choice for musselcracker [white and black].

Any large bottom feeder will go for a crayfish tail bait. Avoid buying it illegally – you may get more than you bargained for. Crayfish have been known to be thrown into pit latrines where they develop at a phenomenal rate. Chances are, when someone is standing on the side of the road, kilometers from the sea, with live crayfish, chances are....

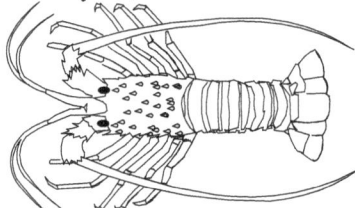

You can catch your own crayfish quite easily. Diving for them is great fun - check out my short story about the crayfish king in my story book.

You will need gloves, a snorkel and a bag to put them in – but most crayfish infested waters are rough and unforgiving so be careful.

Crayfish trap

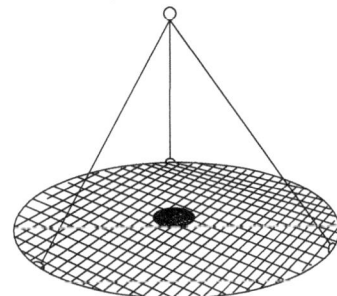

Check regulations for the diameter of the hoop – I have not included this information because they could change at any point.
Crayfish can also be caught with a wire net platform [illustrated alongside].
It is basically a wire hoop with fine mesh netting over it and a little compartment in the centre to hold fish and mussel bait. The hoop has three wires attached to it at 120° for keeping it level. The wires are linked together at the top and fishing line is attached to it. You basically use a fishing rod to lower the baited hoop to the sea bed alongside reef.

Allow it to stand until crayfish are feeding [you can feel them feed because you have to keep a tight line], then you raise the trap and catch the surprised creature.

Wear gloves. And watch the water. NEVER turn your back on the sea!!!

Crayfish jig

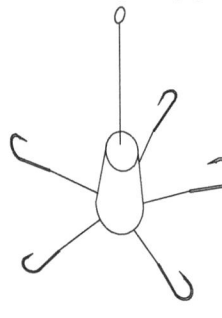

The third way involves the use of a weight into which five wires have been cast. Each wire end has a hook and each hook is oriented facing inwards with the points facing up as illustrated.
Bait comprising a cocktail of sardine, fish fillet and mussel is built up around the central column, above the sinker.
The rig is then cast out and will land facing upwards as illustrated. When a bite is felt all you have to do is reel in rapidly and maintain line tension.
The downside to this rig also foul-hooks fish.☹

Fish bait

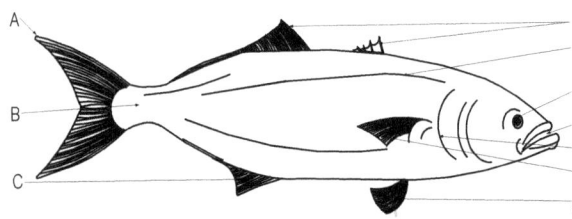

Legend: *Pictured is a shad. A: Tail fin, aka Caudal fin; B: Caudal peduncle [base of the tail]; C: Anal fin; D: Dorsal fin [this bugger has two]; E: Lateral line [any damage on or near this line will almost certainly kill the fish]; F: Eye; G: Mouth [this particular fish has razor sharp teeth – be warned!]; H: Gill slit [fish hooked in the gills are not likely to survive]; I: Pectoral fin; J: Pelvic fin. The heart of the fish is generally situated in a straight line between the pelvic fin and the eye, in front of the gill slit.*

You can catch many small fish for use as bait in estuaries and gullies. Species are glassies [left – 'transparent'], mullet, pinkies, karanteen, blacktail, mackerel, scavengers.... If the fish are small enough and caught in the protection of reefs, they will make good live bait.

Most species can be filleted and used for bait too. Live bait / dead bait. Small fish can be caught either by rod or with a cast net. If you don't have a cast net, your option is to use hook and line. Most reef fish are easy to catch using sardine culets pinned to size 8 - 14 hooks.

Sardines

Sardines are by far the most popular bait used in lagoons and saltwater.

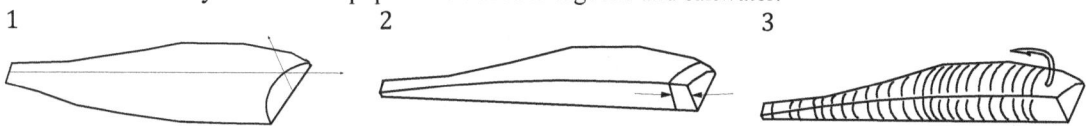

Use whole or filleted. No 1 is a schematic of a normal full-side fillet. Remove any scales. [The knife is inserted behind the gill and an incision is made until the blade reaches bone. At this point, the knife is turned to a horizontal position and the side of the fish is cut away until the blade reaches the tail.] People normally use the entire fillet as a bait. Don't. Turn the fillet so that the skin faces upwards on the cutting board. Split the fillet into two longitudinal pieces - you now have two slim fillets. [top right is a wrapped fillet]

4

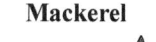

If you are targeting small pan fish, the fillet is sliced into 6 – 8mm slices [see 3 & 4]] with size 8 or 10 hooks passed through the skin and back out the skin – if you do it this way it stays on the hook longer. No 3 is a fillet that has been wrapped in latex for shad.

Mackerel

Mackerel are caught off the backline using *yo-zuri* traces which resemble small squid – I dress long shank size 4-6 hooks with these lures and, as a result, do not lose many to shad. The trace can be fished with or without bait, normally sliced sardine.

It is held on the bottom and lifted and dropped repeatedly to make the *yo-zuri's* seem alive. Shad seem to have a tendency to bite these off – if this happens, you will need to use long shank *yo-zuri* or attach them using steel wire.

Marine worms

Most worms have tough flesh that doesn't come off a hook easily and the truth is that if one person is using marine worm, most of the fish in that area will go off the bite and be looking for marine worm – I classify them as a *superbait*.

Mussel worm

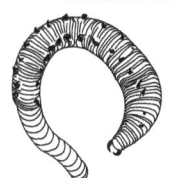

These are found, as the name suggests, between mussels and in their calcium rich burrows [also known as reef worms or coral worms] they are also found under rocks, also in the intertidal zone – catching these worms means destroying reef so – don't. Take those you find whilst picking mussels – leave the others alone. And remember – *the worm has jaws and if they bite you, can transmit a venom that is similar to bee-sting venom.* Clean and store the same as bloodworms.

Blood worm

In fresh water, these are the aquatic larvae of the midge and are very small, impractical to put onto a hook.

The marine bloodworm is found in burrows in the sand. They live in u-shaped burrows, one opening is raised – this is the outlet – worms feed by passing water carrying nutrients through from their mouths and out the other end.

They can be caught using a pump. You will need a floating sieve if you are in shallow beach / lagoon water. You pump at one end of the hole evacuating the pump in the floating sieve. Once you reach the end of the pump [in depth, get your hand in the hole, and feel for the worm – it should be there. It will be full of sand and water and you must eject this by pinching your fingers together and squeezing out the contents. I find this easier to do by cutting it into bait sized pieces [2 inches [50mm] and it is then easier to squeeze out the contents from shorter pieces. Dry each piece off on some paper towel or a squeezed rag and store it on ice wrapped in newspaper or in a freezer in plastic bags. Keep on ice when on an outing.

Tubeworm

These are normally found in estuaries on the edge of mangroves.

Going after them is a waste of time without a floating sieve if the soil is muddy [and it almost always is!]. You will see the top of their 'tubes' exposed art low tide. Watch out for mosquitoes and leeches. Catch and store these just like you would a bloodworm. Please don't destroy corals!!

Wonderworm

Wonderworm occur near bedrock in gravel on beaches or at estuaries. It is too much trouble to find them because you might just ruin your manicure. But they are worth the effort…

Tapeworm

These have the typical 'T'-shaped tapeworm head and can be pumped out or found swimming, particularly at night. The worm is generally white and has a "T" shaped head. Take heed! This creature is also a human parasite!

Warning!!! – the marine tapeworm is a parasite to humans as well!! You do know that this creature can easily become a human parasite and can grow to lengths exceeding 20m, don't you? Keep your hands away from your eyes, nose and mouth when handling them.

Mussels [Black]

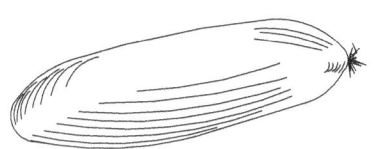

Black mussels are bivalves. Bivalve means that mussels have two shell - halves. They are delicious to eat and also make excellent bait. They occur in large colonies and can grow to sizes in excess of 100mm [about 4 inches]. They are attached to the rocky substrate by fibrous strands at the narrow end.

They open to feed when submerged and keep your skin away from the open end! If it closes on your skin, you will be missing a strip of skin! As with all marine creatures, you need a license to pick these and a good knife / lever. Be sure to pick the current daily legal limit – unfortunately, having a license doesn't mean you can pick your daily limit in the morning and then again… *on the same day…*

Personally, I prefer eating them! Keep them wet, not submerged using sea water splashed on them from time – to time. Be careful when opening them, I have seen quite a few people stab themselves! Oh yes, and when you pry them loose from rocks, keep a sharp eye out for the mussel worm which may become exposed once you remove the mussel.

Octopus

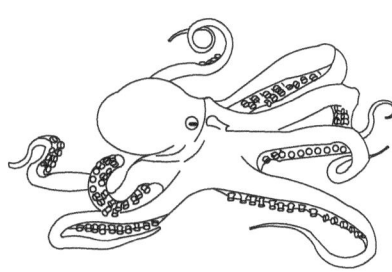

Octopi occur naturally in tidal reefs and in deeper water, also near reefs. They can be very hard to spot as they are masters of camouflage. One needs to carefully scrutinize the area, look for sand / dust being disturbed and watch for movement. Ironically, the same rubber strips used to resemble an octopus and catch crabs is the octopus's own undoing. If confronted by the rubber strips dressed over a gaff, the octopus will attack and wrap itself around the rubber strips, and you can capture it once it has been gaffed.

The tentacles are used for bait – only strip the skin of the tentacle when you're ready to use it as bait. Store on ice until needed.

Good bait whilst the flesh remains white. Very tough meat. I carry a meat tenderizing mallet especially for this bait form. Needs to be 'tenderized' and then skinned [the act of 'tenderizing releases juices- translates into *scent* in the water]. Only the tentacles are used as bait. Be careful of the beak! If the suckers get a grip of your skin, they are capable of leaving scars and tearing skin. They normally have eight 'legs' but the one that posed for me lost one. [don't worry, they grow back!]

Perlemoen [Abalone]

Roughly a third of the creature comprises the shell with the balance split evenly between edible meat and innards. Hmmm. I remember fishing in the Cape with *Bapu*. There were no restrictions then and it drove the fish wild.... Times have changed. Abalone is ***totally restricted. PLEASE DON'T.***

It was on the menu at ***Panama Jacks***, one of the best seafood restaurants in Cape Town.... I remember when I heard that it declared prohibited, I asked a Parks Board officer if I could use the trimmings and guts from a restaurant and he said that it was illegal.

On the far left is a depiction of the shell and to the right is the view from below the muscular foot.

The holes on the shell are for ejecting water that has passed over the gills.

Because of poaching, we cannot use this wonderful bait. ☹ Be proactive - Report poaching. **Please remember that this creature is seriously threatened**, it's up to us to ensure that it survives.

Prawn

There are many species of prawn. Most of them make excellent bait. Some species develop in the sea under rocky overhangs and in rock pools.

Swimming prawn is excellent bait and can be caught using a large flat-lipped [triangular] fine mesh net in lagoons [just make sure you don't try netting them in a protected area!

It's easier to hunt them at night in the shallows in lagoons – their eyes reflect light as red dots so they are easily spotted – if you see two large red dots – you are looking at a crocodile...***GET OUT OF THE WATER!!!***

Prawns can be used whole or cut into pieces. If you are going to keep them in water, make certain that you have an aerating pump. As a live bait, it is excellent. As a dead bait, it can be fished so that it looks alive, or static as a dead bait.

It is best to freeze prawns and keep them on ice to preserve their freshness. The swimming prawn is much more effective than the pink 'bait' prawn you buy as bait in those pathetic tiny boxes.

Razor clams / pencil bait

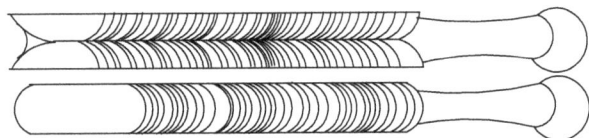

The razor clam or pencil bait is a bivalve [two shell halves] mollusc. Excellent bait for grunter and Steenbras [and anything else.com in the vicinity]. It lives in the sand and can burrow to a safety of 1m in a matter of seconds.

I was taught to catch them using a piece of wire with a bent end – but that really is a waste of time. If you want to catch this bait all you really need is salt [fine salt] – now – when you are near the sea, fine salt does not flow too easily – so make up a salt slurry [mix salt and water until you have a thick, highly concentrated consistency that can be poured].

Most people have been taught to look out for holes in the sand that resemble a keyhole – this will make you successful only part of the time. Look out for water being squirted up from the sand or for small egg-shaped depressions in the sand in areas where these creatures abound. Pour some of the slurry into this depression and wait. You might need to pour in a little more. If you are successful, you will see a squirt of water whereupon the creature will eject itself from the sand – all you then have to do is grab a firm hold of it and gently ease it out of the sand – do not pull too hard or you will break off the creature at the 'foot'. To remove the flesh from the creature, break off one of the shell halves and scoop the remains out of the other half using a sharp knife. The bait can be use whole or cut into pieces and retained on the hook with latex bait cotton.

Red bait / rock bait

Redbait grows in leathery pods in the tidal zone. At low tide, and always keeping an eye on the waves, you will notice water being squirted out, particularly from objects under overhanging rocks and on the sides of rocks normally covered by high tide. Do not reach into areas where your vision is restricted. When you see water being squirted out, first look out for spikey black / brown objects called sea urchins. The spikes are nasty if they get into your flesh – they don't just pull out – they break into pieces upon penetration and they hurt like hell and they're not good for your feet either, and to top it all, some can be venomous. Now you can feel under the rock. Pods feel leathery and yield to pressure. Look for large clusters. Take a sharp knife and cut them off as close to the rock face as possible. Keep the pods in a bag whilst always watching the surf – you can be easily swamped by a rogue wave. Once you have them, cut them open and remove the bait. Place bait into a sealable container. Seal and leave in the open for at least 24 hours. Best after 2-3 days. When you are ready to use the bait, make sure you are wearing old clothes – the bait can really stink and stain. Note that it can also be used fresh.

Sometimes, after heavy seas, pods are washed ashore so it does pay to scout the beach after high tide following heavy seas. Some of the contents of the pods may already be nice and rotten, so careful when you cut into a pod   it may be under pressure! You really don't want to get that ripe juice in your eyes or in your mouth....

This natural food is eaten by all reef fish. The 'ripe' flesh is preferred by our national fish, the galjoen.

Saltwater shrimp

These juvenile swimming prawns are classified as ***super bait***. Threaded on a number 4 short shank / circle hook is a fish every time.

Sand mussels / clams / white mussels

These are bivalves found in the intertidal zone [The area in the sand between low and high tides] in the Cape but can be bought as bait at many bait outlets. Good bait. Can be eaten and good bait. You will need a license to collect mussels – make sure that you respect bag limits.

Bait must be kept fresh and is useless if it starts to rot. Keep it fresh by rolling in wet newspaper do not store IN water, just keep the rolled-up newspaper wet with sea water. Avoid freezing these critters – the freezing action ruins the flesh as it tears easily. Thank goodness for latex bait cotton!

Sea Cucumber

The sea cucumber is a leathery, cucumber-shaped creature that is found on or below the seabed. It is easy to catch and makes good bait. It can be anything from a few centimeters to a few meters in length. ***Be warned*** *that some of the body fluids can cause extreme skin reactions*, so use a suitable barrier cream [like Vaseline] when handling them or simply use surgical or rubber gloves. Cut of the head, and a flood of body fluids will be ejected. Then slit it along the length and scoop out the body parts using a spoon or flat-bladed knife. You will be left with the tough, leathery skin which can be cut into bait-sized pieces and placed on a hook. The bait keeps well if kept cool. Use fresh.

Sea lice [mole crab]

These regulated creatures [*all bait you collect is regulated*] live on the surf line in the intertidal zone.

Legend: A: It [not a true crab] grows to around 30mm long and 20mm wide and high. Firm carapace, easily crushed, can be flipped open; B: hairy appendages; C: Centre 'breast' plate; D: Appendages tucked in below carapace when captured.

They can be spotted as the water recedes, you will notice a *vee* left them as they search for drifting food particles – make sure that the '*vee*' you see is not created by snails that also feed in the same manner you can do this easily by disturbing the sand at the *vee* and you will see the snail not more than 20mm below the sand. If it's not snails, chances are that you are looking at a mole crab. Once you get acquainted with spotting the *vee*-formation, you will need to watch out for two little projections in front of the *vee*. These are the eyes of the sea lice. When you get to spot them like this, you can actually quite easily capture them by hand or you can also use a trap – basically a triangular frame covered with wire mesh. Place the trap in the sand as the wave comes up the beach, holding it with the opening facing away from the water as the water recedes through the trap. After the water has receded beyond the trap, lift it to check if you have caught any. Keep them in a container with sand and enough water to keep the sand wet. Excellent bait for kob, pompano and grunter. Use a drop shot hook cast into white water and retrieve slowly on beaches that have sea lice.

Squid [chokka]

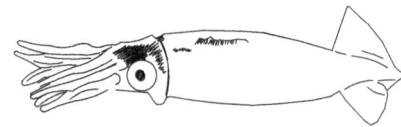

This natural bait is best used fresh. It can be caught on hook and line but is more commonly purchased from bait outlets.

It is cleaned by pulling the head away from the body making sure that the clear cartilaginous 'quill' is removed along with the innards. I keep the tentacles for attaching to trolling squid imitations. *That's why my rig always gets 'smashed'!* Next, cut off the fins and rub off the skin covering. The exposed flesh is white. If it isn't white, it isn't right… seriously – the flesh must be a clean white or you won't even hook scavengers… cut into the tube and open the meat up into a flat sheet. Cut into strips along the length of the tube, not more than 20mm wide. The bait is now ready for use. As with all bait, keep it on ice – once it turns yellowish, it is accompanied by a peculiar smell of decomposition and you will have to dispose of it – it is now useless as bait. I remember once throwing in some yellow strips of squid into the sea and a gull picked it up and dropped it immediately – that must mean something!!!

I like using whole baby squid as bait when shore fishing. For deep sea I secure it to a hook with a skirt over it…. Works every time!

I had the privilege of going on a squid boat some years ago when I was x-raying some steel tubes bound for *Koeburg Power Station… Squid was caught by hand line but there is no 'bite' as such. I held a line and couldn't feel anything and the fishermen were laughing at me saying that they don't take bait like fish.*

The creatures settle on the lure and you are supposed to suddenly feel the extra weight [how you do that with the boat bobbing this way and that – I don't know, but they knew what they were doing, and each time one of the fishermen pulled his line up, there was a squid!]

Venus Ears

You are **prohibited** from using this bait as it is on the endangered list. The creature looks like scaled-down abalone.

Chapter 15: Casting

Notes:

- Reel maintenance is very important. If you are unable to do this yourself, take your reels to the specialists. In Pietermaritzburg I use *Atlas Sports* and *Rochester Tackle* for mention-worthy service. Small baitcasters and other bass reels should be serviced at least once annually.
- NEVER cast with a spool that is overfull.
- When using heavy sinkers, you can easily subject your line to near - breaking strain during the casting process. It is therefore important to use a shock leader that will easily handle the stress caused during the casting process when heavy sinkers are used. The shock leader should be a minimum of two rod lengths when extended. Make sure before you start fishing that the knots run freely through the line guides or you will come short. All leader knots should be tapered by whipping so that they do not impact on the line guides.

  The sketch alongside shows a knot joining line-to-line that has been whipped with cotton and superglued. The taper produced by whipping facilitates the line moving through the line guides and reduces impact of the knot with the line guides.

- Also note that the techniques described here are for those who are right handed, please invert if you are left handed.
- Remember – when your line is stuck or when you have fought in a big fish, that your line is reeled in mostly under tension. Line under tension tries to relieve that tension, and it does this by biting in between the existing line and backing. What does this do? It can burst or distort your spool at its worst, and at the very least, it makes the next cast a problem because it hampers the release of line from the spool. It is good practice to make a cast with just a sinker so you can power out your line, and then reel it in under the required tension. After that, it's back to normal fishing. Always make sure that you reel in your line with adequate tension – loose line on a spool stays loose – this means that other line can cut through….
- When you're done with fishing, loosen your drag and clean your reel. Lubricate every 2-3 months – if you don't know how, take it to your local tackle shop. Don't dismantle anything if you can't put it back together correctly. Drag washer assemblies will malfunction if incorrectly sequenced. You more than likely have a camera phone – take sequential pictures if you want to do it yourself.
- Whenever you cast and are looking for that extra distance, pull the butt back into you at the end of the cast. Try it. Adding extra weight to the butt will also help you get a little more casting distance – see Chapter 1.
- In my opinion braid casts better than monofilament [if you are using 20lb braid and 20lb monofilament, for example – to beat a 'braid' cast, you would have to use a lighter monofilament line]. Watch out when there is a cross wind – braid is light and limber, so keep your cast low. That's why you need a shock leader – you can power the cast *while keeping your weight closer to the water*. Do not practice where you are fishing – go to a sports ground [make sure that there are no people / animals in your target zone! I once hit a gull with my cast and the poor creature was killed. Accidents happen – just be vigilant!
- Remember, if you are using braid, that it has almost zero stretch. This means that all your power in your cast comes from the rod. It is very easy to break a graphite rod by using too much of power or by breaking your casting rhythm. [when you cast with mono and fluoro lines, the line stretches during the cast and this provides additional acceleration in the form of a 'catapult effect' over and above the power from the rod.
- ***Check your hooks after every cast!!!!!*** *You may have bumped the hook against a hard object on the previous cast. The hook must be sharp!!!*

Using a centre pin reel

This type of reel may be pooh-poohed at by many of you, but, in the hands of a master it becomes a veritable weapon. And you can become a master! It is easy. If it is windy, using this reel will only frustrate you unless you are fishing a shallow cast. If you are using braid, do not attempt this method of casting in windy conditions. You do not want to encounter a tangle with braided line – hold on there!! You do not want to encounter a tangle – period.

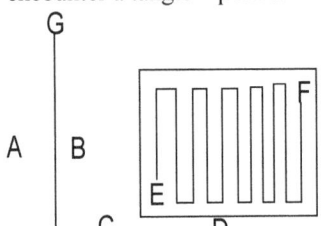

Legend: Preparing to cast with centre pin reel. A: Water; B: Land; C: Stand here when ready to cast [right-handed]; D: Mat / tarp / groundsheet / cardboard; E: Start de-spooling here and follow the line to "F" Don't overlap the coils of line! F: stop de-spooling here; G: Water's edge.

You will need to carry a piece of tarp [or a mat "D"]. Set up the tarp at the point you intend to fish from, out of the water. If you are fishing on sand, you will not need a mat or tarp. Make sure that the sand/tarp/mat is clear of any debris [bits of grass, leaves, stones…]. Weigh down the corners so they do not flip over. If you are left handed, you will need to set up your rod stand to the right of the mat/tarp, and if right handed, to the left of the tarp/mat.

Once baited up, you are ready to cast. If your bait is heavy enough, you will need a small sliding sinker to take your bait into the depths, and if it is light, you may elect to use a heavier sinker. Make sure that the sinker is not too heavy for the rod you are using.

Start de-spooling line onto the mat/tarp from "E" the rod-stand and working your way to the other shore-bound edge, continuing de-spooling line. When you reach the edge of the tarp, continue despoiling, moving back towards the rod stand without overlapping coils of line. Once you feel you have enough line out "F", you are ready to cast.

Stand either facing the water directly, or, if you are right handed, with your left side facing the direction you intend casting in. Make sure your stance is solid so that you do not over-balance at any time during your cast. It is advisable that you stretch your shoulders, back and legs before casting. Whilst standing next to your rod stand, at "C", pull your line until the sinker is 300mm – 450mm from the rod tip. Now cast whilst holding the line in your left hand and the rod in your right, releasing the line just before the rod is vertical, pointing your tip in the direction you intend your bait to land [practice a few times – if you release the line too early, it will achieve more height and less distance; if you release too late, it will have very little height and land like a bomb, close to you. Remember that the power you use will vary the distance considerably. Your action must be smooth. Jerking the rod forward puts stress onto your trace and you risk losing your bait. When you complete the swing of your cast, your rod should remain pointed in the direction of the cast and held steady. This is when you will appreciate a graphite rod as it straightens out very quickly, reducing resistance to the rapidly speeding line.] You will be very surprised at the distance you can achieve. Reel up the slack line and raise the rod tip to mend the line [by raising the tip and pulling in slack line without disturbing the sinker], especially if there is a cross wind blowing [it will carry your line to the side]. If you are happy with the distance you have achieved, mark your line using a black marker [mark about 1m of line] – this will allow you to cast the same length of line again. If you want to extend the cast, the mark will give you an idea of how much more line you need to de-spool.

This method of casting, once mastered, will beat all the other reels [within reason, dammit! ☺]. The only real problem is the speed of retrieval. Just remember that if it is windy, it is not a good idea to use a centre pin reel [unless you build up a windbreaker around the mat/tarp that protects the coils of de-spooled line from tangling whilst preparing to cast.

Using a centre pin reel with side-cast facility

You will not need to de-spool line when using a reel with this ability. Note that some reels have a separate spindle to which the spool has to be installed when casting [night hawk].

Stand either facing the water directly, or, if you are right handed, with your left side facing the direction you intend casting in. Make sure your stance is solid so that you do not over-balance at any time during your cast. It is advisable that you stretch your shoulders, back and legs before casting. It is a bad idea to try a balancing act on rocks whilst casting.

Set the spool into the casting position. Make sure that the line is not caught up in the eyes or around the reel and reel handles. Set your sinker to within 300mm – 450mm from the rod tip. Use your pointing finger to stop line from falling off the spool [some people use the free hand to do this]. Now cast your bait out [practice a few times – if you release the line too early, it will achieve more height and less distance; if you release too late, it will have very little height and land like a bomb, close to you. Remember that the power you use will vary the distance considerably. Your action must be smooth. Jerking the rod forward puts stress onto your trace and you risk losing your bait and / or trace. When you complete the swing of your cast, your rod should remain pointed in the direction of the cast and held steady. [This is when you will appreciate a graphite rod as it straightens out very quickly, reducing resistance to the rapidly speeding line.]

Return the spool to the normal fishing position. Reel up the slack line and raise the rod tip to mend the line [by raising the tip and pulling in slack line without disturbing the sinker], especially if there is a cross wind blowing [it will carry your line to the side]. If you are happy with the distance you have achieved, mark your line using a black marker [mark about 1m of line] – this will allow you to cast the same length of line again. If you want to extend the cast, the mark will give you an idea of how much more line you need to cast. Once you have achieved your range, mark your line again.

When fish bite on this type of reel, minimal resistance is felt, even with the ratchet on.

I have beaten casting distances achieved with multiplier reels and fixed spool reels with the de-spooling casting method using a centre pin reel. You can too.

Using a Scarborough reel

A Scarborough reel is extremely well balanced and spins very freely. It is a difficult reel to cast with but can be mastered with practice. This reel has no drag or ratchet and will need to be 'palmed' to slow it down and held when striking a fish.

Set the sinker to within 200mm - 400mm from the rod tip. Make sure that the line is not entangled on any part of the reel or rod, especially the rod tip. On this type of reel, the line sometimes wraps around the reel boss, between the frame and the spool – check for this – if this happens, do not try and remove the line by hand. Spin the reel backwards, handle facing down – the line should unwind and come free [note that this may also happen at the end of your cast or whilst you are fishing as well].

Stand with your back facing the water, right foot forward [right-handed stance], into the direction of your intended cast. Make sure your stance is solid so that you do not over-balance at any time during your cast. It is advisable that you stretch your shoulders, back and legs before casting. It is a bad idea to try a balancing act on rocks whilst casting. Set the sinker to within 200mm - 400mm from the rod tip. Make sure that the line is not entangled on any part of the reel or rod, especially the rod tip. If you are right handed, hold the rod with your right hand on the butt, thumb/index finger on the spool. Your left hand should be 300 – 500mm away from your right hand, on the rod. Maintain pressure on the spool [remember that when the spool is spinning, too much pressure will literally burn the skin off your thumb / finger – you should first practice wearing a soft leather glove to save your thumb]. Watch you knuckles when the reel is spinning!!!

Swing the sinker to your right, and at the end of the swing, pivot your body smoothly to the left, bringing the rod over your left shoulder, allowing the reel to free-spool with your finger / thumb standing by to slow the spinning spool down. Keep your eyes on the spool, watching the line stream out. Your rod should now be pointing over your left shoulder in the direction of your cast – keep your rod in this position until your cast is complete. Apply pressure to the spool to avoid an overwind [practice a few times – if you release the line too early, it will achieve more height and less distance; if you release too late, it will have very little height and land like a bomb, close to you. Remember that the power you use will vary the distance considerably. Your action must be smooth. Jerking the rod forward puts stress onto your trace and you risk losing your bait and / or trace.

When you complete the swing of your cast, your rod should remain pointed in the direction of the cast and held steady. This is when you will appreciate a graphite rod as it straightens out very quickly, reducing resistance to the rapidly speeding line.]

Once your cast is complete, take up any slack line and wait for the bite. You will need to continually keep pressure on the reel.

You should practice until it is second nature because you will need to cast at night too!

Note that there are fittings available which if attached to your reel will allow for a tangle free cast. These items do work but they severely limit the distance you can cast.

Using a multiplier reel

Make sure that the line is not 'peaked' on the spool. Line should be distributed evenly on the spool. Set the sinker to within 200mm - 400mm from the rod tip. Make sure that the line is not entangled on any part of the reel or rod, especially the rod tip.

Place your right thumb on the reel and set the reel to free-spool, the casting position for the reel. Hold the rod up so that the sinker is elevated. Release your thumb and allow the sinker to free-fall. If the spool continues to fall after the sinker hits the ground, quickly stop it from spinning. Tighten the spindle-float nut [on the side of the reel, in the centre]. Repeat the process until the spool stops spinning when the sinker [or lure] hits the ground. You are now ready to cast. Please use a sinker that is suited to your rod – if too heavy, you will almost certainly break your rod during the cast.

Stand facing the water, right foot forward [right-handed stance], into the direction of your intended cast. Make sure your stance is solid so that you do not over-balance at any time during your cast. It is advisable that you stretch your shoulders, back and legs before casting. It is a bad idea to try a balancing act on rocks whilst casting. Set the sinker to within 200mm - 400mm from the rod tip. Make sure that the line is not entangled on any part of the reel or rod, especially the rod tip. If you are right handed, hold the rod with your right hand on the butt, thumb on the spool. Your left hand should be 500 – 750mm away from your right hand, on the rod. Set the reel to free-spool, keeping your thumb on the spool. [Remember when the spool is spinning, too much pressure will literally burn the skin off your thumb – you should first practice wearing a soft leather glove to save your thumb].

And to those who proudly say that they have hard fingers and they don't get burnt just remember this means that the energy is going somewhere else – slowly fraying your line. Seriously.

Facing the water, swing the sinker until it is behind you, almost touching the ground. Turn your head and look over your left shoulder to ensure that you have achieved this, and that there is no risk of hitting anything during your cast, thumb still on the spool. Your left hand should be holding the rod just behind your left shoulder. The rod should be butt-up, tip down. Power down with your right hand whilst simultaneously pushing your left hand forward, releasing the spool just after your rod passes the vertical position [roughly just after the 11 o' clock position]. Now apply gentle pressure to the spool, slowing it down. If you watch the spool during your cast, you will see when over-winding starts – increase pressure of your thumb on the reel [practice a few times – if you release the line too early, it will achieve more height and less distance; if you release too late, it will have very little height and land like a bomb, close to you. Remember that the power you use will vary the distance considerably. Your action must be smooth. Jerking the rod forward puts stress onto your trace and you risk losing your bait and / or trace. When you complete the swing of your cast, your rod should remain pointed in the direction of the cast and held steady. This is when you will appreciate a graphite rod as it straightens out very quickly, reducing resistance to the rapidly speeding line.]

Once your cast is complete, switch the reel to disengage the free spool action, set your drag [drag is set to below your line breaking strain – you achieve this by tightening the drag and manually pulling on the line until the spool releases line – do not set it too loose or you will release line when you strike, reducing the effectiveness of your strike!], take up any slack line and wait for the bite.

You should practice until it is second nature because you will need to cast at night too!

Using the 'eezi-cast' device

If your reel can take this device, it will prevent overcasts. Useful at night for those of you who are new to multiplier reels. It is a nice-to-have for beginners. I have found that I cast much further without one.

Using a baitcaster reel [small multiplier, normally used for bass]

Line should be distributed evenly on the spool. Set the lure / bait to within 200 - 400mm of the rod tip. Make sure that the line is not entangled on any part of the reel or rod, especially the rod tip.

Place your right thumb on the spool. Press the free spool button [normally situated on the reel, between the spacer bars above the spool]. Hold the rod up so that the lure / bait is elevated. Release your thumb and allow the lure / bait to free-fall. If the spool continues to fall after the sinker hits the ground, quickly stop it from spinning with your thumb. Adjust the spindle-float nut [on the side of the reel, in the centre]. Repeat the process until the spool stops spinning when the sinker [or lure] hits the ground. You are now ready to cast.

Stand facing the water, right foot forward [right-handed stance], into the direction of your intended cast. Make sure your stance is solid so that you do not over-balance at any time during your cast. It is advisable that you stretch your shoulders, back and legs before casting. It is a bad idea to try a balancing act on rocks whilst casting. Set the lure / bait to within 200 – 400mm of the rod tip. Make sure that the line is not entangled on any part of the reel or rod, especially the rod tip. If you are right handed, hold the rod with your right hand on the butt, thumb on the spool. This reel requires a one-handed casting technique. Do not use your whole arm – start by using your forearm and wrist to cast. You will get to the point where you are only mostly wrist to cast.

Facing the water, swing the rod so that the lure / bait is behind you, over your right shoulder, rod almost between the 2 and 3 'o clock positions behind you. Swing your forearm forward, flicking your wrist to get maximum acceleration – you will need to use your thumb to stop the spool and prevent overwind [note that some reels have a magnetic brake that slows the spinning spool down quite effectively. You will find after practicing that you can cast quite accurately. Remember that you will need to adjust your spool float nut every time you change a lure. [Practice a few times – if you release the line too early, it will achieve more height and less distance; if you release too late, it will have very little height and land like a bomb, close to you. Remember that the power you use will vary the distance considerably. Your action must be smooth. Jerking the rod forward puts stress onto your trace and you risk losing your bait and / or trace. When you complete the swing of your cast, your rod should remain pointed in the direction of the cast and held steady. This is when you will appreciate a graphite rod as it straightens out very quickly, reducing resistance to the rapidly speeding line.]

Once your cast is complete, turn the handle to disengage free spool. set your drag, take up any slack line and wait for the bite [drag is set to below your line breaking strain – you achieve this by tightening the drag and manually pulling on the line until the spool releases line – do not set it too loose or you will release line when you strike, reducing the effectiveness of your strike!]. You should practice until it is second nature because you will need to cast at night too!

Using a fixed spool reel 'coffee grinder'

Warning: Some of you have already experienced the heavy duty extended spool reels available on the market. They are fantastic and. I daresay, will match or out-cast any baitcasting reel. Really. Having said that [and I believe its true], please do not be a hero. **Use a glove or casting clip, <u>especially when using heavy sinkers</u>**. *When you cast a 6 or 8ounce sinker [170 / 226 grams approximately], the line becomes a guillotine and can remove not just your skin....* **Please take heed of this warning**.

And to those of you who hold the line against the rod when casting, you are dicing with the devil. If one loop of line gets caught on your finger, the pressure of the cast, you will find, is as efficient as a scalpel. Please refrain from this practice.

The coffee grinder is aptly named because it does resemble hand operated grinders used to reduce coffee beans to granules. It is a reel that can be mastered with ease.

Line should be distributed evenly on the spool. Set the sinker to within 300mm - 400mm from the rod tip. Make sure that the line is not entangled on any part of the reel or rod, especially the rod tip.

Stand facing the water, right foot forward [right-handed stance], into the direction of your intended cast. Make sure your stance is solid so that you do not over-balance at any time during your cast. It is advisable that you stretch your shoulders, back and legs before casting. It is a bad idea to try a balancing act on rocks whilst casting. Set the sinker to within 200mm - 400mm from the rod tip. Make sure that the line is not entangled on any part of the reel or rod, especially the rod tip. If you are right handed, hold the rod with your right hand on the butt, thumb on the spool. Your left hand should be 500 – 750mm away from your right hand, on the rod.

Open the bail arm whilst keeping your index finger against the spool to stop the reel from releasing line [some people physically trap the line with their index finger – I do not like this technique as line can get caught on your finger.

Facing the water, swing the sinker until it is behind you, over your left shoulder, almost touching the ground. Turn your head and look over your shoulder to ensure that you have achieved this, and that there is no risk of hitting anything during your cast, still holding your finger against the spool. Your left hand should be holding the rod just behind your left shoulder. The rod should be butt-up, tip down. Power down with your right hand whilst simultaneously pushing your left hand forward, removing your finger from the spool just before your rod passes the vertical position [roughly just after the 10 o' clock position] [practice a few times – if you release the line too early, it will achieve more height and less distance; if you release too late, it will have very little height and land like a bomb, close to you. Remember that the power you use will vary the distance considerably. Your action must be smooth. Jerking the rod forward puts stress onto your trace and you risk losing your bait and / or trace. When you complete the swing of your cast, your rod should remain pointed in the direction of the cast and held steady. This is when you will appreciate a graphite rod as it straightens out very quickly, reducing resistance to the rapidly speeding line.]

Once your cast is complete, re-engage the bailing arm, set your drag [drag is set to below your line breaking strain – you achieve this by tightening the drag and manually pulling on the line until the spool releases line – do not set it too loose or you will release line when you strike, reducing the effectiveness of your strike!], take up any slack line and wait for the bite. You should practice until it is second nature because you will need to cast at night too!

Press button reel / push button reel

Set the lure / bait to within 200 - 400mm of the rod tip. Make sure that the line is not entangled on any part of the reel or rod, especially the rod tip.

Stand facing the water, right foot forward [right-handed stance], into the direction of your intended cast. Make sure your stance is solid so that you do not over-balance at any time during your cast. It is advisable that you stretch your shoulders, back and legs before casting. It is a bad idea to try a balancing act on rocks whilst casting. If you are right handed, hold the rod with your right hand on the butt, thumb on the spool. This reel requires a one-handed casting technique. Do not use your whole arm – start by using your forearm and wrist to cast. You will get to the point where you are mostly using wrist to cast.

Facing the water, swing the rod so that the lure / bait is behind you, rod almost horizontal behind you. Swing your forearm forward, flicking your wrist to get maximum. You will find after practicing that you can cast quite accurately [practice a few times – if you release the line too early, it will achieve more height and less distance; if you release too late, it will have very little height and land like a bomb, close to you. Also remember that the power you use will vary the distance considerably. Your action must be smooth. Jerking the rod forward puts stress onto your trace and you risk losing your bait and / or trace. When you complete the swing of your cast, your rod should remain pointed in the direction of the cast and held steady. This is when you will appreciate a graphite rod as it straightens out very quickly, reducing resistance to the rapidly speeding line.]

Once your cast is complete, turn the handle to disengage from casting mode. set your drag, take up any slack line and wait for the bite [drag is set to below your line breaking strain – you achieve this by tightening the drag and manually pulling on the line until the spool releases line – do not set it too loose or you will release line when you strike, reducing the effectiveness of your strike!]. You should practice until it is second nature because you will need to cast at night too!

Note – for fly fishing – please refer to Chapter 22.

Casting beneath overhanging branches / ledges / casting at wary fish

It is possible, with practice, to cast at likely lies located beneath overhanging branches / overhangs. This technique is also used for casting at fish that are skittish. It involves a low splash, just above the water cast.

For a right-handed person, stand with your right shoulder pointing in the direction of the intended cast. It is essential that the target area is in range of your casting capability, with the rig you are using. Let out line so that the weight / lure hangs just above the fishing reel. Now hold the sinker / lure in your left hand please don't hook yourself!]. Lower the rod tip so that it is just above the water level, whilst still holding the sinker / lure in your left hand. Pull your left hand back and behind you whilst pulling with your right hand, resulting in bending the rod. Release the sinker / lure whilst simultaneously swinging the rod to your right.

Practice this cast on grass first then over open water until you feel confident to cast the right amount of line out. Practice aiming for targets on a field – you will need this skill if you need to cast to a particular zone. Practice, practice, practice.

Note: There are pneumatic tube casting and mechanical auto-casting devices available on the market. I do not have any experience with these items and will appreciate feedback from any of you who have experience with these devices.

Radio-controlled bait boats are also used to take offerings out in a both salt- and freshwater.

Chapter 16: Fishing using natural bait in freshwater

Some notes:

- If you are going to return a fish to the water, always avoid handling it by the soft underbelly area as this can easily cause injury to the creature *no matter how gentle you are*. In this area of the body, they are extremely vulnerable to injury as any direct pressure could easily be on vital organs.
- Prepare traces in advance and get a supply of plastic bank bags to store them in. You maximize your fishing time by doing this.
- Natural bait cannot be used to catch trout in South Africa unless it is your own farm dam or if you have the permission of the owner.
- Eels are delicious. They are nocturnal feeders [although I have caught many during the day]. Eels will feed where there is a change in the gradient [shallower to deeper / deeper to shallower] and the current is not strong. The best bait I have used is earthworm and fish fillets although they are partial to chicken liver. When landing an eel – beach it – avoid using the net as the creature can entangle itself and the net will be liberally coated in slime.
- In autumn, early winter tilapia are caught using carp tackle [boilies and pips]. When fishing in a shoal of fish, avoid casting over the shoal – you will spook the shoal if you bring a fighting fish through the shoal. Rather cast at the edge of the shoal closest to you.
- Tigerfish – warm water fish.
- Smoked tilapia, bass – excellent eating

Fishing for Carp [and tilapia and yellowfish and sometimes barbel]

Carp can sometimes breed twice in a South African summer. They do not like cold weather and move into the deepest areas in winter. Boiled / steamed peas.

You must try and locate carp before trying out a fishing spot. The rule of thumb is that if carp are jumping in an area, then they will be feeding in the same area. You generally see carp jumping more frequently in the mornings – a jumping carp is generally trying to get rid of parasites [it is also jumping to look for you so that it can avoid you! ☺. Locating carp in this way will contribute to your fishing success. In smaller dams, this will not matter. Look out for masses of small bubbles rising to the surface – this is a sure sign of bottom feeding fish foraging in the area. Look out for carp skimming the surface with their mouths. If you are going to catch carp on / near the surface, you have to be vigilant for fish cruising the surface scum line. [you will see their orange=yellow lips breaking the surface repeatedly as they suck down fragments from the floating scum – The scum line is a floating layer of fine matter. This is found when the surface of the water is 'like glass', mainly in the mornings].

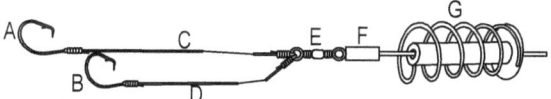

Most people believe in using a 'bomb'. This is a ball of sometimes flavoured mealie-based dough that is pressed onto a spring or around a swivel. The spring rig looks something like "G" alongside.

Legend [above]: Carp rig. A: Hook, size 8-12, depending on bait used; B: Hook, size 8-12, depending on bait used; C: Snoot, not more than 100mm; D: Snoot, 50mm shorter than "C"; "C" and "D" are 4-10pound line; E: Two-way swivel, size 8 – 20 – you may substitute it with a three-way swivel: F: Ball point ink tube positioned over knot, protecting the knot from impact damage with the sinker; G: Bomb sinker – groundbait is pressed around this to form a ball with the spring wires helping to anchor the groundbait.

Legend: Light running sinker rig. A: Circle hook, size 6-12; B: 250mm Snoot, 6-10pound breaking strain; C: Swivel, size 7-10; D: Section of ball-point pen tube protecting the knot from the sinker and prevents the knot from getting stuck in the sinker; E: Small barrel / bullet sinker. This trace can also

exclude a sinker for close-range fishing. Definitely better without a sinker – this is my preference.

If you do not have a spring rig, simply push a matchstick halfway through the swivel on your trace and press your bomb mixture around it. It will hold.

Material for the 'bomb' sinker may vary from wire to plastic and the structure is sometimes a plastic 'cage'.

A mixture of 'bomb' bait is generally compressed bread or special 'bomb' mixtures which are mixed with water and compressed, increasing the weight of the rig. I suggest that the compressed 'bomb' should be wrapped in a layer of surgical gauze and held in position by elastic bands / bait cotton.

This way you do not leave too much of bait behind and run the risk of feeding the fish more than you intended. Two hooks are generally tied below the rig, onto the line that passes through the rig. Baiting of the hook is then carried out with the bait of your choice [in this case, maggots], as depicted in 1 – 5 below.

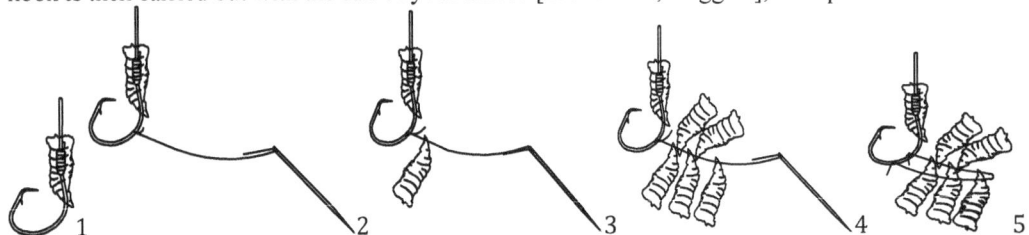

You can use boilies, pips, lentils, beans, sweet corn, flying ants – whatever you like. Though, once you go with maggots, you are more than likely going to stay with that choice.

Do not remove the residual cotton that will accumulate on your hooks. As it is absorbent material, it retains a residue of the last fish you caught – this means that when fish approach your bait, after you have caught a fish, the bait will not smell foreign to them because they will smell the previous fish!

Use a very fine needle to avoid splitting baits. You may need to use a metal thimble to push the needle through some of the harder baits. Preformed baits like boilies can be dipped in the flavour of your choice. Just remember that carp show a preference to salty and hot [chilli]. Sweet baits like *'tutti fruiti'* also work well.

Everyone who knows me knows that I am not in favour of using the 'bomb' use it if you prefer – just note that I have out-fished most people who use the 'bomb' with just a running sinker and single hook trace.

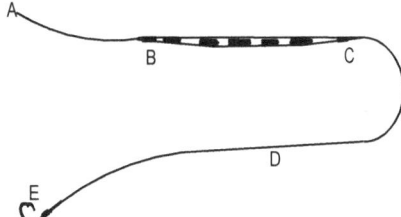

Legend: *Rig for fishing bread crust. A: Main line to reel; B: 'Blunt' end of quill attached to line by means of 2-3 wraps of insulation tape; C: Sharp end of quill attached to line by 2-3 wraps of insulation tape; D: 50-100mm of line leading to the hook; E: Circle hook [can be "J" hook], size 4/5.*

Carp can also be caught close to the surface, especially when they are visibly 'mouthing' the surface 'scum line'.

Try floating out some crust or use a quill with a short hook line.

Do not aim your cast at the fish – rather aim for an area immediately in the anticipated path of the fish.

Some notes:

- *Particularly early in the morning and at dusk, avoid long casts. The fish approach the shoreline. You may very well scare them off by bringing a fighting fish through the shallower water. Start by fishing close to you.*
- *Fishmeal-based boilies are generally more successful in warmer months. Birdseed-based boilies work better in the colder months.*
- *When the water is cold, remember that fish are cold-blooded. They will not expend energy searching for food so vary your cast and cover more ground. Carp will be in deeper water where there is mud – gravel, hard and stony bottoms just mean more work for them to find food.*
- *If your boilies and pips and other seeds are not working, carp love earthworms and shrimp bait. I consider Maggots as a **superbait**. You may think that these creatures are dirty – they are not, they can be bred quite easily and are incapable of biting you as they can only feed on decaying, festering matter – they must just be hooked without perforating the body of the creature this is achieved by running the hook through the skin of the creatures – 4 or 5 on a number 12 hook is perfect.*

- *If you are using the 'bomb' technique, each time you reel out, your bomb should not disintegrate. This ensures that you do not put out too much of groundbait as the fish will have plenty to eat without touching your baited hooks.*
- *If there is plenty of fish activity, you can attract the fish to where you are fishing by ground-baiting your area. You can be creative when getting groundbait out. Using just a sinker, place some bait in the centre of a doubled paper towel – tie this to your main line with some bait cotton and swing it out. Paper towel does not tear when casting, even when wet [as long as you don't 'whip' the rod in the cast]. When you cast, mark the line with a black marker and allow the line to settle for at least a minute then strike hard – the bait is left behind, ground baiting compete. Don't put in too much of ground bait – this may just mean that the fish will have too much to eat and diminishes your chance of catching.*
- *If you're catching carp in a certain area, then you want to place your rigs in the exact same spot every time you cast. To help do this, mark your line using a black marker when your line is in the water – you can then slow down or stop your line when you see the colour change once you have your bait in your preferred area. Some reels have a memory clip that allows you to target the same distance each time you cast.*
- *Don't throw leftover bait in the water. Too much organic matter in the water will rob the water of oxygen take the bait home and freeze it.*
- *If you are battling to remove the hook from a struggling fish, cover the eyes with a wet rag – this calms the fish – you can then remove the hook quite easily.*
- *If you are using more than one rod, keep one shallow and one deeper – this will help indicate where the fish are.*
- *Use small hooks. Test your hook after you get stuck – hell – inspect them after each cast – they may have been damaged on the way out.*
- *Try balls of bread / mealie-pap dough. [dough made with cooked mealie-meal [corn flour]*
- *If it starts to rain without thunder and lightning, carry on fishing. The impact of raindrops on water oxygenates the water – if anything, this encourages fish to feed. Heavy rain will drop water temperature quickly – any change in the environment generally causes fish to go off the bite. If you are fishing shallow water, the water temperature will drop quicker than if you are fishing deeper water.*
- *It's nice to experiment, but don't change a winning combination!!! Why do people suddenly decide to stop using a bait that is working?* **If it 'ain't broke, it 'don't need fixing!**
- *Carp will also feed on worm, shrimp and nymphs.*
- *Oh – did I ask you to use maggots? Try them!!!!*

Bread bait / flour dough / mealie meal

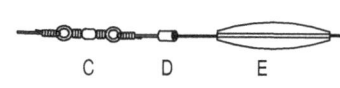

A   B   C   D   E

Legend: Light running sinker rig. A: Circle hook, size 6-12; B: 250mm Snoot, 6-10pound breaking strain; C: Swivel, size 7-10; D: Section of ball-point pen tube protecting the knot from the sinker and prevents the knot from getting stuck in the sinker; E: Small barrel / bullet sinker. This trace can also exclude a sinker for close-range fishing.

Can be used in estuaries [covered under saltwater fishing with natural bait], rivers and dams for yellowfish [freshwater bonefish], mud suckers, tilapia, *nembwe* bream, barbel [catfish], carp, grass carp and bass [yes, bass!! I have caught many a bass whilst reeling in a bread bait!

Normally fished as a dough, natural or flavoured with fruit juice or any dip of your choice, salt, garlic and chilli. In water where a second hook can be a problem, use one hook. I mostly use a single hook. I generally use a 6 or 8 circle / short shank hook and cover the hook with a ball of bait which can be fished off the bottom with a sliding sinker or without any weight [depending on how far you have to cast].

In a river, cast the bait [preferably without a sinker – just swivel] into the current and allow to drift down with the current. Takes can vary from a positive tug to 'taps'. Taps generally mean that there are small fish out there – scale down to smaller hooks if you want to have a chance of catching them or change your spot. The presence of smaller fish generally indicates the absence of larger fish. The problem is that bigger fish sometimes do bite with a series of taps…. Persevere. You can also use a quill when drifting a bait in the current. Just use a small lead shot about halfway down the line between the hook and the float. The line between the hook and the float should not be less than a meter in length.

Crab

Legend: *Light running sinker rig. A: Circle hook, size 6-12; B: 250mm Snoot, 6-10pound breaking strain; C: Swivel, size 7-10; D: Section of ball-point pen tube protecting the knot from the sinker and prevents the knot from getting stuck in the sinker; E: Small barrel / bullet sinker. This trace can also exclude a sinker for close-range fishing.*

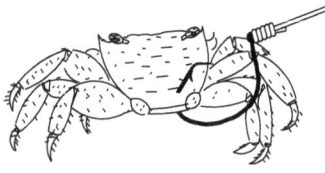

Crab not more than 2cm across the carapace can be fished whole after removing the pincers. Larger crab must be cut into sections big enough for the hook [as a guide for this, remove the carapace by sharply lifting it away from the body, from the side. Cut across the centre of the crab so you have two halves with legs. You can fish pieces of the body with a leg attached. This all depends on the size of the available targeted fish.

Crab is good for barbel [catfish] and yellowfish. You may sometimes be surprised by a bass or bluegill at times. Use a size 6 or 8 hook. For largemouth yellowfish, you can use a size 4 / 5 hook. This will also cater for large barbel. The bait can be cast out totally on the drift [with just a swivel] or using a sliding sinker. You will have to wait for the bite. This could take up to an hour, but when it comes, it will be fast and furious.

If you are using a circle hook – you need not fear – you will almost certainly hook the fish. Remember that if you are using pieces of crab – you will have to check the bait every hour as some fish will pick up the bait and suck out the meat without you ever knowing.

And don't forget to dip the bait into 'essence of crab' made up by crushing all those bits [including the carapace, gills and guts into a little water. Keep the 'dip' in a cooler box or it will go bad.

Nymphs

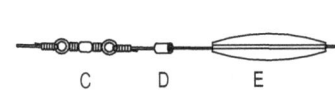

Legend: *Light running sinker rig. A: Circle hook, size 6-12; B: 250mm Snoot, 6-10pound breaking strain; C: Swivel, size 7-10; D: Section of ball-point pen tube protecting the knot from the sinker and prevents the knot from getting stuck in the sinker; E: Small barrel / bullet sinker. This trace can also exclude a sinker for close-range fishing.*

Nymphs can be fished whole, dead or alive. It is always desirable for them to be alive on the hook. You can achieve this by hooking them on the last body segment using a small hook [size 10 / 12]. This is a good bait and must be fished on the bottom or next to weed banks and structure using a quill. Takes are solid. Small fish may pick on the bait but larger specimens will take it whole.

Tadpoles

Same trace as above. [Light running sinker rig].

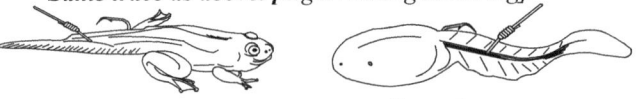

Tadpoles are best used as live bait and will attract bass, bluegill, barbel [catfish] and tilapia.

Remember that bluegill has a small mouth.

Pin a tadpole on a size 6 or 8 hook, in the meat of the tail, away from the centre line of the tail [use smaller hooks based on the tadpole size].

You may elect to use a float or sliding trace. Because it is live bait, do not strike immediately you see a bite – give it at least 5 seconds then strike. If the fish lands behind you, are striking too hard! :D

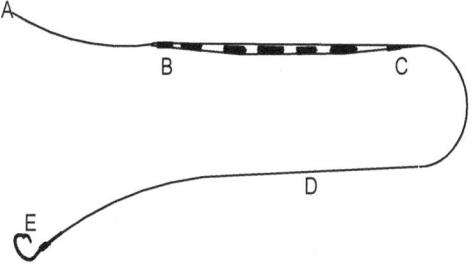

Legend: Porcupine quill rig. A: Fishing line leading to reel; B: Insulation tape attaching line to 'blunt' end of quill, as close to end as possible. Place one wrap of tape around the dry quill before trapping the line to this end; C: Tape wrapping line to sharp end of quill as close to end as possible. Be sure to apply one wrap of tape directly to dry end of quill first; D: 'Pinch on' lead ball [split shot] positioned on line.

The lead weight should not be closer than 300mm to the hook. Use as many weights as necessary to cause the float to just stand erect in the water; E: snoot or line leading to hook. In rapids, this line should be long enough to allow the bait to run as close to the bottom as possible. In still water you need to set it to the depth you want to fish at.

Fish bait

Legend: Light running sinker rig. A: Circle hook, size 6-12; B: 250mm Snoot, 6-10pound breaking strain; C: Swivel, size 7-10; D: Section of ball-point pen tube protecting the knot from the sinker and prevents the knot from getting stuck in the sinker; E: Small barrel / bullet sinker. This trace can also exclude a sinker for close-range fishing. Definitely better without a sinker. Fish should be pinned as shown in the two sketches below.

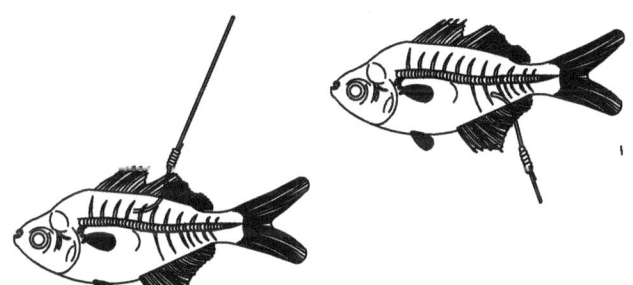

Any small fish can be used as live bait. For bass and barbel, fish of up to 125mm [5 inches] can be used – the perfect size, however would be fish from 75mm to 100mm. Smaller fish are pinned below or behind the dorsal fin, above the lateral line and fished with a float [far left].

The fish pictured here is a 'glassie', a fish generally found in lagoons pinned as live bait the top left sketch illustrates how it is pinned when using a float and the sketch alongside is how it is pinned when fishing off the bottom [in other words, with a sinker].

*Much fun can be had with this method of fishing. Increase your chances of a hook-up by cutting off the long sharp spine on the dorsal fin. The hook size is always proportionate to the size of the fish This bait works well in the surf for shad and salmon on light tackle. Remember that you are forced to use a smaller hook with smaller baits so if something big takes it, you will need to exercise your **skill** muscle! Always scale your hook size in proportion to the size of the live bait you are using.*

As Live Bait: Small fish will be taken readily by other fish, especially bass and barbel. They can be fished in deep water using a running trace

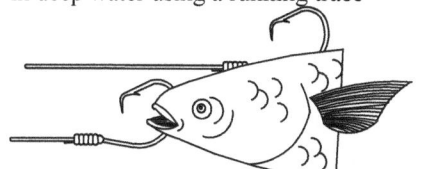

Barbel [catfish] can also be caught using a carp / scalie head. Or a whole carp [150mm – 300mm long]. The head is ideally between 40mm and 100mm in size [from nose to pectoral fin] and is cut off just behind the pectoral fins.

You can use a single hook for smaller heads. Hook size from 1/0 to 4/0. For Vundu you will need up to a 6/0 hook. If you are using a whole fish, pin it as indicated alongside. Line should be 10 to 20pound breaking strain. The head or whole fish needs to be struck a few times with a tenderizing mallet so that body juices are released in the water, acting as a beacon for barbel to zoom in on. The take generally comes in the form of a long run. If you are using conventional "J" hooks, you will need to strike about 3 seconds into the run – with circle hooks – you know the drill, just pick up the rod, reel until you feel the fish and then keep a tight line! Only use this bait if you have sound tackle and plenty of line. A barbel in the 10 – 20kg range will give you a run for your money. And just when you are believing that the fish is tired – it will make a dash. Bring it to the net only when you believe that it is tired out.

Striped frogs and *platanas*

These will attract bass and barbel [catfish]. The hook is placed in the meat of the leg, as close to the body as possible. Use a size 5 / 6 hook. Again, do not strike immediately on getting a bite – give the fish at least 5 seconds before striking unless you have a solid run. Use with a sliding sinker around ½oz in weight [about 14g]. *Platana* may be fished deeper and with a heavier running sinker as these will more than likely attract barbel.

Fruit

You really don't need to use any actual fruit because most fruit are available in juice / concentrate form. Mix the juice into a bread / mealie meal bait and fish as recommended above, for bread bait. This will attract carp, yellowfish, tilapia, *mudsuckers* and barbel.

Insects and spiders

Remember if it's brightly coloured it generally means that it shouldn't be handled. Spiders make good bait but one wrong move and you could be bitten. If the insect floats naturally, use a quill with a short line between the hook and quill. You shouldn't need to use a hook larger than 8. Crickets are excellent bait, as are small locusts. You can alternatively fish them as you would a nymph. Terrestrial insects are a big part of a fish's diet. Keep the insect alive – use latex bait cotton to attach to the hook. Dead insects will also be taken – but better alive than dead. And don't get bitten.

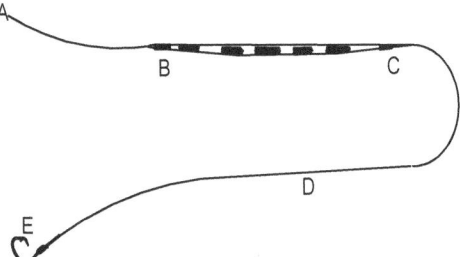

Legend: Porcupine quill rig. A: Fishing line leading to reel; B: Insulation tape attaching line to 'blunt' end of quill, as close to end as possible. Place one wrap of tape around the dry quill before trapping the line to this end; C: Tape wrapping line to sharp end of quill as close to end as possible. Be sure to apply one wrap of tape directly to dry end of quill first; D: 'Pinch on' lead ball [split shot] positioned on line.

The lead weight should not be closer than 300mm to the hook. Use as many weights as necessary to cause the float to just stand erect in the water; E: snoot or line leading to hook. In rapids, this line should be long enough to allow the bait to run as close to the bottom as possible. In still water you need to set it to the depth you want to fish at.

Flying ants are best used alive. Use a size 10 / 12 hook threaded through the last segment. Do not swing too hard when casting – their bodies are soft and they will come off the hook. You can also 'bunch' them on a hook – 3-5 insects should do it. All fish will take these. Can be fished on the surface or deep. Make your decision based on what you see happening. Remember though, fish expect them to be on the surface although they are pretty good bait when submerged. If you are lucky enough to be at the water when they emerge, be prepared for some action!

Get one or more on the hook with a short trace from the hook to the quill. cast it into the water and keep still. These are taken very violently by very excited fish – these fish will feed only on flying ant bait.

You cannot really scare off fish when they are in a feeding frenzy over these creatures!

When fishing this way, do not [try not to break off the wings – they float on water and allow the creature to float]. Flying ants may also be used with a carp rig, on the bottom.

And on the far side, dry the flying ants out completely and grind them into powder – keep the bottle sealed with silica gel packs to keep out all moisture. Mix a little at a time into dough and you are fishing with essence of flying ant – it hasn't failed me.

Maggots

These have been covered well enough in Chapter 14 and for carp above. A superbait and will attract anything. Remember to use small hooks and to fasten your seatbelt!

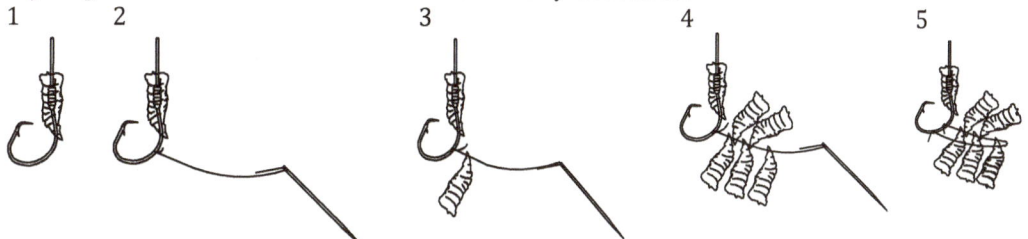

Use size 10 – 14 'J' or circle hooks. "1" First thread one maggot onto the shank.

"2" Tie cotton to hook, thread the other end onto a needle.

"3" Introduce a maggot onto the needle by going through the thinnest piece of skin. Slide the maggot gently up onto the thread near the hook.

"4" Repeat this process with 4 – 6 maggots.

"5" Use the needle to tie the other end of the line to the hook, forming as small a loop as you can.

Go fish! **This method can be used with MANY bait varieties – use your imagination!**

Shrimp

Legend: Light running sinker rig. A: Circle hook, size 6-12; B: 250mm Snoot, 6-10pound breaking strain; C: Swivel, size 7-10; D: Section of ball-point pen tube protecting the knot from the sinker and prevents the knot from getting stuck in the sinker; E: Small barrel / bullet sinker. This trace can also exclude a sinker for close-range fishing.

You can use a fine needle and with some cotton, attach the bait to the hook [see above for maggot bait].

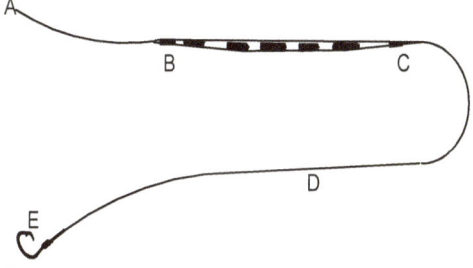

Legend: Porcupine quill rig. A: Fishing line leading to reel; B: Insulation tape attaching line to 'blunt' end of quill, as close to end as possible. Place one wrap of tape around the dry quill before trapping the line to this end; C: Tape wrapping line to sharp end of quill as close to end as possible. Be sure to apply one wrap of tape directly to dry end of quill first; D: 'Pinch on' lead ball [split shot] positioned on line.

The lead weight should not be closer than 300mm to the hook. Use as many weights as necessary to cause the float to just stand erect in the water; E: snoot or line leading to hook. In rapids, this line should be long enough to allow the bait to run as close to the bottom as possible. In still water you need to set it to the depth you want to fish at.

This is a natural food and is best used alive. Use a small hook and hook them by the last segment before the tail. Avoid threading them onto a hook. Use up to a size 10 hook using a terminal / running trace. Hooked this way, if you have a take and you miss the fish, it was more than likely a small fish.

Shrimp is threaded onto a hook tail-first. Keep the body straight. You will need to use latex bait cotton if you are using a circle hook.

Best used in a river with a quill with at least a meter of line between the quill and hook, on the drift in the current. In dams can be used with a quill near structure and grass near drop offs though is better

to use at the bottom in dams. Expect any fish to take this bait.

If you are fishing for greedy fish like bluegill, thread the bait fully onto the hook by the tail and fish with a quill. Tighten line, reel in and strike by tightening line and reeling quickly when the quill moves. Don't take too many fish out!

Snails and slugs

I have never had any success with large specimens, but in a river, drifted downstream in the current works for yellowfish.

This bait is hard work and really not worth the effort.

The smaller aquatic snail works a little better.

Pierce 3 – 5 onto a number 10 or smaller hook using the technique described above for maggots *[remember that aquatic fresh water snails carry Bilharzia – make sure you have no open wounds!]*

Fish off the bottom with a running trace or with a quill float alongside reeds and structure.

Worms

I have found that the large worms [about a meter long] do not work – try it and see. For pan fish, thread the worm onto the hook [10 or 12] and use a quill. For larger fish, fishing off the bottom, bunch the worms on the hook leaving ends sticking out. You want to pierce the worm every 30mm. Fish off the bottom with a running trace. It is advisable to use just one hook, size 6 or 8.

For yellowfish in rivers, fish a size 8 - 10 hook with the earthworm pinned once in the centre and drift it in the current using a quill and tighten your line *every* time the float moves. Fish suck in the whole worm and can also eject it easily if they become spooked. By tightening your line when the float moves, you are engaging the hook while it is in the fish's mouth increasing your chances of a hook-up.

For large bass and tilapia, pin each worm twice using two worms on a size 6 - 8 hook and use a quill near the edge of a drop off or if you are sight-fishing [and you should always try to!] cast the quill in the path of the fish. The distance between the quill and hook should be just less than 500mm [about 19.5 inches]. You can also fish off the bottom with a small split shot sinker [small enough to cast with. The shot should be placed 300mm from the hook. If using the famous Kariba worm, you cannot use a hook bigger than a size 8. The worms are small and thin. Hook them once in the center.

You would normally use split shank hooks [barbs on the shank] to hold worm baits. I have been more successful with hook-ups because I break the worm into pieces and thread each piece across the body onto the hook [see middle sketch]. This way, you are releasing more of the worm's juices, increasing your chances of fish finding your bait and, of taking the bait. Also, if you thread a worm onto a hook and a fish bites, it has a better chance of taking the entire worm. With pieces, as illustrated in the middle sketch .... DO THE MATH.

*When fishing in current, hook worms up as illustrated by the sketch on the right. Fish do not have time to take a bite / nibble in flowing water. As the worm is about to pass them in the current, they open their mouths, creating a vacuum effect, sucking the entire worm in. This is when you should be most vigilant and simply tighten your line. You **will** get a*

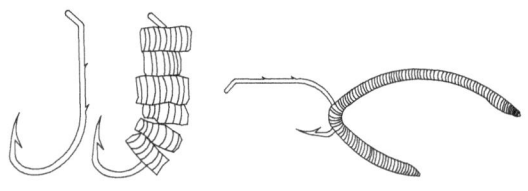

hook-up.

Chapter 17: Fishing using natural bait in salt water

If you are going to return a fish to the water, always avoid handling it by the soft underbelly area as this can easily cause serious injury to internal organs. If you must touch the underbelly, be gentle.

Pay attention to closed seasons, minimum sizes and bag limits for fish species. Should you catch a fish during closed season, please return it to the water – take a picture if you must! Be aware that it is ***illegal*** to buy and sell most species of fish [unless they are canned, or you are in a fishery].

Use extra strong hooks. Period.

Alikreukel [periwinkle]

Mollusc- shell needs to be broken to get the meat out – as with all saltwater bait it is *regulated*. This is excellent bait for all species of fish and is best used cut into strips just under 20mm X 20mm for larger fish or smaller blocks that just fit onto a hook. Keep the guts etc. – make a 'dip' and dunk bait in it before you cast. As with all 'dips' keep it on ice or will go bad and be rendered useless. Follow instructions as stipulated for rock bait below.

Armadillo / Chiton

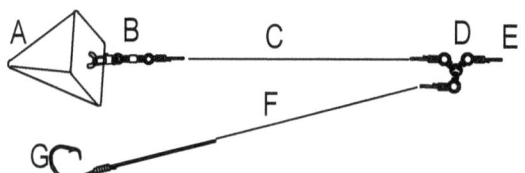

Legend: *Terminal sinker rig. A:4 – 6oz pyramid sinker; B: Snapper swivel; C: 200mm – 350mm sinker line 12kg breaking strain; D: size 2 – 4 three-way swivel; E: Main line, 15 – 25kg breaking strain; F: Snoot – 25kg, 400mm – 600mm; G: Extra strong circle hook, 4/0 to 6/0.*

Armadillo bait "A" and the meat under the shell segments must be cut away from the shell segments "B" alongside.

Once removed from the shell segments, the bait is oval in shape – it is not uncommon to find species as big as the sketch above and bigger. For example, the specimen would be cut down the length. Tenderize the bait to release juices. There are three main options for bait presentation [there is a fourth, but if you didn't read the section on circle hooks in the chapter on hooks….:(

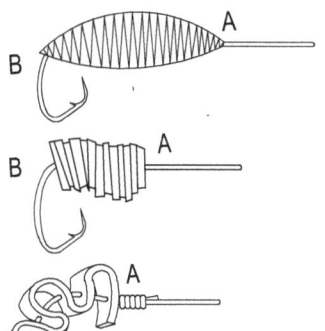

– the first would be to use both halves, 1 on each side of the hook – if the bait is longer than the hook, you will need to keep it straight by wrapping a shaved toothpick to the hook, and then binding the halves back-to-back on the hook as indicated alongside.

The other way to present the bait would be to cut each of the halves referred to above into slices/squares and then pierce each slice in the centre, 'stacking them on the hook as shown alongside.

A strip of bait can also be used as illustrated alongside. Use bait cotton to stop the strip from blocking the tip. The end of the strip near the eye of the hook should not pass over the eye or onto the knot. You will need to wrap latex cotton tightly at "A" and "B" so that the bite does not slide.

Expect violent takes from musselcracker and rock cod. Be prepared to power the fish away from the rocks!

If you downsize your hook and bait you can catch all manners of reef fish. Remember to keep the shell and body fluids on ice so you can dip your bait before you cast and re-cast.

Cheese

This bait is amazing when used in river mouths and estuaries. South of Durban it never fails to catch Steenbras. I have hooked Steenbras, Perch and various river snappers upwards of 2kg and even grunter. Sometimes you will be plagued by various smaller, undersized fish but if you persevere early and late in the day [especially if you are in the high tide zone [2-3 hours before, 3 hours after], you may be rewarded by a decent fish. Don't give up when the *'smallies'* are taking – you may well be surprised every now and then. Prepare to be frustrated – some of the *takes* are VIOLENT!

Legend: Light running sinker rig. A: Circle hook, size 6-12; B: 250mm Snoot, 6-10pound breaking strain; C: Swivel, size 7-10; D: Section of ball-point pen tube protecting the knot from the sinker and prevents the knot from getting stuck in the sinker; E: Small barrel / bullet sinker. This trace can also exclude a sinker for close-range fishing.

Make a bread dough using brown bread and water from the area you are fishing. The consistency of the dough should be such that you can cast it without it flying off the hook. You should also be able to easily pull the hook free. You will need to mix in about a third of the volume in cheese into the dough until it is of a smooth consistency. You are now ready to fish.

You will want to use light tackle and a single hook. The hook size should not be bigger than 6, short shank – circle hooks are best. Make a ball of bait just larger than the hook bend. It should completely cover the hook and you can taper it around the hook shank so that the entire bait is teardrop shaped.

Fish drop-offs and deep water without a sinker from three hours before and after high tide. Mark your line or use a policeman as a bite indicator. Do not hold the rod in your hand – use rod stands. ***You will catch fish – Return** undersized ones please.*

CRAB

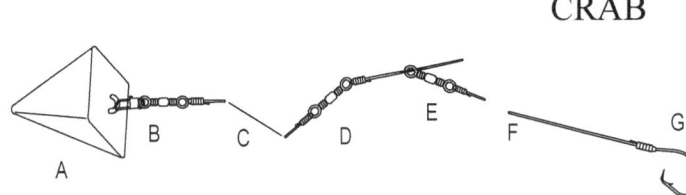

*Legend: Heavy running sinker rig. A: 1 – 5oz Pyramid sinker for low-risk snag areas **[Use a spoon / pear-shaped sinker for the rocks]**; B: Snapper swivel; C: Line between main line swivel and snapper swivel 150mm to 300mm – not more than 12kg; D: main line swivel; E: Snoot swivel; F: Snoot - 400mm to 600mm 50pound line [about 22kg]; G: Circle hook, size as recommended. For musselcracker use a 4/0 to 6/0 good quality hook.*

This is a great bait when fishing from the rocks or deep sea. You could get lucky with rock salmon between dusk and dawn in lagoons, in deep water where grunter will take small crab as well. When fishing for rock cod, *baardman* and musselcracker, a heavy main line is essential as these species need to be powered away from rocks and snags and a good reel with a powerful drag mechanism is indispensable. And then there is the pompano that also loves this bait.

Scale your hook according to the size crab you are using. Use extra strong hooks. Larger crab should be cut up and used.

The parks board never gave me problems with crab bait – but please clarify this with the authorities in the area you are fishing. I mean the license gives you a minimum size for crab you can catch but this is specific to mud crabs. You will be using the scavenger crab that races across the rocks or ghost crabs. Whole Crab should be up to 50mm [2 inches] across the carapace.

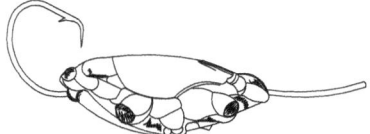

Pin the crab as shown after removing the pincers and set up a running trace. In lagoons, you shouldn't need more than a 1oz ball / bullet sinker and the crab should not be more than 35mm across the carapace.

Cast out, open the drag, set the ratchet and wait. You want to be fishing two - three hours before – during, and after high tide.

In the surf, the crab should be up to 50mm across the carapace although I have seen larger specimens put on a hook. Alongside is a drawing of a crab body on a circle hook. Remove carapace [by lifting it away from the body until it comes free], legs and claws and flap [from underside of body]. Pass a bait needle through the crab body and pull the line [preferably braid, 10-20 pound and then tie it to the hook. Pull the hook into the body so it sits as shown. You can slide the bait up to the bend of the hook. Great for pompano, grunter, musselcracker, baardman and salmon. Other species will also find it attractive. Use on a running trace. Allow fish to run for at least 5 seconds before raising the rod, reeling quickly until you feel the fish if you are using circle hooks. The circle hook will do its job.

For whole crab [up to 5 cm across the carapace – but LARGER crab can and has been used...], remove pincers and pin it as shown or between the 4 legs and cast into the white water on a sandy bottom at any tide using up to a 5ounce running sinker. The hook should be size 1 – 2/0 and the line between the swivel and the hook should be about 300mm. Set the rod in a stand and open the drag and engage the ratchet. Don't stray too far from the rod!!!

The crab body alongside has been cut into half, the flap on the underside removed and sections of the leg have been cut off. The claw has been removed up to the second segment from the body. The hook has been passed through the hard section of the body. All crab baits are generally fished in white water. Note that all crab baits can also be used when bottom fishing from the shore or deep sea. This is a magical bait and will not disappoint you. It does, however require for you to be patient. Allow the fish to take the bait – when the bite develops into a pull, strike lightly and Bob's your uncle [and the rod will be 'bobbing'].

Use a drop-shot hook with a live crab pinned to it [must pin the crab so it moves sideways – it is generally unnatural for a crab to move forwards and backwards].
Keep the rod tip down so that you can strike – you will need to strike with this type of rig. This is magical in the white water next to rocks.

Be flexible with any bait using like this using a drop shot hook – you are no longer using an artificial lure – purists may not like it, but this is *fusion* fishing! Can you see the possibilities? They are endless, what with a natural scent emanating from the pinned bait!!!! If you use a circle hook, pick the tip up and reel fast until you feel the fish.

In lagoons, you can use smaller crab and pieces with lighter tackle using a running trace as shown below.

 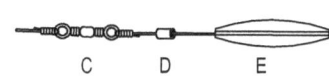

Legend: Light running sinker rig. A: Circle hook, size 6-12; B: 250mm Snoot, 6-10pound breaking strain; C: Swivel, size 7-10; D: Section of ball-point pen tube protecting the knot from the sinker and prevents the knot from getting stuck in the sinker; E: Small barrel / bullet sinker. This trace can also exclude a sinker for close-range fishing. Look for drop-offs.

Remember from Chapter 14 – dip the bait into the liquefied crab waste each time you cast.

Cracker shrimp, mud prawns and sand prawns

Avoid using heavy sinkers with this bait [unless you are lucky enough to be hit by a '*beeeg feesh*', you are unlikely to feel the bite].

 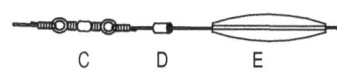

Legend: Light running sinker rig. A: Circle hook, size 3-5; B: 250mm Snoot, 6-10pound breaking strain; C: Swivel, size 7-10; D: Section of ball-point pen tube protecting the knot from the sinker and prevents the knot from getting stuck in the sinker; E: Small barrel / bullet sinker. This trace can also exclude a sinker for close-range fishing.

Cracker shrimp is mostly used to catch grunter and is best used where the shrimp occur naturally – this means anywhere that you can catch them. Any other fish can and will take it. It is best used in the period ranging from 2 hours before and after high tide. This is when big fish are around. This bait is best used with light tackle.

*There are a few ways of presenting this bait. I will describe the common ways but there is one **BEST** way of presenting it when there are big fish around. This is by simply passing the hook carefully through the large claw. If you do this properly, the claw will remain attached to the body and you will have a live shrimp that will jiggle the "EAT ME" dance much more effectively than using a shrimp that dies when you hook it. Use a running trace. Hook size is dependent on the bait size and ranges from an 8 to a maximum of 4. Do not swing too hard on your cast.*

The alternate methods involve piercing the body section. I would suggest that you have several hooks ready, tied to braid or light monofilament. The length of line from the knot on the hook should be between 250 and 400mm. Attach the free end of the nylon to a fine bait needle and pass the needle through from the head, down the centre of the body and out of the tail meat.

Then pull the hook through until the bend gets to the head. Now tie in the loose nylon to the swivel on your trace and cast.

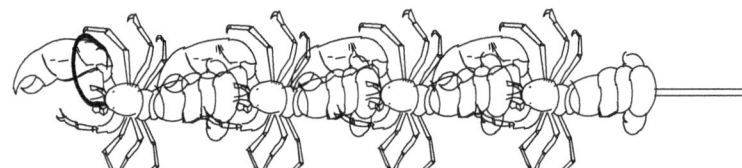

The final method would be using 3 to 5 shrimp. Using the bait needle as above, pass it through 3 to 5 shrimp and pull the one closest to the hook onto the hook.

If you are careful – you can thread the creature directly onto the hook, slide it up the line and repeat without using a bait needle. This form of presentation [pictured below] is called a 'garland'.

This bait is also effective in the surf zone and backline but should be fished using a terminal sinker heavy enough to stand in the current. Because the bait is so soft, you will not feel individual bites – just wait for a positive take. I would suggest extra strong hooks if you are fishing close to structure as it will be scooped by musselcracker, baardman, rock cod and anything else.com.

Crayfish [rock lobster]

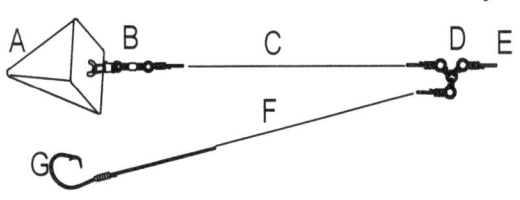

Legend: Terminal sinker rig. A: 4 – 6oz pyramid sinker; B: Snapper swivel; C: 200mm – 350mm sinker line 12kg breaking strain; D: size 2 – 4 three-way swivel; E: Main line, 15 – 25kg breaking strain; F: Snoot – 25kg, 400mm – 600mm; G: Extra strong circle hook, 3/0 to 6/0.

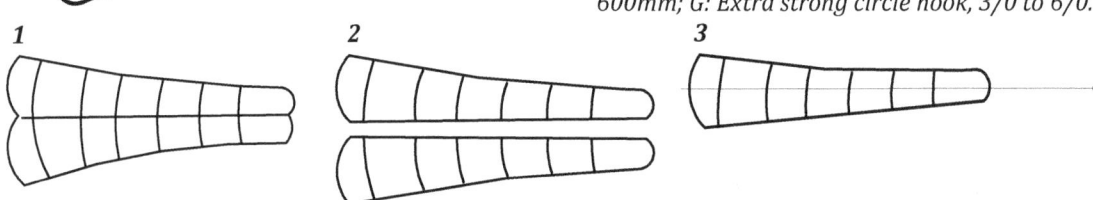

Crayfish bait is wasted where there are 'nibblers' around. It is a favourite food of the black musselcracker [poenskop] and Pompano and will be readily taken by other big reef fish. Stumpnose love it. I have caught salmon as well on this bait. If the flesh has a tint of yellow, toss it away. Remove the hard bits of shell – watch your fingers! The tail should look like the picture above [1].
Cut the flesh down the centre line to create two strips of bait [2]
I prefer thin long baits [3] as opposed to bulky baits – by the way – so do the fish!!!
Take one of the pieces ["3" above], and cut a groove along the length, halfway through the meat. You are creating a slot to accommodate your line so that you can bind the bait in position using latex bait cotton.

4

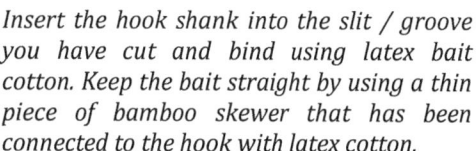

Insert the hook shank into the slit / groove you have cut and bind using latex bait cotton. Keep the bait straight by using a thin piece of bamboo skewer that has been connected to the hook with latex cotton.

Straight baits rock! [see "4" above] Remember from Chapter 14 – dip the bait into the liquefied crayfish waste each time you cast. Bait can also be cut into pieces to catch reef fish. Use size 1 to 1/0 round hooks.

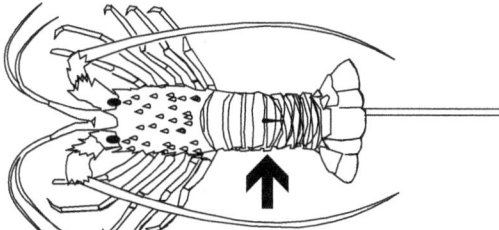

If you are lucky enough to have langoustines,[Yes, I am crazy enough to buy a few for bait] then pin them using a 4/0 or 5/0 hook [hook embedded] in the third section and cotton the hook in place. Refer drawing alongside. The arrow alongside points at hook point just showing with hook shank and line against the body and bound in place using latex bait cotton.

Do not fish lighter than 20kg line on the hook trace. You will feel the bite - takes are savage and you will need to power the fish away from reef structure immediately – pump and reel, pump and reel....!

Oooooh – writing all this just makes me want to GO FISH!!!!!

Fish bait

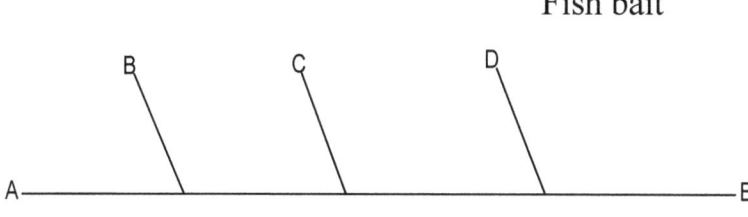

Legend: Banana bunch trace for catching pan fries and bait fish. Refer to Chapter 10 for the tying of this trace. A: tie sinker here; B, C, D: tie hooks here – size 8-12 "J" or circle hooks; E: tie to swivel on mainline.

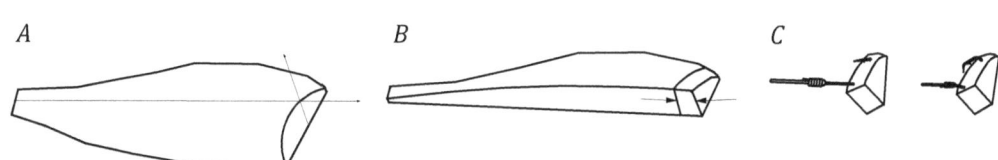

Legend: Baiting up for pan fries / live bait [pinkies, mackerel, karanteen...] A: 1 side fillet from sardine / baitfish; split bait into two pieces by cutting as shown; B: Cut each fillet into slices [cutlets] about 8mm wide; D: Showing width of slice, about 8mm wide; C: "J" Hook and circle hook inserted correctly on bait cutlet.

Once baited up, cast into gullies or alongside reef on the down-current side, keep the line tight so you can feel the sinker, wait for the 'knocks' and reel in quickly – no striking necessary with circle hooks. You will need a minor strike with "J" hooks.

Fishing for biggies

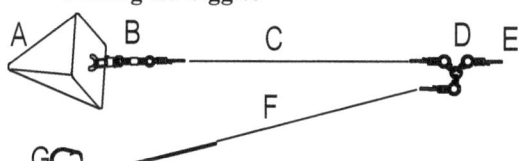

Legend: Terminal sinker rig. A:4 – 6oz pyramid sinker; B: Snapper swivel; C: 200mm – 350mm sinker line 12kg breaking strain; D: size 2 – 4 three-way swivel; E: Main line, 15 – 25kg breaking strain; F: Snoot – 25kg, 400mm – 600mm; G: Extra strong circle hook, 3/0 to 6/0.

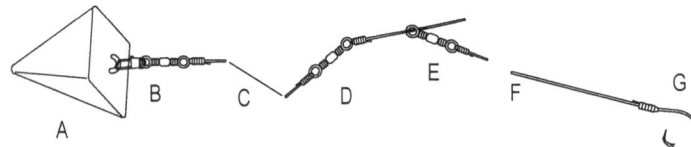

Legend: *Heavy running sinker rig. A: 1 – 5oz Pyramid sinker for low-risk snag areas **[Use a spoon / pear-shaped sinker for the rocks]**; B: Snapper swivel; C: Line between main line swivel and snapper swivel 150mm to 300mm – not more than 12kg; D: main line swivel; E: Snoot swivel; F: Snoot – 400mm to 600mm 50pound line [about 22kg]; G: Circle hook, size as recommended. For musselcracker use a 4/0 to 6/0 good quality hook.*

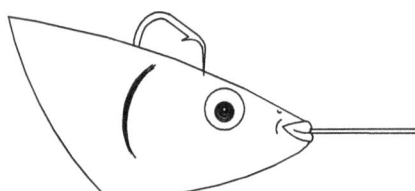

Anything big will tackle a fish head, particularly brusher [white musselcracker], poenskop [black musselcracker], salmon and rock cod. The best fish heads to use are mullet and karanteen. Sardine heads work as well but are quickly stripped of meat. Use a curved bait needle inserted through the mouth to pull the line through then tie on the hook and push the knot and shank into the head so it resembles the schematic picture alongside. Do not strike immediately on take – wait for the run! No bait cotton required.

If you are intend using filleted linefish, Cut the fillet from the head to the tail. Cut into tapered strips up to 20mm wide – wider strips make bulkier baits. Avoid bulky baits. [Refer to Chapter 27 for instructions on cleaning and filleting fish].

Keep fillet baits straight and slim. Pass the hook through the skin first on the wider end of the fillet about 8mm from the end of the fillet.

For musselcracker and rock cod use a combination of mullet and karanteen / blacktail / slinger with the skins back-to-back against the hook then bind with latex bait cotton. For grunter, use the belly section with the guts and blood facing outwards and wrapped tightly [releases the juices] with latex bait cotton.

Remember to dip the bait into freshly liquefied fish remains each time you cast. Keep the dip on ice.

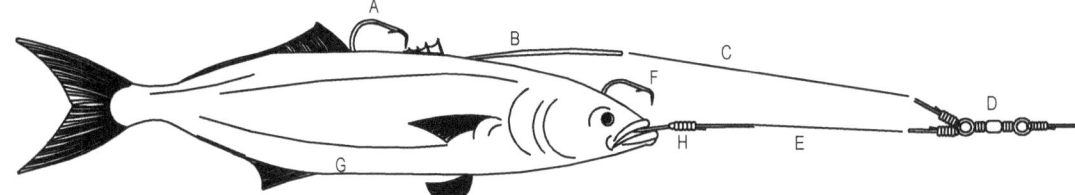

Legend: *Dead shad [elf] bait. A: Circle hook 5/0 to 9/0 with shank pulled into the flesh; B: 15-35kg fluorocarbon mono. This line is pulled through the flesh in front of the first dorsal fin and out just in front of the second dorsal fin using a curved needle. Circle hook "A" is then tied on. Push the shank into the flesh while gently pulling the line. This line must not take up any load when casting or the hook will tear the flesh; C: [same as "B", 15-35kg fluorocarbon line]; D: Power swivel, large enough to accommodate two knots on one side. The other end of the swivel can be attached to a terminal or running sinker; E: 15-35kg snoot, 300-900mm long. This line must take up the strain of casting. No strain must be exerted on "C"; F: 5/0-9/0 circle hook with the point brought through between the eyes of the fish; G: Make an incision in the anus of the bait and sew in a barrel sinker to help keep the fish upright and to retard any 'spinning' action when reeling in; H: Knot on hook "F" must be clear of the teeth of the shad. Do not make the mistake of threading the line leading to hook "A" through the mouth. Once you have rigged the bait, take some latex bait cotton and wrap "C" and "E" together lightly.*

This bait does not have to be fished far from you. Scout river mouths for deep channels. Between dusk and dawn use nothing bigger than a 4oz sinker – salmon do not like heavy sinkers. For salmon, the bigger the shad, the bigger the salmon [kob]. If you are fishing the backline, drift this out with a large float for Garrick. You may also get a surprise from a kingfish as well…

During the day, fishing from the shore, cast this bait alongside structure with a running trace for Garrick and kingfish early mornings till 10am and afternoon from 4pm till you hear the "CLUNK" of darkness falling… From then on the kob will be calling…

If you are fishing deep sea this bait should be drifted out without a float but use wire on your hooks – depending on the current, you may need to use a barrel sinker to keep the bait at the depth you require. Refer Chapter 10 for my recommended method of tying the wire to the hooks and swivel. Beware! Sailfish and billfish will take this bait as well!! And if this happens, fasten your seatbelt!!!!!

Head and sides bait for rock cod, salmon [kob, geelbek]

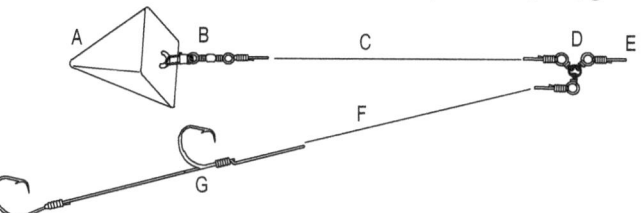

Legend: Rig may be terminal sinker or running sinker. Alongside is a terminal rig. A: 4 – 6oz pyramid sinker; B: Snapper swivel; C: 200mm – 350mm sinker line 12kg breaking strain; D: Size 2 – 4 three-way swivel; E: Main line, 15 – 25kg breaking strain; F: Snoot for "G" – 25kg, 400mm – 600mm; G: Circle hook, 5/0 - 9/0; H: Circle hook, 5/0 - 9/0; I: Snoot for "H" about 100mm longer than "F", 25kh line. Note that the gap between "G" and "F" is dependent on the bait size.

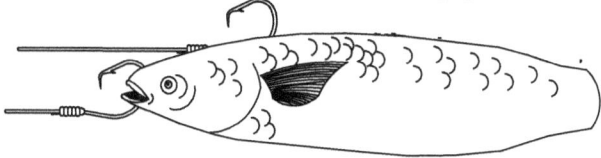

Take a whole baitfish [preferably not sardine, note that mullet is used here] and from the tail, cut both sides away from the bone, leaving the flaps of fillet attached to the head.
Cut off the centre bone with the dorsal, anal and tail fins attached. Wedge and tie in a cork float in the head from the fillet end. This will keep the bait just off the bottom and will cause it to move enticingly with the currents.

Trace for barracuda [below]

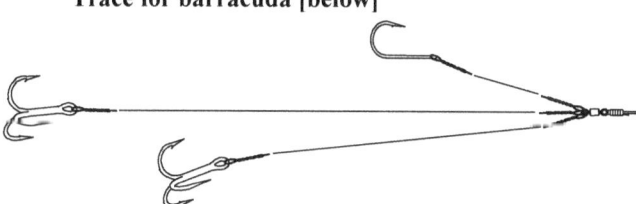

Using the haywire loop, tie three consecutive traces onto the same swivel so that it resembles the same trace illustrated alongside. This is for a mackerel bait, live or dead. Mullet or shad can also be used. One hook in the jaw [upper and lower (or just upper), one treble in the side, the other treble in the opposite side.

Live bait

Just about any small fish can be used as live bait – my preference is pinkie, glassie, mullet, shad. Live fish are pinned differently. Smaller fish are pinned below or behind the dorsal fin, above the lateral line and fished with a float. The inset pictures below show on the top, a glassie pinned as live bait when using a float and the sketch below it how it is pinned when fishing off the bottom [using a sinker].

Much fun can be had with this fish which doesn't grow much bigger than 75mm. I caught some decent rock salmon in the Isipingo lagoon before industrial effluent struck and totally ruined the fishing. Increase your chances of a hook-up by cutting off the long sharp spine on the dorsal fin. The hook size is always proportionate to the size of the fish which is kept just off the bottom at a drop off. Much fun can be had with shad, 'pickhandles' [juvenile 'couta], kingfish and Garrick. This bait works well in the surf for shad and salmon on light tackle. Remember that you are forced to use a smaller hook with this bait so if something big takes it, you will need to exercise your **skill** muscle!

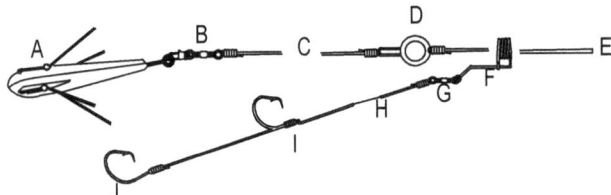

Legend: Live bait 'non-return' running trace. A: Grapnel sinker [adjustable with grapnels set in grooves on sinker; B: Snapper swivel linked to grapnel sinker; C: line between sinker and live bait ring stop. This line is always weaker than the main line but strong enough for casting – normally 12kg – line is tied to weak link on ring stop; D: Ring stop, part of live bait rig; Shock leader is tied directly to the main ring on the ring stop; E: Shock leader normally minimum of 1.75 X rod length, best at three times rod length; F: Non-return coil spring with clip – attached to main line by opening press-release clip. Do not forget to close clip after installing over main line; G: Built in swivel on coil spring; H Snoot – normally minimum 25kg braid, 500mm – 1500mm long from swivel to first hook; I: First circle hook on tandem trace [4/0 – 9/0] – refer Chapter 10 for instructions on how to tie; J: Terminal hook on tandem trace – the positioning of this hook depends on the size of the live bait. Hook is normally 4/0 – 9/0.

When fish takes, allow at least 8 seconds. If you are using circle hooks, raise rod whilst reeling rapidly until you feel the fish.

Mullet – anything from 100mm to 300mm. Best hooked just behind the beginning of the anal fin and allow to swim out ["B" on sketch]. If fishing deep sea, [refer "A" on sketch] set up a running trace with a 1 or 2ounce barrel sinker above the power swivel [to keep the fish below the surface on the drift]. Use a steel wire trace because you can be smashed by 'couta you will need a guide hook to pin just behind the upper lip in the mouth to keep the fish pointed into the current and the main hook is pinned behind the first dorsal fin. You can catch any game fish, including the rare prodigal son or cobia.

The sardine / pilchard

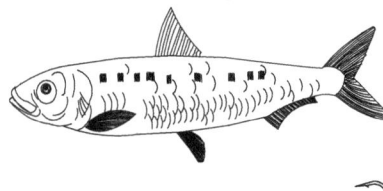

Probably the most common saltwater bait in use in South Africa. It can be use whole or in fillets of various sizes and is still a favourite food for many of our saltwater species.

They are best used fresh and bait that is yellow and soft is a waste of time – better used to catch crab or to make chum.

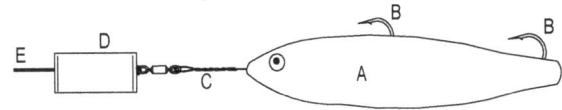

Legend: Whole sardine bait. A: Whole sardine with all fins snipped off. Sardine is butterflied from the belly almost through to the top – just so you can get the hooks through and bury the steel wires. The bait is then wrapped with latex with extra wraps around the front to lock it in position and around the hooks to hold them in place; B: 3/0 – 6/0 hooks - half the bend is exposed. Latex is wound around the shank at the point where the hook emerges to hold them in place. Each hook has its own wire attached to the swivel; C: Steel wire – can be single strand or multi strand; D: The 'bung' or cork is placed at least an inch away from the bait; E: Main line

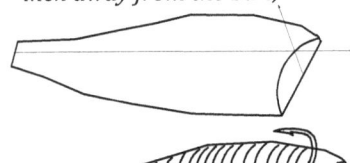

This is a fillet from one side of a sardine. I normally cut it into two pieces along the length.

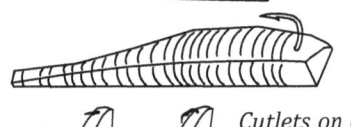

And a shad bait from one of the fillets.

Cutlets on a 'J' and circle hook [for smaller fish, (generally from size 10 to size 1 hook) depending on what is biting].

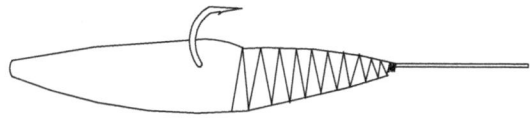

For fish like *geelbek* [Cape salmon], a whole side fillet is hooked as illustrated alongside and fished off the bottom using a long snoot [up to 1m] of 20+kg line using a 4/0 – 9/0 hook. Must have a swivel as this bait will spiral whilst going down. Whole sardine can be used this way too.

For shad, the fillet is wrapped over the steel wire. A float should be used to keep the bait off the bottom and drifting enticingly. Circle hooks should only be used with slimmer, smaller baits when using sardine [unless the hook is passed through the mouth, and through the upper jaw.

Mackerel

Mackerel are caught off the backline using yo-zuri rigs [left]. Mackerel bait is generally wasted for shore fishing and is best used alive or dead when fishing deep sea. Use of this bait is described in Chapter 19.

Fishing with a top bung

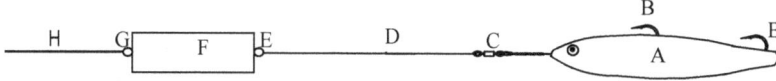

Legend: *Top bung trace for float fishing for shad, large gamefish and shark near the surface. A: Whole fish [can be fillet]; B: Tandem hooks with half bend exposed. Hooks can be "J" or circle. Hook size can be 3/0 – 6/0, depending on what you are targeting. For Shark, you will need larger, stronger hooks; C: Steel wire trace [use only with shad and other razortooth fish]. For fish like Garrick, you can leave out the steel wire, tying your trace directly to the shock leader; D: Leader line – 40-80pound, 1-3m; E: wire ring on bung, attach leader to here; F: bung float 'top bung'; G: Ring on bung float. If this does not have a swivel, attach one here using a split ring or a secure clip on swivel; H: main line [must be attached to swivel].*

Marine worms

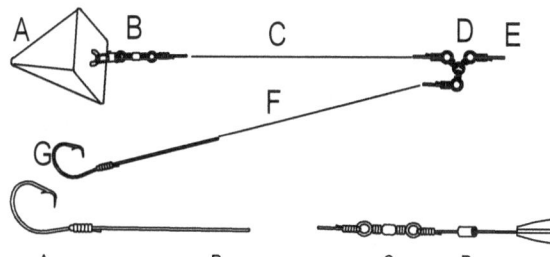

Legend: *A:4 – 6oz pyramid sinker; B: Snapper swivel; C: 200mm – 350mm sinker line about 8kg breaking strain; D: size 4 - 6 three-way swivel; E: Main line, 10 – 15kg breaking strain; F: Snoot – 25kg, 150mm – 200mm; G: Circle hook, size 4 to 1.*

Legend: *Light running sinker rig. A: Circle hook, size 6-12; B: 250mm Snoot, 6-10pound breaking strain; C: Swivel, size 7-10; D: Section of ball-point pen tube protecting the knot from the sinker and prevents the knot from getting stuck in the sinker; E: Small barrel / bullet sinker. This trace can also exclude a sinker for close-range fishing.*

This superbait class is normally cut into sections which are **threaded** onto a hook. I use single hook traces with a terminal sinker. If you are using this bait you will be sending a 'telegram' to all fish in the area and they will start feeding selectively, searching for worm. Use extra strong hooks. Please. If big fish are around, they **WILL** take it – you might have to be patient, though.

Left: Marine worm section on a hook. Use latex bait cotton to fix the end of the worm on the centre of the hook bend so that the worm does not slide down the hook.

Warning!! If you are using the marine tapeworm as bait, you risk being infected – yes – the marine tapeworm can have a human host! [and one adult marine tapeworm can grow to about TWENTY METRES!]

Black mussels

Years ago, in the Eastern Cape I saw a fisherman tapping away at a mussel with a spike and cursing every now and then. He was trying to make a hole in the shell so that he could pass a hook through and the shells were just shattering in the process. I thought about it and used an extra strong 4/0 circle hook held against a mussel [*over* the shell] as shown and bound in place using bait cotton [now replaced by latex]. I have caught several musselcracker using this rig.

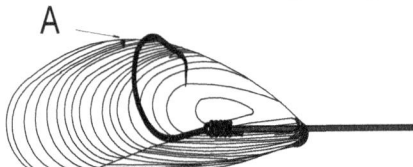

What I also do at point 'A', using a side-cutter, I make small nibbling cuts into the shell until I get to about 4mm into the shell. This causes the scent of the fresh, vital mussel to permeate the water. The shell cracks a little but the cut is not enough to shatter it – even if it does shatter a little, it is okay. Smaller fish leave it alone.

Musselcracker jaws are so powerful that the teeth just crush at the mussel – by this time the circle hook is in the fish's mouth, and when the fish turns to swim away, the circle hook does its job. Raise the rod and reel in rapidly until you feel the fish. Get it away from reef quickly or you will lose it [pump and reel!!]!

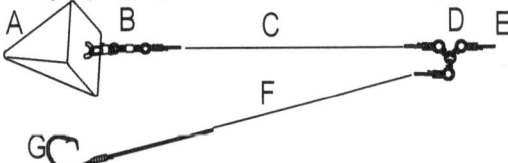

Legend: A:4 – 6oz pyramid sinker; B: Snapper swivel; C: 200mm – 350mm sinker line about 8kg breaking strain; D: size 4 - 6 three-way swivel; E: Main line, 10 – 20kg breaking strain; F: Snoot – 25kg braid, 150mm – 200mm; G: extra strong circle hook, size 3/0 – 6/0 [dependent on the size of the mussel]

Mussel meat can be stripped from the shell. Be careful. Use a ***dull bladed knife*** to lever the shells open then scoop out the meat without breaking it up.

Bind a shaved toothpick to the hook shank using latex and build it up into a straight, long and tapered fillet [as illustrated]. In this case, you will be using extra strong hooks, size 1 to 3/0.

White mussels [clams]

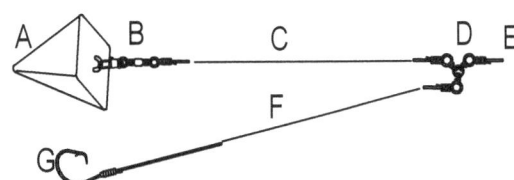

Legend: A:4 – 6oz pyramid sinker; B: Snapper swivel; C: 200mm – 350mm sinker line about 8kg breaking strain; D: size 4 - 6 three-way swivel; E: Main line, 10 – 20kg breaking strain; F: Snoot – 25kg braid, 150mm – 200mm; G: extra strong circle hook, size 3/0 – 6/0 [dependent on the size of the mussel]

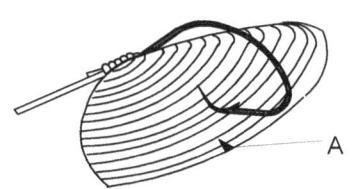

Place the hook as shown, ***over*** the shell [hook should not stick out, size proportionate to the mussel] and bind to the mussel using latex bait cotton.

Take a side-cutting pliers and make small nibbling cuts into the shell until about 4-6mm deep as shown by "A" alongside. When the bite comes, be prepared to bully the fish away from reef or all will be lost!

*White m*ussel meat can be stripped from the shell. Be careful. Use a ***dull bladed knife*** to lever the shell halves open then scoop out the meat without breaking it up.

Bind a shaved toothpick [whittle it down] to the hook shank using latex and introduce the meat to the toothpick and hook, building it up into a straight, long and tapered fillet [as illustrated] bound with latex.

In this case, you will be using extra strong hooks, size 1 to 3/0. Much fun can be had with the meat on smaller hooks. Remember to present the bait as a scaled down version of the last illustration above - and use latex bait cotton.

Octopus

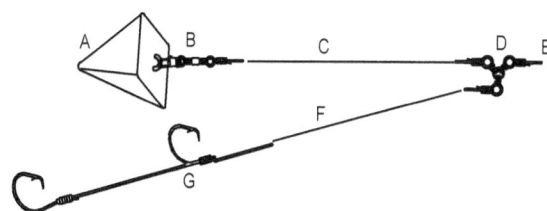

Legend: A: 4 – 6oz pyramid sinker; B: Snapper swivel; C: 200mm – 350mm sinker line about 8kg breaking strain; D: size 4 - 6 three-way swivel; E: Main line, 10 – 25kg breaking strain; F: Snoot – 25kg braid, 300mm – 600mm to the first hook; G: Tandem extra strong circle hook, size 4/0 – 9/0 [dependent on the size of the octopus' leg]. The last hook should be just past the middle of the leg and the first hook should have about 40mm of bait over the knot.

Take a 'leg' and tenderize by striking repeatedly with a mallet until it is possible to slide off the tough skin. The skin comes off with the suckers. Use only if white – yellowish or yellow/brown tinge is unacceptable. Make a shallow slit in the leg to slot in the hook shanks and line [the preparation of this trace is covered in Chapter 10]. Bind in place with latex. If the octopus' leg is too thin, double up or use three or more. Bait should not be too thin and hooks must protrude as illustrated. Best used from dusk to dawn for salmon [kob].

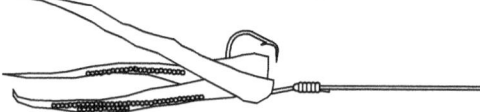

If you have smaller appendages, mount them like this. Use extra strong hooks.

Perlemoen [abalone]

It is indeed a pity that this creature has been so heavily exploited. It is a superbait and is used as stipulated for Armadillo above. Note that it carries severe penalties should you be found in possession of it or using it. Until it is de-restricted [and that will only happen shortly after hens grow teeth], please refrain from capturing or using this creature. Many years ago, I used this bait with old man *Bapu* from *District 6*. Even the guts were great bait. It would be a pleasure to see numbers increase so that abalone is no longer a threatened species. ☹ ***PROHIBITED.***

Prawn

This natural bait is eaten by all fish. It is best used whole although, upon occasion it may be fished minus the head or in sections. Try and keep the bait straight because it emulates a living prawn [obviously more desirable to the fish].

 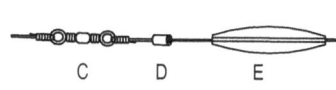

Legend: *Prawn running trace for use in estuaries. A: Circle hook, size 4 - 6; B: Snoot -300mm – 500mm; C: Swivel; D: Section of ball point pen tube to slide over knot and protect knot from impact with sinker, also prevents knot from fouling in the sinker and impeding the running action; E: Sinker – small – medium weight barrel / ball, the lighter the better. Note that a terminal trace may also be used.*

Peeled prawn bait. Most people make the mistake of locating the hook end in the thick meat – do it the other way around.

Try and keep the bait straight by using a shaved toothpick.

Tandem peeled prawn bait. Use at high water when the small fish are in hiding. Make a cut into the prawn and position the hook shank and line inside the meat. Bind the meat in position.

Prawns may also be cut into segments or the meat used in small pieces. These can be threaded directly onto the hook sized or the bait. You may or may not elect to use latex bait cotton. This is used in conjunction with a running trace.

For this and the next presentation, the prawn is cut in half down the centre line from between the eyes to the middle of the tail. Both halves are then brought together so that the drop shot hook is sandwiched as illustrated and then bound together with latex [you can just see the drop shot weight below the hook eye and the head of the prawn]. This bait can be retrieved [yes, retrieved –it also can be fished static] super-slow. Be wary – takes are so fierce you may have a heart attack!!

Larger prawn should be fished with a tandem hook trace [alongside] with the first hook being a drop shot hook and the trailing hook a normal hook. Split the prawn in half as before and sandwich the trace between halves and bind with bait cotton. The drop shot hook weight is just visible below and in front of the head. Tying of the tandem hook trace is covered in Chapter 10. A prawn bait presented like this with a terminal sinker and normal hooks in tandem will attract any big fish.

Razor clams / pencil bait

Species in Cape Town-surrounds are at least 6inches long!!! Remove the flesh from the creature, break off one of the shell halves and scoop the remains out of the other half using a sharp knife. The bait can be use whole or cut into pieces and retained on the hook with latex bait cotton. The bait is long and worm-like. It can be threaded onto a hook using a bait needle or threaded directly onto the hook and bound in place using latex bait cotton. Keep the bait long and slim. The other option is to wind the meat around a toothpick that has been whipped to the hook shank and then binding it with cotton. Saves time. Great for grunter and Steenbras. A superbait.

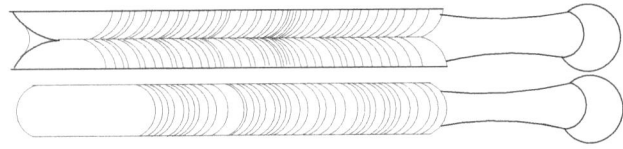
Legend: Prawn running trace for use in estuaries. A: Circle hook, size 4 - 6; B: Snoot -300mm – 500mm; C: Swivel; D: Section of ball point pen tube to slide over knot and protect knot from impact with sinker, also prevents knot from fouling in the sinker and impeding the running action; E: Sinker – small – medium weight barrel / ball, the lighter the better. Note that a terminal trace may also be used.

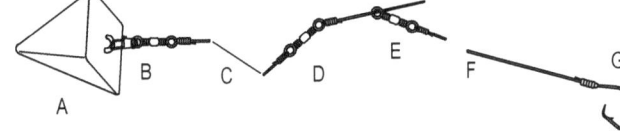
Running sinker rig for 'biggies'. *Legend:* A: 1 – 5oz Pyramid sinker for low-risk snag areas **[Use a spoon / pear-shaped sinker for the rocks]**; B: Snapper swivel; C: Line between main line swivel and snapper swivel 150mm to 300mm – not more than 20pound breaking strain; D: main line swivel; E: Snoot swivel; F: Snoot – 400mm to 600mm 20-pound line; G: Circle hook, size as recommended. Use a size2 – 2/0 hook. Main line can be about 20pound.

Rock bait [red bait]

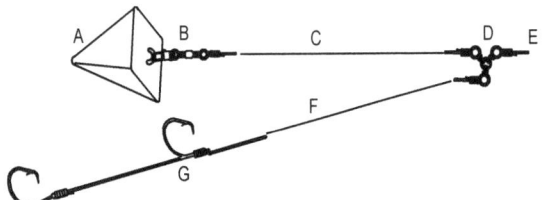
Legend: A:4 – 6oz pyramid sinker; B: Snapper swivel; C: 200mm – 350mm sinker line about 8kg breaking strain; D: size 4 - 6 three-way swivel; E: Main line, 10 – 25kg breaking strain; F: Snoot – 10-25kg braid, 300mm – 600mm to the first hook; G: Tandem extra strong circle hook, size 1 - 4/0. The last hook is tied 40mm from the first. A toothpick about 50 mm long is first attached to the bottom hook a using latex and then the top hook.

This a favourite bait of *Baardman* and *galjoen* although any species present will take it. Red bait is normally a bunch of 'gloop' and can be used fresh or rotten, when it is at its most effective for large fish – it stinks and is correspondingly staining. I run a sharp knife through it, reducing it to strips. Take a shaved toothpick cut down to around 50mm and use latex to fix it to the bottom hook shank and then the second hook shank, creating a 'backbone' that will keep your bait presented straight and slim. Work the bait around the toothpick holding it in place with latex until it is built up to around 10 – 15mm diameter and covers the entire toothpick. The bend of both hook [and the points] should not be covered. Remember to use extra binding where the bait meets the hook – this will prevent the bait from sliding further down the hook. You may elect to use a single hook trace and/or smaller hooks for pan fries.

Sea Cucumber

Be warned that some of the body fluids can cause a skin reaction

Use a suitable barrier cream [like Vaseline] when handling them. Cut of the head, and a flood of body fluids will be ejected. Then slit it along the length and scoop out the body parts using a spoon or flat-bladed knife. You will be left with the tough, leathery skin which can be cut into bait-sized pieces and placed on a hook.

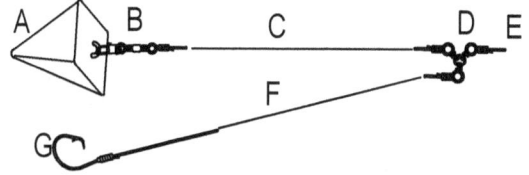

Legend: *Terminal sinker rig. A:4 – 6oz pyramid sinker; B: Snapper swivel; C: 200mm – 350mm sinker line 12kg breaking strain; D: size 2 – 4 three-way swivel; E: Main line, 15 – 25kg breaking strain; F: Snoot – 25kg, 400mm – 600mm; G: Extra strong circle hook, 1/0 to 4/0.*

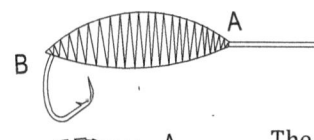

Using two strips, 1 on each side of the hook – if the bait is longer than the hook, you will need to keep it straight by wrapping a shaved toothpick to the hook, and then binding the halves back-to-back on the hook as indicated alongside.

The other way to present the bait would be to cut each of the halves referred to above into slices/squares and then pierce each slice in the centre, 'stacking them on the hook as shown alongside.

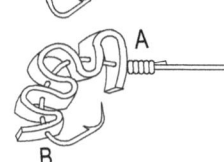

A single strip of bait can also be used as illustrated alongside. You will need to wrap latex cotton tightly at "A" and "B" so that the bait does not slide.

Expect violent takes from musselcracker, baardman and rock cod. Be prepared to power the fish away from the rocks! If you downsize your hook and bait size, you can catch all manners of reef fish. Mixed strips of squid and sea cucumber with a strip of sardine sandwiched between these two tough baits also works very well – all manners of large fish will take this bait.

Just remember – not all fluids are not dangerous but please, take no chances: use glasses, gloves / barrier cream to protect yourself from the fluids. Fluid will squirt out when you cut the head off.

Sea lice [mole crabs]

Legend: *Running trace. A: Circle hook / "J" hook, size dependent on the size of the creature and should not have a bend wider than the width of the creature though the shank may be longer; B: Snoot around 500mm; C: Swivel; D: Section of ball point pen tube to slide over knot and protect knot from impact with sinker, also prevents knot from fouling in the sinker and impeding the running action; E: Sinker 3 – 5ounce barrel sinker – if there is a strong side wash, use a pyramid or grapnel sinker. A terminal trace may also be used.*

This bait is great for Stumpnose and pompano which are normally caught on beaches where sea lice occur naturally.

You need to cast into the white water with a sandy bottom – your selection of sinker is as surf conditions warrant.

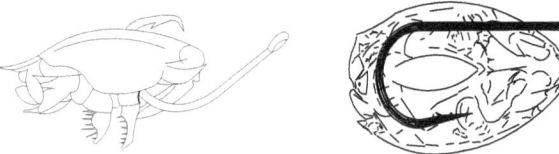

Place the hook on the flat section of the creature, the hook should not be wider than the creature. Wrap some latex around the bend of the hook and then using a figure of eight wrap, place the hook as shown, taking the line over the back of the creature and back around to hold the eye-end of the hook. From here, take the latex around the back of the creature and over the bend of the hook. Repeat at least ten times. Before you cut off the latex, make a few wraps around the shank of the hook then break it off. Alternate bait presentation on the extreme left.

Be warned – *do not stray too far from your rod* – and be prepared for a fight if you are lucky enough to be hit by a pompano *although large stumpnose are also worthy adversaries*.

You may also be surprised by Steenbras and grunter and other fish big enough to eat the sea lice.

Where there is a side-wash, cast in the direction of the side wash so that the trace line does not foul with the main line. This bait is normally used in open water below beaches where the creatures occur naturally.

Squid [*chokka*]

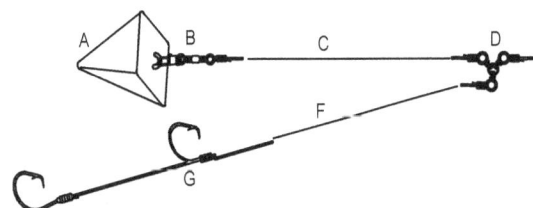

Legend: A:4 – 6oz pyramid sinker; B: Snapper swivel; C: 200mm – 350mm sinker line about 8kg breaking strain; D: size 4 - 6 three-way swivel; E: Main line, 10 – 25kg breaking strain; F: Snoot – 10-25kg braid, 300mm – 600mm to the first hook; G: Tandem extra strong circle hook, size 1 - 4/0. The last hook is tied 40mm from the first. A toothpick about 50 mm long is first attached to the bottom hook a using latex and then the top hook.

Squid may be cut into strips, squares or used whole. The strips may be threaded onto a hook or as a long-tapered fillet.

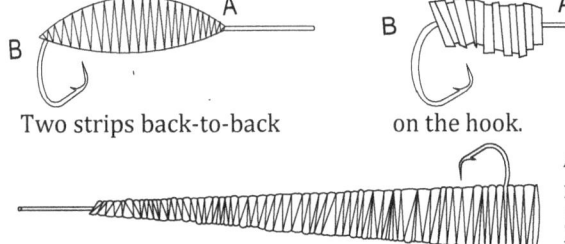

Two strips back-to-back   on the hook.   Pieces stacked   A strip fed on to the hook.

As a fillet bait: Cut a triangular strip of flesh – for normal fishing, from a width of 10mm to a width of 5mm over a length of 80mm. Place the strip on a bait board and tenderize with a mallet to allow the juices to escape [yes, keep the waste juices for dipping]. Poke the hook through the centre of the narrow end of the strip – slide the bait a little up the hook and poke it through again, repeating the process. Carry on with this process until you poke the hook through the broad end of the fillet, 5mm to 10mm from the bend of the hook. Wrap the sides of the fillet around the back of the hook, leaving the point and bend exposed. Start by winding the latex around the bend of the hook and securing the end of the fillet so that it will not slide down the bend. This bait is easy to keep straight and will not need a skewer.

If you use a tandem hook trace, the presentation will be as illustrated alongside. For kob and geelbek, bait strips are tapered from 15mm to 25mm over a length of 150mm – 180mm and presented as above.

The hook size will be 4/0 – 9/0, and if a tandem trace is used, the hooks should be 100mm apart. The trace line should be upgraded to a minimum of 15kg and a skewer should be used to keep the bait straight.

For deep sea fishing, strips are cut roughly 40 mm long and 20mm wide – these are simply threaded onto a size 1 – 2/0 hook and fished off the bottom.

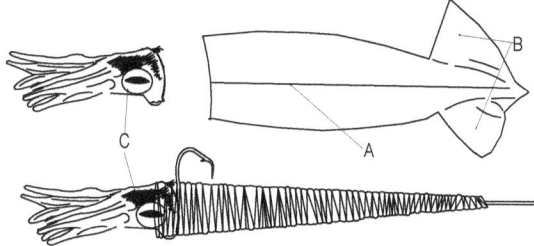

To use baby squid whole, you will need to clean the squid as described in Chapter 14.

Slit the tube along one side ["A"], cut off the fins ["B"], tenderize to release the juices and hook the broad end on the hook about 5mm from the end. You may use a single or tandem hook rig as directed above. Wrap the bait as described above using latex and hook on "C" the head tentacles after wrapping. Give these a few wraps to secure.

Larger squid may be presented using the trace described for kob and geelbek.

Venus ears

It is indeed a pity that this mollusc has been so heavily exploited (it resembles abalone but is a scaled-down size). It is a superbait and also carries severe penalties should you be found with it or using it. **Prohibited** for possession or use.☹

THE FISH [Note that *superbaits* will work for almost all species]

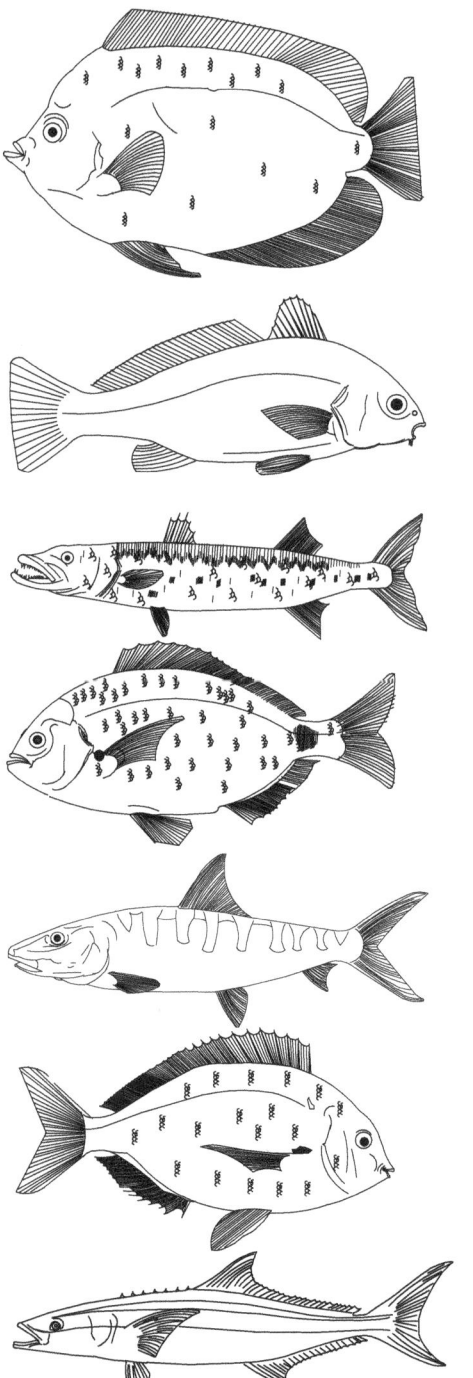

Angelfish. *Size 1-1/0 hook; Bait: shellfish and shrimp; trace: terminal, sometimes mid-water around reef.*

Baardman *is a slender brown / silver fish with stubby barbels growing below a short chin. These fish live below ledges and must be moved away from the reef or they will be lost to the rocks. If you catch one, chances are there's more out there. Excellent eating. Hook size: 1-1/0; Bait: crab, prawn, worm and red bait; trace: terminal.*

*Great **Barracuda**. Hook size: 'couta trace; Bait: mackerel fillet or whole mackerel, shad, pinkie, sardine, karanteen, mullet - alive or dead; trace: 'couta.*

Blacktail*. Hook size: 6-8; Bait: sardine cutlets, chicken guts cut into half inch pieces [must not be rotten]; trace: terminal / drift.*

Bonefish.*, Hook size: 1 -1/0; Bait: Sardine chunks, crabs, shrimp, small live bait; trace: terminal / running. Good eating but very bony.*

*Bronzie [Bronze **bream**]. Light tackle in the white water in and around gullies. Look for bronze – gold flashes in the water. Hook size: 3; Bait: pieces of crayfish / prawn trace: Use a stick float with 1m line to the hook with split shot pressed onto the line about 300mm from the hook.*

Cobia *[Prodigal son] Hook size: 3/0; Bait: live fish, live eel; trace: Running / drift. Can be caught from the beach or off piers. "Luck of the draw."*

Eel. *Moray Hook size: 3/0 – 6/0 – use wire leader. Bait: live bait or fillet held near lair; trace: terminal. I leave them alone.*

Eel *catfish. Excellent eating.* Great eating – beware of the spines, one in front of dorsal fin and 1 on either side of the head, part of the pectoral fins. No scales. immediate first aid is required if scratched / poked by these spines – *the fish's normal mucous is harmless. The venom is broken down by heat – bleed the wound out as much as you can and bathe the area with water as hot as the person can tolerate.* **Find medical treatment.** *Hook size: 1; Bait: small fish, crabs, prawns and crayfish and will readily take fillets and squid; trace: terminal.*

Galjoen. *Cold water. in white water in gullies or slightly discoloured water, particularly where kelp is growing. Can be caught using a float [quill] and a size 3 hook] – same as for bronze bream above. Can also be fished using a terminal trace, size three hook with a 500mm snoot. Hook size: 3; Bait: Red bait, white & black mussel strip bait, small crab, worm, sea lice and juvenile molluscs; trace: terminal.*

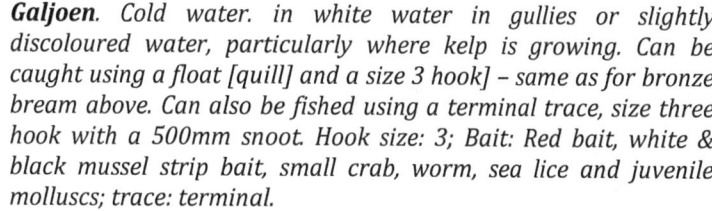

Garrick. *Has fine rasping teeth – a heavy trace line is needed. 4/0 – 8/0 size hook, 40pound snoot. Early mornings and late afternoons, better when these times are synchronized with high tides; Bait: Pinkie, shad, mullet, karanteen; trace: running non-return trace. Can be fished for using a large float with live bait. You will have to cast the bait out and reel in slowly to maintain tight line and re-cast periodically.*

Geelbek *salmon Hook size: 5/0 – 9/0; Bait: live bait or whole sardine; trace: terminal, long snoot [1-1.5m]. Nocturnal feeder.*

Grunter *[spotted grunter]. Warmer months, – light tackle. Size 5-6 hooks, strike on steady take. Hook size: 4-6; Bait: shrimp, prawn, sea lice, razor clams; sardine belly fillet trace: running.*

Karanteen *aka 'strepie' has orange-gold stripes. Cold water around reef and structure. Hook size: 8 – 10; Bait: Sardine cutlets, sardine guts, red bait, prawns, baitfish cutlets; trace: terminal / drift.*

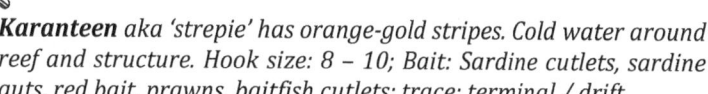

Giant ***Kingfish*** *[GT]. Use a 150mm knife-edged spoon on a medium trolling speed. Use up to a meter of 40pound line attached to your leader using a power swivel. Hook size: 1/0 – 4/0; Bait: Will also take a mackerel fillet or whole mackerel. Live or dead mullet / shad / karanteen on the drift. Also, prawn on the drift.; trace: terminal / running / drift.*

Threadfin trevally, mirrorfish, indian mirrorfish, threadfin ***kingfish***. *Good eating – not many caught in our waters. Warmer waters, Hook size from: 2 – 2/0; Bait: Sea lice, baby squid [I caught one near Tugela Mouth with whole baby squid], and small live bait. Pinky strip bait.; trace: running.*

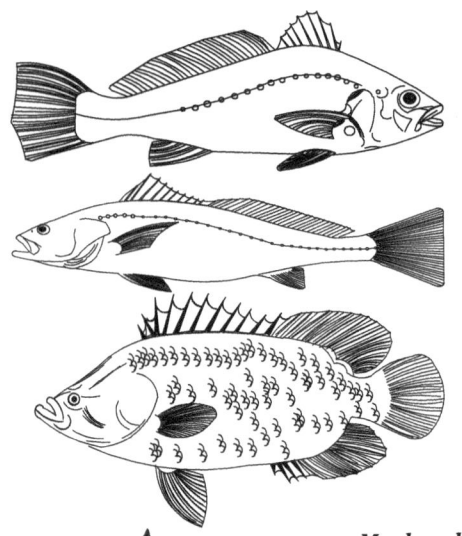

Kob [salmon – or affectionately known as Simon ☺]. Cold water. Do not use steel wire. Preference for discoloured water near rivers. Fish at night. Likes octopus and squid. Hook size: 1/0 to 9/0; Bait: Live bait – mullet [even glassies and pinkies]; trace: running for live bait / terminal.

Squaretail **Kob.** Hook size: 1-1/0; Bait: Sardine fillet, octopus, prawn; trace: terminal.

Lobotus – Triple tail bream – Only caught around the Tugela Mouth area and slightly north of the mouth. Hook size: 2/0 – 4/0; Bait: Use live mullet; trace: running.

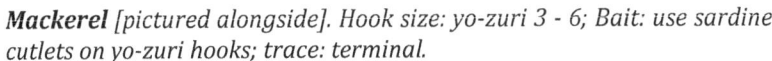

Mackerel [pictured alongside]. Hook size: yo-zuri 3 - 6; Bait: use sardine cutlets on yo-zuri hooks; trace: terminal.

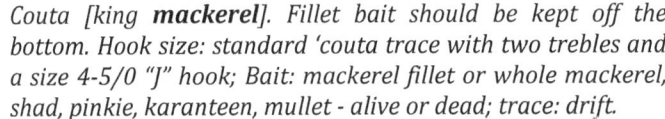

Couta [king **mackerel**]. Fillet bait should be kept off the bottom. Hook size: standard 'couta trace with two trebles and a size 4-5/0 "J" hook; Bait: mackerel fillet or whole mackerel, shad, pinkie, karanteen, mullet - alive or dead; trace: drift.

Mullet. Use size hooks depending on the size of the fish [I use a 10 mostly]. Fish with a float. Sight fishing ahead of the shoal. Hook size: 12 – 5; Bait: Loves mussel bait, sardines, bread, insects [especially flying ant].

Black **Musselcracker.** Same as for white musselcracker below.

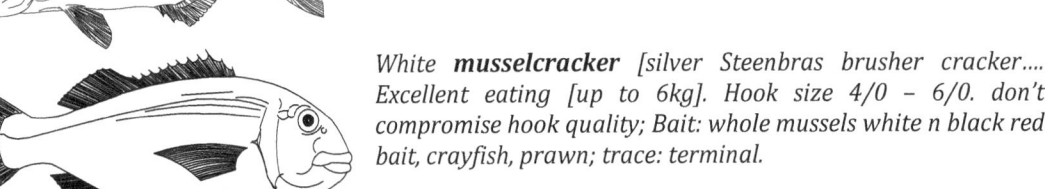

White **musselcracker** [silver Steenbras brusher cracker.... Excellent eating [up to 6kg]. Hook size 4/0 – 6/0. don't compromise hook quality; Bait: whole mussels white n black red bait, crayfish, prawn; trace: terminal.

Estuary **Perch.** Don't fish deep. Hook size: 5 – 8; Bait: Cheese and bread, shrimp, small crabs, sardine; trace: running / drift

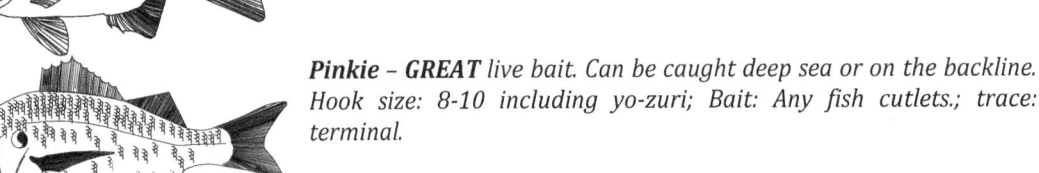

Pinkie – **GREAT** live bait. Can be caught deep sea or on the backline. Hook size: 8-10 including yo-zuri; Bait: Any fish cutlets.; trace: terminal.

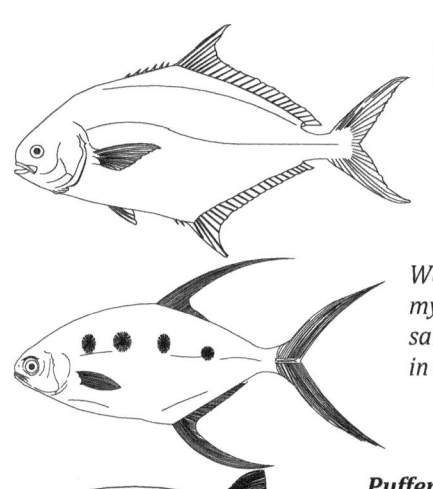

Pompano. *– sandy bottom. Hook size: 6 – 1/0; Bait: Sea lice, crabs, shrimp, small live bait.; trace: Running.*

Wave Garrick, large spot ***pompano****. Fine-scaled. White water. Use my live drop shot presentations…. Hook size: 1-6; Bait: Sea lice, sardine belly, crab, whole and fillet white and black mussel, worms in the shallow wave zone.; trace: running.*

Puffer fish*.aka 'tobee' Hook size: blah; Bait: blah; trace: blah. Doesn't matter how hard you try, You will catch them. Its magic.*

Queenfish. *[Natal snoek]. Normally takes well on small spoons and squid imitations. If you have access to deep water, float fishing with pinkie is a winner [provided that nothing else takes the pinkie first!]. Hook size: 4/0 – 5/0; Bait: sardine fillet; trace: steel. Us a skirt. Can be caught off piers and places where the backline is accessible.*

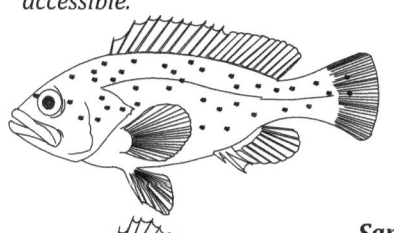

Rock cod *[Captain Fine]. Others: half-moon, spotted, swallowtail, yellow belly…] From a depth of 3m near rocks. Power away from reef! Hook size: 1/0 – 5/0; Bait: Flapper bait, any other bait, particularly fish heads. Will also readily take crab.; trace: terminal in water 3m and deeper, near rocks.*

Sand soldier. *Hook size: 1; Bait: squid; trace: terminal. Deep water, in bays and off piers accessing deeper waters.*

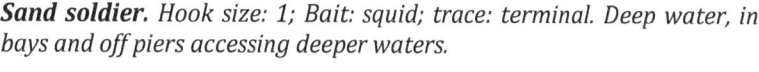

Scottsman. *Hook size: 1-2/0; Bait: squid; trace: terminal.*

Sea barbel *[sea catfish]. Great eating – beware of spines, one in front of dorsal fin and on either side of the head. immediate first aid is required if scratched / poked.* ***Find medical treatment****. Bait: small fish, crabs, prawns and crayfish. Readily takes fillets and squid. Hook size: 1; trace: terminal.*

Shad. *Winter to summer. Hook size: 2/0 -6/0; Bait: Sardine fillet. Baitfish fillet; trace: Use steel wire.*

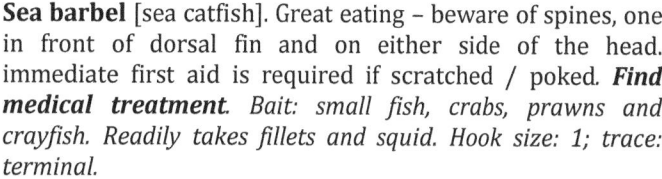

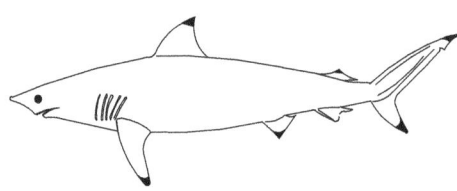

*Black Tip **Shark**. Don't go after shark without experience. It is a hard fighter and will test you and your tackle to the limit. Use only the best tackle and book a massage. And make sure you have enough line on your reel. Hook size: 'beeg and strong [10/0 upwards]; Bait: best bait is bonito – any other fish will do; trace: heavy. You are not playing around – don't go after any shark unprepared – and don't kill if you are not going to eat. The wire leader used should be heavy and at least 5m.*

*Hammerhead **Shark**. As above.*

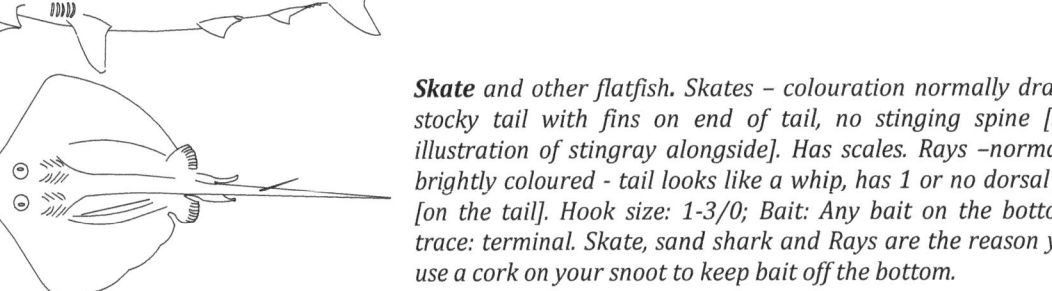

***Skate** and other flatfish. Skates – colouration normally drab - stocky tail with fins on end of tail, no stinging spine [see illustration of stingray alongside]. Has scales. Rays –normally brightly coloured - tail looks like a whip, has 1 or no dorsal fin [on the tail]. Hook size: 1-3/0; Bait: Any bait on the bottom; trace: terminal. Skate, sand shark and Rays are the reason you use a cork on your snoot to keep bait off the bottom.*

***Sole**. Hook size: 6 -8; Bait: marine worm; trace: terminal – affix split shot to snoot close to hook [about 3" from hook] to keep the bait on the bottom. Keep rod low so that the snoot is not elevated by the tip – to – sinker angle.*

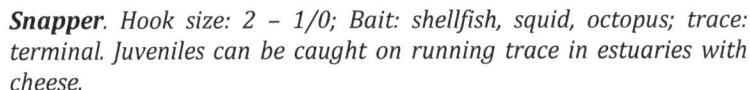

***Snapper**. Hook size: 2 – 1/0; Bait: shellfish, squid, octopus; trace: terminal. Juveniles can be caught on running trace in estuaries with cheese.*

*Blood **Snapper.** Hook size: 2 – 1/0; Bait: shellfish, squid, octopus; trace: terminal. Juveniles can be caught on running trace in estuaries with cheese.*

***Snoek.** [Cape snoek] Hook size: 7/0 – 12/0; Bait: chopped sardine; trace: drift.*

***Springer** [skipjack]. Use size 1 hook. Warmer months. Hook size: 2 - 2/0; Bait: Will readily take any small live bait, particularly pinkie, glassies and mullet; trace: float.*

*Red **Steenbras**. **Prohibited.** Aggressive predator – small fish, octopus and squid bait. Hook size: **Prohibited**; Bait: **Prohibited**; trace: **Prohibited**.*

*White **Steenbras** - in lagoons, cheese. In the surf: Hook size: 1 – 4/0; Bait: worm crab crackers small shellfish, shellfish strip baits, razor clams; trace: running.*

*Natal **stumpnose** and other stumpnose. Grows to just under a meter! Good eating. Fish at night. Hook size: 4 – 6; Bait: Sea lice, crab, mussel and other shellfish, worm, fish fillet from pinky, sardine, cracker shrimp, redbait and prawn; trace: Running trace. White stumpnose and cape stumpnose [not illustrated]*

*Oxeye **tarpon** Hook size: 3 – 1/0; Bait: marine worms, razor clams; trace: float with 1m snoot.*

__Walla walla__ [ribbonfish]. Mid-water biter – you will normally hook into these whilst reeling in from the bottom. Hook size:6 - 1; Bait: ribbonfish fillet, baitfish fillet; trace: can be terminal – preferably drift.

Five fingers [__wildeperd__ – any bait like blacktail, preference for. Normal gulley trace [size hook]. Sardine, shellfish, shrimp, prawn. Hook size: 5-6; Bait: prawn and shrimp chicken guts; trace: terminal.

Chapter 18: Fishing using artificial bait in freshwater

The only fish I have not caught on any type of lure is an eel – and I am not particularly broken-up by that. I have even caught grass carp on fly and broke my rod in the process… The smallest fish I took on fly measured 3cm – yes, 30mm.

You have to persevere. But don't just mechanically cast and retrieve. Pay attention to the type of creature you are imitating. Pay attention to the water and literally the birds and the bees. Don't make the lure move unnaturally. Don't slow down when you see a fish chasing – this is unnatural. And when the water temperature is down, slow down your retrieve. Look out for tell-tale signs broadcasting the presence [or absence] of fish.

And start with short casts. Your trophy could be right in front of you. Why do people start with long casts? In rivers and where there is flow of water, always start by casting upstream and bringing the lure down – fish are facing upstream waiting for food to come down with the current. *Gettit*?

*When you can see fish and they are not taking your lure, do not cast over them. Cast in the projected path of the fish [NOT on its nose!]. If the lure doesn't work – change to a suitably sized general attractor pattern and carry on casting and retrieving to trigger an aggressive attack. It **WILL** happen.*

Remember the advantages of using artificial lures from Chapter 13…?
- They are easily switched. If you are not in a tigerfish area [tigerfish will readily strike at a swivel], use a suitable clip-on swivel so that you can quickly change lures.

The sketch alongside shows the type of clip to use. "A" is the bent wire end that positively closes the clip. This clip will not open under load. Remember that if you are using light lures, the weight of the clip may negatively influence the performance of the lure.

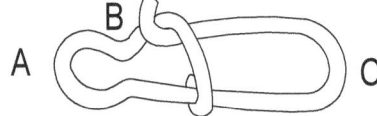

Legend: *Clip for easy knotless attachment of lures / traces to your line. A: Tie this end to the main line; B: This end is pushed inwards to open the clip. The lure is then slipped on here where it will sit on "C"; C: This is where the lure sits when it is attached – remember to close "B" after inserting the lure! This clip is only used for fast changeover of lures where a swivel is not required. Note that it may be installed onto a swivel if need be. To think that I actually made my own line clips when I was 14 years old – never thought about patenting it… I used to make and sell wire and bead jewelry. ☺*

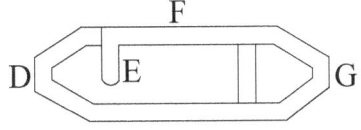

Legend: *Heavy-duty clip for easy knotless attachment of lures / traces to your line – the wire wraps sit tightly against each other and you have to pry them apart to slide a hook between the wraps. D: Tie this end to the main line; E: Slide the lure / the split ring on the lure onto the clip by introducing it in on "E" and sliding it along "F" until it reaches "G". This clip is only used for fast changeover of lures where a swivel is not required. Note that it may be installed onto a power swivel if need be.*

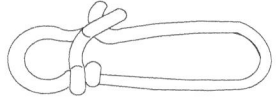

Alongside is the line clip I designed when I was 14. It worked well. Line was knotted at the far side and the clip would accommodate any lure, heavy or light. ☺

- You can cover much more water than you would when bait fishing, and covering more water means more chances of encountering fish. Make sure that you have a good selection of lures. Be familiar with the various types of bait species that exist in the area and use lures that most closely resemble these species.
- Using artificial baits also allows you [mostly] to target specific species. Most people think that lures are used only to catch bass and that flies are used only to catch trout. This is not true. Most of the lures available are specifically for bass, and pike. These lures are large and will not fit into the mouth of smaller omnivorous fish. But there are scaled-down versions, and omnivores can be caught on them,

- In areas where natural bait fishing presents you with a high-snag potential, artificial bait can be rendered 'snag-less' or 'weedless'. Most people don't like reeded-up areas – but these areas contain a variety of life-forms and also provide cover to these life-forms, so it stands to reason that bigger fish will feed in reeded-up areas. For heavily reeded up areas, I carry a length of ski rope with a section of 10mm steel rod shaped into a double hook attached to it. I tie a loop at the other end, and throw out the hook and pull in clumps of reed, creating channels. Now most people would think that the sound of this disturbance would scare fish away – you are right!

  But disturbing the reed disturbs the creatures living in the reed and this assures that fish will return – quickly! And again – most people would just leave the clumps of reed that have been pulled out. Don't do this. Examine the reeds carefully – you will get valuable information on what creatures live in the reeds and therefore be better guided on what types of lures to use.

  If your lure picks up bits of weed – be sure to remove the weed from the lure or it may compromise the performance of the lure.
- Also – apart from the occasional risk of foul-hooking fish – you hook most fish in and around the mouth and not in the throat and stomach, so if you are practicing catch-and-release, survival statistics are higher because you virtually eliminate injuring the fish anywhere but in the mouth.
- You control the action of the artificial bait. Convince the fish that it is alive – or injured. Work the lures you have in a pool and see what effect the different rod, hand and reel movements make, in combinations.

As I said before – lures can be quite costly – so if you have a lure with treble hooks that you know works well, and the trebles increase the chances of losing the lure, change the hooks to *weedless* hooks. It is quite easy to modify a hook to render it *weedless*. Even trebles can be rendered *weedless*. Refer to Chapter 4.

Make sure that you understand the lure you have acquired – this is why those that come with instructions are generally of higher quality. A lure that dives won't necessarily return to the surface. Read the instructions and specifications that accompany the lure. Create a database on your phone / tablet along with a picture of the lure lest you forget the name of the lure like I do!

You should always use a leader with lures – this ensures that you do not lose line from your reel every time you change a lure. You must also use a clip like the one illustrated above. But a word of caution! – do not use a fluorocarbon or braid leader if you are using a floating lure – fluorocarbon and braided line are denser than water and will almost certainly compromise the action of the lure because they will sink quickly. For floating lures, use ordinary monofilament line leaders.

When using surface lures, you will probably have the most dramatic experiences – you will generally see a bow wave, when a fish is chasing the lure – don't slow down your retrieve! Continue as normal.

Would you slow down if someone/something was chasing you?

And, with all lures, always make sure to check that your line is not tangled with hooks on the lure, and continuously check the hooks to see that they remain sharp.

IMPORTANT!!! When it is time to strike, <u>NEVER EVER</u> strike vertically upwards when fishing with a lure [or any other rig fished within 10m of you]. If you do, the lure will naturally be propelled directly to your mid-section or face. Always strike slightly to one side, so if the lure is propelled out of the water, it will not hit you. I have removed many treble and single hooks from bellies and cheeks.

Spinner blades

Very few people use a blade the way I do. I have spent years experimenting and have successfully caught most freshwater - and many saltwater species. The only problem is that the spinner blades cannot be cast very far as they are extremely light. They operate very well on fly tackle and I am certain that they will catch trout too – although *I* have never tried it.

They come in all shapes and sizes, some are circular with the others tending to be streamlined with one end smaller than the other and some are elongated and symmetrical. There is advantage in this as all manners of baitfish can be imitated. They can be made from various metals and come in many colours.

Use as light a line as possible to maximize your casting distance. It flits about like a coin dropped into water, reflecting light in all directions and attracting attention of many fish.

The retrieve is slow with light flicks of the rod, allowing it to rise and drop.

Takes can be so violent that your rod can be pulled free from your hands.

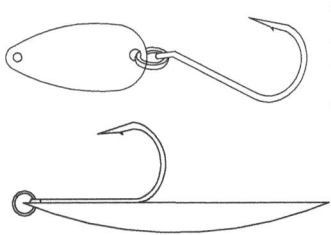
The smallest I have used was 12mm in length and oval. I have caught all manner of fish with it and lost a few to shad in the surf. The larger blades mostly have two holes. Use split rings – never tie line directly to the blade as it will cut your line when under tension!

Legend: The smaller blades have only one hole. Mount the hook as shown with the point pacing outwards. This lure should be used with a medium action rod on or near the surface and in the deep – they are, after all, mini spoons and can be fished as a spoon, but because of weight, cannot be retrieved too quickly.

These are very successful when fished into deep drop-offs. The only fish I haven't caught with it are mud suckers [mud fish] and eels.

Study the movement of fry and emulate that movement. Enjoy. Because these lures are so light, you will continually have to make sure that your line is reeled in with adequate tension or you will have loose coils of line sitting on your reel and the increased chance of a tangle.

Spinners

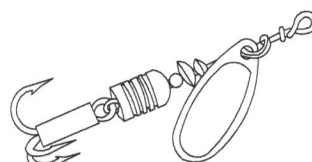
The **MEPPS** spinner design – the *best* spinners I have ever used. In fresh water – very effective when the water is 18°C+. Bass, bluegill, *scalies* [and other yellows] and tilapia.

Spinners are activated by drawing them through the water using a fast – medium action rod – this causes the blade / blades to rotate. This rotation causes vibrations in the water and reflects light just as light is reflected off the sides of a baitfish.

You can catch yellows, tilapia and bluegill with sizes 00 and 0, and bass with the larger spinners, size 3 / 4. For this you should use as light a line as you dare – sizes 00 and 0 spinners are very light and best cast using light lines.

For bass and other large-mouthed fish you are forced to use at least 14pound line for you will need to power fish away from structure.

Remember that the trebles can always be removed and replaced with a single "J" hook. And that they can be rendered *weedless*. If you do this, you can stop your retrieve at any time and allow the spinner to drop to the bottom – this increases the potential of this lure in attracting fish.

Spinner baits

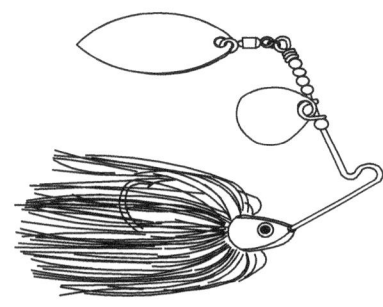
These lures are used predominantly to catch bass using a fast action rod with at least 14pound line. I have not caught anything else on them in freshwater but am certain that they can be used successfully to catch barbel and African pike and certainly Nile perch. They are available in a wide range of sizes and are better used in shallow waters. I use them in deep water at various depths. Properly used, they swim upright sending flashes of light and vibrations announcing their presence. If the lure swims skew and not upright – simply re-shape the wires to their original shape and all will be well. This lure should **NEVER** spiral when retrieved – only the spinner blades should rotate. It also performs well on a slow troll, fresh water.

Drop shot hook [aka 'jig', 'jig head']

These hooks are superior to normal bass hooks in that they do not easily allow the bait to spin and twist your line. You do not need a swivel with these – just a line clip for fast changeover of hook types. Use a fast-action rod with at least 14pound line for bass and other large-mouthed predators.

When fishing for other species, you will need smaller drop-shot hooks and smaller grub-like plastic baits attached on 8 - 10pound line using a medium action rod.

Use heavier line if you are fishing near structure. When using these lures and you feel a strike, do NOT strike immediately – wait 1 to 2 seconds.

Sometimes the tails and appendages on these plastics get torn off – replace the plastic because the action will become compromised.

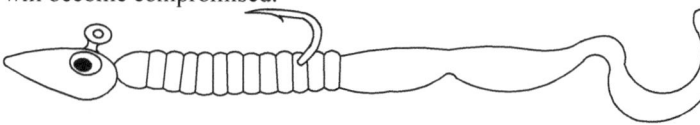

Lures having this basic shape are worm / eel / leech imitations. These creatures should be presented as such. Cast out and retrieve with small twitching movements, also moving the rod from side-to-side, much like the slow-moving creatures you are imitating. Each cast should pick the lure off the ground and then allow it to realistically return to the ground.

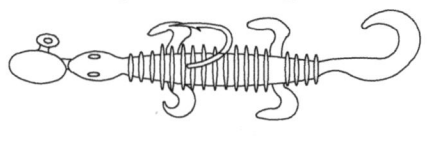

The plastic bait alongside and immediately below resembles a lizard / aquatic swimming creature. Because it is on a drop shot hook, it has to be fished on the bottom, so it must naturally be moved as though it is a swimming creature, small darts, keeping to the bottom – it can also be retrieved smoothly for a short while before being allowed to sink down to the bottom. It also can be used as a general-attractor pattern with erratic and rapid movements for stubborn fish.

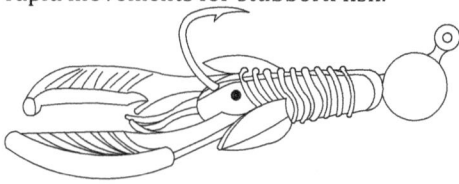

This type of lure is a prawn / crayfish / shrimp imitation. It can be mounted facing towards or away from the hook. If mounted as illustrated alongside, it is retrieved with short darts [prawns move in this direction with sharp flicks of their tails, producing a series of short darts, followed by periods of non-movement]. If you mount the lure on head first, it should be retrieved at a crawl with interspersed dashes and periods of inactivity, much like the creature is mobile and feeding – which is the only time it moves forwards.

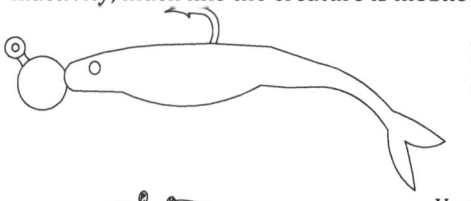

All fish / fry imitations can only be fished on the bottom when using drop shot hooks. They should be fished erratically to resemble feeding and/or injured baitfish.

You do know that crabs move *sideways*? Mount plastic / real crab as shown [if you elect to use a real crab - mount it as shown – you can avoid piercing the creature by using latex bait cotton to fasten it to the rig]. Retrieve is super slow to slow. Rod tip down...

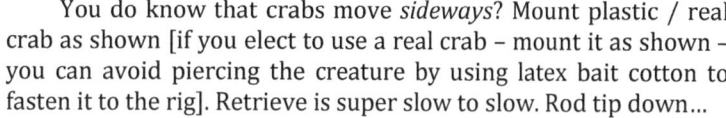

As with the crab, bloodworm imitations must be retrieved very slow. Every now and then, raise the rod to pick it up off the bottom and allow it to fall naturally. Most strikes occur when this happens. About ten minutes per retrieve.

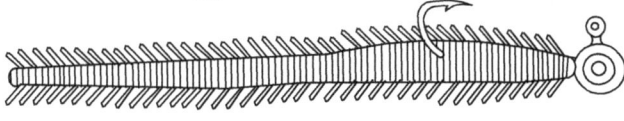

Paddle tail lures are **DEADLY**.

Can be retrieved on the bottom with darting movements or can be fished mid-water at various depths. Vary movements, sweep rod from left to right. Keep rod tip down – to horizontal.

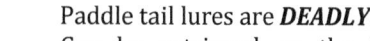

This is a grub. Darting retrieves on the bottom combined with lift and drop movements. Can also fish mid-water. Rise and fall in one position and while retrieving. The hook size must be proportionate to the size of the grub used.

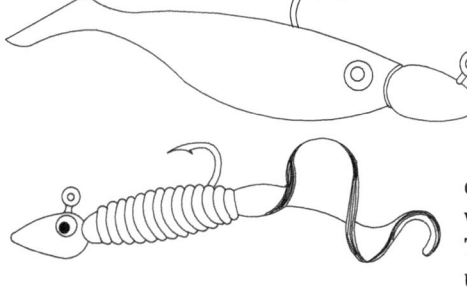

By now you understand how the hook is to be located – go fourth and fish! Just remember not to retrieve without simulating the movements of the creature you are imitating. The same if you are using actual bait.

Don't just cast out and reel in. Imitate the creature you have on. Prawns / lobsters need to be crawled. Mingle this with a few short, darting retrieves.

Some of the plastics [like the prawn, can be put on facing forwards or backwards. Facing backwards means short darting movements followed by periods of no movement. Take full advantage of the rod you are using [fast action – in other words, just the tip bends when it is pulled until it is at 90° to the butt].

Movements can be combined with reeling whilst simultaneously pulling / jerking / vibrating the rod or just by moving he rod then reeling.

And then, after you consider the thousands of plastics available on the market – get this…. You can use real bait too! Real frogs, real hoppers, real fish, real crab – *gettit*?

Some of these creatures will need to be pinned – but where you can get away with attaching them to the hook using latex bait cotton, DO IT! [crabs, hoppers, crickets, shrimp…]

'Dressed' drop shot hooks [aka 'Jigs']

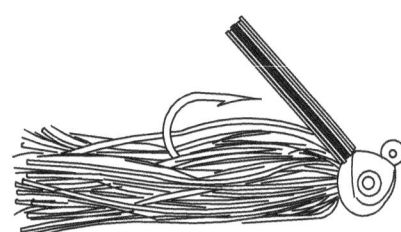

These are used as described in the preceding section.

They are available in various sizes and combinations and colours. They can also be used with plastic / real bait – use your imagination. Retrieve a little quicker with minor pauses – it imitates swimming creatures and can be used as a general attractor pattern. They are generally used for bass but can be used for other small mouthed species when scaled-down.

Spoons

Use only light spoons in fresh water – generally the ones made from metal strip. In freshwater – only really effective when water temperature is > 17.5°C. Spoons should be fished to imitate escaping baitfish / squid. Some of the heavier spoons will work for pike and Nile perch.

This spoon is made from metal strip [it is actually a modified spinner blade] and is concave, forcing it to spiral and gyrate in the water. It is suitable for freshwater applications – refer section above for 'spinner blades'. Use a clip-on swivel to attach to line.

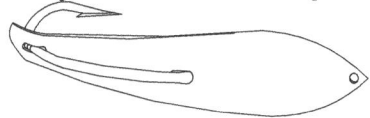

This spoon is curved and convex and designed for tiger fish. It can be used with or without a fillet on the hook and is brightly polished, sometimes having reflector tape on the outside. It will need a split ring through the hole and a clip-on swivel – it moves like a baitfish – the action may be compromised when you put on a fillet. Make the fillet as slim as possible. And don't forget to use steel wire leaders!

Crankbaits

These lures work well during the warmer months, in water 18°C or warmer. You are generally wasting your time using them after a storm when rain has caused a drop in water temperature.

The lures will work for tiger fish but this becomes a costly exercise as they are quickly damaged by the fish. You will need a minimum of 14pound line to power fish away from structure.

Smaller versions can and will land you tilapia and yellows during mid- and late summer with barbel also taking a crankbait.

When you first start fishing, cast to one side [e.g. to the right-hand side] towards the water's edge. Your retrieve should be interrupted periodically, allowing the crankbait to rise – beware – this is generally when strikes occur – also note that some lures do not rise when you stop the retrieve – make sure that you read the instructions/specifications for the lure. From your original cast, fan out until you are casting to your left.

Bass are predators and you will often find them, mornings and evenings, in the shallows where the water temperature is higher.

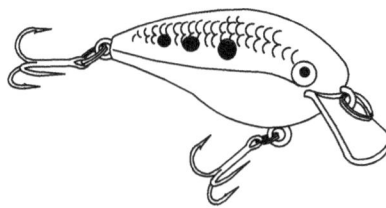
The secret to using crankbaits successfully is by fishing them with a rod that is not too fast-actioned. To test a rod for this, get someone to hold the line and pull until the tip is roughly at 90° to the butt. At least half the rod should bend when you do this. If the rod is too fast actioned [just the first quarter bends when the tip is at 90°, you will more than often pull the lure out of the fish's mouth – so please use a medium action rod with a 1-2 second pause before striking. The fish being targeted here is generally bass.

Surface fish imitation lures

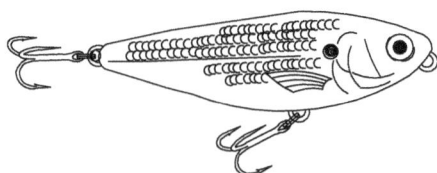
Use a medium action rod. Keep the rod horizontal. Lower the tip from time to time making alternating small and large sweeps with the rod, from left to right, resembling an escaping baitfish. Use where there is evidence of surface feeding and / or visible sub-surface fish.

It is a valuable addition to your arsenal and the best imitation is **Heddon's "spitting image"**. Note that this lure needs a split ring attached to the nose. Fish will strike at surface lures so violently that you may develop a heart condition!

Surface Creature imitation lures

Use a medium action rod. These lures may be frogs, other creatures or just general attractor patterns. They must be used when water temperature > 17°C. Especially when there is surface activity, However, if retrieves are super-slow, they could induce a take.

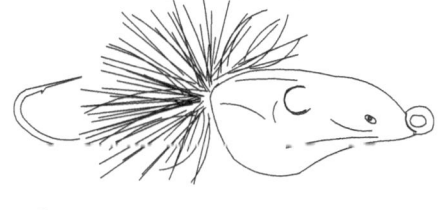
Mouse imitation lure – this is a GREAT lure – can't remember where I bought it and who makes it... ☹ When retrieved, it 'swims' nose-up, much like a mouse does and should be retrieved slowly to imitate a swimming mouse. Retrieve with a smooth action whilst vibrating the rod tip, but sweep the rod from left to right whilst retrieving. Keep rod tip down.

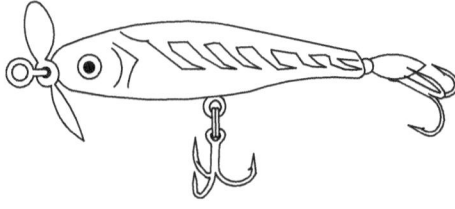
This floating lure should be retrieved so that it skips across the water with periodic phases where it actually goes below the surface film. It is streamlined and has two 'propellers' [blades] at either end which reflect light and create vibrations in the form of 'buzzing' sounds in the water. Make it look like a panicking baitfish. Or at times an unsuspecting baitfish. Rod tip should be kept down whilst working this lure. Sweep rod from left to right when retrieving, giving it the appearance of a creature changing direction.

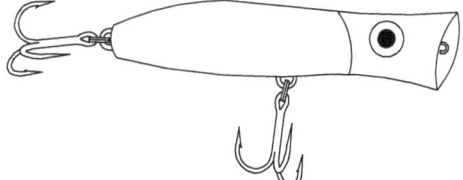
All 'popper' type lures have a concave face and you generally tie your line to a split ring located in the centre of the 'dished' face. This lure is used when there is surface feeding activity or when you spot fish near the surface. Best time is late afternoon when the water is at its warmest, in the shallows or close to drop-offs. It is retrieved with a combination of a sideways jerk of the rod whilst simultaneously reeling [it can be done just with the jerking motion too]. When you make this motion, the dished shape forces water forward and creates a 'popping' sound. This popping sound is interpreted as a frantically feeding [or frantically escaping!] baitfish. It can also be interpreted as something landing in the water. The lure should be retrieved with long periods of sitting static on the surface. As with all surface lures, keep your eyes on it – it can vanish leaving a small whirlpool or it can vanish in a loud splash that is likely to scare the pants of you!

Sub-surface [diving lures]

Use a medium action rod. These lures may be heavier than water or buoyant and are induced to dive whenever dragged through the water [by YOU, of course!].

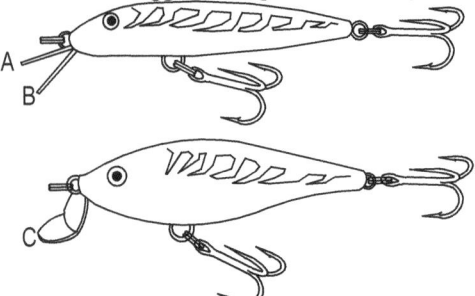

The lure patterns alongside are fish representations and are sometimes made of more than two segments [broken-back] These swim very realistically and are worth including in your arsenal. They are made from various materials. They normally float well and have a little blade at the front called a diving vane.

The size, angle and design of this vane determines how deeply the lure dives. Vane "A" is a shallow diving lure, vane "B" is a deep-diving lure and vane "C" is a shallow running lure. These lures will float and only dive when you retrieve line. When the retrieval is stopped, they will float back to the surface. Some of these lures are heavier than water and some will not rise or sink when you stop reeling.

Good lures come packaged with performance specifications that describe how to retrieve and the depth the lure will dive to. Read the instructions and understand how the lure is to be used. Don't limit the action by the manufacturer's recommendations – experiment with all lures.

You will generally regret buying 'cheapies'.

Smaller lures can be used in the warmer months for other species.

Plastic fish and creature imitations

Use a fast action rod with these. It is essential that when you feel a 'take', you wait for 1 to 2 seconds before striking.

For bass, barbel and other large mouthed predators, you will need at least 14pound breaking strain line. For other species, you will need to scale down the hook size and plastic lure combination.

There are hard plastic capsules filled with shot *[rattlers]* that cause rattling sounds when they are moved – these capsules must be pushed into the head of lures to make them emit additional noise down there.

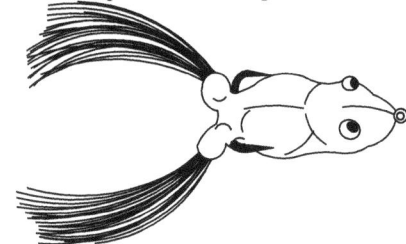

The plastic frog is a great lure. These lures are generally made *weedless* and are very light. Always check the legs – in this case [alongside] crystal flash was used] the legs must move when the lure is moved and should never be rigid. Keep two handy. Make a slit on the top of one of them and slip in a little sinker in to make it sink. This way you can fish one lure deep or the other on the surface. Cast it onto a lily pad or on the bank and drag it into the water. Frogs move with powerful kicks, so the motion should incorporate dashing movements and can be interspersed with static moments.

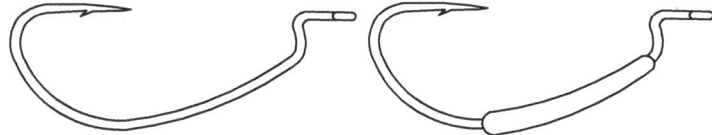

The special hooks alongside are mainly for use with plastic lures. The difference between the two is that the hook on the right is weighted with lead on the shank.

Plastic lures have soft bodies – this gives you that extra bit of time to strike as the fish, by feel, thinks it has taken a living creature. The additional advantage is that some of them are scented.

These hooks are deadly when properly inserted into the plastic bait. Follow the instructions below and learn how to do this properly because incorrectly inserted hooks could mean that you will either miss fish or become snagged if the hook point sticks out of the plastic bait. You may use a weighted hook or the normal hook – it all depends on the creature you will be using and how you want to present it. The weighted hook is best used when you are using *'this way up'* baits. Some hooks have a spiral spring or a spike attached to the eye whilst some have split shanks to hold the plastic bait in place.

Refer to the sketches below:

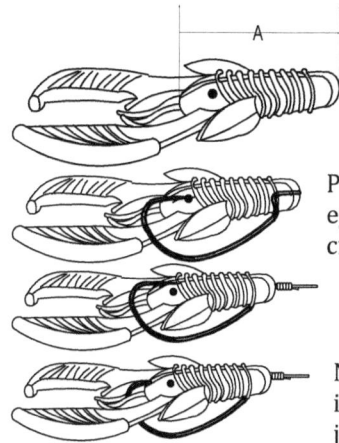

The length of the creature's body "A" is the deciding factor for the size of hook to be used. This helps determine the size of hook that can be used. *Note that some baits have a cavity at the bottom – this is to accommodate the bend of the back of the hook, on the shank.*

Place the hook alongside the body to gauge if it will fit in the body. The eye and the tip should easily be accommodated by the body of the creature being imitated. And yes, it can actually be a living creature!

Pass 8 to 10mm of the hook point through the centre of the body and bring the point out at the base of the creature. Now gently slide the bait until it passes over the 'dog's leg' on the hook.

Now pull the body towards the eye of the hook and introduce the hook into the head of the creature, close to the top-side so that the point is just below the top of the head as illustrated alongside – the rule-of-thumb is that the hook point should just be below the outer skin, close to the top, and the body of the creature should be straight and not twisted.

You are ready to fish! Check the location of the hook after every cast – as depicted in the last picture above, it is *weedless* – once the point of the hook comes free, it is no longer *weedless*. Reinsert the hook point when this happens. The plastic bait may also slide down the hook, particularly when you have had a strike. Always check and reposition the hook. You may also need to replace the plastic bait from time to time – so make sure that you have a good supply at hand.

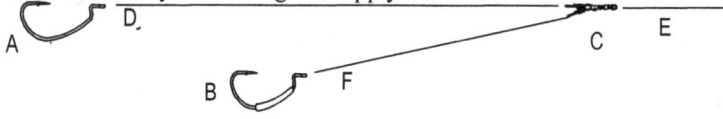

Legend: Tandem plastic bait fishing rig. A: Trailing hook – normally used in conjunction with a fish representing – you want the bass to think that a small fish is chasing down something. Hook size is dependent on the size of the bait; B: Leading hook – normally a smaller fish or creature representation. The hook illustrated is a weighted hook and can be switched for a normal hook ["A"]; C: clip-on swivel; - can be replaced by a clip alone if the bait you are using does not spiral or spin; D: Trailing hook line. Normally minimum 14pound breaking strain minimum – this line is 300mm – 450mm long; E: main line, normally minimum 14pound breaking strain minimum; F: Leading hook line, normally a minimum of 14pound breaking strain minimum – this line should be 150mm shorter than "D". Sliding sinkers ['bullet" sinkers can be placed at "D", "E" and/or "F". An egg-shaped brass sinker can be placed at "E". the trace can also be rigged with one hook, TEXAS – style, with a bullet sinker in front of the hook, between the hook and the swivel / clip. It can also be fished CAROLINA – style, with an egg-sinker on the main line, above the swivel / clip. A sinker enhances the action of the plastic bait on the bottom, causing the bait to nose-dive immediately when the retrieve is interrupted. The CAROLINA rig makes it seem as though the plastic bait is chasing down the sinker as it raises plumes of dust on the bottom. Scaled-down hooks and plastic baits can be used for species other than bass. Plastic baits work well on tigerfish but you will need to carry a lot of plastic bait because ...

I normally fish plastic baits in tandem with a smaller bait on the shorter line – this gives the predator the impression that the smaller bait is being 'chased' by the larger – an excellent *trigger* for the predator to join in!!

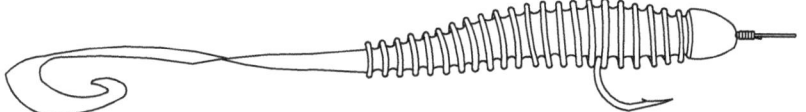

The extra-long worm baits you see are excellent when presented in open water, as a swimming bait – you can use a size 1 to 3/0 "J" hook [you can go larger with the baits that are longer than 6 inches]. Don't think these baits too big!! Only really works for bass – when a bass takes the bait, it opens its mouth in one quick motion – this 'vacuum' effect can pull an entire bait into the mouth of the fish. This is partly why you do not strike immediately – 1 to 2 seconds then pump. They also do well with a small 3 or 4mm weight pinched just in front of the knot at the arrowhead. Make the bait look like it is swimming by reeling in whilst constantly changing the side you are holding the rod on, and by periodically raising and lowering the rod, with occasional jerks.

Flies

The action of the rod is not important – what is important is that your line weight is not more than 2 sizes above or below the rated line weight in the rod. *Refer Chapter 22* for more details. The heavier line class rods are *generally* faster action rods.

Flies are used to resemble and imitate existing life forms or, as general attractor patterns, to induce takes simply because they are *foreign* to the fish. There are literally thousands of fly patterns. The key is to find out what creatures abound at the waters you are fishing. Once you do this, you can use the pattern that most closely resembles the life-form you are imitating – correspondingly, you can then fish the pattern on the surface, in mid-water or off the bottom, as required.

And don't think for one moment that you only use fly fishing equipment to cast a fly out. You can fish successfully using flies with conventional tackle – use a float to get the fly out. Try it!!

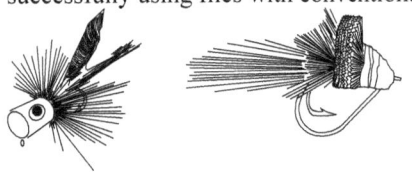

These two flies are poppers, surface ['dry'] flies that create a 'popping' sound when retrieved with a combined snap of the wrist and / or flick of the rod. The one on the right has been rendered *weedless*. It is a pattern called the *Dahlberg Diver*. Both flies are imitations of several terrestrial, aquatic and amphibious creatures; and is also a general attractor fly.

These must also be allowed to stand static after each mini retrieve. The fibres and feathers move in the water and give it signs of being alive. It can be taken violently or vanish leaving a tiny whirlpool...

'Wet' flies are designed to be fished on the bottom. The pattern alongside is a depiction of a caddis pupa / larva – an essential part of every fish's diet. I have caught very large tilapia with this baby. Also, large bass with a size 12.

Dry fly. Designed to float on the water. Must have floatant applied. All dry flies should be generously coated with a floatant to ensure that they float above the surface film. Dry flies are generally made with modified hooks that are lighter than conventional hooks. Entire fly must float on water if fished as a dry fly. Dry flies can also be used submerged.

Chapter 19: Fishing using artificial bait in salt water

If you are going to return a fish to the water, always avoid handling it by the soft underbelly area as this can easily cause injury to the creature.

Using artificial lures in salt water isn't an art – it's a passion. Whatever the rig you choose to use – it has to be part of you, like a bad habit. The salt is unforgiving – most artificial bait you use is subjected to an extremely high risk of being damaged or lost to reef or fish alike. So, whatever the rig you choose to use, you must master fishing with it. Your casting accuracy, your ability to compensate when casting with a combination of wind, water current, wave and wash direction, the dangers that certain creatures and conditions pose, and, watching for large breakers trying to swamp you must be fine-tuned and dynamic. Most fish that you will catch will be near reef. You will need to know in advance where you can land a fish and how you are going to do this. You may get more than you bargained for in the surf for there is a multitude of fish that may accept your offering and you will require skill because there is almost always something bigger. People with legendary casting skills did not just become like that without practice – you too, can be legendary. Practice.

You have to persevere. But don't just mechanically cast and retrieve. Pay attention to the type of creature you are imitating. Pay attention to the water and literally the birds and the bees. Don't make the lure move unnaturally. Don't slow down when you see a fish chasing – this is unnatural. And when the water temperature is down, slow down your retrieve. Look out for tell-tale signs broadcasting the presence [or absence] of fish.

And start with short casts. Your trophy could be right in front of you. Why do people start with long casts? Most fish that will take artificial baits will be lurking under cover. If someone is fishing the gullies for pan fish and they suddenly stop biting – it could more than likely mean that predators are around.

Oh – and artificial lures are best used up to three hours after sunrise and three hours before sunset. They can also be used through the night.

Remember the advantages of using artificial lures from Chapter 13…?

- They are easily switched. Use a suitable clip-on swivel or clip, as applicable, so that you can quickly change lures. The sketch alongside shows the type of clip-on swivel to use. "A" is the bent wire end that positively closes the clip. This clip will not open under load. Use the heavy-duty clip illustrated below if your choice of lure does not warrant a swivel.

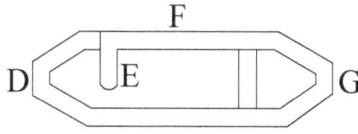
- *Legend: Heavy-duty clip for easy knotless attachment of lures / traces to your line – the wire wraps sit tightly against each other and you have to pry them apart to insert a hook [introduce the hook onto "E" and slide it along "F" until it sits at "G" – normally used in heavy applications. D: Tie this end to the main line; E: Slide the lure / the split ring on the lure onto the clip by introducing it in on "E" and sliding it along "F" until it reaches "G". This clip is only used for fast changeover of lures where a swivel is not required. Note that it may be installed onto a power swivel if need be.*

- You can cover much more water than you would when bait fishing, and covering more water means more chances of encountering fish. Make sure that you have a good selection of lures. Be familiar with the various types of bait species that exist in the area and use lures that most closely resemble these species.
- Using artificial baits also allow you [mostly] to target specific species.
- In areas where natural bait fishing presents you with a high-snag potential, artificial bait can be rendered 'snag-proof'.
- Also – apart from the occasional risk of foul-hooking fish – you hook most fish in and around the mouth and not in the throat and stomach, so if you are practicing catch-and-release, survival statistics are higher because you virtually eliminate injuring the fish anywhere but in the mouth.
- You control the action of the artificial bait. Convince the fish that it is alive – or injured.

As I said before – lures can be quite costly – so if you have a lure with treble hooks that you know works well, and the trebles increase the chances of losing the lure, use snag-less hooks. Even trebles can be rendered snag-proof. Refer to Chapter 4.

Make sure that you understand the lure you have acquired – this is why those that come with instructions are generally of higher quality. A lure that dives won't necessarily return to the surface. Read the instructions and specifications that accompany the lure. Create a database on your phone / tablet.

Saltwater is corrosive – rinse it off your lures after use and store your lures in boxes that have silica gel packages.

You should always use a leader with lures – this ensures that you do not lose line from your reel every time you change a lure and that you can put additional effort into casting. You must also use a clip like the one illustrated above. But a word of caution! – do not use a fluorocarbon or braid leader if you are using a floating lure – fluorocarbon and braided line are denser than water and will almost certainly compromise the action of the lure because they will sink quickly. For floating lures, use ordinary monofilament line leaders.

When using surface lures you will probably have the most dramatic experiences – you will generally see a bow wave, when a fish is chasing the lure – don't slow down your retrieve! Continue as normal. Would you slow down if someone/something was chasing you?

And, with all lures, always make sure to check that the hooks on the lure are not wrapped around the lure or line, and continuously check the hooks to see that they remain sharp.

IMPORTANT!!! When it is time to strike, <u>NEVER EVER</u> strike vertically upwards when fishing with a lure [or any other rig fished within 10m of you]. If you do, the lure could be propelled directly to your mid-section or face. Always strike slightly to one side, so if the lure is propelled out of the water, it will not hit you.

I have removed many treble and single hooks from bellies and cheeks of hapless fisher folk. Please don't become a statistic.

Spinner blades

Very few people use a blade the way I do – strange – they are after all, spoons. I have spent years experimenting and have successfully caught many saltwater species. The only problem is that the spinner blades cannot be cast very far as they are extremely light. They operate very well on fly tackle and I am certain that they will catch trout too – although *I* have never tried it. All manners of reef fish can and will take a spinner blade.

They come in all shapes and sizes, some are circular with the others tending to be streamlined with one end smaller than the other and some are elongated and symmetrical. There is advantage in this as all manners of baitfish can be imitated.

They can be made from various metals and come in many colours.

The smallest I have used was 12mm in length and oval. I have caught all manner of fish with it and lost a few to shad in the surf.

The sketches below illustrate how the blades are rigged. You are looking at a side view of each below.

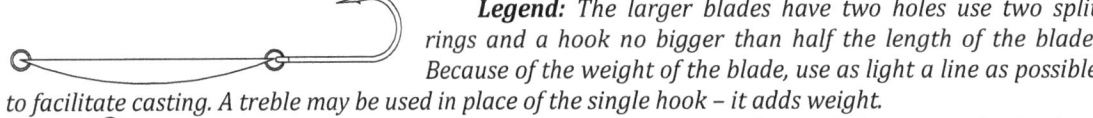

***Legend:** The larger blades have two holes use two split rings and a hook no bigger than half the length of the blade. Because of the weight of the blade, use as light a line as possible to facilitate casting. A treble may be used in place of the single hook – it adds weight.*

***Legend:** The smaller blades have only one hole. Mount the hook as shown with the point pacing outwards.*

This lure should be used with a medium action rod on or near the surface and in the deep – they are, after all, mini spoons and can be fished as a spoon, but because the weight, cannot be retrieved too quickly. Use as light a line as possible to maximize your casting distance. It will flit about like a coin dropped into water, reflecting light in all directions and attracting attention of many fish. The retrieve is slow with light flicks of the rod, allowing it to raise and drop. Takes can be so violent that your rod can be pulled free from your hands.

Perfect for use in lagoons, fishing channels or into deep drop-offs.

It is very successful when fished into deep drop-offs from the rocks and off sandbars. Study the movement of fry and emulate that movement. Enjoy.

Because this lure is so light, you will continually have to make sure that your line is reeled in with adequate tension or you will have loose coils of line sitting on your reel and the chances of a tangle.

You will also have to be very in tune with the wind direction and periodic gusts which can blow your offering way off target – compensate!

Spinners

*The **MEPPS** spinner design – the best spinners I have ever used. In fresh water – very effective when the water is 18°C+.*

Spinners are activated by drawing them through the water using a fast – medium action rod – this causes the blade / blades to rotate. This rotation causes vibrations in the water and reflects light just as light is reflected off the sides of a swimming baitfish.

Because the entire spinner body also ends up turning as well, you will need to use it in conjunction with a clip-on swivel. Split shot can be added in front of the swivel to increase casting potential.

You can catch all manners of pan fish. Cast into gullies between waves and on the side of large rocks / reef. Fish at various depths. These lures are easily distorted by the take and fight. You can only reshape the wire so many times before it is weakened. If there are shad around, use a steel wire trace. Remember that the trebles can always be removed and replaced with a single "J" hook. And that they can be rendered snag-proof. If you do this, you can stop your retrieve at any time and allow the spinner to drop to the bottom – this increases the potential of this lure in attracting fish.

Spinner baits

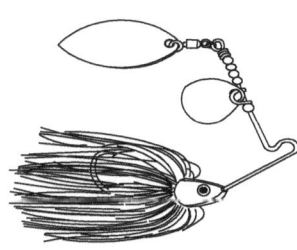

These lures work in the salt but get smashed and the wire needs to be re-shaped. Use various sizes of these in estuaries, into drop-offs and channels in shallow waters. I use them in deep water at various depths. Properly used, they swim upright sending flashes of light and vibrations announcing their presence.

If the lure swims skew and not upright – simply re-shape the wires to their original shape and all will be well. This lure should **NEVER** spiral when retrieved – only the spinner blades should rotate.

Drop shot hook [aka 'jig', 'jig head']

These hooks are superior to normal bass hooks in that they do not easily allow the bait to spin and twist your line. You do not need a swivel with these – just a line clip for fast changeover of hooks. Use a fast-action rod with at least 14pound line. When fishing for other species, you will need smaller drop-shot hooks and smaller grub-like plastic baits attached on 8 - 10pound line using a medium action rod. Use heavier line if you are fishing near structure. When using these lures and you feel a strike, do NOT strike immediately – wait 1 / 2 seconds. Sometimes the tails and appendages on these plastics get torn off – replace the plastic because the action will become compromised.

Most plastics used in freshwater can be used in lagoons and gullies.

Larger hooks can be used with larger baits for kob and bottom-feeding predators.

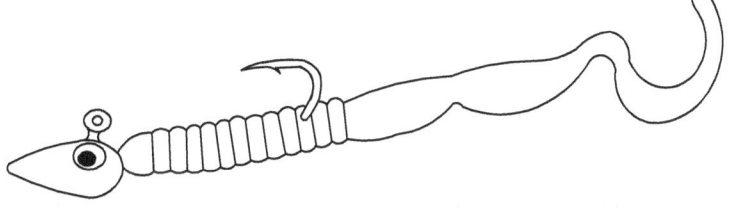

Lures having this basic shape are worm / eel / leech imitations. These creatures should be presented as such. Cast out and retrieve with small twitching movements, also moving the rod from side-to-side, much like the slow-moving creatures you are imitating. Each cast should pick the lure off the ground and then allow it to realistically return to the ground. If there are cobia around, fish this lure mid-water and fasten your seatbelts.

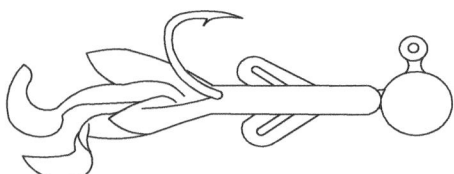 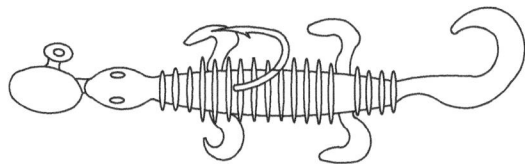

The two plastic baits immediately above resemble a lizard-shaped terrestrial / aquatic creature. With this hook, it has to be fished on the bottom, so it must naturally be moved as though it is a swimming creature, small darts, keeping to the bottom – it can also be retrieved smoothly for a short while before being allowed to sink down to the bottom. It also can be used as a general-attractor pattern with erratic and rapid movements for stubborn fish.

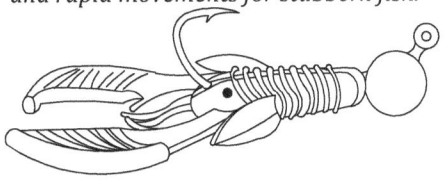

This is a prawn / crayfish / shrimp imitation. It can be mounted facing towards or backwards. If mounted backwards, [see sketch], retrieve - short darts [prawns move with sharp flicks of their tails, producing a series of short darts, followed by periods of non-movement]. If you mount the lure on head first, it should be retrieved at a crawl with interspersed dashes and periods of inactivity, much like the creature is mobile and feeding – which is the only time it moves forwards.

All fish / fry imitations can only be fished on the bottom when using drop shot hooks. They should be fished erratically to resemble feeding and/or injured baitfish.

You do know that crabs move *sideways*? Mount plastic / real crab as shown [if you elect to use a real crab – mount it as shown – you can avoid piercing the creature by using latex bait cotton to fasten it to the rig]. Retrieve is super slow to slow. Rod tip down. You will easily be smashed by pompano, grunter and large stumpnose, to name a few. Fish sand banks and sandy bottoms as well as alongside reef.

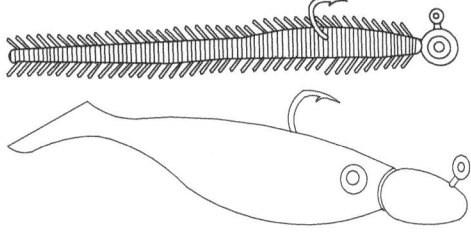

As with the crab, bloodworm imitations must be retrieved very slow. Every now and then, pick it up and allow it to fall naturally. About ten minutes per retrieve.

Paddle tail lures are deadly. Can be retrieved on the bottom with darting movements or can be fished mid-water at various depths. Vary movements, sweep rod from left to right. Keep rod tip down – to horizontal. Double deadly for large predators – look for holes in the surf and around river mouths. Kob find them irresistible.

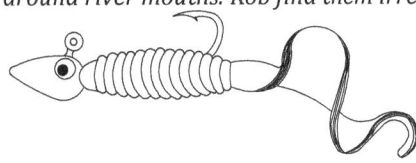

This is a grub. Darting retrieves on the bottom. Can also be fished in mid-water. Raise and allow to fall. Deadly if allowed to raise and fall repeatedly on the same spot. Raise and allow to fall whilst retrieving as well.

By now you understand how the hook is to be located – go fourth and fish! Just remember not to retrieve without simulating the movements of the creature you are imitating. The same if you are using actual bait.

Don't just cast out and reel in. Imitate the creature you have on. Prawns / lobsters need to be crawled. Mingle this with a few short, darting retrieves. Some plastics [like the prawn, can be put on facing forwards or backwards. Facing backwards means short darting movements followed by periods of no movement. Take full advantage of the rod you are using [fast action – in other words, just the tip bends when it is pulled until it is at 90° to the butt].

Movements can be combined with reeling whilst simultaneously pulling / jerking / vibrating the rod or just by moving he rod then reeling. And then, after you consider the thousands of plastics available on the market – get this…. You can use real bait too! Real prawns, real fish, real crab – gettit? Some of these creatures will need to be pinned – but where you can get away with attaching them to the hook using latex bait cotton, DO IT!

Dressed' drop shot hooks [aka 'Jigs']

These are used as described in the preceding section.

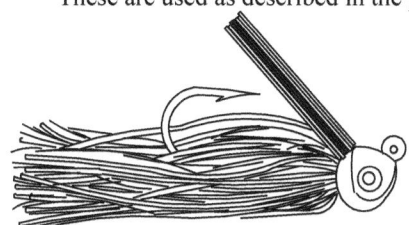

They are available in various sizes and combinations and colours. They can also be used with plastic / real bait – use your imagination. Retrieve a little quicker with minor pauses – it imitates swimming creatures and can be used as a general attractor pattern. It is generally used for bass but can be used for other small mouthed species in the scaled-down versions.

Spoons

These lures are very successful in the surf.

S-bend spoon – use in estuaries and from the beach. Retrieve to be medium to fast, vary your depths.

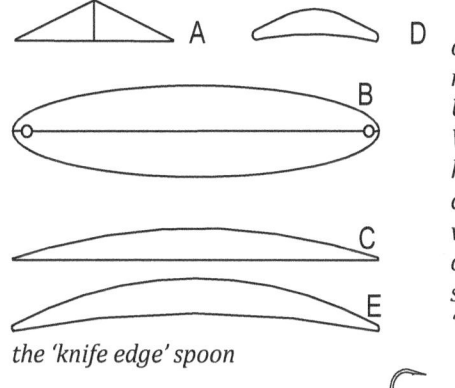

the 'knife edge' spoon

Legend: 'Flat" spoons. "A", "B" and "C" are different views of the 'knife-edged' flat spoon, designed for high speed retrieval. "A" = end view, "B" = top view and "C" = side profile. Use oval split rings on these lures to attach line and hooks. Whilst most people use trebles on these lures, I prefer single 'J' hooks [obviously extra strong designs only]. I have not tried circle hooks on spoons although I am certain that they will work. "D" and "E" are views of the 'curved' flat spoon. This type of spoon is curved along its length [refer view "E"], and sometime features a curvature across the width [refer view "D"]. This type of spoon is retrieved at a much slower rate than

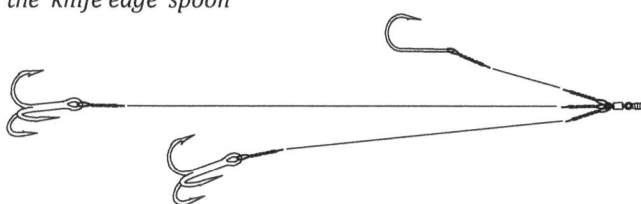

Trace for Great Barracuda / Couta. *Using the haywire loop, tie three consecutive traces onto the same swivel so that it resembles the same trace alongside. This is for a mackerel bait, live or dead. Mullet or shad can also be used. One hook in the jaw [upper and lower, one treble in the side, the other treble in the opposite side. Use a grapnel sinker to keep you anchored and stop live bait from swimming to cover along with a sliding trace [non-return]. You will need to cast out the sinker first and then clip on the live bait. Short distance casts can be made with the live bait on the hook. Do not attempt long casts with the live bait on the hook – you will tear the flesh and probably kill the live bait. As with all live bait, allow at least 4 seconds before responding [no strike necessary for circle hooks – just tighten up and keep a tight line] – you will need to strike with "J" hooks]. It may also be used with a plastic ribbonfish or rubber squid imitation with or without a fillet attached to the "J" hook – a killer presentation*

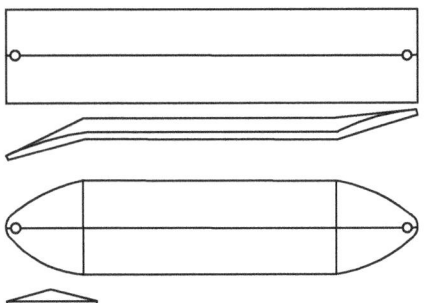

Here is the killer kob spoon design. You will need copper busbar [I originally used a CuNiSi material which is harder and slightly darker than copper], 38mm X 8mm, solid bar. Cut off 150mm length. Mark off longitudinal centreline. Mark off from each end a transverse line 38mm from the ends. Mark and drill 4mm holes at either end, leaving 4mm of material to hold split ring. Machine away from the ends up to the 38mm line, leaving a 2mm face at either end. Now using the centre line as a reference, machine each long side leaving a 2mm face on each side and the centreline as a witness. Grind away the corners to round the ends as illustrated alongside. Bend the ends using the base as a reference to around 15°.

Polish spoon and lacquer-coat to sustain the shine. Insert split rings – tie 80pound leader to one split ring and attach a heavy duty 6/0 – 9/0 hook to the other end. Find the 'holes' in the seabed during the day, and fish the spoon slowly, bumping along the sandy bottom at night.

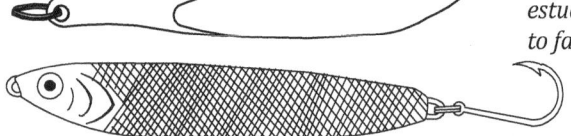

A variation of the s-bend spoon design. *Use in estuaries and from the beach. Retrieve to be medium to fast, vary your depths.*

This heavy metal spoon looks like a baitfish. *Use in estuaries and from the beach. Retrieve to be medium to fast, vary your depths.*

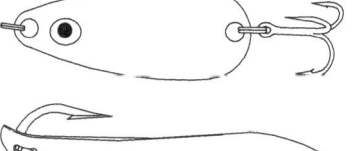

This spoon is made from metal strip [it is actually a modified spinner blade] and is concave, forcing it to spiral and gyrate in the water. Refer section above for 'spinner blades'. Use a clip-on swivel to attach to line.

This spoon is curved and convex and designed for tiger fish. It can be used with or without a fillet on the hook and is brightly polished, sometimes having reflector tape on the outside. It will need a split ring through the hole and a clip-on swivel – it moves like a baitfish – the action may be compromised when you put on a fillet. Make the fillet as slim as possible – fillet should be attached to the back of the spoon, not on the hook.

Garrick plugs

Use a fast – medium action rod.

These normally solid polyurethane lures are fished an hour before and up to three hours after sunup and three hours before and an hour after sundown. They are cast out – if you can reach the backline or beyond, better!

Retrieve is with the rod at 45°, varying the angle from below the horizontal and back again, very fast and interspersed with jerking motions of the rod with the lures being kept on and at times just below the surface. It resembles a panicked baitfish / squid and if retrieve properly will jump out of the water at times.

Because of the weight, and as for spoons as well, they will sink if retrieved slowly and therefore must be used with a fast retrieve

They will also work retrieved fast below the surface and deeper with sideways, jerking motions of the rod whilst retrieving.

Lobotus [triple tail bream] can also be caught with a Garrick plug – only in the Tugela Mouth area.

Crankbaits

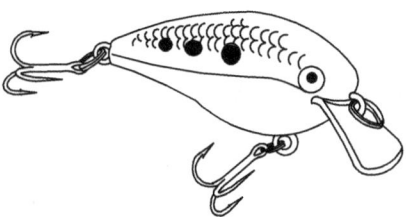

These lures work well during the warmer months, in water 18°C or warmer. You are generally wasting your time using them after a storm when rain has caused a drop in water temperature – that's kinda the rule of thumb for all fishing, in general.

The secret to using these lures successfully is by fishing them with a rod that is not too fast-actioned. If the rod is too fast actioned [just the first quarter bends when the tip is at 90°, you will more than often pull the lure out of the fish's mouth – so please use a medium action rod with a 1-2 second pause before striking.

All estuarine fish can be targeted here – the smaller 3cm lures are best in estuaries and gullies. The bigger ones? – Bigger fish! You will need a minimum of 14pound line to power fish away from structure.

Smaller versions can and will land you a myriad of fish. When you first start fishing, cast to one side, angling the rod downwards [e.g. to the right-hand side] towards the water's edge.

Your retrieve should be interrupted periodically, allowing the crankbait to rise – beware – this is generally when strikes occur – also note that some lures do not rise when you stop the retrieve – make sure that you read the instructions/specifications for the lure.

Like with all other lures, from your original cast, fan out until you have covered the immediate area, then take a few steps and do it again. Keep me a river snapper please!

Surface fish imitation lures

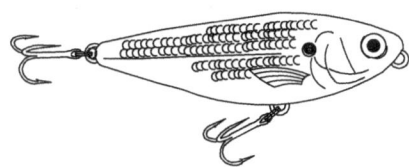

Use a medium action rod. Keep the rod horizontal. Lower the tip from time to time making alternating small and large sweeps with the rod, from left to right, resembling an escaping baitfish.

Use where there is evidence of surface feeding and / or visible sub-surface fish. It is a valuable addition to your arsenal and the best imitation is **Heddon's "spitting image".**

Note that this lure needs a split ring attached to the nose. Fish will strike at surface lures so violently that you may develop a heart condition! This lure is deadly when baitfish are being chased – keep your eyes open!!!

Surface Creature imitation lures

Use a medium action rod. These lures may be frogs, other creatures or just general attractor patterns. They must be used when water temperature > 17°C. Especially when there is surface activity, However, if retrieves super-slow, they could induce a take.

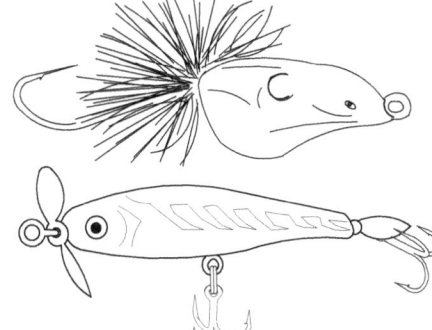

Mouse imitation lure – this is a GREAT lure. When retrieved, it 'swims' nose-up, much like a mouse does and should be retrieved slowly to imitate a swimming mouse. Retrieve with a smooth action whilst vibrating the rod tip, but sweep the rod from left to right whilst retrieving. Keep rod tip down.

This floating lure should be retrieved so that it skips across the water with periodic phases where it actually goes below the surface film.

It is streamlined and has two 'propellers' [blades] at either end which reflect light and create vibrations in the water. Make it look like a panicking baitfish. Or at times an unsuspecting baitfish. Rod tip should be kept down whilst working this lure. Sweep rod from left to right when retrieving, giving it the appearance of a creature changing direction. These lures should not be fished with line lighter than 14pound breaking strain.

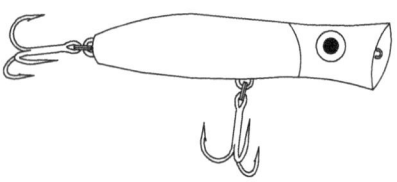
All 'popper' type lures have a concave face and you generally tie your line to a split ring located in the centre of the 'dished' face. This lure is used when there is surface feeding activity or when you spot fish near the surface.

Best time is late afternoon when the water is at its warmest, in the shallows or close to drop-offs. It is retrieved with a combination of a sideways jerk of the rod whilst simultaneously reeling [it can be done just with the jerking motion too]. When you make this motion, the dished shape forces water forward and creates a 'popping' sound. This popping sound is interpreted as a frantically feeding [or frantically escaping!] baitfish. It can also be interpreted as something landing in the water.

The lure should be retrieved with a series of pops and twitches of the rod and long periods of sitting static on the surface. As with all surface lures, keep your eyes on it – it can vanish leaving a small whirlpool or it can vanish with a loud splash that is likely to scare the pants of you.

Sub-surface [diving lures]

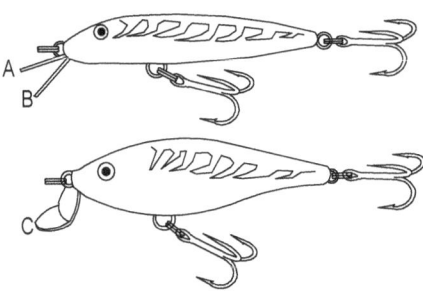
Use a medium action rod. These lures may be heavier than water or buoyant and are induced to dive whenever dragged through the water [by YOU, of course!].

The lure patterns alongside are fish representations. They are made from various materials. They normally float well and have a little blade at the front called a diving vane. The size, angle and design of this vane determines how deeply the lure dives. Vane "A" is a shallow diving lure, vane "B" is a deep-diving lure and vane "C" is a shallow running lure. These lures will float and only dive when you retrieve line.

When the retrieval is stopped, they will float back to the surface. Some of these lures are heavier than water or they take in water and so do not rise back to the surface.

Good lures come packaged with performance specifications that describe how to retrieve and the depth the lure will dive to. *You will generally regret buying 'cheapies'*. Smaller lures can be used in the warmer months for other species.

Plastic fish and creature imitations

Use a fast action rod with these. It is essential that when you feel a 'take', you wait for 1 to 2 seconds before striking. For bass, barbel and other large mouthed predators, you will need at least 14pound breaking strain line.

For other species, you will need to scale down the hook size and plastic lure combination.

There are hard plastic capsules filled with shot that cause rattling sounds when they are moved [ratlers] – these capsules must be pushed into the head/body of lures to make them 'rattle' down there.

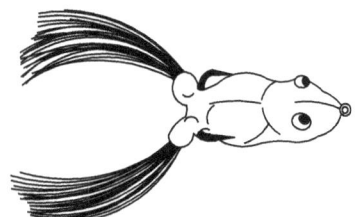
The plastic frog pictured below is a great lure and can be used in estuaries as a general attractor lure where they are mistaken for squid and cuttlefish.

*These lures are generally made weedless and are very light. Always check the legs – in this case [alongside] crystal flash was used] the legs must move when the lure is moved and should **never** be rigid. Keep two handy. Make a slit on the top of one of them and slip in a little sinker in to make it sink. This way you can fish one lure deep or the other on the surface. Cast it onto the bank and drag it into the water.*

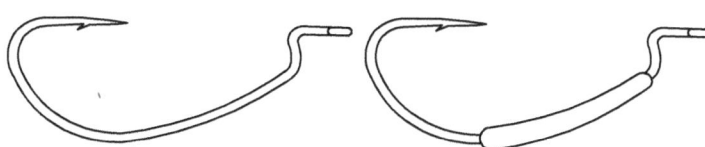

The special hooks alongside are mainly for use with plastic lures. The difference between the two is that the hook to the right is weighted with lead on the shank.

Plastic lures have soft bodies – this gives you that extra bit of time to strike as the fish, by feel, thinks it has taken a living creature. The additional advantage is that some of the are scented.

These hooks are deadly when properly inserted into the plastic bait. Follow the instructions below and learn how to do this properly because incorrectly inserted hooks could mean that you will either miss fish or become snagged if the hook point sticks out of the plastic bait. You may use a weighted hook or the normal hook – it all depends on the creature you will be using and how you want to present it. The weighted hook is best used when you are using 'this way up' baits. They sometimes have a spiral spring attached to the eye – this is for securing plastic baits by literally screwing the bait onto the spring. Some hooks have barbs on the shank to help hold the plastic bait in place.

Refer to the sketches below: The length of the body "A" is the deciding factor for the size of hook to be used. This helps determine the size of hook that can be used. Note that some baits have a cavity at the bottom – this is to accommodate the bend of the back of the hook, on the shank-section *['kinda like a hook-bend housing]*.
Place the hook alongside the body to gauge if it will fit in the body.

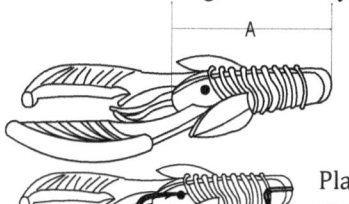

The length of the creature's body "A" is the deciding factor for the size of hook to be used. This helps determine the size of hook that can be used. *Note that some baits have a cavity at the bottom – this is to accommodate the bend of the back of the hook, on the shank.*

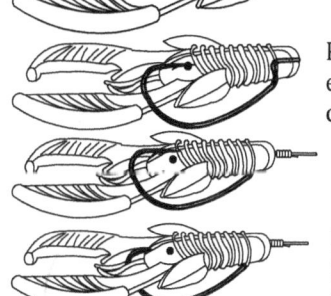

Place the hook alongside the body to gauge if it will fit in the body. The eye and the tip should easily be accommodated by the body of the creature being imitated. And yes, it can actually be a living creature!

Pass 8 to 10mm of the hook point through the centre of the body and bring the point out at the base of the creature. Now gently slide the bait until it passes over the 'dog's leg' on the hook.

Now pull the body towards the eye of the hook and introduce the hook into the head of the creature, close to the top-side so that the point is just below the top of the head as illustrated alongside – the rule-of-thumb is that the hook point should just be below the outer skin, close to the top, and the body of the creature should be straight and not twisted.

You are ready to fish! Check the location of the hook after every cast – as depicted in the last picture above, it is *weedless* – once the point of the hook comes free, it is no longer *weedless*. Reinsert the hook point when this happens. The plastic bait may also slide down the hook, particularly when you have had a strike. Always check and re-position the hook. You may also need to replace the plastic bait from time to time – so make sure that you have a good supply at hand.

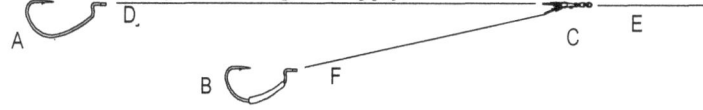

Legend: *Tandem plastic bait fishing rig. A: Trailing hook – normally used in conjunction with a fish representing – you want the bass to think that a small fish is chasing down something. Hook size is dependent on the size of the bait; B: Leading hook – normally a smaller fish or creature representation. The hook illustrated is a weighted hook and can be switched for a normal hook ["A"]; C: clip-on swivel; - can be replaced by a clip alone if the bait you are using does not spiral or spin; D: Trailing hook line. Normally minimum 14pound breaking strain minimum – this line is 300mm – 450mm long; E: main line, normally minimum 14pound breaking strain minimum; F: Leading hook line, normally a minimum of 14pound breaking strain minimum – this line should be 150mm shorter than "D". Sliding sinkers ['bullet" sinkers can be placed at "D", "E" and/or "F". An egg-shaped brass sinker can be placed at "E". the trace can also be rigged with one hook, TEXAS – style, with a bullet sinker in front of the hook, between the hook and the swivel / clip. It can also be fished CAROLINA – style, with an egg-sinker on the main line, above the swivel / clip. A*

sinker enhances the action of the plastic bait on the bottom, causing the bait to nose-dive immediately when the retrieve is interrupted. The CAROLINA rig makes it seem as though the plastic bait is chasing down the sinker as it raises plumes of dust on the bottom. Scaled-down hooks and plastic baits can be used for species other than bass. Plastic baits work well on tigerfish but you will need to carry a lot of plastic bait because ...

I do not advocate tandem hooks for presenting plastic baits in the sea. You may attract two predators...this reminds me of a line by Confucius: "if you chase two rabbits, both will escape". ☺

I normally fish plastic baits in tandem with a smaller bait on the shorter line in lagoons – this gives the predator the impression that the smaller bait is being 'chased' by the larger – an excellent *trigger* for the predator to join in!!

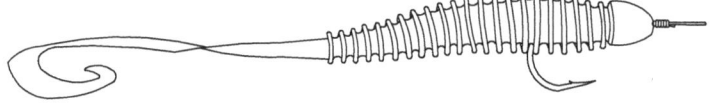

The extra-long worm baits you see are excellent when presented in open water, as a swimming bait – you can use a size 1 to 3/0 "J" hook [you can go larger with the baits that are longer than 6 inches]. Don't think these baits too big!! Only really works for bass – when a bass takes the bait, it opens its mouth in one quick motion – this 'vacuum' effect can pull an entire bait within the mouth of the fish. This is partly why you do not strike immediately – 1 to 2 seconds then pump. But I have to tell you that I have caught prodigal son with it as well!

Make the bait look like it is swimming by reeling in whilst constantly changing the side you are holding the rod on, and by periodically raising and lowering the rod, with occasional jerks.

Flies

The action of the rod is not important – what is important is that your line weight is not more than 2 sizes above or below the rated line weight in the rod. **Refer Chapter 22** for more details. The heavier line class rods are *generally* faster action rods.

Flies are used to resemble and imitate existing life forms or, as general attractor patterns, to induce takes simply because they are *foreign* to the fish. There are literally thousands of fly patterns. The key is to find out what creatures abound at the waters you are fishing. Once you do this, you can use the pattern that most closely resembles the life-form you are imitating – correspondingly, you can then fish the pattern on the surface, in mid-water or off the bottom, as required. And don't think for one moment that you only use fly fishing equipment to cast a fly out. You can fish successfully using flies with conventional tackle – use a float to get the fly out. Try it!!

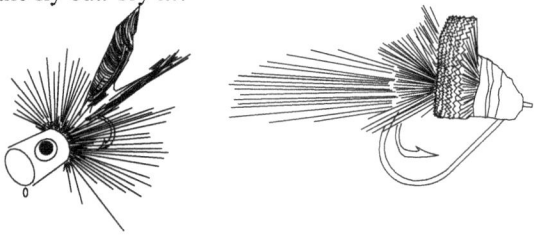

These are poppers, surface ['dry'] flies that create a 'popping' sound when retrieved with a combined snap of the wrist and / or flick of the rod. The one on the *right is a special popper*. It is a pattern called the Dahlberg Diver. Both flies are imitations of several terrestrial, aquatic and amphibious creatures; and also general attractors.

It must also be allowed to stand static after each mini retrieve. The fibres and feathers move in the water and give it signs of being alive. It can be taken violently or vanish leaving a tiny whirlpool...

Wet' flies are designed to be fished on the bottom. The pattern alongside is a depiction of a caddis pupa / larva – an essential part of every fish's diet. I have caught very large tilapia with this baby. Also, large bass with a size 12.

Dry fly. Designed to float on the water. All dry flies should be generously coated with a floatant to ensure that they float above the surface film. Dry flies are generally made with modified hooks that are lighter than conventional hooks. The entire fly must float on water. Dry flies can also be used submerged – you do know that whatever floats has to sink – so it is natural for them to be found on the bottom – static.

THE FISH [Note that *superbaits* will work for almost all species]

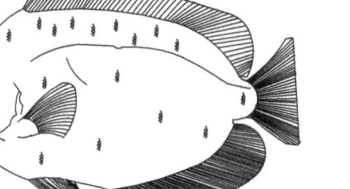

Angelfish. *These fish will probably take small grub imitations on a size 1 drop shot hook. Haven't caught them on artificial lures – yet.*

Baardman *is a slender brown / silver fish with stubby barbels growing below a short chin. These fish live below ledges and must be moved away from the reef or they will be lost to the rocks. If you catch one, chances are there's more out there. Excellent eating. I haven't caught these on artificial lures but am sure that they will take crustacean soft plastics presented on a drop shot hook, say size 1.*

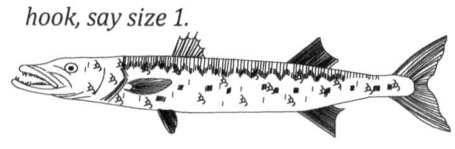

Great **Barracuda**. *Young 'cuda are referred to as 'pickhandles'. Large Rapala type lure, squid imitations.*

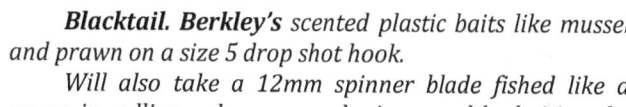

Blacktail. Berkley's *scented plastic baits like mussel and prawn on a size 5 drop shot hook.*

Will also take a 12mm spinner blade fished like a spoon in gullies – chances can be increased by baiting the hook.

Bonefish. *Can be caught using drop shot hooks, size1 with shrimp and crab [and fry] imitations.*

Bonito. *You will probably catch this species in deep water around bay inlets and off deep-water piers – normally caught offshore, but I have heard stories of bonito being hooked in the bay. Will take fast moving fish and squid imitations fished on and below the surface and in mid-water.*

Bronzie [Bronze **bream**]. *Swimming prawn plastics on a size 3 hook with light lead shot to allow for casting and sinking. I don't see why it won't take swimming plastic worms and grubs as well – better fished for near the surface or in mid-water in rough water and in gullies. Better do some sight fishing – spot them then target them.*

Cobia *[Prodigal son] Hook size: 3/0; Bait: live fish, live eel; trace: Running / drift. Can be caught from the beach or off piers.*

Use long plastic grubs - very effective for Cobia [6 – 12inch versions of the plastic used with a light bullet sinker use mid-water or on a sandy bottom 4/0 / 5/0 hook.

Dorado. *Same as for 'couta. Not caught off the beach. Beware when targeting this species – you may get much more than you bargained for – sailfish sometimes move with dorado!*

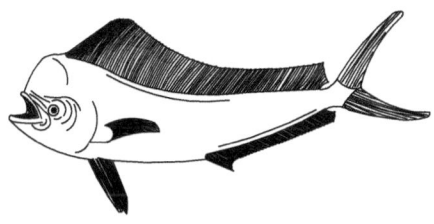

Eel *catfish. Excellent eating. Great eating – beware of the spines, one in front of dorsal fin and 1 on either side of the head, and in front of the pectoral fins. Immediate first aid is required if scratched / poked by these spines.* **Find medical treatment.** *I have not caught this creature on artificial lures though I see no reason why they won't take scented soft plastics presented on the bottom with a size 1 drop shot hook.*

Eel. *Moray I don't see why this creature won't take scented soft plastics presented on the bottom using a 4/0 – 5/0 drop shot hook. But why would you want to target it?*

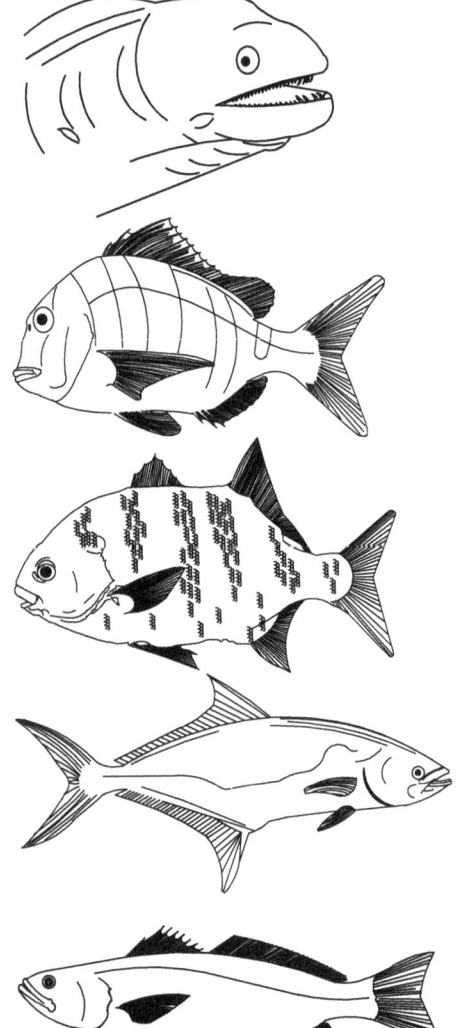

Englishman. *Not normally caught from the beach [unless they're wearing speedo's].*

Galjoen*. Cold water. in white water in gullies or slightly discoloured water, particularly where kelp is growing. Use a size 4-5 drop shot hook with bloodworm, crab and prawn imitations.*

Garrick*. This fish has fine rasping teeth – therefore a heavy trace line is needed. 1 – 4/0 size hook, 40pound snoot. Early mornings and late afternoons, better when these times are synchronized with high tides.*
Use a Garrick plug or a 125mm knife-edged spoon fished on and just below the surface at high speed. Garrick will also take popper-type plugs if you can get them close to the backline.

Geelbek *salmon [below]. Drop shot size 5/0 – 9/0 with paddletail fish imitation. Use my killer spoon design or bi-metal spoons. Nocturnal feeder.*

Grunter *[spotted grunter]. Warmer months, – light tackle. Drop shot size 6 with prawn / crab imitations. Will also take a small spinner blade with a size 6 hook in lagoons. Also use surface lures.*

Hake.*I have included a drawing of hake head just to dispel rumours about the fish's looks. How do you like those teeth??!! Hake are normally netted by trawlers. It is easy to catch but only if someone throws it at you – just avoid the teeth!*

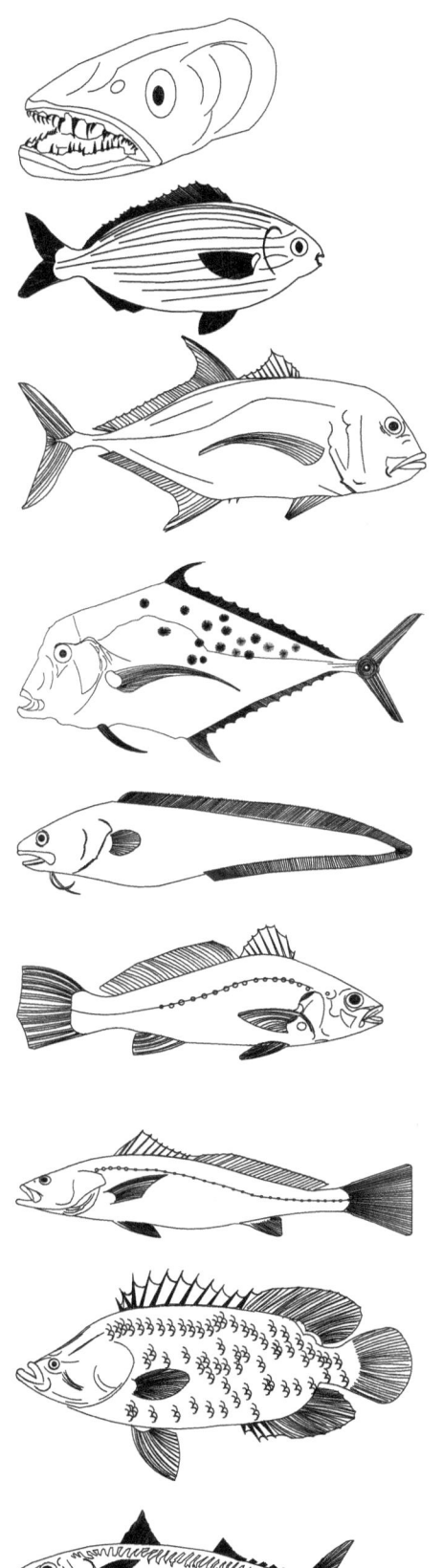

Hake head....

Karanteen aka 'strepie' has orange-gold stripes. Cold water. Small grubs fished with size 6 drop shot hooks. Yo-zuris.

Giant **Kingfish** [GT]. Use a 150mm knife-edged spoon on a medium trolling speed. Poppers and surface lures fished in panic-mode. Early mornings and late afternoons, particularly when high tide coincides with these times.

Threadfin trevally, mirrorfish, indian mirrorfish, threadfin **kingfish**. The threadfin is good eating – not many caught in our waters. Warmer waters. Poppers and surface lures fished in panic-mode. Early mornings and late afternoons, particularly when high tide coincides with these times.

Kingklip. Not normally caught from the beach – you think??! ☺Use cash and catch in the fresh fish section of the supermarket.

Kob [kabeljou, salmon – or affectionately known as Simon ☺]. Cold water. Do not use steel wire. Large flat spoons, copper coloured – fished at night at river mouths in and around holes. Retrieve – slow and off the bottom. You can use drop shot hooks as well – size 4/0 with fish and crustacean representations. Best choice is drop shot size 5/0 – 9/0 with paddletail fish imitation

Squaretail **Kob.** Large flat spoons, copper coloured – fished at night at river mouths in and around holes. Retrieve – slow.

Lobotus [below] – Triple tail bream – Only caught around the Tugela Mouth area and slightly north of the mouth. Knife edged spoons retrieved at high speed. Don't forget to fasten your seatbelt!!!

Mackerel Yo-zuris. Small grubs mounted banana-style on a terminal sinker. Dance them with the sinker just on the bottom.

*Couta [king **mackerel**]. Large Rapala type lure, squid imitations.*

***Marlin.** Hook size: blah; Bait: blah; trace: blah. Don't be trying to catch these off the beach.*

***Mullet.** Tiny surface lures, **Mepps** spinners. Surface and just below. Cast just in front of a shoal.*

*Black **Musselcracker [below]**. Scented plastic baits like mussel and prawn on a size 4/0 drop shot hook.*

*White **musselcracker** [silver Steenbras brusher cracker.... Excellent eating [up to 6kg]. Scented plastic baits like mussel and prawn on a size 4/0 drop shot hook.*

*Estuary **Perch**. Don't fish deep. Hook size: 5 – 8; Bait: Cheese and bread, shrimp, small crabs, sardine; trace: running / drift. These fish will take small floating, sinking, diving and drop shot-presented lures near and around structure. Anything goes. **Mepps** spinners work as well.*

***Pinkie** – the BEST live bait. Large pinkie can be caught deep sea or on the backline. Yo-zuris, small grubs.*

***Pompano.** – sandy bottom. Fine-scaled. White water. Use my live drop shot presentations.... Drop shot size 2 hook, any crustacean imitator. See that nose? Watch for them in lagoons and over prawn banks, tails sticking up – look for flashes in the water in these areas.*

Wave Garrick, large spot **pompano**. *Fine-scaled. White water. Use my live drop shot presentations.... Drop shot size 2 hook, any crustacean imitator.*

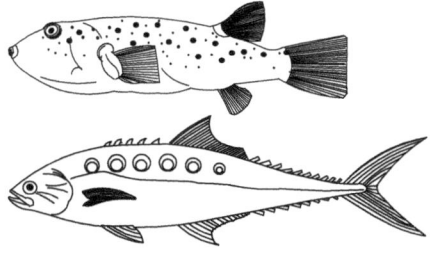

Puffer fish. *Hook size: blah; Bait: blah; trace: blah. Doesn't matter how hard you try. You will catch them. Its magic. Moving on...*

Queenfish. *[Natal snoek]. Normally takes well on small spoons and squid imitations. Will take any lure up to 5inches long. Fast retrieve off piers and harbour mouths, especially when you can reach over the backline. Mid- and top-water fishing.*

Redfish. *Grubs fished off the bottom with size 1 drop shot hook.*

Rock cod *[Captain Fine]. Various species [half-moon, spotted, swallowtail, yellow belly...] water more than 3m deep near rocks. Must power away from reef or will be lost. Drop shot with baitfish / prawn imitations, size 2/0 – 6/0 hook.*

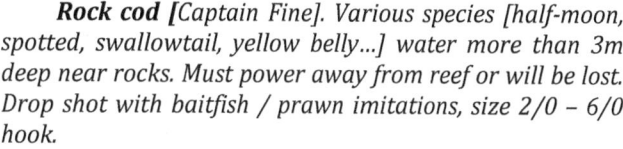

Sailfish. *Better to crack a beer and start a braai – offshore species.*

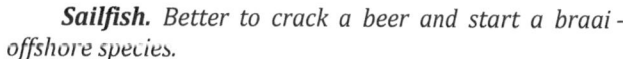

Sand soldier. *Small grubs on size 1 drop shot hooks.*

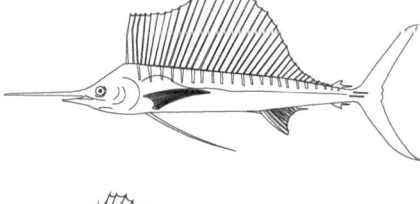

Sea barbel [sea catfish]. Great eating – beware of the spines, one in front of dorsal fin and 1 on either side of the head, part of the pectoral fins. No scales. immediate first aid is required if scratched / poked by these spines – *the fish's normal mucous is harmless.* **Find medical treatment**. *I see no reason why these will not take plastics on drop shot hooks, size 1.*

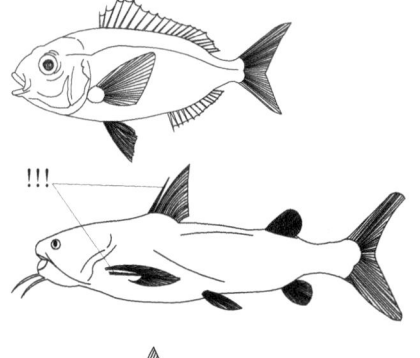

Sardine *Hook size: you will need a bait shop; Bait: money; trace: cooler box*

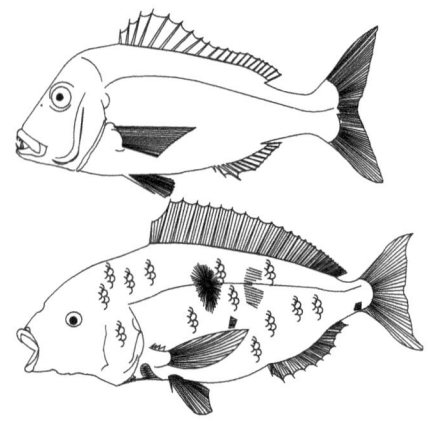

Scottsman. Scented plastic baits like squid, prawn and fry on a size 1 drop shot hook.

Seventy-four. The best lure to use for these is: **Prohibited**.

Shad. (Elf) Winter to summer. Hook size: 2/0 -6/0; Bait: Sardine fillet. Baitfish fillet; trace: Use steel wire. Medium speed slim spoons with "J" hooks, size 2/0 and steel wire. They will take and destroy soft plastics, spinners, spinnerbaits, floating and sinking lures, best choice is fish imitations. Shad will often strike a lure just before you lift it out of the water – be warned.

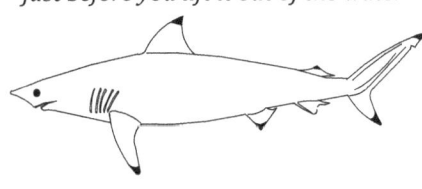

Black Tip **Shark.** Don't go after shark without experience. It is a hard fighter and will test you and your tackle to the limit. Use only the best tackle and book a massage. And make sure you have enough line on your reel. Hook size: beeg and strong – and don't kill if you are not going to eat. If they are going to take a lure – it will have to be chum flavoured.

Hammerhead **Shark.** Instructions as above, for black tip shark.

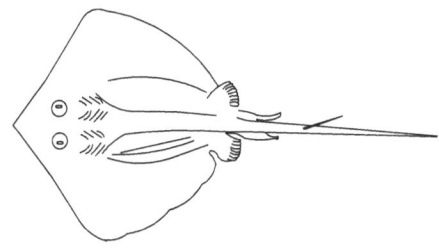

Skate and other flatfish. **Ray.** Skates – colours normally drab - stocky tail with fins on end of tail, no stinging spine [see illustration of stingray alongside]. Has scales. Rays – colouration normally has brighter colours - tail looks like a whip, has 1 or no dorsal fin [on the tail]. I have never caught these creatures on artificial lures but see no reason why they can't be tempted with a drop shot rig with scented plastics.

Sole. Dunno – but would suggest drop shot hook with scented bloodworm bounced very slowly off the bottom.

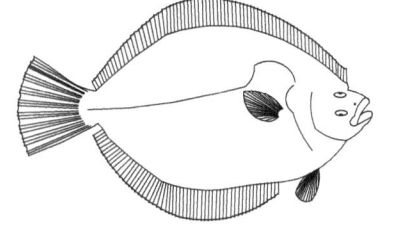

Snapper. Drop shot hook, size 1 – 1/0 with plastic fish imitations [green works best]. 4-5inch lures. Squid imitations also work.

Snoek. [Cape snoek] Large spinners and spinnerbaits. Slim **Rapala** lures. Fish deep and with wire leader [> 15m]. Will also take plastic baits fished deep [but say goodbye to the lure!].

Blood **Snapper.** Drop shot hook, size 1 – 1/0 with plastic fish imitations [green works best]. 4-5inch lures. Squid imitations also work.

Springer [skipjack, lady]. Set up a running trace with a small barrel sinker [heavy enough to cast]. Tie in a 40mm spinner blade with a size 1/0 hook on a 400 – 500mm snoot. Cast out and retrieve in top- and mid-water in short fast bursts. When you slow down, the sinker goes down and gives the spinner blade a lovely action. Any slim, shiny **Rapala** type surface or diving lure. Any popper. Lures should not be longer than 100mm. Responds well to soft plastic fish imitations fished on or just below the surface. Will also take slim spoons fished on and just below the surface. Fast retrieve.

Red **Steenbras**. **Prohibited.** Aggressive predator – small fish, octopus and squid bait. Hook size: **Prohibited**; Bait: **Prohibited**; trace: **Prohibited**. Please return if you catch this or any other prohibited beauty.

White **Steenbras** Drop shot with size 1 – 4/0 hooks and suitable bloodworm, crab, shrimp, prawn and fry imitations [scented]. Will also take a 12-20mm spinner blade fished like a spoon in gullies and lagoon dropoffs – chances can be increased by baiting the hook.

Natal **stumpnose** and other stumpnose. Drop shot with size 4 – 6 hooks and suitable crab, shrimp, prawn and fry imitations. Good eating. Fish at night. Will also take a 12mm spinner blade fished like a spoon in gullies – chances can be increased by baiting the hook.

Oxeye **tarpon.** Drop shot with bloodworm, shrimp imitation lures. Tie in a 25mm spinner blade with a size 3 hook on a 400 – 500mm snoot. Cast out and retrieve in mid water in short fast bursts at drop-offs in estuaries.

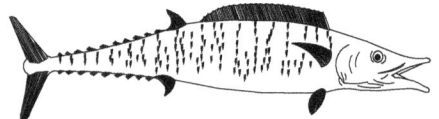

Wahoo. Mackerel with blue, pink or white skirts. **Halco** twisty lures. S-bend spoons retrieved at high speed. Mostly caught offshore.

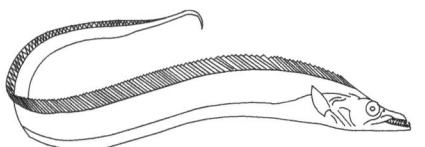

Walla walla Using a size 1 hook on a spinner blade. If it is windy use a barrel sinker. Tie in a 25mm to 40mm spinner blade with a size 1 hook on a 400 – 500mm snoot. Cast out and allow to drop and retrieve in mid water. Oh, and make sure you have a wire leader! Any slim, shiny type surface or diving lure. At night, fish off the pier on in a lagoon with a mini light stick attached to your bait – ribbonfish will come up to investigate and find your bait.

Five fingers **[wildeperd]** – Scented plastic baits like mussel and prawn on a size 5 drop shot hook. Will also take a 12mm spinner blade fished like a spoon in gullies – chances can be increased by baiting the hook.

Chapter 20: Offshore fishing

If you are going to return a fish to the water, always avoid handling it by the soft underbelly area as this can easily cause injury to the creature. The prime time for catching most game fish is early in the morning and late in the afternoon. Incoming tide [two hours before and after high water].

Refer Chapters 13 and 14 for natural and artificial baits [respectively].

Top and mid-water fishing

[note that ***ANYTHING*** will take a superbait]

Great **Barracuda**. Use a 150mm knife-edged spoon on a medium trolling speed. Use up to a meter of braided steel wire attached to your leader using a power swivel. Will also take a mackerel fillet or whole mackerel. Also, whole shad. Hook size: couta trace; Bait: mackerel fillet or whole mackerel, shad, pinkie, sardine, karanteen, mullet - alive or dead; trace: couta. Use a skirt / duster mounted over the bait, above the swivel.

Bonito. Will take fast moving fish and squid imitations fished on and below the surface and in mid-water. Hook size: 1-3/0; Bait: fish fillets; trace: single hook, mid water with running barrel sinker to keep bait below the surface, drift baiting. Not good eating – excellent shark bait – fillets can be used for reef fish and shad. Fish on the drift or trolling.

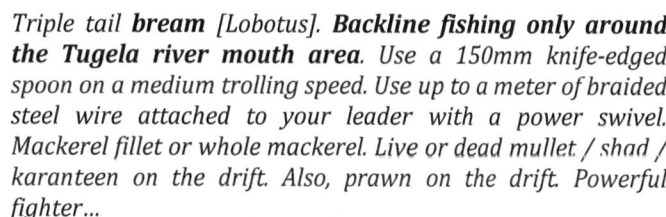

Triple tail **bream** [Lobotus]. **Backline fishing only around the Tugela river mouth area.** Use a 150mm knife-edged spoon on a medium trolling speed. Use up to a meter of braided steel wire attached to your leader with a power swivel. Mackerel fillet or whole mackerel. Live or dead mullet / shad / karanteen on the drift. Also, prawn on the drift. Powerful fighter...

Cobia [Prodigal son] Hook size: 3/0; Bait: live fish, live eel; trace: Running / drift. Can be caught from the beach or off piers. Use 6 – 12inch plastic eel imitations midwater or on sandy bottoms.

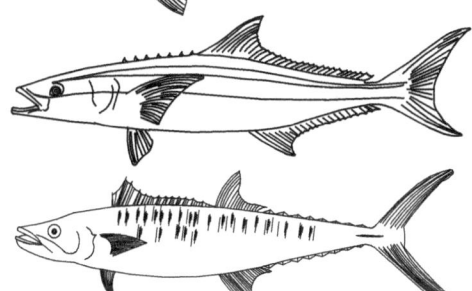

Couta [king **mackerel**] Use a 150mm knife-edged spoon on a medium trolling speed. Large **Rapala** type lure, squid imitations, feathers. Use up to a meter of braided steel wire attached to your leader using a power swivel. Will also take a mackerel fillet or whole mackerel. Also whole shad. Use a skirt / duster mounted over the bait, above the swivel. Fillet bait should be kept off the bottom. Hook size: standard 'couta trace with two trebles and a size 4-5/0 "J" hook; Bait: Will also take a mackerel fillet or whole mackerel, shad, pinkie, karanteen, mullet - alive or dead; trace: drift. **Tandem peeled prawn bait.** Prawns may also be cut into segments or the meat used in small pieces. A whole large prawn may also be used with a tandem / single hook on steel wire. You may or may not elect to use latex bait cotton. This is used in conjunction with a running trace. Braided steel wire is used to attach the hooks to the line which should be up to 1m in length. Can also be used to catch Dorado, sailfish and sometimes prodigal son [Cobia].

Dorado. Same as for 'couta. Beware when targeting this species – you may get much more than you bargained for – sailfish sometimes move with dorado! Dorado [alongside] will readily take a rapala, squid imitation as well. Fish as for 'couta. Bait: Same as for 'couta.

Garrick [backline and around river mouths only] – topwater flies - floating, midwater – intermediate. Early mornings and late afternoons, better when these times are synchronized with high tides. Garrick have fine rasping teeth that can wear through your tippet during a prolonged fight – rather use a 20-25kg nylon / braid leader/tippet. Any popper or fly resembling small baitfish will work. Colour is not important. Make up flies that resemble these baitfish [mullet – white bottom, black top.... Translucent flies resemble smaller baitfish... best midwater = clouser minnow. Use a Garrick plug or a 125mm knife-edged spoon fished on and just below the surface at high speed.

Garrick will also take popper-type plugs if you can get them close to the backline. If the fish follows a popper but does not strike, change to intermediate and use a baitfish imitator – usually works. This fish has fine rasping teeth – therefore a heavy trace line is needed. – size hook, minimum 40pound snoot. Hook size: 3/0 – 5/0; Bait: Pinkie, shad, mullet, karanteen; trace: running non-return trace. Can be fished for using a large float with live bait. You will have to cast the bait out and reel in slowly to maintain tight line and re-cast periodically.

Giant **Kingfish** [GT]. **Backline fishing, warmer months**. Early mornings and late afternoons, particularly when high tide coincides with these times. Use a 150mm knife-edged spoon on a medium trolling speed. Poppers and surface lures fished in panic-mode. Use up to a metre of braided steel wire attached to your leader using a power swivel. Will also take a mackerel fillet or whole mackerel. Live or dead mullet / shad / karanteen on the drift. Also, prawn on the drift. Be-double-ware – you are in for a fight! Hook size: 1/0 – 4/0; Bait: Will also take a mackerel fillet or whole mackerel. Live or dead mullet / shad / karanteen on the drift. Also, prawn on the drift.; trace: terminal / running / drift.

Threadfin trevally, mirrorfish, indian mirrorfish, threadfin **kingfish**. Good eating – not many caught in our waters. Warmer waters. Poppers and surface lures fished in panic-mode. Early mornings and late afternoons, particularly when high tide coincides with these times. Hook size from. Hook size: 2 – 4/0; Bait: Sea lice, baby squid [I caught one near Tugela Mouth with whole baby squid], and small live bait. Pinkie strip bait.; trace: drift.

Marlin. Trolling a large rapala or coner. Ribbonfish also a great lure.
Hook size 14/0 – 16/0; bait live/dead mackerel or bonito on a skirt; Trace – drift – trolling.

Queenfish. Backline and around river mouths. [Natal snoek]. Normally takes well on small spoons and squid imitations. Will take any lure up to 5inches long. Hook size: 3/0 – 5/0; Bait: sardine fillet; trace: steel. Us a skirt.

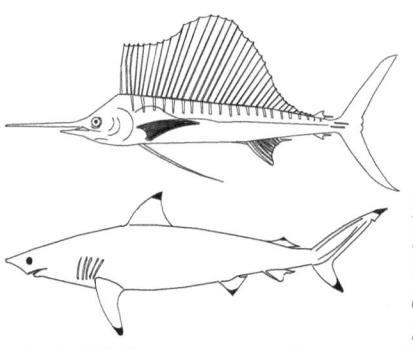

Sailfish. *Will take trolled large rapala, ribbonfish or coners. Hook size 12/0-16/0; bait live / dead mackerel / bonito trolled or drifted. Sometimes moves with dorado.*

***Black Tip* Shark.** *Don't go after shark without experience. It is a hard fighter and will test you and your tackle to the limit. Use only the best tackle and book a massage. And make sure you have enough line on your reel. Hook size: 'beeg and strong 16/0. You are not playing around – don't go after any shark unprepared – and don't kill if you are not going to eat. If they are going to take a lure – it will have to be dipped into blood-flavoured chum. Opportunistic feeder – waits under the boat for his order. Great eating.*

***Hammerhead* Shark.** *Instructions as above, for black tip shark.*

Snoek. *[Cape snoek] Large spinners and spinnerbaits. Slim **Rapala**-type lures. Fish deep and with wire leader [> 15m]. Will also take plastic baits fished deep [but say goodbye to the lure!]. Hook size: 7/0 – 12/0; Bait: chopped sardine; trace: drift.*

Springer *[skipjack, lady]. Mainly backline and around river mouths and in bays. Set up a running trace with a small barrel sinker [heavy enough to cast]. Tie in a 40mm spinner blade with a size 1/0 hook on a 400 – 500mm snoot. Cast out and retrieve in top- and mid-water in short fast bursts. When you slow down, the sinker goes gown and gives the spinner blade a lovely action. Any slim, shiny **Rapala** type surface or diving lure. Any popper. Lures should not be longer than 100mm. Responds well to soft plastic fish imitations fished on or just below the surface. Will also take slim spoons fished on and just below the surface. Fast retrieve. Warmer months. Hook size: 2 – 2/0; Bait: Will readily take any small live bait, particularly pinkie, glassies and mullet; trace: float.*

Tuna. *Just like a typical man, will chase anything in a skirt. Will take almost anything trolled behind a boat. Has a preference for mackerel – yes, wearing a skirt / duster. Fasten your seatbelt. Feathers, small coners, squid....*

Wahoo. *Mid- and surface fishing. Mackerel with blue, pink or white skirts. Halco twisty lures. S-bend spoons retrieved at high speed.*

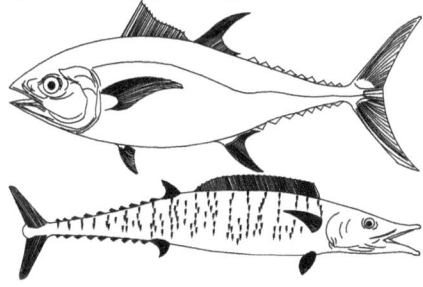

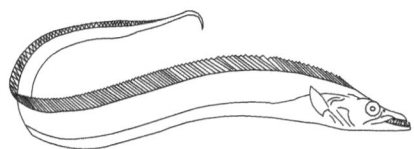

Walla walla *[ribbonfish] Using a size 6 hook on a spinner blade. For short casts, you are at the mercy of the wind. What you can do if it is windy [or if you need to cast deeper], is to set up a running trace using a barrel sinker. Tie in a 25mm to 40mm spinner blade with a size 1 hook on a 400 – 500mm snoot. Cast out and retrieve in mid water in short fast bursts. When you slow down, the sinker goes down and gives the spinner blade a lovely action. Oh, and make sure you have a wire leader! Any slim, shiny **Rapala** type surface or diving lure. At night, fish off the pier on in a lagoon with a mini light stick attached to your lure – ribbonfish will come up to investigate and find it. This is excellent large gamefish bait.*

Bottom fishing [Note that superbaits will work for all species]

Note that gamefish can and will also be hooked on the bottom.

Angelfish. *These fish will probably take small grub imitations on a size 1 drop shot hook. Haven't caught them on artificial lures – yet. Hook size: 1-1/0; Bait: shellfish and shrimp; trace: terminal, sometimes mid-water.*

Baardman *is a slender brown / silver fish with stubby barbels growing below a short chin. These fish live below ledges and must be moved away from the reef or they will be lost to the rocks. If you catch one, chances are there's more out there.*
Excellent eating.
I haven't caught these on artificial lures but am sure that they will take crustacean soft plastics presented on a drop shot hook, say size 1. Hook size: 1-1/0; Bait: crab, prawn, worm and red bait; trace: terminal.

Blacktail. *Use **Berkley's** scented plastic baits like mussel and prawn on a size 5 drop shot hook. Will also take a 12mm spinner blade fished like a spoon in gullies – chances can be increased by baiting the hook.*
Hook size: 6-8; Bait: sardine cutlets, chicken guts cut into half inch pieces [must not be rotten]; trace: terminal / drift.

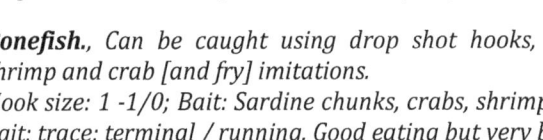

Bonefish., *Can be caught using drop shot hooks, size1 with shrimp and crab [and fry] imitations.*
Hook size: 1 -1/0; Bait: Sardine chunks, crabs, shrimp, small live bait; trace: terminal / running. Good eating but very bony.

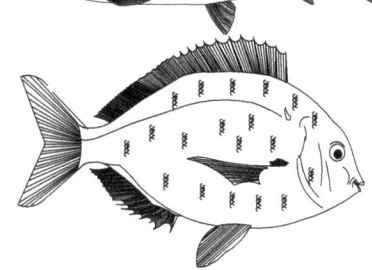

*Bronzie [Bronze **bream**]. Swimming prawn plastics on a size 3 hook with light lead shot to allow for casting and sinking. I don't see why it won't take swimming plastic worms and grubs as well – better fished for near the surface or in mid-water in rough water and in gullies. Better do some sight fishing – spot them then target them. Hook size: 3; Bait: pieces of crayfish / prawn; trace: Use a float with 1m line to the hook with split shot pressed onto the line about 300mm from the hook. I have never caught this species offshore though I am sure that you will if you are fishing backline and shallow reefs, you do have a chance.*

Eel *catfish. Excellent eating. Great eating – beware of the spines, one in front of dorsal fin and 1 on either side of the head, part of the pectoral fins. No scales. immediate first aid is required if scratched / poked by these spines – the fish's normal mucous is harmless.* **Find medical treatment.** *I have not caught this creature on artificial lures though I see no reason why it won't take scented soft plastics presented on the bottom with a size 1 drop shot hook. Hook size: 1; Bait: small fish, crabs, prawns and crayfish and will readily take fillets and squid; trace: terminal.*

Eel. *Moray I don't see why this creature won't take scented soft plastics presented on the bottom using a 4/0 – 5/0 drop shot hook. But why would you want to target it? Hook size: 3/0 – 6/0; Bait: live bait or fillet held near lair; trace: terminal. I leave them alone.*

Englishman. *Swimming prawn plastics on a size 3 hook with light lead shot to allow for casting and sinking. I don't see why it won't take swimming plastic worms and grubs as well. Hook size: 1 - 1/0; Bait: squid; trace: terminal.*

Galjoen. *Cold water. in white water in gullies or slightly discoloured water, particularly where kelp is growing. Use a size 4-5 drop shot hook with bloodworm, crab and prawn imitations. Hook size: 3; Bait: Red bait, white & black mussel strip bait, small crab, worm, sea lice and juvenile molluscs; trace: terminal.*

Geelbek *salmon. Drop shot size 5/0 - 9/0 with paddle tail fish imitation. Use my killer spoon design or bi-metal spoons. Nocturnal feeder. Hook size: 5/0 - 9/0; Bait: live bait or whole sardine; trace: terminal, long snoot [1-1.5m].*

Grunter *[spotted grunter]. Warmer months, – light tackle. Drop shot size 6 with prawn / crab imitations. Will also take a small spinner blade with a size6 hook in lagoons.*
I have not caught this species offshore, but am sure that you can when fishing backline near river mouths in warmer waters. Hook size: 4-6; Bait: shrimp, prawn, sea lice, razor clams; trace: running.

Hake. *I have included a drawing of hake just to dispel rumours about the fish's looks. These creatures are normally netted by trawlers. It is easiest to catch one if someone throws it at you – in a fish shop.*

Karanteen *aka 'strepie' has orange-gold stripes. Cold water. Small grubs fished with size 6 drop shot hooks. Yo-zuris.*
Backline: Hook size: 8 - 10; Bait: Sardine cutlets, sardine guts, red bait, prawns, baitfish cutlets; trace: terminal.

Kingklip. *Deep drops, more than 90m. Incidental catches on bottom fishing with squid.*

Kob *['kabeljou'. salmon – or affectionately known as Simon ☺]. Cold water. Do not use steel wire. Large flat spoons, copper coloured – fished at night at river mouths in and around holes. Retrieve – slow and off the bottom. You can use drop shot hooks as well – size 4/0 with fish and crustacean representations. Best choice is drop shot size 5/0 – 9/0 with paddletail fish imitation. Hook size: 1/0 to 9/0; Bait: Live bait – mullet [even glassies and pinkies]; trace: running for live bait / terminal.*

*Squaretail **Kob**. Large flat spoons, copper coloured – fished at night at river mouths in and around holes. Retrieve – slow. Hook size: 1-1/0; Bait: Sardine fillet; trace: terminal.*

Lobotus – Triple tail bream – Actually a topwater and midwater feeder. Only caught around the Tugela Mouth area and slightly north of the mouth. Knife edged spoons retrieved at high speed. Hook size: 2/0 – 4/0; Bait: Use live mullet; trace: running.

Mackerel. Backline reefs. Yo-zuris. Small grubs mounted banana-style on a terminal sinker. Dance them with the sinker just on the bottom. Hook size: yo-zuri 3 - 6; Bait: use sardine cutlets on yo-zuri hooks; trace: terminal.

Mullet. Backline, off sandbanks and near river mouths. Tiny surface lures, **Mepps** spinners. Surface and just below. Cast just in front of a shoal. Hook size: 12 – 5; Bait: Loves mussel bait, sardines, bread, insects [especially flying ant].; trace: float.

Black **Musselcracker.** Scented plastic baits like mussel and prawn on a size 4/0 drop shot hook.
Same as for white musselcracker below.

White **musselcracker** [silver Steenbras brusher cracker…. Excellent eating [up to 6kg]. Scented plastic baits like mussel and prawn on a size 4/0 drop shot hook. Hook size 4/0 – 6/0. don't compromise hook quality; Bait: whole mussel white n black red bait, crayfish, prawn; trace: terminal.

Estuary **Perch.** Backline and reefs near river mouths. Hook size: 5 – 8; Bait: Cheese and bread, shrimp, small crabs, sardine; trace: running / drift. These fish will take small floating, sinking, diving and drop shot-presented lures near and around structure. Mepps spinners work as well. Hook size: 5 – 8; Bait: Cheese and bread, shrimp, small crabs, sardine; trace: running / drift.

Pinkie – the BEST live bait. Large pinkie can be caught deep sea or on the backline. Yo-zuris, small grubs. Hook size: 1-3 including yo-zuri; Bait: Any fish cutlets.; trace: terminal.

Pompano. Backline near sand bars – sandy bottom. Fine-scaled. White water. Use my live drop shot presentations…. Drop shot size 2 hook, any crustacean imitator. See that nose? Watch for them in lagoons and over prawn beds, tails sticking up – look for flashes in the water in these areas. Hook size: 6 – 1/0; Bait: Sea lice, crabs, shrimp, small live bait.; trace: Running.

Wave Garrick, large spot **pompano**. Backline near sand bars – sandy bottom. Fine-scaled. White water. Use my live drop shot presentations…. Drop shot size 1 hook, any crustacean imitator. Hook size: 1-6; Bait: Sea lice, sardine belly, crab, whole and fillet white and black mussel, worms in the shallow wave zone.; trace: running.

Puffer fish. Hook size: blah; Bait: blah; trace: blah. Doesn't matter how hard you try, you will catch them. Its magic. Moving on….

Redfish. Grubs fished off the bottom with size 1 drop shot hook. Hook size: 1; Bait: squid; trace: terminal.

Rock cod [Captain Fine]. Various species [half-moon, spotted, swallowtail, yellow belly...] water more than 3m deep near rocks. Must power away from reef or will be lost. Drop shot with baitfish / prawn imitations, size 2/0 hook. Hook size: 1/0 – 5/0; Bait: Flapper bait, any other bait, particularly fish heads. Will also readily take crab.; trace: terminal in water 3m and deeper, always near reef.

Sand soldier. Small grubs on size 1 drop shot hooks. Hook size: 1; Bait: squid; trace: terminal. Deep water, in bays and off piers accessing deeper waters.

Sardine Hook size: you will need a bait shop; Bait: money; trace: cooler box. Go and buy some, silly – try and salt this bait to make it tougher.

Scottsman. Scented plastic baits like squid, prawn and fry on a size 1 drop shot hook.
Hook size: 1-2/0; Bait: squid; trace: terminal.

Sea barbel [sea catfish]. Great eating – beware of the spines, one in front of dorsal fin and 1 on either side of the head, part of the pectoral fins. No scales – *the fish's normal mucous is harmless*. **Find medical treatment**. I see no reason why these will not take plastics on drop shot hooks, size 1. Hook size: 1; Bait: any fish fillet bait and squid; trace: terminal.

Seventy-four. The best lure to use for these is: **Prohibited**. And PROHIBITED is NOT the name of a lure.

Shad. Winter to summer. Hook size: 2/0 -6/0; Bait: Sardine fillet. Baitfish fillet; trace: Use steel wire. Medium speed slim spoons with "J" hooks, size 2/0 and steel wire. They will take and destroy soft plastics, spinners, spinnerbaits, floating and sinking lures, best choice is fish imitations. Shad will often strike a lure just before you lift it out of the water – be warned. Hook size: 2/0 -6/0; Bait: Sardine fillet. Baitfish fillet; trace: Use steel wire.

Snapper. Drop shot hook, size 1 – 1/0 with plastic fish imitations [green works best]. 4-5inch lures. Squid imitations also work. Hook size: 2 – 1/0; Bait: shellfish, squid, octopus; trace: terminal.

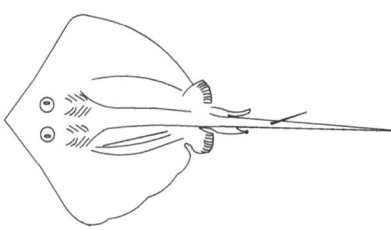

Skate and other flatfish. **Ray.** Skates – colouration normally drab - stocky tail with fins on end of tail, no stinging spine [see illustration of stingray alongside]. Has scales. Rays – colouration normally has brighter colours - tail looks like a whip, has 1 or no dorsal fin [on the tail]. I have never caught these creatures on artificial lures but see no reason why they can't be tempted with a drop shot rig with scented plastics. Hook size: 1-3/0; Bait: Any bait on the bottom; trace: terminal. Skate, sand shark and Rays are the reason you use a cork on your snoot if you do not want to catch them – the cork or 'float' keeps the bait suspended above the bottom. If you are targeting skates and rays, your bait will have to lie on the bottom

Sole. Dunno – but would suggest drop shot hook with scented bloodworm bounced slowly on the bottom.
Hook size: 6 -8; Bait: marine worm; trace: terminal – affix split shot to snoot close to hook [about 3" from hook] to keep the bait on the bottom. These fish normally 'flounder' about.

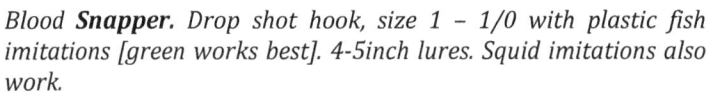

Blood **Snapper.** Drop shot hook, size 1 – 1/0 with plastic fish imitations [green works best]. 4-5inch lures. Squid imitations also work.
Hook size: 2 – 1/0; Bait: shellfish, squid, octopus; trace: terminal.

Red **Steenbras**. **Prohibited.** Aggressive predator – small fish, octopus and squid bait. Hook size: **Prohibited**; Bait: **Prohibited**; trace: **Prohibited**.
Please return any prohibited species.

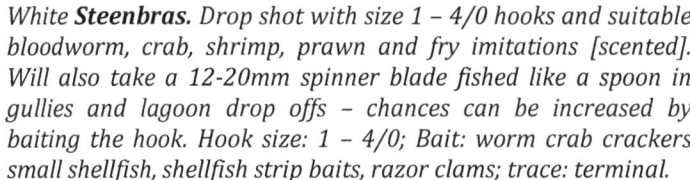

White **Steenbras.** Drop shot with size 1 – 4/0 hooks and suitable bloodworm, crab, shrimp, prawn and fry imitations [scented]. Will also take a 12-20mm spinner blade fished like a spoon in gullies and lagoon drop offs – chances can be increased by baiting the hook. Hook size: 1 – 4/0; Bait: worm crab crackers small shellfish, shellfish strip baits, razor clams; trace: terminal.

Natal **stumpnose** and other stumpnose. Drop shot with size 4 – 6 hooks and suitable crab, shrimp, prawn and fry imitations. Good eating. Fish at night. Will also take a 12mm spinner blade fished like a spoon in gullies – chances can be increased by baiting the hook.
Hook size: 4 – 6; Bait: Sea lice, crab, mussel and other shellfish, worm, fish fillet from pinky, sardine, cracker shrimp, redbait and prawn; trace: Running trace.

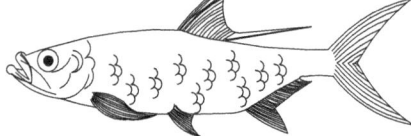

Oxeye **tarpon.** Backline and around river mouths. Drop shot with bloodworm, shrimp imitation lures. Tie in a 25mm spinner blade with a size 3 hook on a 400 – 500mm snoot. Cast out and retrieve in mid water in short fast bursts at drop-offs in estuaries.
Hook size: 3 – 1/0; Bait: marine worms, razor clams; trace: float with 1m snoot.

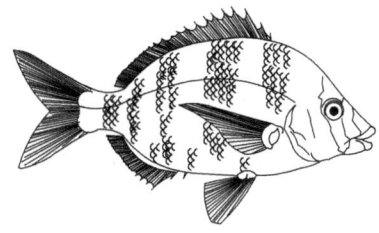

*Five fingers [**wildeperd**] – backline and shallow reefs. Scented plastic baits like mussel and prawn on a size 5 drop shot hook. Will also take a 12mm spinner blade fished like a spoon in gullies – chances can be increased by baiting the hook.*

Chapter 21: The fight

Typical and literally the 'tiger by the tail' scenario: You have done it all correctly up to now. Some of you never thought you'd get this far – as a matter of fact, some of you never expected this….
Something has taken your bait and there is a fish at the end of the line!
Now you have to land it! And you had better be using a rod-bucket around your waist!

If you are fishing with monofilament and normal 'J' shaped hooks, you will need to strike and set the hook. Setting the hook means that the barb [if any] has to be engaged. A surprisingly large amount of energy is involved in getting the barb to penetrate fully and it doesn't help that much of the 'striking' energy is lost because of the elasticity [stretch] of the line. Consider that normal monofilament can stretch as much as 30% before returning to its original length [3m in 10!!!!] – this is why I recommend that you reel in, bring the tip down and then strike.

Never strike directly overhead, but a little to the left or right – if the line flies out of the water with the effort put into the strike, it will pass you on the side that you strike, thereby minimizing the chance of the hook lodging itself in you or being struck by whatever else is on the line.

If you are using fluorocarbon, the stretch is a little less than monofilament, therefore the strike energy required is lower.
If you are using braid, your strike action is automatically converted to raising the rod sharply and reeling in rapidly until you feel the fish. The lack of stretch sets the barb! [significantly less strike energy required]
Get this: *if you were using circle hooks, you wouldn't need to strike! Just raise the rod, reeling in until you feel the fish.*

You will have to first consider the breaking strain of the line – this will determine how much of pressure you can put on the fish – the weaker the line, the less the pressure. But the converse is not true – if you put on too much of pressure, you may pull the hook free. You may also be using a small hook – too much pressure, and the hook straightens or pulls free. In striking, the rod is swept up and backwards and slightly to one side, in the opposite direction of the bite. Put the butt of the rod into the rod bucket or you will hurt yourself badly.
Remember that the fight is shared between the stretch of the line and the action of the rod. The fish will naturally do everything in its power to try and escape. Some fish will try and make for cover and try to break you off. Your advantage is that you know what type of bait you are using -
Now before you cast the bait out and ended up with this scenario, you would have [naturally] set the drag [assuming your reel has one]. This is your protection during the fight – if you put on too much pressure during the fight, the reel must protect you by releasing line, even while you are reeling in.

At <u>no point</u> during the fight should you tighten the drag to the extent that you run the risk of breaking your line. Your drag should release line even whilst you are reeling in, should the fish make a run. You must always be aware of how strong your line is, coupled with knowledge of how strong a mouth the fish you have on has.

Develop good habits – learn to pump and take the strain off the reel. This action must become automatic. Lower the rod, reeling in what you can whilst lowering, then stop reeling when the rod is as low as possible in front of you, raise the rod [without reeling], pulling the fish towards you. When you have raised the rod to its maximum, start reeling again, as you simultaneously lower the rod. This action must be repeated. Pull the rod back whilst not reeling, lower the rod, reeling rapidly and bringing the rod down as you reel in, pull, repeat… Avoid holding the rod upward and reeling in – this causes line to bite into the reel and this can reduce the efficiency and protection of your drag and will certainly compromise your next cast.
You slow down a run and turn the fish by applying strain. This is most effectively done by keeping the rod in as close to a vertical position as possible. If the fish turns left or right and there are no rods in the way, you can choose to 'walk' the fish or apply side strain – If the fish is running to your right, angle the rod to the left and try and hold it and force the fish to turn. The objective of these antics is to tire the fish as quickly as possible so it can be landed. Keep the line tight at all times – give no slack line. A prolonged fight will tire both you and the fish. You have to keep the pressure on and not give the fish a chance to recover.

Always use the water and never work against the water. If there are waves, use the forward momentum of the wave to bring the fish closer. When the wave recedes, hold the fish and allow some line to be stripped. Your drag will automatically compensate if the fish attempts a run whilst you are reeling in.

Should the fish go into a reed bed or become stuck, maintain strain until the fish gets out. You will sometimes lose fish like this, but having slack line is not a good idea.

You must continue until the fish tires – this will immediately be evident because the fish will swim on its side when tired. It is now safe to land the fish. At this point you are ready to take it out of the water. If using a landing net, hold the net static in the water *whilst bringing the fish to the net*. If someone is helping you to land the fish, make sure that they know this. Never allow the person to hold the line and ***never*** hold the line. That last dash that could cause you to lose the fish. Be prepared to release line if the fish does this.

If you resort to gaffing a fish, aim for the head, under the jaw. Do not lunge, and avoid the line. Stab the fish in the body only if you have to. Once gaffed, lift the fish as clear of the water as possible in one motion, to one side of you, with the stabbing action and get the fish away from the water. Only attempt to remove the hook once the fish is clear of the water. If the fish is actively trying to escape, flapping all over the place, cover the eyes with a damp cloth [this is when you will be glad that you are using a single hook].

Never bring the net to the fish. Any sudden movement or lunge will spook a fish. Always have the net ready, held in position and bring the fish to the net. If a gaff is to be used, the same principle applies – hold the gaff in the water, and bring the fish to the gaff. And be prepared, *all the time* for the fish to make sudden dashing runs even though it is tired. So, do not tighten your drag!

If you intend to return the fish to the waters, please ensure that you do the following:
- If you've used a gaff, you've missed the plot.
- Get the fish out as quickly as possible. *Remember the first time you over-exerted yourself and the resulting stiffness and soreness due to acid build-up in your muscles?* This happens to fish as well. *Fish are not likely to survive the pressure of an extended fight.*
- Make sure the landing net is clean and made from soft material. It is better if you do not use a net. Most fish can be 'tailed' [landed by holding the tail]. Some can also be lip-landed. Do not put your fingers into a fish's mouth if you are not sure of the species. If you are attempting to 'tail' a fish, make a fast, firm grab at the tail [not the fin!!! The body just before the fin.
- Be wary of toothy fish – you may be on the receiving end of a bacterial infection if bitten / scratched by teeth. You may also lose fingers.
- Make sure that your hands are wet – you are less likely to remove much protective slime from the fish with wet hands. *Slime protects the fish from parasites and bacteria.*
- Avoid handling the fish roughly on the soft underbelly as you may injure them.
- Fish dragged on sand, rocks or over the side of a boat are not likely to survive.
- Hooks do not ***have*** to be removed. Have you ever seen humans with piercings? *Fish can have them too!* If it is a problem to remove the hook [even with a disgorger] – don't. Cut the line off close to the hook [as close as possible], before releasing. The hook will corrode away with time. Stainless steel hooks take a lot longer to corrode, but they will corrode. Use a hook disgorger – this minimizes the handling time and allows you to focus more time on fishing.
- Fish that have been foul-hooked in the gills / gut should not be released unless they are prohibited species [*you are obliged to release prohibited species*]. Survival odds are poor.
- If it is a prohibited species or you have caught your daily limit, the fish *must* be returned regardless. If a bag limit is 4 fish, you don't have to take 4 if less will suffice.
- Fish brought up from very deep water will have high air pressure in their swim bladders [not present in all fish] this may manifest as one or more of the following:
    - Bulging eyes
    - Bloated belly
    - Bloated intestines showing through anus
    - Stomach protruding from the mouth

I have heard stories about returning them to the depth they were captured from but I just don't see any people practicing this. I once went on a boat in Port Elizabeth where the skipper just pierced

the side of the fish with a clean, sharp needle and then returned the fish to the water... I must investigate this further....
- I have seen fish being unceremoniously tossed back into the water. This is not a good idea as they could be stunned by the impact.
- And finally, don't just release the fish – revive it first by forcing water over its gills.

If you are keeping the fish, take adequate measures to ensure that it is safely stored. Also – put it out of its misery by striking it over the head just behind the eyes. It is also good practice to allow fish to bleed out. You can do this by making a cut through the lower part of the head from the gills towards the lower jaw where the heart is situated. Suspend the fish by the tail and allow to bleed out.

Chapter 22: Fly fishing

In my wanderings, I have only encountered one trout fishing venue that allowed the use of spinning reels for catching trout – that was the reservoir near Cape Town – I wonder if this still applies?

The sad perception that many people share is that when one speaks of 'fly fishing', one refers specifically to trout. Thank goodness for the media for helping to change this perception. In South Africa, trout is an alien species. It is far too late to reverse whatever damage has been done and the impact on our aquatic biodiversity. It is too late now to do anything about it – it has become a part of South Africa and we now live with it and enjoy the challenge of catching the species.

We must focus on conservation and do what we can when to ensure that all species of fish endure in our beautiful country – both the alien and indigenous.

Your Tackle 'Box'

- What fish are present in the area you will be visiting? [your tackle choices will need this as a decision rule]
- What rod/s will you require?
- Reel/s and line weight combination?
- Thermometer.
- Leader material.
- Tippet material. And extra tippets.
- Selection of flies – fly boxes. Also, a patch on your cap for sticking flies, allowing them to dry.
- I sometimes carry fly-tying equipment.
- Fly floatant and wetting agent.
- Will I need camouflage gear?
- Hat, hiking boots and glasses. The hat should have provision for holding flies while they dry.
- Waders.
- Gloves – protection from cold and spines. Buy the Kevlar gloves – a worthy investment!
- Lined track pants and a hooded top.
- Reading glasses / magnifying glass [because I sometimes battle with the lighter tippets under poor light conditions].
- Head lamp [no matter what].
- Superglue.
- Clipper, priest [to administer the coup' de grace], landing net.
- Scale to check if you've put on weight ☺.
- Longnose and normal pliers, cutters & hook disgorger.
- Hook sharpening stone.
- If you are taking fish home, how are you going to transport them?
- Sharp knife that stays on your person.
- Lanyards to hold thingies around your neck.
- Materials for strike indicators. You do know that I use a black marker – no kinks on *MY* line!
- Thermal blanket
- Kick boat / float tube and accessories including flippers and/or motor and battery [fully charged]
- Patches and adhesive for kick boat / float tube.
- Pump for inflating.com.
- Life jacket / pool noodle just in case!
- Rope & anchor.
- Emergency water and rations.

- Aquarium net, stomach pump.
- Whipping material for knots.
- Airtight & watertight bag / container to keep electronic devices in.
- Natural soap to be used as a wetting agent for flies and line intended to sink.
- Fish finder – not just to find fish, but to mark spots you intend returning to!
- Back packs and storage packs.
- Bait just in case your flies don't work. :D.
- Me [last resort].

In conventional fishing, a weight is used to cast the line out – in fly fishing, the line is the weight. Fly fishing, I have always said - is misnamed. It should really be called "Line Casting" because we actually cast out the line and the offering at the end of the line ends up in the water as a result. Fly line is much thicker than standard lines to add to the weight of the line so that it can be cast. [It is extremely difficult to use normal monofilament line [I know! The first time I went fishing with my friend and brother *Ilan Lax*, I didn't have tackle other than a 10foot [about 3m] Fenwick wood-stream slow action freshwater rod and a centre pin reel with 8pound [3.6kg] line. Fortunately, I had the wind blowing in my favour, and I actually managed to get the line out 4 – 8m! and for my troubles, I hooked, landed and took home a 2.55kg [5.62lb] brown trout!]

The rod.

Your selection of rod. As a guideline, the range of rods available for this sport extends from a 1 weight to a 16 weight. Try and avoid rods rated for more than two – line class weights – from my experience, these combinations compromise performance. If you have a split-cane rod, you own a formidable weapon. It is powerful with the action directly proportionate to the combination of thickness and taper. It requires real skill to handle and is much heavier than normal, newer fly rods. Personally, if I owned one, it would be well oiled and mounted on the wall as a trophy. *I* wouldn't use it.

You will notice that a typical fly rod has little or no butt. This design feature exists because a normal rod design would impede the necessary casting motions.

- 1 – 4weight would be used in small streams for small fish. Tippet should be stepped down to at least 4lb [1.8kg]. Yes, you can hook and land larger fish. Let me tell you three stories here – the first goes like this. I was fishing Gareth Olivier's farm dam in *Eston* when one of his friends / relatives arrived with a 1 weight rod. I had never fished one before and was delighted with the performance. I hooked into a 2.5 kg bass and the fight lasted more than 15 minutes. The fish was exhausted but I could not bag it as it had an old injury from an encounter with what must have been a king cormorant on its side. The wound had all but healed. Gareth's relative volunteered to revive the fish and did a pretty good job of it because five minutes later it vanished in a tremendous surge. Later that evening, as I made my way to my vehicle with my fine catch of tilapia, I saw a fish lying dead in the shallows. It was the same bass.... Under similar circumstances I hooked a yellowfish, this time with my very own 1-weight [acquired from Rochester Tackle in my hometown, Pietermaritzburg]. I had already caught my planned bag limit of 4 fish so I revived the 2kg yellow and allowed it to go, to live to fight another day. I was fishing at *Midmar* mouth and while paddling my kick boat out some 2 hours later, encountered the fish lying on its side, dead. I recognized the fish because it had one pectoral fin smaller than the other, a fact I had noted when I landed the fish some hours earlier.... The third experience was when I had flown to Botswana to fish the *Okavango Delta* at a lodge near *Maun International Airport*... I caught a 2kg Nembwe bream which fought as though possessed. When I landed the fish, it just lay on its side – I didn't even need a priest.... Anyway – I planned on only taking one fish, so I kept it and carried on fishing, landing another specimen just over 2 kg – the fight taking much more than 15 minutes with my 4pound leader.... And try as I might, I could not revive the fish – it just lay in the water, feebly mouthing in water on its side.... It was absolutely awesome – the fight was something else!!! Every time!!! But too much acid in the muscles after an extended fight.... Maybe some of you have experienced success stories with larger fish, but I am sure they are few and far between. Give it a thought....

- 5-weight - Tippet should be stepped down to at least 6lb [2.7kg]. – this is my rod of choice for trout and all freshwater – I caught an 8.1kg largemouth yellowfish in the Vaal river below the caravan park at the steel bridge in Vereeniging. I have caught carp, *mudsuckers*, trout, tilapia, bass, barbel and bluegill on fly with my trusty 5-weight.
- 6-8 weight. Rivers. Tippet should be stepped down to at least 8lb [3.6kg].
- Rods from 9-weight upward have what we called a 'fighting butt' which is a short, domed section extending from the rod blank, behind the reel mount. Tippet should be stepped down to at least 15lb [6.8kg]. 9-weight. Bass, barbel [catfish], light surf. I have caught dorado up to 8.5kg on my 9 weight.
- 10-13 weight. Tippet should be stepped down to at least 22lb [10kg]. Surf, gamefish, especially kingfish and Garrick, large bottom fish like grunter and Steenbras and species of rock cod.
- 14-16 weight. Tippet should be stepped down to at least 35lb [15.8kg]. Powerful rods. Offshore, barracuda, wahoo, prodigal son, sailfish, marlin. I have not tried this – I am not quite sure that it constitutes fly fishing – but who wouldn't want one of these fish at the end of their line, using a rod well capable of fighting these respected denizens of the deep blue yonder.
- **NOTE:** When selecting the final diameter of tippet, you step your line down to, **MAKE CERTAIN** that the line diameter you have selected will fit the hook you intend using. The smaller flies are much more effective. Much more successful. But smaller flies like sizes 16 to 20 require finer tippet material. NOW you're fishing! If you decide to use one piece of line as a leader / tippet combined, it will be difficult to do this with smaller flies – the line has to 'turn over' at the end of the cast. A stepped leader & tippet combination facilitates this 'turning over' process, giving the fly a very natural action.

Legend: Overhead view: "C" represents the end of the fly line. The broken lines represent the leader and tippet for two separate casts. If the fly lands at "A", it has not 'turned over' this mostly 'spooks' fish because the fly line impacts hard with the water. If it lands at "B", the line has 'turned over,' with the fly landing at the end of the cast, looking very natural ☺.

The reel.

You will find that the fly reel is basically for holding line. For reels used with rods up to 8 weight class, the arbor diameter is small so you will want to maximize on getting the most from these reels. Without tying your fly line to the reel, wind in the fly line and without joining it to the backing, reel in backing over the fly line to within 3mm of the reel rim. De-spool the backing onto another reel, remove the fly line from the reel and tie in the backing and reel in the backing, making sure that it is under tension and evenly spread on the reel. Tie the backing to the correct end [where applicable] of the fly line and reel in the fly line, spreading evenly on the reel, under tension. Tie in leader and required tippet lengths. Refer sketch below for recommended applicable knots.

Once you have maximized on the spool diameter [standard protocol for lines 9-weight and above], other reel features come into play when selecting a reel:
- Spool interchangeability– this feature is most essential. It allows you, at any stage to change line from floating to intermediate to sinking to a lower weight to a higher weight…. See? You don't have to change the reel – just the spool. Saving time.
- A ratchet system. Especially if you put your rod down – an audible alarm to make you drop your phone or the oars…. I love the sound of a screaming ratchet – who doesn't?
- An efficient, effective drag system. Disk drag systems improve with increased reel diameter, great for rods 9-weight and higher but will not work on smaller rods. This is essential when we are dealing with

powerful fish. But a well-timed palm and rod angle can easily compensate for the lack of a mechanical drag.

The Line.

Fly line differs from normal line in that it is much thicker in diameter and heavier than normal fishing line. It consists, generally, of a core which can be normal monofilament or fluorocarbon or braid, depending on the make and type. The core gives the fly line its rated strength. Wrapped around [well – not 'wrapped', but 'injected'] around the core is an artificial layer of special plastic which is treated, giving it properties that make it so slick that it slides *'frictionlessly'* through the line guides, [also properties to make it buoyant / intermediate / sinking]. When you buy fly line, you get between 23 and 27m [26 - 30yards] – there are longer lines for specialized distance casting. All fly line comes with a double taper [it is tapered at both ends because it has to slide through the line guides].

So, there you have it – fly line comes in three main classes

- **floating** [The entire line floats – when used in conjunction with a dry fly, both the fly and tippet must be treated with floatant] – avoid using fluorocarbon here – it is denser than water and will drag the fly down, beneath the surface. *I recommend this line for those starting out in this sport in the WF [weight forward] type.* Best used early mornings and late afternoons.
- **sinking** [There are various types of sinking lines. A normal sinking line will sink at various rated rates; the entire line sinks. Sinking line is categorized by the rate at which it sinks, normally in inches per second. It is best used in deep bodies of water during the day and is described in seven categories at which the various lines sink in inches per second, from category 1 which sinks at 1.5 – 2.5inches per second to category 7, which sinks at a rate of 7 – 8inches per second.

   A sink-tip line – only the tip sinks whilst the rest of the line floats.
- **intermediate**. These are present across the range of sizes of fly rods. These sizes ranged, the last time I checked, from size zero [super – ultra light] to size sixteen [extra-heavy]. Note that when the term 'buoyant' is used – this does not necessarily mean that the line floats. Some buoyant lines may be suspended in water. Best used early mornings and late afternoons and during the day.

Amongst the classes of line, you get the following basic line designs:

- DT – [Double taper] – If it were to be cut in half, both ends would be almost identical. This line can be reversed on the reel. This line allows for better, low splash presentations of the fly.
- WF [Weight forward] – If this line were to be cut in half, the majority of its mass would be in the front end ['the belly'] which is the only end that is designed to be used for a leader to be attached to. There are many variations to this and the other line classes. Investigate them all – new lines are being developed…This line gives you more power in the cast, enabling you to achieve bigger casts.
- D - Shooting head – designed for distance casting. Make sure that the entire shooting head is airborne or your cast will be compromised.
- Parallel – 'Level" lines. The entire line is the same diameter. This design only really exists to make fly line more affordable.

When you buy fly lines, make certain that you confirm that the line is suitable for the conditions in which you intend fishing, particularly for salt water applications. Whatever you decide to buy should be matched. As far as lines go, I have found that a lower rated line works better on a rod with a higher rating [up to two sizes bigger]. My 5-weight rod performs exemplarily with a 3weight line but avoid using a line that is heavier than the rod's rating [having said that I must say that I once fished my 8weight rod with 9 weight line, and it did perform well. I wouldn't recommend more than 2 sizes up or down. But things like this must be tried – and if you must try it, try it away from the water – until you are comfortable with it and you can see the advantages and disadvantages.

Now there is a basic rule that applies to combined leader and tippet size. In still water, use as long a leader as you can. The faster the movement of the water, the shorter your required leader/tippet combination. The main reason for this is simple – a short leader on calm water brings the splash of the fly line closer to the fly. So now you suddenly think – but a longer leader is going to be harder to get out with the required action and with the rod-reel-line combination – more than often, the impact of the fly on the water will be less if you use a lighter line on your rod – also, the impact of the lighter line on the water is significantly less.

Now consider this – you are using a 6-weight rod and 4 weight line. The rod is designed to cast a heavier line and, with a 6-weight line, it amounts to your casting limit of say 'x' meters. But a 4-weight line is lighter than a 6-weight line, so your casting limitation translates to a given mass of line that is airborne – you therefore increase your casting distance!!! Remember that the line thickness is smaller and therefore the wind-resistance [even in zero wind conditions] is less for a thinner line.

Heavier line with a lighter rod? Only where the swim is like 20m or less and there are snags present behind you. I really don't know why, but this is the only condition I have identified that supports the use of a heavier line / lighter rod combination. Not recommended for long casting unless you are using a fast sinking line.

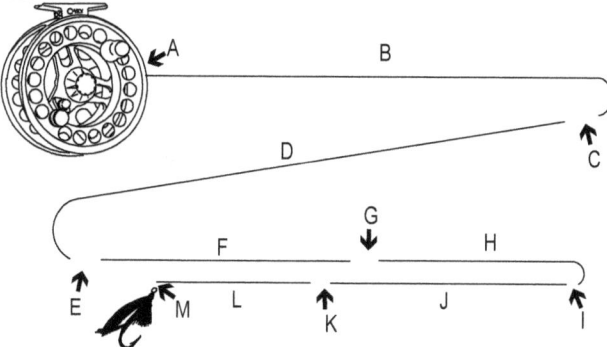

Legend: A: FAV knot, backing to reel; B: Backing – anything from 50m to 400m; C: Nail knot, Backing to Fly Line; D: Fly line; E: Nail knot, Fly line to Leader; F: Leader; G: Fav – FAV knot, Leader to Step 1 tippet;:; H: Step 1 Tippet; I: FAV – FAV knot, Step 1 & 2 tippets; J: Step 2 Tippet; K: FAV – FAV knot, Step 2 & 3 tippets; L: Step 3 Tippet; M: FAV knot, step 3 tippet to fly. Refer to Chapter 10 for a description of how to tie the knots you will need.

NOTE: *H, J and L can be substituted with a tapered tippet / leader. If D is substituted by a tapered leader, I always recommend that you tie on a tippet. Tapered leaders are available and rated as 0X; 1X; 2X; etc. The "?X" refers to the strength of the smallest part of the tapered line. I suggest you buy one size heavier than you need then you can add a weaker line [step] to the tapered leader, extending the life of the tapered leader.*

You will need long-shanked flies for toothy fish shad [razor tooth clan – includes barracuda, wahoo, queenfish and cape snoek] and tiger fish – the latter have formidable teeth capable of crushing line and causing it to break. The best wire leaders you get are made from a titanium – nickel alloy. Well worth the investment as it outlasts even stainless steel and is very flexible and can be reused and can be tied and is only kinked under exceptional circumstances. Some of us prefer to use a heavier line but this must be inspected on every cast as they get nicked by the razor tooth clan. Fish like salmon, Garrick and kingfish must be fished for with a heavier nylon / fluorocarbon leader.

Strike Indicators

Once you get your line in the water, how do you know if there was a strike? I do not advocate the concept of tying bite / strike indicators to your line.

For more than twenty years I have been marking my line with a black permanent marker. As soon as I cast, I dump any excess line into my stripping basket, keeping an eye on my markings which are made on the line before I arrive at the fishing grounds. There is no apparent damage / deterioration to my line which has always been *Airflo*.

This means that I can identify strikes irrespective of whether I am fishing dry, intermediate or bottom flies [provided, of course, that I avoid slack line....

How to cast.... My way

A. Please don't think that the further you cast, the better. You could easily be scaring off fish that are between you and where you are casting. Start close and work your way out. Especially when you have just arrived at the fishing grounds. Before you learn how to cast, remember that you must avoid hitting your rod with the fly as this will cause 'wind' knots or worse still, cause your rod to break. You therefore need to keep the path of the fly away from the rod by false-casting to the side or way above the rod. Also – don't be disappointed if your casting distance is not far enough. You had to learn to walk as a child, didn't you? You can improve your casting distance by finding your sweet spot – once you do, focus on it. There is a select handful out there who can cast the entire fly line and more.

B. Ok…. Don't worry about the 11h00 and 13h00 positions when casting…. Remember that a 'cast' is when your line actually hits the water – to achieve a cast, you make several 'false' casts – this allows you to progressively let out more line on each forward and backward false cast. You will soon learn your limits.

C. Safety first. Wear glasses and a hat. Make sure that your back cast are is clear and that no-one tries to walk behind you whilst casting. Always check for possible snags – this may include animals as well. You need wide open space, preferably grassed. You will need as much space in front of you as there is behind you.

D. My method for you to learn is unorthodox – but it hasn't failed.

E. Lay your rod flat on the ground with the line threaded through the guides and a 'stupaad' fly tied on [picture of 'stupaad' fly alongside; it is actually any fly with the entire hook bend cut off☺]. Pick up the fly and walk your line about 30 paces away from your rod. Lay fly on the ground. Please note that the 'stupaad' fly can actually hurt you ***so wear glasses and a hat and a jacket – and pay attention to wind direction and speed***. **Safety first!!**

F. Put on your stripping basket. Pick up the rod. DO NOT EVEN ***THINK*** OF TRYING TO CAST AT THIS STAGE. *RESIST* the temptation.

G. Retrieve your line by hand with 30 cm pulls directly into the stripping basket. You are preparing your line so that it will feed out naturally when you start casting. Stop when there is between 2 and 3metres of fly line beyond the last guide [if you leave too little line outside the last guide, it will slide down the rod, pulling the leader along with it, down into the line guides.

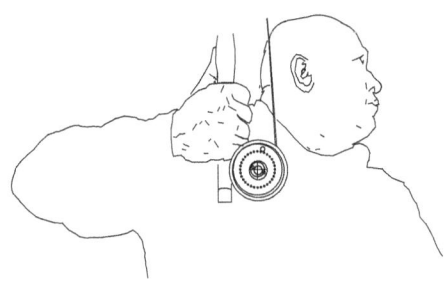

H. Hold the rod just above the reel, small finger riding against the top of the spool, acting as a break. You want to start off by stripping out some line so that the fly line extends at least 2m beyond the rod tip, making sure that you have clear space behind you so your line will not foul on objects behind you. Whilst you are learning, do not fasten a fly to the end of your line.

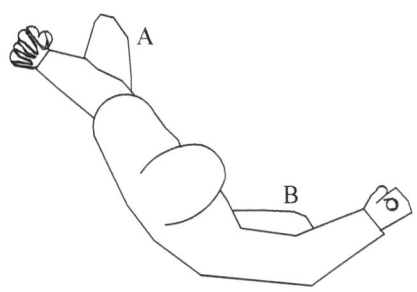

I. STANCE. Right-handed stand with "A" left leg forward, pointing in the direction of your intended cast, and "B" your right leg roughly one step behind perpendicular to the left foot – your body should be roughly at 45º so that you can turn and watch your back cast without falling over. At all times, your fist is kept at shoulder height holding the rod sticking vertically upwards.

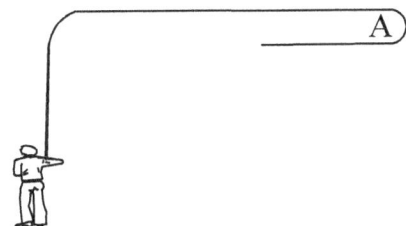

J. *[False cast to the rear – the line is streaming out – watch the bend ["A"] for the line to straighten out.]* Now hold the rod in a closed fist, in a vertical position with your fist at shoulder height, rod vertical, left hand holding the line at chest height. Start the first false cast by pulling your fist back until it is just behind your shoulder, preparing to throw a punch - swinging the line behind you in the process. Freeze in this position. Turn your head to look behind you at the line, releasing line but allowing it to slip through the fingers of your left hand – the trick is not to allow the line in the cast to start dropping before you begin the forward punch [swing].

K. *[False cast backwards – begin your forward false cast as the line straightens out ["B"] behind you.]* Now hold the line at chest height, and as the line straightens out behind you, haul the line sharply down [from chest height and ending just below your navel] at the same time, punch forward, keeping the rod in a vertical position, at shoulder height, now allowing the line to stream through your fingers. Watch the line, keep it horizontal.

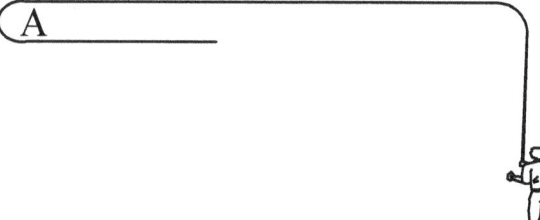

L. *[Forward false cast – as long as there is a bend in the line ["A"], it is still streaming out.]* At the end of your punch stroke, freeze, allowing the line to stream through your fingers, watching the line, and as it straightens out in front of you, haul the line sharply down with your left hand [from chest height and ending just below your navel] at the same time, pull your fist back, keeping the rod in a vertical position, at shoulder height, now allowing the line to stream through your fingers. Watch the line, keep it horizontal.

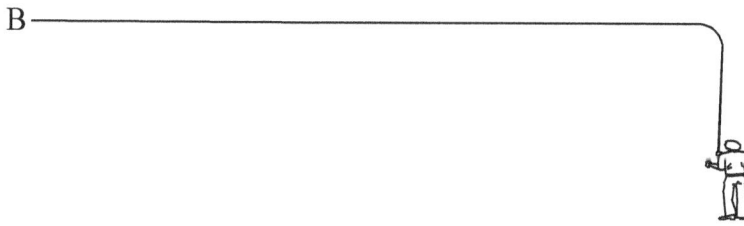

M. *[Forward false cast – the line has straightened out, begin your next false cast to the rear.]* Now hold the line at chest height [yes, your left hand], and as it straightens out behind you, haul the line sharply down [from chest height and ending just below your navel, always with your left hand] at the same time, punch forward, keeping the rod in a vertical position, at shoulder height, now allowing the line to stream through your fingers. Watch the line, keep it horizontal.

N. Repeat the process until all the line from the stripping basket is out and airborne. Now for the real cast, on the forward cast, bring your rod down, pointing in the direction you want it to land. The line should stream out in front of you, and if your technique is good, the leader and tippet should land **in front of the fly line**. [you should also practice allowing the line to settle behind you [backwards casting. This just means bringing the rod down in the final cast, behind you.]
O. You can continue practicing by retrieving line into the stripping basket....
P. Once you are comfortable with casting, from the stripping basket, you will find that it is quite easy to strip line off your reel – either incorporate it with each 'haul', or between hauls.
Q. If you are right handed:
    o Wind blowing from the left means you can fish facing the water and casting with the line to your right.
    o Wind from the right means that there is a risk of the line running into you. I would recommend that you cast backwards, keeping the line on your left where it cannot be blown into you.
    o Wind blowing in your face is the biggest challenge. Use a shooting head for this. Depending on the intensity of the wind, you can use a rod with line rated not more than two weights below the rod. The thinner line does not have as much wind resistance as the normal thicker line.

- A tailwind [wind blowing from behind you] is your best friend. Remember this is the best situation but don't make the mistake of trying to cast at maximum distance, using the wind. *WHY?* The fish know the direction of the wind and will be lying in wait for terrestrials to be blown into the water – so you may be casting too far when the fish are right in front of you!

Roll-casting

This technique is used mainly when you cannot false cast [due to obstacles behind you].

A. Safety first. Wear glasses and a hat on. Always.
B. You want to start off by stripping out some line so that the fly line extends at least 2m beyond the rod tip, making sure that you have clear space behind you so your line will not foul on objects behind you.
C. Stand with [right-handed] your left leg forward, pointing in the direction of your intended cast, and your right leg roughly one step behind with the right foot perpendicular to your left foot – your body should be roughly at 45° to your left foot so that you can turn and watch your back cast.
D. With your right index finger pointing down the length of the rod, bring the rod forward. The line should land in the water. Strip out a little more line, allowing it to slide through the eyes.
E. Now gently sweep the rod, tip down until the rod tip is over the water's edge.
F. Sharply raise the rod tip vertically to about shoulder height and rapidly execute a casting motion ending with the rod tip just below chest level, in front of you with right arm fully extended. The line should draw naturally out of the water and shoot out naturally.
G. Your casting distance is limited and this technique is only recommended when using floating line although it is quite possible to execute using intermediate and sinking lines.
H. ALWAYS control the outgoing line with your line hand – and yes, USE a stripping basket.

What species are you targeting?

For most freshwater fish, you will do well with a 4-weight – 8-weight rod. Remember, the larger the fly you use, the heavier the rating of the rod required. For barbel [catfish] and for bass, you will need a 9-weight rod as the flies are much larger. Make sure that you have at least 50m of backing and a good reel. The larger the diameter of the reel, the faster your retrieval rate when reeling in. For both bass and barbel you will easily get away with only floating and intermediate lines. Your tippet class should not be less than 4.54kg [about 10 pounds].

Tippets should be chosen according to the species currently on the go / targeted. Leader and tippets should not reflect sunlight as line-flash can and will scare off fish. Do not use fluorocarbon tippets for dry flies as this line is designed to sink as it is denser than water.

Always inspect the hook for sharpness before you tie it on. Test for sharpness. The smaller the fly you use, the greater your chances of a hook-up.

Here's the good news: you don't have to remember the names of the flies you use. What you need to know is what type of life-form you are attempting to simulate in order to get fish to accept your offering. So before you select a fly to tie onto your leader, it would be a good idea to look around and take note of the water-side environment. Please don't be alarmed. You do not have to learn zoological and botanical names – you just need to relate the appearance of any creature you wish to simulate back to a fly that best represents / resembles it. Take note of the terrestrial and aquatic life forms in the areas you are fishing… You can do this in many ways:
- ✓ Examine the surface of the water for floating evidence of a hatch – use binoculars if available.
- ✓ Look for flying and crawling insects – do not waste time with the brightly coloured life forms – these are generally poisonous or nasty-tasting.
- ✓ Pick up rocks and gravel that is just at the margin, in the water and look for life forms.
- ✓ If you are downwind, examine what has been washed up in the scum line and on the shore.
- ✓ Carry an aquarium net, you may find that there is shrimp in the water. Wade quietly in the shallows and have a look.
- ✓ Look for feeding fish and identify the different forms of 'takes' when they "swish" something off the surface. Each disturbance is a tell-tale sign of what trout and yellowfish are feeding on. If it makes a

"*gloop*" sound, it's a barbel taking a gulp of air; splashy rises means that there are large caddis flies on the go; if you see a typical ring rise, fish are feeding on mayflies or small caddis flies; violent splashes next to structure means that bass are feeding and it would be a good time to use poppers; a ring rise accompanied by a "sucking" noise indicates that some terrestrial insect / spider has been taken; If you see the fish's head followed by the tail ["*porpoising*"], the fish are feeding on sedge pupae or midges; if you see a rise with a trace of bubbles after the rise, nymphs are hatching and being taken; if you see a swirl, you have either scared off a fish or it is feeding on damselfly nymphs; and, carp jumping out of the water generally means that the carp are actively feeding below – they are merely jumping to clear their gills and mouth of mud / sharp objects / parasites. This gives you an idea of what fly to select.

- ✓ If you catch a fish, you must examine the stomach contents by using a pump [the typical orange rubber bulb with a long nozzle]. If the fish is not going to be returned to the water, administer the 'coup de grace' using a priest and cut it open and check the stomach contents. Remember that some of the contents may be partly [or more] digested so try and identify what you find in the stomach.
- ✓ If you catch some of the insects [don't go wildly chasing them using a butterfly net – you might scare the fish off!] you can attempt to tie a fly to mimic it. It doesn't have to be too neat – only humans are fussy about how well a fly is tied!
- ✓ Locals may also have an idea of what works in a particular stretch of water, and their advice may save you time but don't let this stop you from trying out patterns that resemble life forms you encounter at the water,
- ✓ Remember if you are using a floating / intermediate line and you want surface presentation of the fly, do not use fluorocarbon line for tippet as it will sink and probably cause the fly to sink as well.

Have you been underwater? Go on, put on a pair of goggles and put a well proofed fly on the surface. Now go underwater and look up at the fly. You can't really see it. All you see are the little prick marks from the surface tension where the fly is sitting on the water. Floating objects are hard to see [recognize], especially if they are sitting ON the surface film. Other submerged flies are quite recognizable when you look at them – but what happens when factors like clouding, dust, discolouration and depth come into play? Fish don't look for a perfectly dressed fly – the fly that you choose has to move like it is alive and resemble some food form. Except two other circumstances: the first is when the lure triggers an aggressive response – the fish simply strikes out of aggression [here it wouldn't matter what the fly / lure looks like], and when the feeding has become selective. When this happens, fish will touch nothing else and if they strike, then your offering looks like what they are selectively feeding on.

What I do is categorize flies by what they are designed to resemble. Once you know what life form you are imitating, you have the upper hand in that you know what action to use when retrieving your fly. I have categorized flies by the various groups of life forms they are meant to depict and included recommendations on the retrieval method that I have found to work. The fly that you choose should closely match what you actually find at the water. Be sure to coat dry flies with a floatant to assure buoyancy [**NB: a dry fly when fished as a dry fly should float on *TOP* of the water**]. If you are fishing just below the surface film, grease your line to within 150mm of the hook. Remember that if you are fishing a dry fly, never to use fluorocarbon tippet material. It is denser than water and will sink.

And if you think these flies are only for trout, think again. I have caught all the common species of fish on fly. Don't judge your anticipated catch by selecting larger hooks – you will find that the fly patterns incorporating smaller hooks can and do catch large fish. My first and largest trout was caught on a size 14 black tadpole whilst fishing with my friend and brother, *Ilan Lax* in one of the *Brown family dams* in *Nottingham Road*.

And remember – all dry fly patterns can and must be fished as wet flies too. When fishing a dry fly, the tippet should always be greased to within 150mm of the fly – do not use fluorocarbon tippets when fishing a dry fly. The fly should also be thoroughly treated with a floatant. Flies fished just below the surface film should only have the tippet greased to within 150mm of the fly with no waterproofing on the fly itself [if, however, the fly insists on sinking, especially during a slow, in-the-surface-film-retrieve, please waterproof the fly.

And don't pooh-pooh small hook flies – you will be surprised at how much more successful the smaller hooks are on light tackle!

Remember the bigger the barb on the hook, the harder you need to strike to set the hook [if you are using barbed hooks]. And the converse: use flies tied onto circle hooks – it will change your life – you just need to tighten your line! Rather go barbless – you won't regret it.

ANTS

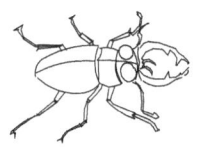

Trout; yellowfish; tilapia; barbel.

These insects sometimes land in the water. Generally static in water with small vibrations from wildly flailing legs. Use floating line, grease tippet to within 150mm of the fly. Fly must be waterproofed. Retrieval should be super slow with long static periods. Tap on your rod gently with your fingertips to generate some vibrations. Hook sizes 12 - 22.

The following flies can be used:
- ❖ *Black Ant [as per above paragraph].*
- ❖ *There are many small flies that can be used.*

ATTRACTOR PATTERNS [see General Attractor patterns below]

BEETLES

Trout; yellowfish; tilapia; Carp; bass; barbel [catfish].

These insects sometimes land in the water and generate some powerful vibrations with their wings. The legs also cause vibrations. Use floating line with a tippet that is greased to within 150mm of the tied fly [waterproof all flies unless pattern is being fished 'drowned' in which case an intermediate or slow sinking line should be used with a very slow retrieval]. Retrieval should be slow with some static periods [5 - 20 seconds] and should incorporate a slight jerky motion as well. Hook sizes 6, 8, 10, 12, 14, 16.

The following flies can be used:
- ❖ *DDD [Duckworth's Dargle Delight – dry fly, should be treated with a floatant as well];*
- ❖ *Black Phantom;*
- ❖ *Hamill's Killer;*
- ❖ *Black and Peacock spider;*
- ❖ *Orange fuzzy wuzzy;*
- ❖ *Coch-y-bonddoo [dry fly];*
- ❖ *Royal Coachman [dry fly];*
- ❖ *Chomper;*
- ❖ *Red-tag Palmer.*

BLOODWORM [BUZZER LARVAE]

All species.

The bloodworm is generally the midge larva. It propels itself with a lashing motion which is impossible to imitate. It is best fished right on the bottom with an extremely slow retrieve [10-25 minutes to retrieve the average cast]. Note that the bloodworm can sometimes be green in colour. Use sinking or intermediate line. Hook sizes 10, 12, 14, 16.

The following flies can be used:
- ❖ *San Juan Bloodworm fly [red / green];*
- ❖ *Digger's red;*
- ❖ *Red Nymph.*

BUTTERFLIES AND MOTHS

Trout; yellowfish; Carp; bass; barbel [catfish].

These insects sometimes land in the water. The powerful wings cause ripples around the creatures. Best used first thing in the morning. Use floating line with a tippet that is greased to within 150mm of the tied fly. Retrieval should be slow with you tapping on your rod with your fingertips during static periods [5 – 20 seconds] to transmit vibrations to the floating fly. Hook sizes 6, 8, 10, 12, 14.

The following flies can be used:
- *DDD [Duckworth's Dargle Delight – waterproof the fly thoroughly – use for sight fishing as well, casting no closer than 2m of the projected path of the fish].*
- *Soldier palmer pink [dry fly]*

BUZZER [see midge below]

CADDIS FLY

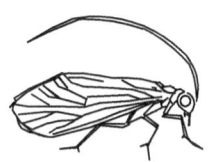

Trout; yellowfish; tilapia; Carp; bass; barbel [catfish], mudfish [strangely enough, most of the mudfish I have caught were foul-hooked!].
Use floating line with a greased leader [do not coat the last 150mm of the tippet]. If fished just sub-surface, retrieval is slow; if a dry fly is used, the fly must be coated with a floatant and should literally be skimmed across the surface with a fast strip action in the evening. Hook sizes 8 - 22.

The following flies can be used:
- *Goddard and Henry's Sedge [dry fly, floating line, greased tippet to within 150mm of the fly, fly well waterproofed, fished static, about 20 minutes per retrieve];*
- *Henryville special [dry fly];*
- *Highfield dun [dry fly];*
- *Greenwell's glory [dry fly]. Use the smaller flies in winter.*

CADDIS LARVA.

Trout; yellowfish; barbel [catfish]; carp; mudfish.
Use sinking or intermediate line. Hook sizes 10 - 22. Retrieval should be very slow.

The following flies can be used:
- *Zak nymph;*
- *Steve's olive caddis;*
- *Black and peacock spider;*
- *Steele's Taddy;*
- *Hot spot;*
- *Walker's Killer [sinking / intermediate line, slow retrieve with sudden darting movements of 50-75mm interspersed into the slow retrieve; The fly also works well fished just below the surface film using floating line with the tippet greased to within 150mm of the fly; an 'anytime' fly];*
- *Joe's hopper [dry fly fished as a wet fly].*

CADDIS NYMPH.

Trout, all species.

This creature mostly lives in a case made from pieces of reed or sand/rock fragments. It is slow moving. Use sinking or intermediate line. Fish right on the bottom, retrieval is very slow [5 – 10 minutes to retrieve a cast]. In a river / stream, allow to dead drift after casting upstream retrieve slowly. Hook sizes 10 - 22. The following flies can be used:
- *Gold ribbed hare's ear [GHRE];*
- *High country nymph;*
- *Peacock woolly worm*

CADDIS PUPA.

Yellowfish, trout, mudfish, barbel [catfish]

Pre-hatching pupa of the Caddis fly. This is the creature to simulate after sudden weather changes. Use sinking or intermediate line fished just under the surface film or up to 500mm below the surface. Works well in rivers and streams at the end of runs / pools – achieve this with a floating line, greased tippet, waterproofed fly on a well-mended drift and allow to reach the end of the pool. Retrieval should be very slow and static at times and must incorporate a short burst of speed [not more than 75mm] every 2-3m of line retrieved.

The fly can also be fished using a floating line and retrieved very slowly, just below the water surface – this technique can be complemented with a few *sink-and-draw* retrieves. In rivers and stream, cast into the current and dead-drift. Hook sizes 10 - 22.

The following flies can be used:
- *Walker's nymph;*
- *Gold-ribbed hare's ear [GHRE];*
- *Peacock woolly worm;*
- *Invicta;*
- *Red-tag Palmer*
- *Emerging nymph;*
- *Zak nymph;*
- *Charcoal nymph;*
- *Woolly bugger;*
- *Coch-y-bonddoo [dry / wet fly]*
- *Pearl Pushkin;*
- *Hot spot nymph*

CORYXID [see water boatman].

CRABS.

Yellowfish; barbel [catfish]; bass; trout.
Use sinking or intermediate line. Hook sizes 10, 12, 14, 16. Retrieval should be very slow with occasional short darting movements.

The following flies can be used:
- *Walker's Killer [sinking line retrieved slowly off the bottom, 15 – 20 minutes to retrieve a cast, an 'anytime' fly for all species]*
- *Crab imitation flies.*

CRICKETS

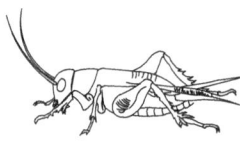
Trout; yellowfish; Carp; bass; barbel [catfish]. These insects sometimes land in the water. The powerful legs propel it forward for about 75mm.
Use floating line. Retrieval should consist of 75mm darting jerks and some static periods [5 – 20 seconds]. Can also be fished drowned using sinking line with a very slow retrieval rate. Hook sizes 8, 10, 12, 14, 16.

The following flies can be used:
- *Van's cricket;*
- *DDD [Duckworth's Dargle delight*

DRAGONFLIES AND DAMSELFLIES.

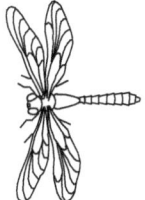 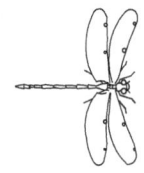

Trout; yellowfish; bass; barbel [catfish].
Use sinking or intermediate line. Hook sizes 10, 12, 14, 16. Retrieval should be slow and on the bottom.
The following flies can be used:
- *Peacock woolly worm;*
- *Charcoal nymph*

DRAGONFLY AND DAMSELFLY NYMPHS.

Trout, yellowfish

These are carnivorous slow moving, crawling aquatic insect larvae, living underwater and capable of short bursts of speed when feeding. Use fast sinking line. Retrieval should be very slow and static at times and must incorporate a short burst of speed [not more than 75mm] every 2-3m of line retrieved. Retrieval just below the surface film is fast [not two handed] with the fly being maintained just below the surface skin of the water. A fast sinking line can also be used along with 200mm retrieves whilst raising the rod tip and then allowing the fly to sink [sink & draw] – from time-to-time, use a fast strip retrieve – and hold on to your rod when you do! In rivers / streams, look for lies and cast upstream but never directly on the lie as you may spook fish that are facing upstream, waiting for *'yum yums'* [use an intermediate line]. Hook sizes 6, 8, 10, 12.

The following flies can be used:
For the Dragonfly nymph:
- *Mrs Simpson;*
- *Black Phantom;*
- *Hamill's Killer;*
- *TVN [a fly created by Theo van Niekerk];*
- *Parson's Glory [this should be described as a 'killer' pattern];*
- *Olive woolly bugger;*
- *Woolly bugger;*
- *Don's dragon;*
- *Dragonfly nymph;*
- *Viva Booby;*
- *Green mamba;*
- *Montana Nymph;*
- *Viva Tadpole;*
- *Woolly worm;*
- *Adolf;*
- *Orange fuzzy wuzzy*

For the Damselfly nymph:
- *Hamill's Killer;*
- *Parson's glory*
- *Green mamba;*
- *Walker's nymph;*
- *Montana nymph;*
- *Red-eyed damsel [near structure, reeds and weeds – just below the surface];*
- *Woolly bugger;*

❖ *Viva tadpole*

FISH.

Trout; yellowfish; bass; tigerfish; barbel [catfish]; African pike.

Little fish are seldom found in open water. They are generally in the shallows close to structure and reeds and make little darting movements. They are generally in groups, so I always use flies in tandem when simulating them. When tying on patterns simulating little *fishies*, always use a loop knot – this knot does not snug against the hook eye, but has a loop in which the hook sits. When you retrieve the fly, it has an articulated and more realistic action. Use intermediate or floating line with darting strip retrieves and short static periods – remember – little fish are not found in open water, so use it close to structure, weeds and reeds. Remember that any fish feeding on fry will find something that looks injured much easier to eat, so sometimes a slow, erratic retrieve is worth practicing. Hook sizes 6, 8, 10, 12, 14, 16. The following flies can be used:

❖ *Walker's Killer [sinking / intermediate line, slow retrieve with sudden darting movements of 50-75mm interspersed into the slow retrieve; The fly also works well fished just below the surface film using floating line with the tippet greased to within 150mm of the fly; an 'anytime' fly. All species of fish, particularly yellowfish];*

❖ *Zonker Killer [sinking / intermediate line, slow retrieve with sudden darting movements of 50-75mm interspersed into the slow retrieve; The fly also works well fished just below the surface film using floating line with the tippet greased to within 150mm of the fly; an 'anytime' fly. All species of fish, particularly barbel and yellowfish];*

❖ *Mrs Simpson [sinking / intermediate line, slow retrieve with sudden darting movements of 50-75mm interspersed into the slow retrieve; The fly also works well fished with a slow darting retrieve just below the surface film using floating line with the tippet greased to within 150mm of the fly; an 'anytime' fly. All species of fish, particularly bass & yellowfish];*

❖ *Dullstroom Orange;*
❖ *Green mamba;*
❖ *Woolly bugger;*
❖ *Vleikurper;*
❖ *Pink Panther;*
❖ *Viva Booby;*
❖ *Silver darter;*
❖ *Adolf;*
❖ *Black Phantom;*
❖ *Catlet Muddler;*
❖ *Viva Tadpole;*
❖ *Teal and Red;*
❖ *Parson's Glory;*
❖ *Machadodorp;*
❖ *Clouser minnow;*
❖ *Jersey herd.*

FISH EGGS.

All species.

Trout attempt to spawn during the winter months in dams but fail because they need strong currents over a gravel bottom to succeed at this. They drop their eggs in winter in still water gravelly environments. Fast sinking line with the fly on the bottom. The colour is critical and the fly should be fished static and retrieve extremely slowly [15 – 25 minutes per cast]. Hook sizes 10 – 22. The following patterns can be used:

❖ *Egg Booby;*
❖ *Red setter;*
❖ *Marabou whiskey;*
❖ *Adolf;*

- ❖ *Pink Panther;*
- ❖ *Dullstroom Orange.*

FLIES [TWO-WINGED].

All species.
Flies are most frequently found in spring through to early autumn. They sometimes land on the water [alive or dead] and are trapped by the surface tension. When this happens, and if there are no rises at the time, these beauties can entice fish to feed. Use floating line, ensure that the tippet is greased to within 150mm of the fly. Render the fly waterproof using a floatant. Use in summer on overcast days and hot evenings. Hook sizes 8 - 22. Retrieval should be in the form of a re-cast. Normally roll-casting. Tap at the rod with your fingers to send vibrations running to the floating fly from time to time.

The following flies can be used:
- ❖ *Blue dun;*
- ❖ *Black gnat [note that all imitation of this species can also be fished wet, allowed to be static and retrieved slowly using intermediate line]*

FLYING ANTS.

All species.
These insects come out in hordes on hot summer evenings and just after a storm – they land on the water and the fish go crazy – it is essential that you make the most of it as soon as the flying ants emerge as the fish will get extremely selective and ignore your presented fly if you are too late. Use floating line with a tippet that has been greased to within 150mm of the fly. Hook sizes 8, 10, 12, 14, 16. Retrieval should be in the form of a re-cast. Normally roll-casting. Tap at the rod with your fingers to send vibrations running to the floating fly whenever static.

The following flies can be used:
- ❖ *Flying ant [dry fly, should be treated with a floatant as well]*

FROGS.

Trout; yellowfish; bass; barbel [catfish].
Use sinking or intermediate line. Hook sizes 10, 12, 14, 16. Retrieval should be about a 75mm strip retrieve whilst 'snapping' the wrist.

The following flies can be used:
Frog imitations, streamers

GENERAL ATTRACTOR PATTERNS.

Trout, bass, yellowfish.

These patterns may incorporate basic characteristics exhibited by several creatures but really resembles no actual living form. They are used to induce an aggressive take as they are perceived as intruders.

Having said this, sometimes, a fish will take one of these patterns simply because it is hungry. Use intermediate or sinking line with darting retrieves and short static periods – you may also elect to allow the fly to sink progressively deeper each time, and retrieve it using a figure of eight retrieval method. These flies should be cast over an area repetitively as they are designed to produce an aggressive response from fish encountering them. When repeating casts, fish progressively deeper with each cast. Hook sizes 6, 8, 10, 12, 14, 16. The following flies can be used:

- ❖ *Walker's Killer [sinking / intermediate line, slow retrieve with sudden darting movements of 50-75mm interspersed into the slow retrieve; an 'anytime' fly];*
- ❖ *Viva Tadpole;*
- ❖ *Woolly bugger;*
- ❖ *Orange fuzzy wuzzy;*
- ❖ *Pink Panther;*

- *Adolf;*
- *Sunset;*
- *Red-tag Palmer;*
- *Dullstroom Orange;*
- *Viva Booby;*
- *Red setter;*
- *Teal and Red;*
- *Montana nymph*
- *Catlet Muddler*
- *Royal coachman [dry fly]*
- *Jersey Herd*

GRASSHOPPERS.

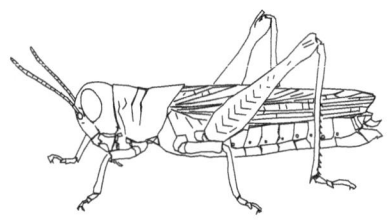

Trout; yellowfish; Carp; bass; barbel [catfish].

These insects sometimes land in the water. Observe a grasshopper in the water and copy the movement. The powerful legs propel it forward for 75-150mm. You will also note that it attempts sometimes to fly whilst in the water, causing powerful ripples. Use floating line with a tippet greased to within 150mm of the fly – remember to waterproof the fly. Retrieval should consist of 75-150mm darting jerks and some static periods [5 – 20 seconds]. To copy the ripples from the wings, tap on your rod using your fingers whilst static.

Note that all these patterns can also be fished wet using a sinking line with a short tippet. This appears as though the insect has drowned. Fish static with very slow retrieve, making it sem like some current is moving the fly.

Hook sizes 6, 8, 10, 12, 14, 16 – you will be surprised to find out that no pattern is too big to fish.

The following flies can be used:
- *Mrs Simpson [waterproofed];*
- *Joe's hopper [dry fly];*
- *DDD [Duckworth's Dargle Delight, dry fly];*
- *Muddler minnow [dry fly]*

HOPPER [see 'grasshopper' above]

LEECHES

Trout, barbel [catfish], yellowfish.

I have only had success in early spring when there are not many other food forms and the trout resort to feeding on leeches. Use sinking or intermediate line. Retrieval is super slow. Hook sizes 10 - 22. The following flies can be used:
- *Viva tadpole*

LIZARDS

Trout, bass.

These creatures sometimes land in the water. They have spurts of frantic 'running on the water' dashes and quiet spells. Copy the movement. The powerful legs propel it forward for 75-150mm. Use floating line. Retrieval should consist of 75-150mm darting jerks and some static periods [5 – 20 seconds]. Hook sizes 6, 8, 10, 12, 14, 16. The following flies can be used, well-greased:
- Lizard fly
- Dragon patterns
- Streamer pattern, greased

MAYFLIES

Trout, all species.

Always try and identify whether the mayflies that are hatching are dark or light winged – this will ensure your success. If you have no means of doing this during an active hatch, try each one over several casts. Use floating line with a tippet that is greased to within 150mm of the fly. Fish the fly just under the surface film with a steady figure of 8 retrieve. You may also use a fast sinking line with a slow strip retrieve method in deeper waters. Hook sizes 8 - 22.

The following flies can be used:
- *RAB [red-arsed bastard – dry fly]*
- *DDD [Duckworth's Dargle Delight – dry fly, should be waterproofed for floating line and allowed to sink for sinking line presentations];*
- *Walker's nymph;*
- *Red-tag Palmer;*
- *Machadodorp;*
- *Mooi moth – [dry fly, spring through summer, fish over channels];*
- *Henryville special [dry fly, should be treated with floatant as well];*
- *Emerging nymph;*
- *Coch-y-bonddoo;*
- *Pheasant tailed nymph;*
- *Blue dun [can be fished wet or dry – if fished dry, tippet should be coated with a floatant grease to within 150mm of the fly. Fly should also be treated with floatant and used during misty weather];*
- *Soldier palmer spinner [dry fly] – warm months only*
- *Sherry spinner [dry fly]*
- *Black gnat [can be fished wet or dry – if fished dry, tippet should be coated with a floatant grease to within 150mm of the fly. Fly should also be treated with floatant and used during misty weather];*
- *Greenwell's glory [can be fished wet or dry – if fished dry, tippet should be coated with a floatant grease to within 150mm of the fly. Fly should also be treated with floatant].*

NYMPHS

Trout; yellowfish; tilapia; Carp; bass; barbel [catfish].

These are crawling aquatic insect larvae, living underwater, but are capable of shorty bursts of speed when feeding. Use sinking or intermediate line. Retrieval should be very slow and static at times and must incorporate a short burst of speed [not more than 75mm] every 2-3m of line retrieved. When fished with a floating line, it should be fished slowly, just below the surface film. In a stream / river, cast upstream using the beaded version and dead drift the fly down the current at the same speed as the current. Hook sizes 8 - 22.

The following flies can be used:
- *Gold-ribbed hare's ear [GHRE];*
- *Zak nymph;*
- *Ammonite nymph*
- *Pheasant tail nymph [PTN]*
- *Charcoal nymph;*
- *Walker's nymph;*
- *Dragonfly nymph;*
- *High country nymph;*
- *Emerging nymph;*

- *Orange and black nobblers [dog];*
- *Strip dragon and nymph;*
- *Coch-y-bonddoo;*
- *Pheasant tailed nymph;*
- *Hot spot nymph;*
- *Montana nymph;*
- *Leptophleba nymph*

MIDGE LARVA. [see 'bloodworm' above]

MIDGE PUPA. [Buzzer]

Trout.

This form of the midge's life-cycle, after the bloodworm stage, is most commonly located just below the surface. Use a floating line. Retrieval is slow but keep the fly just below the surface film – start retrieving the line as soon as the cast is complete. Hook sizes 6 - 22. The best time to use this type of fly would be at the end of the day when the hatch volume is at its largest.

The following flies can be used:
- *Claret buzzer*
- *Midge pupa fly*
- *Black fly patterns*
- *Hot spot*
- *PTN*

MOLLUSCS.

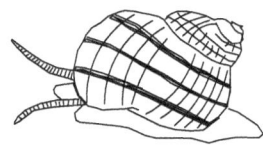

Trout, yellowfish, barbel [catfish].

Snails are slow moving creatures that live mainly at the bottom of rivers and dams. They also sometimes migrate to the surface and become stuck in the scum-line. Use sinking or intermediate line. Hook sizes 12, 14, 16. Retrieval should be extremely slow [10-15minutes per cast] when fishing on the bottom. When fishing the surface film, fly must be static and suspended in the scum- line using floating line.

The following flies can be used:
- *Orange fuzzy wuzzy;*
- *Black and peacock spider*
- *DDD [Duckworth's Dargle delight – do not waterproof – ensure leader is greased to within 150mm of the fly and fish the fly just below the surface film – retrieve should be up to 15 minutes per cast]*

MOUSE.

Bass, barbel, large yellowfish.

Use floating line AFTM 8 / 9. Hook sizes 1, 2, 1/0, 2/0. Retrieval should be smooth whilst vibrating the rod tip with your fingers to simulate a swimming mouse. To use the popping action, jerk the retrieve at the end until the mouse action is just audible. The following flies can be used:
- *Mouse fly,*
- *Waterdog,*
- *Dahlberg diver.*

MOTHS [see butterflies above]

SEDGE [see caddis above]

SHRIMP.

Classified as a super bait – appeals to all types of fish.
Shrimp live on the bottom in colonies. They walk forward when trying to find titbits to eat but will rocket off backwards when alarmed. Use sinking or intermediate line in still water. Hook sizes 10, 12, 14, 16. Retrieval should be based on the orientation of the shrimp pattern on the hook. If the shrimp pattern is tied so that the head is facing the eye of the hook, retrieval should be a creeping movement, inching in slowly, taking 5-10 minutes before it is necessary to re-cast. If the head faces away from the eye of the hook, you may use a darting motion with flicks of the wrist creating the motion, taking in 75mm of line at a time.

The following flies can be used:
❖ Shrimp imitation flies

SNAILS. [refer MOLLUSCS] above.

SPIDERS.

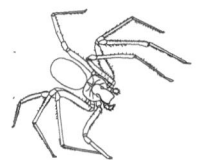

Trout, bass.
Use sinking or intermediate line. Hook sizes 10, 12, 14, 16. Retrieval should be static with periodic slow, twitching strip retrieves.

The following flies can be used:
❖ *Daddy-long-legs [dry fly, grease tippet line to within 150mm of the fly, and waterproof fly well, retrieve to skim slowly over the water, all year round];*
❖ *Black and peacock spider*
❖ *Spider fly*

STONEFLY NYMPHS

Trout.
The third creature in the illustration is an actual depiction of a stonefly nymph. These are crawling aquatic insect larvae, living underwater, but are capable of shorty bursts of speed when feeding. Use sinking or intermediate line. Retrieval should be very slow and static at times and should incorporate a short burst of speed [not more than 75mm] every 2-3m of line retrieved. Hook sizes 10 - 22.

The following flies can be used:
❖ *Peacock woolly worm*
❖ *Stonefly patterns*

TADPOLES.

Trout; yellowfish; bass; barbel [catfish].
Normal tadpoles from all swimming frogs [excluding those of the toad family] remain still for long periods of time, moving once every 15 or so seconds in short bursts unless they are trying to escape being caught. Use sinking or intermediate line. Hook sizes 8, 10, 12, 14, 16. Retrieval should be in short 7.5 cm bursts at the bottom of the swim, then remaining static for 15-30 seconds.

The following flies can be used to imitate tadpoles:
- *Viva Tadpole;*
- *Black Tadpole;*
- *Steele's Taddy;*
- *Black and Peacock Spider.*

WATER BOATMAN [Coryxids]

Trout.
Use intermediate line. Retrieval should incorporate a 'dash' of 10-20 cm and then a static period of say 2 - 3 seconds close to the bottom. Best time is first thing on clear crisp mornings Hook sizes 10 - 22.

The following flies can be used:
- *Silver coryxid;*
- *Olive corixid;*
- *Chomper;*
- *Brown chomper;*
- *Coch-y-bonddoo [dry fly].*

WORMS

All species.

The bloodworm is generally the midge larva. It propels itself with a lashing motion which is impossible to imitate. It is best fished right on the bottom with an extremely slow retrieve [25 minutes to retrieve a full cast]. Note that the bloodworm can sometimes be green in colour. Use sinking or intermediate line. Hook sizes 10, 12, 14, 16. The following flies can be used:
- *Bloodworm fly [red / green];*
- *San Juan bloodworm*

Tigerfish and African pike

100mm steel leader attached to your fly. Make sure hooks are sharp – any fish pattern will work, particularly streamers, deceivers, *clouser* minnows, thumpers.

These fish literally fight to the death. I haven't been able to revive many of them.

Retrieve should be as small fish – small jigging motions – wrap some lead core around the bend of the hook if the fly is not weighted enough to emulate this motion.

SALTWATER FLY FISHING

For saltwater fishing, particularly in lagoons and bays, most of your freshwater flies will work with the same retrievals. You need to bear in mind though that the hooks need to be stronger as saltwater fish are, pound for pound, much more powerful than freshwater fish.

Saltwater flies are made up using stronger hooks that are also resistant to the highly corrosive saline environment, so it will make use of the galvanized and stainless hooks.

Bear in mind that you need to simulate the action of the typical creatures that live in the marine environment. Most flies resemble small fish or squid and need to have the characteristic faster action that can only be achieved with a two-handed retrieval. These flies are seldom fished static. First prize goes to simulating the movement of injured creatures. The only exception is the popper which is fished using a fast, jerking retrieval with scattered pauses. The popper is supposed to resemble baitfish that are escaping from bigger fish.

The slower-moving flies are your crab and shrimp family imitations. These are generally fished on the bottom with the current doing most of the work.

Crabs

[bonefish, kob, mullet, perch, oxeye tarpon, wave garrick]

- Crab imitations
- Sand Crab
- Walker's Crab

Fish & Fry imitations

[all saltwater – barracuda, bonefish, bonito, cobia, kingfish, kob, marlin, mullet, perch, pompano, queenfish, rockcod, sailfish, shad, snappers, snoek, springers, tarpon [oxeye], tuna, wahoo, yellowtail]

- Blonde
- Boobies
- Chartreuse
- Clouser's minnow
- Crazy Charlie
- Deceivers
- Flipper
- Glass minnow
- Gotcha
- Gurgler patterns
- Irish blonde
- Moonfly
- Natal halfbeak
- Poppers
- Red Knight
- Ribbonfish
- Salty bugger
- Streamers
- Surf candy
- White death

General attractor patterns [all saltwater]

- Deceivers
- Minnow patterns
- Rainbow minnow
- Rainbow Mohawk

Molluscs

[all saltwater – jobfish, musselcracker, pompano, rockcod]

- Crazy Charlie
- Freshwater snail fly, weighted
- Periwinkle
- Shrimp & prawn imitations

Squid & Cuttlefish

[all saltwater, barracuda, bonito, couta, dorado, jobfish, kingfish, marlin, sailfish, snoek, tuna, wahoo, yellowtail]

- Streamers and squid imitation flies

Prawn

[all saltwater - bonefish, jobfish, kingfish, musselcracker, perch, pompano, rock cod]
- Deceivers including Lefty's deceiver
- Shrimp & prawn imitations

Worm flies

[all estuarine and saltwater - sandbanks, mud banks – all saltwater – grunter, musselcracker, perch, pompano, snapper]

Use Leech imitations, Red Knight, San Juan Worm, Shimmy Leech.

Chapter 23: Fishing from a float tube / kick boat

- If crocs or hippos are resident in the water, do not use your floatation device. If you are afraid of snakes, remember that you are in their natural habitat – they will assume that you are a safe perch. And if you are in a lagoon, there is always the possibility that you may encounter a shark or four.
- Life jackets can be bulky and cumbersome – carry a pool noodle and link it to yourself with a lifeline – it can easily be trailed alongside.
- If you use a kick boat, carry a knife because your feet could easily become entangled and you will then need to cut yourself free. The knife should have a life line as wet hands are slippery.
- If you are using flippers, make sure that they fit properly – they should not slip off your feet. They should also not be too tight. And if they don't float, don't buy them. If you are using a battery-operated motor, make sure that the battery is fully charged. And do carry flippers / at least one oar.
- I am against float-tubes – to me the two main disadvantages are very significant. The first is that you are a much smaller visual target; you are immersed in the water and are exposed to greater core temperature heat loss; and I don't like them… someone needs to design a cycle-operated propelling device for a kick boat.
- You may need to anchor yourself in certain areas – carry a suitable length of rope with a suitable weight attached and remember that you may sometimes need to cut the anchor line.
- You are limited to what can be carried on a kick boat. What you should be carrying:

  - ✓ Spare tippets / trace line
  - ✓ Hook disgorger
  - ✓ Forceps scale
  - ✓ Line cutter attached to fishing vest by a lifeline
  - ✓ Knife
  - ✓ Floating fly / lure / bait boxes; hooks
  - ✓ Sunblock
  - ✓ Short handled landing net
  - ✓ Rope with rock for anchor
  - ✓ Spare spools with sinking and intermediate lines
  - ✓ Spare rod
  - ✓ Reel with floating line
  - ✓ Stomach pump for checking what fish are feeding on
  - ✓ Soft bag keep net
  - ✓ Water or fluids to rehydrate, salt tablets for cramping
  - ✓ Something to nibble on
  - ✓ If you are carrying a phone, a waterproof bag to keep it in
  - ✓ A priest to administer the last rites
  - ✓ Fine sharpening stone for hooks
  - ✓ An oar strapped to the pontoon

- Don't make noise - sound is transmitted very effectively in water and you can easily spook fish.
- You don't have to cast that often – troll your lures / baits – you will cover much more water this way. You will have to use only lures that can be fished at the speeds you can troll, and remember, trolling is frowned upon if you are fly fishing – *although technically, as long as you are moving, you are always trolling*.
- For lures that need to be fished at faster speeds, you can cast and do this on the move.
- If you are using small fish live bait, you will need to hook the fish through the upper lip.
- In cold water your retrieves will have to be slow – very few fish are going to expend energy chasing down a fast-moving lure / bait. Retrieve slowly. Fish are cold-blooded and their activity is directly proportionate

to water temperature and are less likely to hit a fast-moving bait. Strike whenever you fell a bump. You will need to fish deeper in cold water.
- Be patient.
- You are going to spend some time on the water – make sure that you are protected against the elements.
- You can use a fish finder from a kick boat.
- You can work your way through reed-beds – just make sure that nothing is dangling from you or the kick-boat. When in heavy reed, your flippers should be operated on the water – use an oar in situations where it becomes difficult to use your flippers.

Chapter 24: Boat fishing

This Chapter is not designed to represent the skipper's ticket *body of knowledge*. I have just put together points that I have learnt over the years that can and will benefit you and your fishing whether you own your own boat, are a guest on one, or have chartered one.

Notes:
- The skipper's ticket is as necessary to boating as learning to cast is necessary to fishing. Respect it and make sure that whoever is captaining the boat is suitably qualified and experienced. And you are right – *he/she shouldn't really be drinking.*
- I suppose the first point – whether it is freshwater or saltwater - is motion-sickness, better known as sea-sickness. Please trust me when I say that this is all in the mind – read my stories. But if you must, take the meds – just remember that they do make you drowsy and are by no means a preventative measure. *Make sure that you get good rest the night before and avoid alcohol the night before too.* I once went on a charter with someone who offered to buy the boat in order to get back to *terra firma*. And if someone is sea sick, don't allow them to lie on deck – they must be in a safe area whenever they are horizontal and not feeding fish [yes, that means vomiting!]. People prone to sea sickness should not sit or be at the back of the boat where the exhaust fumes will only exacerbate their condition.
- If you are prone to sea sickness, keep your eyes on the horizon and do not focus too much on the motion of the boat – excitement can and does eliminate sea-sickness.
- It is less likely for people to get sea sick on trolling charters – you pay a little more, but the boat is continually on the move.
- When you make the booking – enquire as to what services are provided, whether you are allowed to keep the fish, that the craft is safety-compliant, whether you can take your own tackle [I always take my own]. Check how many other boats are going out. If it is a surf launch – make sure that your captain is very experienced. Is trolling going to be done – is it a trolling charter, a bottom-fishing charter or a mixture of the two?
- Make sure that you know whether there are meals and [at least] non-alcoholic drinks provided. And water. In many cases, you must provide your own meals and drinks
- If the charter takes 8 – try and pay for 8 but go with a smaller group – you will be happy with the resultant extra space.
- What baits will be provided? You may elect to carry other baits or to pay a little extra if the captain is to provide additional bait. You may need raincoats. Don't forget hats, sunglasses and sunscreen. If you are on a deep-sea boat, take some fresh crab bait – and sardines are a must. It can be miserable out there if you are wet and cold.
- Is there a gaff and/or landing net provided?
- Electronic equipment should be stowed in the cabin with the skipper/captain. No valuables in top pockets – if you bend over, they will fall out of your pocket. Licenses and valuables should be in a plastic bag and stowed safely and securely.
- In freshwater avoid going over the areas you intend to fish – you will almost certainly scare off fish. And never pass an inlet without stopping before it and working it.
- Respect *no-wake zones* – these zones also actually protect your boat as well as the surrounding flora and fauna, and other people around.
- Make sure that someone is provided to assist you and your group with tracing-up and baiting up and everything_else.com.
- It doesn't matter what the reputation of the area you are boating in is – no area produces fish all the time - and inasmuch as it could be the trip where you catch the dream fish, its more than likely that you won't. Don't rate the chances of catching fish with the amount of money you pay.

- If the boat has a fish finder and you plan on going after game fish, enquire whether the fish finder has *side-scanning* capabilities – this increases your chances of catching.
- Please discourage excessive consumption of alcohol on the boat. It is NEVER a good idea. Some people should not be allowed to drink – alcohol is renowned for its ability to change a person entirely [Dr Jekyll / Mr Hyde] – many trips have been ruined because some idiot can't hold his liquor.
- If you are trolling, listen to the captain and/or his assistant. Strike drift baits or lures when told to do so – premature strikes mean lost fish.
- When the boat is under way, no-one should be handling hooks or tying traces. All rods should be stowed with the hooks and sinkers secured. A swinging hook / sinker is dangerous.
- Listen to advice from the crew and locals. Everyone is not out to con you – besides, these guys make a living from what they do.
- You should have done research on the area and should know in advance what weather conditions are forecast and the fish that are in season and/or on the bite and the activities that are prohibited.
- Carry a glove so that you can hold fish without having to be too wary of spines / scalpels. And gill-rakers that can rip your fingers.
- If crocs or hippos are resident in the water, boating can be very dangerous.
- Life jackets can be bulky and cumbersome but are necessary.
- You may need to anchor yourself in certain areas – carry a suitable length of rope with a suitable weight attached and remember that you may sometimes need to cut the anchor line.
- When you are fishing, the deck should be clear – cooler-boxes and bags should not be in the way.
- Avoid fishing alongside the anchor rope / chain.
- If there are shark around, get the fish out as quickly as possible. Shark will prey on a hooked fish – it is easier game for them.
- If you get caught up on the reef, call for assistance – spinning Scarborough handles can break fingers and damage hands or knees. Loose clothing can get caught up in a rapidly spinning reel.
- If the line gets caught between the reel and frame. Hold the reel and call for help. Avoid trying to undo this type of tangle – you could get seriously hurt or you will make the problem worse.
- Be careful when handling fish – most of them have teeth, *and they know how to use them*. Carry and use a disgorger or pliers.
- Sea barbels are great eating, but one prick from the three poisonous spines will require medical attention.
- Don't risk safety by trying to get the hook out of the mouths of barracuda, 'couta or shark. Cut off and re-tie your traces.
- Fish caught should not be thrown on deck. They have teeth and spines… they should go straight into containers or fish holds. Avoid free standing on deck as far as possible.
- When the boat is moving, pull your butt onto the seat. It is very easy to become airborne or lose your balance on a moving boat. Also remember that sharks have been conditioned to look out for fishing boats – they get free meals. If someone falls aboard, bait and blood residue on their hands…do the math!
- Carry rags to wipe your hands with after baiting up / tracing up.
- When you let your line down, allow the reel to spin but not to free-wheel too fast. You will feel a bump when your sinker hits the bottom. Immediately you feel this, tighten your line – you will only catch if you keep your line on the bottom *and maintain a tight line*. Remember that the boat will drift – make sure that you let out line slowly to stay on the bottom. Keep the tip down – when you feel the bite, raise the rod sharply whilst reeling fast. If you hook a fish, the barb will hold – you can either reel up or let your line back down if you have more than one hook.
- I mostly fish two hooks, sometimes just one – and I still manage to catch more fish than most.
- It is always practical to anchor a boat fore- and aft- in flatwater conditions.
- Avoid fishing more than 4 hooks, and the bottom hook should be a 'biggie' for musselcracker or rock cod.
- Don't make noise - sound is transmitted very effectively in water and you can easily spook fish, particularly in fresh water and lagoons.

- If you are using live bait, you will need to hook the fish just below the dorsal fin and the lip.
- Be patient.
- You are going to spend some time on the water – make sure that you are protected against the elements. Dehydration and loss of body salts is a real threat. I was once fighting a shark and had to give up the rod to my buddy Erhard because of hand cramps....
- If you are not holding a rod in your hands, always place it in the rod-holders provided.
- You should be carrying the following with you, as a minimum:

    - ✓ Spare tippets / trace line
    - ✓ Hook disgorger
    - ✓ Scale
    - ✓ Line cutter attached to fishing vest by a lifeline
    - ✓ Knife
    - ✓ Floating fly / lure / bait boxes; hooks and swivels
    - ✓ Sunblock
    - ✓ Landing net
    - ✓ Stomach pump for checking what fish are feeding on
    - ✓ Soft bag keep net
    - ✓ Water or fluids to rehydrate, salt tablets for cramping
    - ✓ Something to nibble on
    - ✓ If you are carrying a phone, a waterproof bag to keep it in
    - ✓ A priest [club] to administer the last rites
    - ✓ Fine sharpening stone for hooks
    - ✓ Don't make noise - sound is transmitted very effectively in water and you can easily spook fish.

Chapter 25: Hand line

Fishing a hand line can be fun – I would almost always have hooks, line and sinkers on me for the times when I find good waters and have no rods with me.

You will be surprised to see just how far you can cast with a hand line and just how much more sensitive your hands are to detecting bites.

For short to medium range casting, you will need a 500ml cool drink bottle [like a coke dumpy bottle]. Fill the bottle with water. Tie the line to the neck of the bottle, just below the ridge on the mouthpiece. Now wind the line firmly around the body of the bottle. You now have a self-casting bottle!

Once your hooks have been baited, you can hold the line in your right hand and the bottle in your left. Spin the bait and let go as the line passes your foot – with a little practice, you will get your timing tuned to achieve a decent cast.

For a long cast – [up to and over 100m – **YES, 100m!!!!**] – you will need a 50mm diameter plastic tube that is between 500mm to a meter in length. You will also need a clear flat area [use a mat] where you can spread out your line with no coils overlapping. Block one end of the tube [you can do this using aluminium foil or an end-cap – do not use cloth or the hook may be caught up in it!

Now slide your baited hook into the tube and then the sinker.

Using a two-handed grip, the left hand on the blocked end of the tube, swing the tube forward, - you should end your stroke with the tube pointing forward just under 45° to the water. Centrifugal force will accelerate the sinker and you will achieve distances you never thought possible, probably out-casting most rods.

Oh – and did I mention that the free end of the line should be firmly attached to a peg securely buried in the ground?

Keep a tight line and feel for that bite. Enjoy!!

Chapter 26: Crabbing

If you should find a dead crab it is *extremely dangerous* to consume it. Once a crab dies, the flesh is rendered *toxic*. Only eat crabs that you have caught alive, or that you have acquired frozen or alive from fisheries and supermarkets. There are three ways to kill a crab: The first way is to freeze the creature whilst it is alive [this is achieved by dropping it into ice or slurry made from water and crushed ice / ice cubes and is the most humane and stress-free {to you and the crab} way of killing the creature]. The second is to drop it into boiling water [I *HATE* this} and the third is to kill it when you are cleaning it in order to cook it [by removing the carapace whilst the creature is alive].

Crabs can be encountered almost anywhere and there are many species. The popular orange crab you see is normally caught off East London and Port Elizabeth by commercial crabbers. It is tasty and probably the easiest to eat. The species you see scurrying off rocks at the beach have very little flesh in them but are excellent bait. The ghost crabs you see scurrying on the beach are very small but very tasty and worth the effort to catch – consuming them takes a little more time…. Most other crabs caught off South African waters are not worth the effort of catching / eating.

Then there is the swimming [mud] crab which is delicious and well worth the effort of catching. Most other crab you see for sale are foreign to South African waters.

And finally, there is the fresh water crab. Excellent eating and proven to be good for people with asthma.

Catching crab for consumption or bait can be such fun even though it requires concentration. Please make sure that you have a valid license – this allows you to catch the mud crab [swimming crab] which is probably the tastiest crab caught off our coastline. The ghost crab is also very tasty and easily caught for consumption or bait – to catch these you need a marine license. And as for freshwater crab, I do not know of any legal requirement for catching them.

So – wherever you are, look for signs of crab. If you don't actually see them, you will see holes in the sand and bank. You will catch crab near rocky areas [estuaries] and freshwater crab just about anywhere. Ideally, you are looking at a spot where the water is at least 500mm deep at the point where you will be netting the crab. You are not allowed to use a crab trap in South Africa.

You will need:
- **To be very careful – those claws can do damage. I handle crabs by holding both sides of the carapace or from behind where the back leg meets the carapace, but however you handle them, be wary!!**
- Onion sack – the plastic woven type, normally orange.
- Some dark, stout thin rope or 100pound nylon. About 6m.
- Some sardine bait [heads, bones and guts and some meat [must not be gone off]. In freshwater, chicken guts and skin and liver].
- Bundle the bait together and wrap it with at least two wraps of onion sacking, knotting it tightly.
- A peg to put into the ground.
- A long handled shallow net with a large mouth.
- A cooler box with ice.

Securely tie the rope / line to the parcel and secure the other end to the peg. Throw the parcel into the water and take out your phone and play some games. Put the long-handled net into the water so it lies below the line.

Watch the line. When you see movement, it is more than likely that a crab has got it. Don't leave it too long or the crab may take your parcel into a hole. Gently coax the line towards you – you will feel the crab. Bring the crab towards the net, and when it passes over the net, raise it sharply.

Drop the crab into the cooler box and re-cast. And call me to have some crab curry.

Cleaning the crab

You will need:
- Crab [duh!]

- A container with a plastic bag opened over it and newspaper in the bag for the waste.
- A cleaver.
- A cutting board
- A nailbrush reserved for this purpose [hard toothbrush can also be used]
- A container for the cleaned crab
- A small screwdriver or a spike to make holes in the pieces to ensure that the spices permeate into *Mr. crab* pieces.

If the crab is frozen, defrost by soaking in cold water.
Place the crab the right way up on a board.
Place your left hand over the legs, alongside the carapace.
Grab the carapace with your right hand and lift it steadily, keeping legs trapped against the board with your left hand.
Remove the carapace completely. Pull out the gills – the bag-like appendages. Under flowing water, remove the guts [the yellow / pinkish gunge]. There is a triangular flap on the base of the crab, pull it off. Pull out the mouthparts [little pieces on the head].
Take the nailbrush and brush the legs and body clean.
Place the cleaver across the centre and split it in two.
Place the cleaver on each leg and claw joint directly to the body and press down, severing each appendage. The claw should be split into two pieces.
Each body half may be split into two or three pieces.
Rinse.
Take the screwdriver / spike and punch a small hole in each leg segments – you are ready to cook the crab.

Chapter 27: Cleaning your catch

Turmeric powder [*hurdhi / manja*] is a natural antibacterial agent that is palatable. It can be mixed with your rinse water and will destroy salmonella, e-coli and most of their cousins.com. 1 tablespoon in 5litres will do it for your rinse water. It will yellow the flesh but will ensure that you don't waste time squatting on the beach [or wherever] with your pants down.

Remember that when you are gutting, try and avoid running the knife through the guts – always try and remove the guts intact. Bury the guts and scales or dispose of them by wrapping in newspaper and freezing and placing in refuse bins at the time of collection.

<u>Never</u> use a bait knife to clean fish you intend eating – you may well contaminate edibles with harmful bacteria and toxins.

Eels.

The meat from edible eels [generally those with gill slits] is very rich and very tasty. Try it sometime.

The creature can live for a long time once out of water. Do the humane thing and kill it by striking the body between the eyes and the gills with a priest or heavy object, then once it stops wriggling all over, you can give it a firm knock on the head. Do not remove the head until you have skinned the eel. The flesh cannot be consumed without first removing the skin.

Some people use ash – for me it is too messy. There is a simpler way. I learnt this from my grandmother who never went to school but was so wise….

When I brought eels home, my granny would wash and dry the skins and they formed a tough leathery twine that some people used as shoe / boot laces. These laces were called 'never break' laces.

To skin an eel, you need to make an incision around the head, below the gill slit. Hook the eel by passing a large hook [or a butcher's hook] through the upper and lower jaws and hang it up [say on the branch of a tree] and, using two pairs of pliers, grab a hold of the skin on either side of the body and pull downwards with a steady pulling motion. The skin should come off like a glove. You can now gut the creature and trim off the fins. Cut off the head and wash the body thoroughly. Cut into slices and it is ready to cook.

Barbel [catfish]

Suspend the barbel in the same manner as you would an eel, hooking the upper and lower jaws together. Make an incision all the way around the head, below the gill slit. Hang it up [say on the branch of a tree] and, using a pair of pliers, grab a hold of the skin on one side of the body and pull downwards with a steady pulling motion – you may need two pairs of pliers for bigger fish]. The skin should come off like a glove. Repeat this procedure on the other side. If strips of skin remain, you will need to work a blunt knife between the flesh and the skin, grab with pliers, and Bob's your auntie. You can now gut the creature and trim off the fins and tail. Cut off the head and wash the body thoroughly. Cut into slices and it is ready to cook.

Scaled species

Some freshwater fish have tasty skins. *Scalie* [yellowfish], bass, bluegill, tilapia, trout are examples of these. Everything else should be skinned. The so-called 'muddy' taste that people complain about comes from the slime. Dead fish continue to produce slime for a while afterwards, so the sooner you clean, the better. Many people freeze fish with the guts and scales intact –avoid doing this as toxins from the gut can be absorbed into the meat.

There are four main ways to prepare a fish – you need to plan this in advance:
- Baked or fried whole, with or without the head. You will normally do this using fish that do not have fine bones,
- Filleted, using only the two sides of the fish [whole or cut into medallions],
- Sliced as steaks for braaing, currying or biryani
- Sliced thinly for frying [bony fish], and,
- Steamed – for when you want just the fish meat for savouries like fish cakes.

You will need to lay out some newspaper – I normally do this outside – but if you are forced to, spread out some newspaper – this is messy business.

Wet the fish to lubricate the scales and make them stick to the knife / fish scaler.

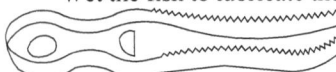 *This is basically what a fish scaler looks like. It is held by the area without serrations, handle ②. [there are various designs]*

Place a sheet of newspaper over the cutting board and wet the newspaper lightly.

If you are right-handed, place the fish on the board, over the newspaper with the head on your left and the tail to you right.

Take note of sharp spines and razor edges on the fins and gill covers – you will need to avoid these whilst you are operating the scaler.

Lightly hold the scaler in your right hand, on the tail and place your left hand over the head, to the left of the gills.

If you do not want the scales to fly everywhere, you need to cover your right hand with a damp cloth, the cloth must be clear of the serrations on the scaler.

Now pressing lightly against the fish, sweep the scaler towards the head of the fish in a crisp smooth motion.

If you are having trouble moving the scaler, you are pressing down too hard. Repeat the motion until all scales are removed.

Pay particular attention to the head [top and sides], the top and sides of the fish, the area before, after and around all fins [the tip of the scaler is normally used for these areas. That's why the scaler ends in a point].

A sharp knife can also be used [I use my Chef's knife] but I suggest this only be done by the more experienced. The knife should have no serrations on the blade. Too much pressure and you will ruin the meat.

You now have a scaled fish. Wash the scales off the fish. Run your fingers from the head towards the tail only – this will ensure that you do not get injured by any sharp spines or edges.

If you find that the flesh is soft or like porridge, do not consume it.

Removing the fins

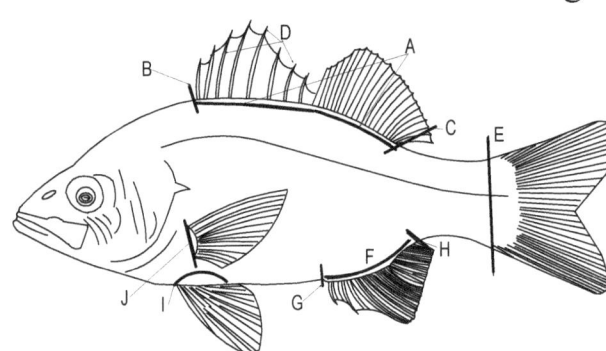

- The pectoral fins [next to the gill slit] can simply be cut off at "J" using a pair of kitchen scissors as close to the body as possible.
- The pelvic fins [just immediately behind the head - on the underside of the fish], can be removed by cutting into the flesh behind both fins, cutting around the bone mounting the fins, and cutting out, in front of the fins "I".
- For the dorsal fins, make a cut "A" on both sides of the fin towards the backbone.
- Make a cut in front of the fin 'B' and behind it "C" and simply pull the fin out "D", complete with the thorns.
- Repeat the same for the anal fin. ["F", "G" and "H"]

If you intend baking the fish

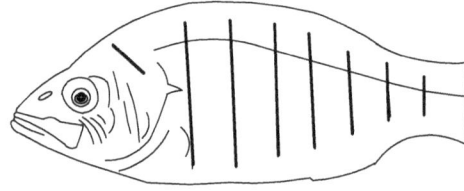

- Make slits [bold lines] into the flesh so that whatever spices you use can penetrate into the meat directly.
- You may elect to keep the head and/or tail on, or remove them.

Slicing the fish

[Note that it is best to slice fish when it is partly frozen]

- If you are going to fillet, you do not have to remove fins or gut the fish.
- Place the fish on a cutting board.
- You will need a sharp chef's knife or cleaver and a mallet.
- Make cuts into the flesh up to the bone using the chef's knife.
- Space the cuts to get the desired slice thickness.
- Place the cleaver / chef's knife into the cut.
- Give it a firm tap with a mallet, just enough to break through the centre bone. Remember that you are not trying to split the board!
- Once through the bone, you can use a sharp knife to cut through the remaining meat.
- Rinse the slices and start your culinary miracle.

Filleting

- You will need a narrow-bladed filleting knife, very sharp.
- Place the scaled fish on a clean cutting board, head away from you, tail towards you, dorsal fin to your right.
- Place the knife just on top of the dorsal fin and cut into the flesh, angling the blade away from you, towards the bone. Cut until you feel the ribs. Cut into the meat of the head and all the way to the tail.
- Turn the fish over and repeat the above step.
- Now lift he flesh and work the knife over the ribs until the blade breaks through the skin. The ribs run all the way from the head to just before the anus.
- From the anus to the tail, lift the flesh and cut away from the bone. Repeat on the other side.
- You now have two fillets from which you may decide to use whole, slice or cut into nuggets. The fillet should look like the bold shape drawn on the sketch above.

Cleaning prawns

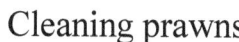

Prawns definitely taste better with the shell on. As a matter of fact, I chew the shell and suck the juices out. Delicious.

Prawns should be allowed to defrost overnight [take out of freezer, and place into a bowl in the fridge and leave overnight] – prawns should thaw sufficiently for cleaning – it is difficult to clean a semi-frozen prawn.

The bold line in the body on the sketch indicates the approximate location of the creature's digestive tract.

You will need:
- Prawns [duh!]
- A container with a plastic bag opened over it and newspaper in the bag for the waste.
- A straight-edged, sharp knife with a pointed end
- A cutting board

A container for the cleaned prawns

Headless and shelled

Hold the head of the prawn, gently squeezing it. Simultaneously twist and pull. The head should come off leaving the legs still attached to the body. Pull off the legs [immediately behind the front of the head, and the swimmerets [fine leg-like appendages between the legs and tails. The shell can now be pulled off from all six segments by hand. Take a small sharp knife and run the blade along the back of the body, until you see the digestive tract [a dark-coloured line running from where the head joined the body, through to the tail. Spread the cut open and use the tip of the knife to dig out part of the digestive tract – grab hold of it and gently pull out the line – with a little practice, you will be able to pull out the entire digestive tract. Rinse each prawn clean.

Shell on

My personal preference… If you want the prawns with the shell on, all you do is make an incision at the back and pull out the digestive tract. Rinse clean and you are ready for the pot.

Chapter 28: Why fish are lost or not caught

Have you ever had reason to *actually* walk into / go into the water? I don't know – salt / fresh? There's a risk that you face each time you do this – a risk so scary and real and so many of you are unaware of this. Every time you go into the water – even walk through it, you face the risk of encountering ghost lines and ghost nets. These are nets, wires, hooks and lines that have been lost. And in the water, in the current – strange things happen – some lines float, some are kept up, suspended by a lost float; suspended between structure, lying on the bottom, waiting for you to bring a fighting fish through = and even worse …. To trap you. Make sure that you heed my advice on waste line, and make sure, that if you have to go into the water, you are carrying a sharp knife so that you can cut yourself free should you get caught up. As to the fish you are fighting – you will almost certainly lose it to these ghost objects. Please remove them from the water when you encounter them and cut them up if you can't take them away, cut them up, and dispose of them safely.

Why do you sometimes go fishing and you don't catch anything despite the fact that people around you are catching? Why do you fail to hook fish when they are biting? Why do you lose fish that you have hooked? This Chapter relates causes for fish not being hooked; not being caught; and, being lost. These tales of tails are based on *my* experience and observations. Just remember that breakage of ANY kind whilst fishing is almost always YOUR fault. You never stop learning – I never stop learning.

If you plan on starting a fire, make sure that it is safe to do so and you can use the vehicle or the natural geography of the area as a windbreak. Be aware of whether fires are allowed in the area before you get there.

Keys

– find a stashing place for keys. I carry a small *Tupperware* container for keys – this can be safely buried close to the vehicle – this way if someone wants to get access to the vehicle for whatever reason, they don't have to hunt the *key-holder* down. Don't bury keys without ensuring that they are in a plastic bag or in a waterproof container. And don't forget *where*.

OH NO! YOU FORGOT SOMETHING…

Forgetting something could ruin a fishing trip. Make a list of the items you would normally take on each type of fishing trip. When you return from each trip, you will find that there were things that were unnecessary, and things that you wish you had carried along with you. Use your phone to do this and keep updating and saving the list. Skim through the list before each new trip…

What!! You forgot the list???!!! I know that spontaneous trips are sometimes so good – but it is essential that some planning is done – begin this planning with a list [refer Chapter 9].

RELATED TO THE FISHING ROD:

Loose binding:

Loose binding can [and generally will] wrap itself around your line, especially when you have a fish on or when you are casting, compromising both…. Be sure to repair it – even if temporarily with insulation tape or a dab of glue or even nail polish. [I always keep some handy]. Some of the binding on your rod is meant for aesthetic impact, making the rod look good. If the binding itself is loose, it means that no varnish / resin was used to lock it in place or that the finish was damaged somehow. You will need to get the binding re-done properly. You do *not* want line guides to come loose whilst you're fishing – tangles tend to occur at the most inopportune moments.

Line guide missing:

This is courting disaster - even worse if it is put back with the wrong spacing. Line guides are not put onto a rod *willy-nilly* – they are there to distribute the load evenly when casting and fighting and to provide a low-friction retrieval for your line. If the spacing between eyes is wrong, the strain of a fighting a fish can result in breaking your rod as well as, ah yes, losing the fish. If you don't have the experience, take it to specialists.

Corroded / damaged / grooved line guides:

Corrosion is like cancer. When metal corrodes it is *seriously* weakened and will more than likely fail when put under stress. If they are corroded, have them replaced. If the guides are damaged or grooved, this will result in line damage and damaged line *will* fail under the strain of catching a fish. Whenever retrieving your line, pass it between your fingers – this almost certainly guarantees that you will feel when your line has been damaged; it also ensures that your line tension on the reel is correct.

Rod broke:

Treat your rod with respect and care. Don't let it get bashed against rocks or by other rods. A rod will break if it is damaged along its length. When you buy a rod [second-hand], it is generally nicely finished off – scrutinize it for defects – defects running across the grain are bad – defects parallel to the grain are generally tolerable [almost every graphite rod has defects along the length!]. A nick along the length of a rod is almost certainly where it will fail when it is placed under load during a fight / casting / striking. When in transit or storage, rods should be placed in a cloth sleeve. Do not place rods side by side in a sleeve – the vibration caused by travelling will result in the sections rubbing together and weakening the rod.

Rod gone:

The story: "I only left it alone for a minute and the next thing I saw was the rod ploughing into the water. I miss my rod." *You really want me to tell you what to do to prevent this? Wake up! Seriously. An unmanned rod is trouble. If you have to leave a rod unmanned, lash it to something that can't move. I believe that there is always a fish out there waiting for you to walk away, relieve yourself, eat, fetch a drink... They are watching us...*

Rod too stiff / whippy:

Each type of rod is designed to deliver a particular type of action. This action is optimized with the correct line, reel and bait-weight combination. If this combination is incorrect, you stand a chance of losing fish. Deep sea rods are not designed for casting, a heavy action rod will generally cause you to lose, for example, a soft-mouthed fish like a scalie [yellowfish]. The general rule is that *soft-mouthed fish require a rod with softer action*. Use the right tool for the right purpose.

Line not threaded through guides properly:

Setting up is important – if you miss a line guide, the line will wrap around the rod, and you stand a chance of losing fish because of the increased friction. Take your time when threading your line through the guides. You will also not be able to cast efficiently. Take the time to inspect the rod once you have threaded the line through the guides.

Line twisted around rod tip:

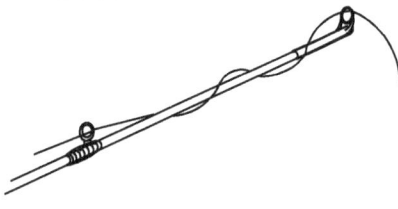

This is a serious problem. If you have a fish on and this happens – you almost certainly will not only lose the fish, but probably break your rod tip as well. Take the time to check before you strike / reel out, and before you cast. This is a problem that can occur at any time. To help prevent this, keep a rod stand handy for when you have reeled out. This way you can check your trace / bait up without exposing your rod to any danger.

Too much pressure:

There will be times when you have to chance that extra little bit of pressure, but mostly, you have no reason to lose a fish due to you applying too much pressure during the fight. A lot can be prevented if your pre-fishing scouting of the area is thorough; if your knowledge of the limits of your tackle [and yourself] is also thorough. Check the area you are fishing in beforehand and plan where and how you can bring a fish to be landed. Learn to use side-strain when a fish is moving too far to your left or right. Side strain is applied by turning you rod to the left if the fish is pulling to the right and vice-versa. Keep it like this and you will see how your rod is designed to work for you. Side strain is a powerful tool in turning fish. Too many people hold the rod straight up. This is only necessary if the fish swims directly in front of you, and NOT to the side.

Fish on, storm starts:

Well, what would you do? I've heard enough stories about lightning strikes – hell – I've worked with high voltage hardware and fear enough for man-generated electricity – but from the heavens! If you're sporting graphite – give it up to fight another day. And if you're so intent on being suicidal, can I have your tackle, please? Seriously now – lightning is a discharge of electricity from the atmosphere to the ground. If you are fishing graphite, it is a superconductor and will almost certainly invite a discharge from the heavens. You could take the risk if your rod is not built of boron or graphite, but a storm is a storm. I know the temptation of playing the fish out is great – but is it worth the risk?

Power lines:

There are those of you out there who are blissfully unaware that you don't have to touch power lines to get shocked. High voltage is quite capable of 'jumping' from the power line, down your rod and through your body, going to ground. How close does the rod need to go? Arcing / tracking can take place from around 2metres with high voltage. This distance can be greatly reduced in heavy mist and rain. Don't catch a spark! Hold rods and any other long equipment flat if you have to pass under power lines. You might wonder how in the blue blazes this will prevent you from catching a fish or cause you to lose a fish.... You really can't fish if you have been electrocuted.

Two / more-section rod comes apart on casting / striking....

Hmmmm.... When you assemble your rod, you have to be aware that handling it during casting, retrieving your line, and fighting a fish, etc, can cause the segments to work loose. Make it a habit of briefly checking it before you cast, each time you cast. *Make it habit.*

Using a rod with "snake" line guides using monofilament line.

When you retrieve your line, the rod picks up some of the moisture – casting becomes a problem because you experience line-stick [to the rod]. This can compromise your cast. Wiping the rod down before you cast will help you avoid experiencing line-stick. If it is raining, you're "stuck" with the problem though wiping the rod just before you cast will make a difference.

RELATED TO FISHING REELS:

Reel broke:

There are times when reel failure can be avoided. If you service reels after use, loose / worn / damaged parts can be identified and replaced / repaired. Go to a reputable dealer for servicing if you can't do it yourself – it is well worth it. Normally, a reel won't just break. If you lose a fish because the reel breaks, chances are it's your fault. There are times when I want to bash someone over the head when I see them straining the reel when the line is snagged [and then blame the reel manufacturer or bad-mouth a reel when it breaks during a fight!

Also never leave a reel with line under tension [this happens after a heavy fight, heavy pulling when line is snagged]. The line is under stress and potentially dangerous to the life of your reel. Strip and re-spool.

Another contributing factor lies with some of the cheaper products on the market. *Cheaper generally implies that the product is sub-standard.* I remember buying cheapies for a whole group of children and Davina Maya, my beautiful niece hooked into a 2.5kg bass [her first fish at age 7]. Well the *cheapie* reel broke and I had to help her fight the fish with a broken reel.

After you fish, take the time to inspect your tackle – you do not want to find problems when you are actually fishing.

Reel jammed:

Wassup? Forgot to clean / service your reel? Would you go hunting without checking and servicing your weapon? Make sure that your reel is well-maintained. If the jam is due to tighter coils that have bitten into the coiled line on the reel, you really have only yourself to blame. When you catch a big fish or when you really strain your tackle, I would recommend that line be de-spooled and re-spooled [generally achieved by casting without bait].

Sandpaper is so named because it is abrasive. 1 grain of sand can do so much damage to bearings and bushes. Avoid placing / dropping your reel in/on the sand / mud. Always have a rod stand handy to keep your reels off the sand / ground.

Get pouches for your reels to keep the dust and sand off. Soak them in warm water after you fish and give them a good cleaning. Learn to apply grease and oil or take them for regular services, minimum once a year. If you use braid, the line should be kept damp.

Drag on too tight / too loose:

When you set your drag, you are protecting your line [and your rod]. Correctly set, the drag should release line when the rod tip is at an angle of about 90° to the rod butt, without the line breaking. Your drag should be set before your first cast. This ensures that when you fight a fish, your reel will automatically release line even whilst you are reeling in. A drag set too tightly could result in tearing of the fish's mouth or your line breaking. A drag too loose could result in failure to obtain a hook-up and worse – a bird's nest [tangle].

Too little line on reel.

You might hook into the fish of your dreams and find that there is inadequate line left on your reel for the fight. Don't let this happen. When you lose line from your reel, it should be replaced. If you must, join another piece of line to make up for the loss, or replace the line. *Do not use line from your reel to tie traces*. Carry separate line to tie traces and use a lower breaking strain line to tie on terminal sinkers. Carry spare line. Note that if your line is twisted it can work its way between the spool and reel body quite easily – This is possible on most reel types.

Too much 'float' on spool:

'Float' refers to movement between the spindle onto which the reel is attached and the spool / reel body, whichever is applicable.

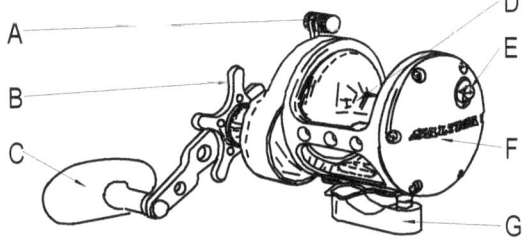

Legend: Multiplier reel. A: This is the free-spool lever. Engages the winding mechanism after casting and disengages the winding mechanism when casting; B: Star drag. Tightening increases drag tension; C: Reel handle / crank; D: Line spool. Do not fill to less than 3 mm from spool edge; E: Ratchet; F: On the centre of the opposite side of the reel is the spool tension adjustment nut – used to adjust the extent of free-spooling for casting; G: Reel mounting block [for mounting reel to rod].

With **multiplier reels**, this is adjustable and controls the spool tension. Too much wear can cause an excessive gap between the spool "D" and reel body "F"; and if your line enters this gap it will either jam the reel, or, more likely, be guillotined, severing it completely.

For your **fixed spool reels 'coffee grinders'** I have noted with the cheaper reels, that the possibility of the line getting jammed under the spool and on the spindle is quite high. This can also happen in two other situations – if you do not maintain adequate line tension, slack line can cause this problem. A loose spindle mounting screw can also cause this problem. You can test for this by pulling and pushing on the mounted spool and checking for excessive movement. There should be none.

Pushbutton reels: I have never experienced this problem with this reel type. Check your line tension and confirm whether the line is twisted.

RELATED TO FISHING LINE:

Always be vigilant.

Check your line after each cast and ensure that you carry adequate spare line / reels with you at all times. If in doubt address line-related problems *before* you lose a fish / risk damaging your tackle / injure yourself or someone else. Don't leave line-related problems to be sorted out on *the next trip*. You may regret it.

Fishing too light:

There is nothing wrong with fishing light – but **be reasonable** - give the fish a sporting chance. There is no cheer in allowing a fish to break you, trailing a length of line with a hook stuck in its mouth. Use the best possible combination of tackle and pay attention to the waters you are fishing. There is no point fishing ultra-light if there is too much of structure / reeds etc. that present a snagging hazard or refuge to a fighting fish....

Besides, I still say that the chances of successfully reviving a fish when fishing ultra-light are pretty slim. You out there with your sub 4-weight rods – give it a thought.

Remember that fishing ultra-light presents an extreme challenge if you are practicing catch-and-release. Remember that fish caught in this manner are subjected to a prolonged fight and severe stress. You have to work hard and spend enough time at making sure the fish has recovered adequately before it is released or it will only go off to die a little later. ☹

Tackle not balanced:

Tackle must be reasonable well-balanced. Refer Chapter 10.

Forgot to use a steel trace.

When fishing for any member of the 'razor tooth' gang [shad, ribbonfish, barracuda, wahoo, tigerfish, snoek, and shark] you should always use the correct gauge of steel wire. In many cases, you may actually use a long shank hook if you do not have steel wire. You will also need a long wire leader where the skin / scales / bill / tail scalpel is rough enough to cause your line to break. Fish like kob and Garrick have fine teeth – a prolonged fight increases the risk of the line being damaged by these fine teeth.

Using braid.

Remember that *all kinds of braid have little or no stretch*. Normal monofilament line has stretch that helps during the hook-up and in the fight – braid does not do this. You should always be vigilant when using braid to ensure that you do not put on too much pressure during the fight because *the fight is now all rod*.

Waste nylon [including tangles].

Waste / discarded / broken line poses a multitude of threats. You could be fighting a fish and lose it when it becomes entangled in line that some other unfortunate has broken off. Any waste line should be disposed of by wrapping it around your fingers, [with the tangle, if there is one] and then cutting through it with a sharp knife or scissors, leaving short pieces that small creatures cannot get entangled with. Do this especially when you pull out or find someone else's old line whilst fishing.

Small creatures [including both larger birds and wildlife]

… can suffer a painful lingering miserable death by entanglement or even become injured and disfigured as a result. Waste nylon also poses a tripping risk to anyone passing by. Imagine a fishing trip that is cut short because someone tripped and got injured. If you use a kick boat, carry a knife because your feet could easily become entangled and you will then need to cut yourself free.

Line frayed from previous cast:

When your line gets frayed, you should generally find out about this immediately after it has happened. Frayed line is weakened line, and weakened line **will** break prematurely under load. Have you ever seen someone cast and the line snaps with the effort of casting? Sometimes the line will also break with the effort of striking. There are different classes of abrasion-resistant lines, some of them, are really good. *Always carry spare line. Always inspect your line.*

Try and use fluorocarbon line for your hook trace [unless you are fishing on the surface]. This line is naturally abrasion resistant.

Many people avoid touching their line when reeling in. Line should always pass through your fingers when reeling in. By doing this, you can feel when there is a knot / tangle or frayed line. Investigate anything that does not feel normal and you won't lose fish through frayed line because you can take preventative measures once you feel the frayed line.

Remove frayed line and dispose of it by wrapping it around your fingers and cutting through the loops so that it is reduced to short pieces that will not cause damage or pose danger. Don't leave it at the waterside, take it home and use a rubbish bin or even better, recycle.

What causes frayed line?

Damaged / grooved eyes [line guides]:

Inspect line guides [commonly called 'eyes'] for damage or wear. Check that bindings are secure.

Don't wait for grooves to develop in your line guides – replace them as soon as you see damage. Don't think that this is limited to the tip guide only. Check *all* guides for wear / damage. If there is damage, establish what is causing the damage and take corrective measures.

Just remember that sand by nature is abrasive and fine particles are always present on your line – this has the effect of converting your line into one long strip of sandpaper…

Fishing over rough stuff

[between rocks, mussel beds, barnacles, rusted metal, razor clams and glass]: Get real – you seldom catch fish in open water without any structure that provides cover for fish against predators. You therefore have to fish in areas that expose your tackle to the risk of loss or damage.

When you're reeling in, always run the line pinched lightly between your fingers as you reel in and you will feel if the line is damaged – this has the additional advantage of ensuring that the line tension on the spool is good.

Watch out for old fences, rocks, razor clams, barnacles and mussel beds! Crabs can also damage your line.

Fishing over sand / soil / rocks into a distant drop-off:

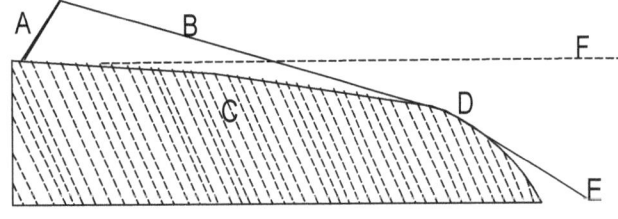

Legend: A: Rod; B: line from rod and before drop-off; C: Sandbank – could well have rocks as well; D: Drop-off; E: line after drop-off – note change in angle – line will bite into the drop-off at D. If there are rocks at "D", you stand a higher risk of experiencing line fray. The line extends from point "A" to the end of the cast at "E". F= water level

Your line will always bite into the shallow soil, particularly if you are stuck or fishing with a sinker. Sand and soil are abrasive. Remember that if your line bites into the sand / soil, it means that your hook and sinker will also be drawn through the sand / soil / stones / rocks at "D". Yes, you WILL get stuck. Be wary of shellfish – your everyday razor clams, mussels, oysters and other shellfish.com are very abrasive. I have found that if you can't get close to the drop-off to prevent your line from digging in, then the use of a float helps. A drop-off is always a wonderful place to fish – just ensure that your line clears the top of the drop-off so that it doesn't bite into the sand. And when all else fails – high abrasion resistant line is the answer – just keep tabs on it!

Damaged reel / guides

Line getting jammed between spool and frame of reel:

Anything that normally contacts with the line should be smooth. When you reel in, make sure that the line is evenly distributed along the width of the spool. Regular servicing and checking of your reels must be done. Line is not meant to go between the spool and the reel body – have your reel checked or change your technique of feeding line into the reel. Remember that there is oil / grease between the spool and reel frame – most lubricants will cause line to deteriorate.

Fraying due to repetitive casting:

[bass-fishing using artificial lures, fly-fishing, using a spoon]. Remember that if you fish artificial lures, it means high frequency repeated casting. The same line is passing through the guides over and over again. As I said earlier, if you are feeling the line onto the reel as you reel in, you will detect problems with the line and will, hopefully be in a position to do something about it.

Rough hands; rough skin:

– believe it! You know what? I generally cover my thumb with a cut-off leather glove. Keep the leather wet and you'll be fine. *Repeated rubbing against rough skin will eventually weaken your line.*

There is too much line on the reel:

And the excess line is being frayed against some part of the reel body. Too much line on a centre-pin or multiplier reel means that before you cast, the line chafes against the reel body or pillars. Spinning reels should be loaded to not less than 3mm the spool lip. Press-button reels will generally not operate if over-filled. Excess line on a reel increases the risk of tangling.

You can't feel the frayed line?

Then you are not pinching your line between thumb and fingers as you reel in, or maybe your fingers are frozen. To know what frayed line feels like, hold a piece at both ends, rub it up against some masonry and run the line through your fingers.

Cheap and nasty:

I don't even know whether this applies to the lines that are available today – I have my brands that I am faithful to and I have no reason to change. If you cannot afford the more expensive proven lines, try out the cheaper varieties – but put them to the test before you actually go fishing. Test line before use.

Fish entangled with someone's old line:

This happens when someone got broken off and the line remains in the water. Remove any waste line you find and cut it up as described above.

Line fraying due to finger/thumb pressure [multiplier reels]:

I try and exert pressure on the side of the spool rather than the line. Pressure on the line is generally light. Slowing a spinning multiplier reel spool down is like touching your lover – do it gently, and your line [and thumb!] will last longer. You'll be pleasantly surprised at what a gentle touch will do for you! Go to a grassy field and practice with short casts first, and as you improve, longer casts.

Line breaks when casting:

You may well ask how fish can be lost when this happens…every time this happens, you have lost the opportunity of catching a fish. Always remember that a motion should be smooth and balanced. Any jerk / interruption in the flow of line exerts an extra load on rod and line alike.

Causes:

Remember to open the reel or let go of the line when you cast!

Poor casting technique, poor coordination can contribute to line weakening / breakage. You subject your rod, reel, line and your body to tremendous stress each time you cast. Any break in the natural casting motion could easily result in some sort of failure. If the line breaks when you're casting, you cannot possibly catch a fish in that cast. Too little line on the reel: Ahem! You're not really trying to catch the fish, are you? Try Russian roulette – you're definitely a player.

Seriously now you need at least 100m on the reel.

In the salt – at least 150m [and that could be cutting it fine if your cast is 80m and longer].

You're fishing too light:

Use at least 9m of shock leader. A shock leader is heavier line fastened to the end of lighter line – this allows you to use more energy in casting. No, you won't be disqualified in a competition, and yes, your casting distances will definitely improve.

Leader knot jams:

When you tie on your shock leader, you have to check that there is adequate clearance between the knot and the line guides [the knot must pass through freely]. What I do to reduce the impact of the knot on the eyes is apply some whipping [binding] between the knot and the line – this creates a natural taper and relieves the stresses applied to the leader knot during casting and reeling [refer Chapter 10].

Line was tangled on rod / line guide before casting:

Wake up! It must be second nature for you to check for this. Automatically.

Old knots on line:

A knot is designed to work as long as all consecutive coils / wraps comprising the knot are uniformly tight. Sudden jerks and heavy fights may cause knots to tighten unevenly. This can cause 'inexplicable' line breakages. Check knots. Check knots. Check knots. Each time you go fishing, tie fresh traces. If you have recovered your line after being stuck, or have had a nice fight with a large fish, check your knots. I have heard people brag about how their favourite traces never fail to catch. Don't get caught up in this potentially tragic situation – you could lose the fish of your dreams because of old knots and damaged line and corroded hooks.

Miss-casts:

When you cast and for some reason the line doesn't go – this can cause the line to bite into the reel and/or cause knots to tighten unevenly. You know the drill from here! *By the way I've seen some mighty fine 'misses' cast and they 'so fine!*

Always do a test-cast especially after a hard fight

– hard fights cause the overlying line to bite into the reel – this results in line being embedded between and under overlying coils and this can cause problems with future casts and fights.

Poor knots / poor knotting technique:

Use the right knot for the job. Ensure that the line is lubricated by saliva / water before pulling evenly and without jerking on the ends to tighten the knot.

Line too old:

What is your problem? I know that line is expensive, but it's like playing chess using 16 pawns against a full set – boy are you going to get destroyed! Don't hoard line! Line life is dependent on a combination of frequency of usage and extent of exposure to the elements. If you are a bass-fisherman using rubber worms and artificial lures, then the act of casting repetitively will wear out line at a greater rate. You should always inspect line for wear / damage and replace it when you are in doubt. Always test the line by feel – you will detect when and where your line is damaged – remove the damaged line.

Please – when you are **disposing of old line**, try and remember that it takes at least 20 years before it degenerates – this is if you're the sort of fisherperson who discards line when you fish. And if you have to discard old line, *roll it up in your hand and cut through it so that you dispose of little pieces and not long pieces that can pose a hazard to bird, plant and animal life, and other people.*

Causes:

Old line breaks without warning:

Remember that old line loses part of its elasticity and that the line strength becomes seriously compromised: When something loses elasticity, it gets brittle, when it gets brittle, it breaks more easily and is unable to take shock-loading [as in casting, sudden dramatic bites, striking].

Line degraded from excessive exposure to the sun's rays:

Protect line from exposure to the sun: You suffer from sunburn and you are a living entity, capable of protecting your own skin – your line can't think for itself – don't leave line exposed to the sun for longer than you have to. Everything is bio-degradable to some extent, and solar exposure increases the rate of deterioration dramatically. *Replace old line.*

Excessive exposure to salt water:

Protect line from exposure to salt water. After you've fished, a couple of soaks in a bucket of warm water should get the salt out. Remember that if you don't, salt crystals will form as the water dries and salt is both corrosive and abrasive. And don't soak the whole reel – just the spool holding the line – remember to re-grease the spool when putting the reel together again! The salt on your line can and will cause corrosion to your tackle.

Line twisted.

This is what twisted line looks like. Highly undesirable as it causes slack line and will tangle with anything it comes into contact with and even compromise your cast – and the worst-case scenario is that it could result in you breaking your rod.

Twisted line will cause tangles [see inset picture]. Twisted line must be de-spooled and untwisted – this is generally accomplished by deep-casting with just a sinker and using a little extra pressure pinching the line whilst reeling in – if this is repeated several times, the amount of line-twist should be reduced. If you are in a boat, let the line out with nothing tied to it whilst the boat is moving – the line should sort itself out while you reel it back in.

Causes:

No swivel:

Cheapskate! Use a swivel whenever required. This is designed to help prevent twist. Fixed spool reels can and will twist line with frequent use. You can untwist the line by making a long cast with a sinker and reeling it in slowly – make sure that you tie in a swivel. Test the swivel and replace old swivels.

Swivel on strike [the swivel is not working properly]:

If you are using a swivel, it is not working properly. Check if it is corroded / damaged, or if its action is impaired by some obstacle like mud/dried bait. Dispose of and replace defective swivels.

The line has been incorrectly spooled onto your reel.

It is important that when you are putting new line onto your reel, that the orientation of the feed spool is correct. Just hold your line up in the air – it should not twist but should hang in waves. If the line gathers, you are looking a twisted line. The correct method of installing new line is described in Chapter 2.

Lure is spinning:

The lure you are using is twisting your line. Lures should not spin when being reeled in. Use a swivel.

Check Chapter 10 on knots for artificial lures.

Slow down your retrieve or use a weight to stop the spinning action. Tweaking the diving vanes on the lure sometimes helps. Use a swivel. Sometimes caused when the lure tangles with the main line.

You are fishing deep water and your bait is spiraling as it goes down / comes up: This can also happen when trolling dead fish / fillets / large baits. Check your bait and make sure it is uniform in shape. If you drop your bait close by, you will see if it is spinning. Use a swivel as well. Reduce the rate at which the bait sinks.

Put 'the Beatles' music off – that's causing your line to do the twist!

Line tangled on reel:

Sort out tangles as soon as possible after they occur. I have seen so many people give up fishing and reel in the tangle to sort out later. Guess what – later is the next time they go fishing! Contrary to popular opinion, tangles are relatively easy to unravel. Make sure that the line is not bunched up – this helps to locate key loops that can be pulled through the bunch, helping undo the tangle. Whenever line on a reel has been spooled with high tension, this causes the line to bite into the reel, with the line becoming jammed between coils of the line already on the reel. In this case, line must be de-spooled and then re-spooled at a lesser tension. You can accomplish this by casting out with a heavy sinker with a swivel and reeling in at the correct tension.

Causes:

High strain fight caused line to bite into remaining line on reel.

Whenever you experience a high-strain fight, de-spool by casting or manually drawing line off the reel and reel in at the right tension.

Line too loose on reel spool.

This causes the loose coils to leave the reel at the same time, causing a tangle.

Like, it's an overwind, dude! Remember – gentle pressure from the moment you cast!

Give anyone that was fishing at the spot total right of way. Two or more lines in the same zone is just asking for it! That's why I'm a loner when I fish. I can't stand rod jungles.

Gap between reel and reel frame.

If you're stuck with the reel, you're stuck with the reel – get used to the action and learn how to disentangle as quickly as possible [mostly experienced with centre pin reels and some multipliers]. Line stuck in this manner generally is damaged when it becomes jammed. Always test the line between your fingers – when you feel damage, remove the line up to that point – replace if you have to.

Overwind.

Pull line off reel slowly and when you come to a tangle, find the main loop causing it [it is easy – this is the line that is stops line from de-spooling], back-wind and continue stripping line from the reel. Repeat until overwind and all loose coils are gone. When casting with a multiplier – type reel, you are generally facing the water and casting from over one shoulder or overhead. Bring the rod forward firmly and smoothly, releasing the free spool just before your rod is vertical. Immediately, lightly tame the free-spinning spool and I promise you, you will not burn your thumb! Make sure that line is evenly distributed across the spool and that line is wound in under reasonable tension.

Line caught in eye / guide:

Keep an *'eye'* out for this. Always look before you cast or strike. Line caught on or in a line guide will almost certainly cause your line to snap and possibly damage the rod. Second nature!!

Causes: Windy.

Eat less cabbage, cauliflower and beans. Seriously, when it is windy avoid slack line on your rod. Come to think of it – avoid slack line – period. The only time you want a little slack line is when you're live-baiting.

You are fishing light and it is raining. Wet rods and guides cause light line to stick to them – it's the power of cohesion. Watch out for this especially more so when you are fishing light.

Swinging rod too far behind on striking:

Like the rod-tip hits the ground behind you when you strike, causing the line to wrap around the tip. Slow down, killer! Down boy! You are striking too hard – remember to reel in as you strike. The striking process is for you to set the hook, not to remove the hapless fish's jaw!!

Your line is twisted.

Hey! None of this is limited to just what I say. There's more out there. If you just open yourself to this, then, like me, *you will learn something new each day*. Untwist the line [see above].

Line caught on rod tip:

Twisted line can cause this to happen. Look before you cast or strike – you run the risk of breaking your rod / losing a fish if you don't. Sometimes the wind can cause this, sometimes the act of striking can cause this – always check for line caught / wrapped around the rod tip. *Be extra vigilant at night*. Use a head lamp – avoid flashing the light from the headlamp in the water – this can and will spook fish.

Causes:

Tangles / knots can do this.

Tangles are quite simply described as undesired knots. A tangle always consists of loops of line and it is not difficult for one of those loops to catch on your tip / line guides. Check for twisted line. You know the drill.

Reeling in and setting your rod down.

Each time you reel in, whether to re-bait, inspect your bait or land a fish, you set your rod down. Make certain that you have a rod stand / rod tube set up to hold your rod whilst you work on the line. This way, tangles on the tip are reduced.

When it is windy avoid slack line:

It can easily be forced to wrap around the tip or any of the guides. If you strike whilst your line is like this, we will more than likely be having a moment's silence for your rod and/or line.

Line caught in tree / telephone & power lines:

Are you nuts? Scout the surroundings well before you start fishing. When it is very hot, your chances are better near shade [sometimes, when Murphey's Law doesn't work, the shade from trees actually falls on the water, and the water is fishable]. You are only forgiven if the tree is in the water.

If you **practice** your casting [hopefully without a hook], you will soon learn that your limits can easily be extended and you will **know** your limits. [Generally, the frequency of 'line caught in the tree' is directly proportionate to the number of empty beer cans]. Safety first – you can afford to drop your guard if it's a tree or telephone line, but power lines? That's shocking man!

Practice is the difference between casting onto the Lilly leaf and sliding smoothly into the water with a bass worm or fly; and casting over the Lilly bed and getting snagged in the papyrus. And for God's sake – **don't** practice when you go fishing - go to a sports ground instead.

Carry 'a flask of wine, a book of verse and y..' sorry! – wrong article! [apologies to Omar Khayyam]

Slack line:

This is the *king* of reasons.

Picture the fish fighting to get free. Remember the natural swimming action of the fish is that the head moves from side-to-side. When the fish is desperate, this action is intensified with the head of the fish frantically moving from side-to-side – this can and will invariably result in the hook becoming loose or free. A little slack line in the fight is all the fish needs to throw a hook, whether the hook is barbed or not. When you're fishing, ensure that once a fish is hooked, you do not give it slack line. Slack line with sinkers and floats shall be dealt with individually – later. Sometimes the fish swims towards you – if it does this fast, check if you can back step and reel like the devil. *Avoid that slack line.*

RELATED TO THE FISH:

Fish breaks free:

Here's a thing. When a fish breaks you, it has won the fight. Sometimes this cannot be helped, but a little attention to detail will help. Study the waters you are fishing, look for possible snags in the form of reef and structure, reed beds, channels, trees and branches, broken off line in the water and other obstacles. Remember – snags can be in, on and above the water.

Learn how to use side-strain

– side strain can effectively turn a fish away from a potential snag / run. Side-strain is turning the rod in the opposite direction to the direction the fish is pulling in. Do everything you can to turn a fish that is seeking refuge for something that will almost certainly result in being broken off. Do everything but compromise the breaking strain of your line. Wherever possible, "walk" a fish away from possible snags, even before they head towards the potential snag [that's why you need to scout an area before you fish!]. As much as I hate to admit it, there is a reason why shad get towed out of the water without any chance of a fight. The same with bass – you power up your tackle so that the fish can be powered away from snagging hazards. Just bear in mind the type of fish you are hunting – if it has a soft mouth, remember that when fighting the fish. And always remember – sometimes the fish is allowed to win. Take a moment and relish the encounter you've had, learn from it and, hard as it may be, celebrate the fish's victory. *It's a challenge.*

If a fish takes refuge in a weed bed, maintain tension and you might win yet. Allow a little slack line and watch closely. If you see movement, the fish is still there. Play the waiting game. Wait for it to get itself loose then take up the fight again.

Always remember – once you have set the hook, the die is cast. There is nothing you can do from this point onwards – the fish may be well-hooked or not.

Fish escapes down / up-stream:

Most of us have seen the movie 'a river runs through it'. Believe me, I've had some hairy scrapes [that's why I'm bald!] in rivers, but I have to say that it would be really nice if a fight like that was possible [without the snags, leftover line, broken bottles, nuclear waste……] There has to be a time when you decide that it would not be safe to pursue the fish any further, put on maximum pressure, and pray for a miracle.

However, something I learnt quite by accident, a few days after the actual incident. I was fishing the cascades at *Midmar* mouth with Sean Pillay. Fishing with bait using a fly rod. I had an incredible take, and the fight was on, the fish shot into the rapids, headed strongly upstream. I then brought it pretty close and when I saw the size of the fish, knew immediately that this was the biggest scalie [yellowfish] I had ever seen. The fish turned and shot downstream. During the fight, my spool came loose, and fell into the water. Luckily the force of the fish speeding away caused it to spin, so it sank really slowly. I grabbed at it and reassembled the reel. I could only feel the current on my line, and thought I'd lost the fish. As I reeled in, I found that the line was actually headed upstream. I bagged that fish and it tipped the scales at 3.2 kg. But it only hit me a few days later: It might have been chance that made the fish turn and head upstream, but I am reasonably confident that this explanation holds more weight:

When my spool was spinning, too much line was released. This line was dragged downstream by the current, below the fish in a loop, giving the fish the feeling that it was being pulled downstream, so it turned! What do you think – worth a try? I think so.

Eels:

If you're fishing for eel, you're okay. You just need to pull the eel out so quickly that it does not have a chance to grab onto some sort of structure. If it does, keep the line taut and keep on twanging the line at high frequency – this helps. Remember that once you catch an eel – if this was not your targeted species, you need to remove all line that has come into contact with the creature and re-tie your traces – the residual scent left in an eel's slime is a strong "**keep away**" signal to fish. Oh yes, and wash your hands too. Remember that the eel has long muscular body – it can wrap around structure and you have no chance of landing it whilst it is gripping the structure. But like all muscles, exhaustion must set in and the eel will tire. Play the waiting game, keep on twanging that line and it will eventually have to relax its grip. There's your chance!

RELATED TO *FISHERFOLK*:

[That's right, it is *all* your fault!]

Forgot to use sunscreen:

A lecture on how harsh the sun is is wasted here. If you are going to be in the sun, protect yourself from sunburn. Fishing with sunburn can very painful. Take adequate precautions.

Snakes:

Most people have an *irrational* fear of snakes. The snake has more right to be there than you have. If you leave it alone, it will leave you alone. Back away from the area and continue fishing. The snake will go away. If it is a spitting cobra [Rinkhals] be sure to have your glasses on. If it is a mamba, change your spot. Mambas are fiercely territorial. Don't be a hero and try to catch the snake and please don't kill the snake unless you have absolutely no other option. There is more on snakes later in this Chapter.

Cheap and nasty:

It's not often that you get lucky buying something cheap and it turns out to be a real bargain because it does what it is supposed to do… The general rule of thumb is that if it is cheap – its nasty. I have seen disappointment on so many faces when tackle fails prematurely….

Striking too hard:

Have you ever seen hook being set into a marlin? I swear that some of you out there strike harder than Marlin fishermen. There must be generations of lipless fish out there! Generally, the smaller the hook, the lighter the strike. Follow this rule and you are well ruled. Generally, striking would involve rapidly dropping the tip as you reel in, then, continuing reeling, raising the rod sharply. "Pumping" is what you would do if you're fishing a live bait: set drag, drop tip whilst reeling in quickly, step back and pump the rod firmly backwards, step back again, dropping tip and reeling fast, repeat. Some people repeat three or four times. Two is good enough for me.

Strike too weak:

Fishing live bait for Garrick. The fish runs, the fisherman picks up the rod, counts his 10 seconds [I told you, I prefer eight seconds] and the fishermen gently pulls the rod back and starts reeling, exclaiming "Bloody fish! I don't know how they get away every time!" I wanted to respond, but didn't – but I thought it anyway – why didn't he just empty that bucket of mullet into the surf if he wanted to feed the fish. Really – remember the rule stated above – unless you are using circle hooks.

When I was learning the game of snooker, the talented old man who taught me the game, *Pa Padayachee*, always said when I played a shot with just too little power so that the ball came to a halt in the mouth of the pocket: *"Son, you rushed all the way to the lavatory [toilet] but you crapped outside!!"*

Your strike should be proportionate to the size of the hook you are using. Smaller hooks always require little or no striking. Bigger hooks have bigger barbs and therefore require greater energy to set the hook, circle hooks just require you to take up the slack and maintain tension.

Fish escapes [idiot holding fish up by line over water.com]:

How many times have I seen some idiot hold a fish up by the line [still hooked] and then stare stupidly as it falls back into the water? When you land a fish, only remove the hook a safe distance away from the water. If you used a landing net, only remove the fish from the net after you have dislodged the hook – *away from the water*. Once you have the fish in your hands, get a secure grip on it if you are keeping it. If you are returning the fish to the water, do NOT apply any pressure to the soft area between the anus and eyes. You can seriously injure the fish by doing this.

Striking too early:

This happens very often in the surf – *fisher folk*, not very familiar with what a bite feels like, strikes a 'wave bite', before the fish bites. I have to say that there are not very many bites that are difficult to discriminate. Of course, as weather conditions worsen, that sorts out the men from the boys. You have to know what a bite feels like. You have to watch the surf.

Key words: ***WATCH THE SURF.***

Experience is key.

Best if you go with someone who allows you to feel what a bite is like [pretty much like when you're holding your rod and someone taps it with their fingertips]. Seriously now – what is the point of setting up that lovely bait and waiting all that time it was in the water, only to pull it out the fish's mouth as it starts biting. It actually is as easy as learning to walk. Just try. The same with striking too late…

Failure to give line:

The reason that you give a fish line is that if you don't, it will snap the line / pull the hook free / causing you to lose it. Make sure that your drag is not locked using a shifting spanner. As I said earlier, your drag is set correctly if the reel releases line when tension applied to the line bends the rod tip to about 90° to the butt. Remember this.

Remember that some fish like those caught on live bait, grunter, Steenbras and kob [salmon] need you to give line before you strike.

Rod strikes obstacle:

What was it? Someone else's head, your own head, tree, cable, tent, rock…? Wake up! Even in the dark you should have extreme confidence of your surroundings. If you don't, you're suicidal – kamikaze. *You should never be performing ANY activity without first scouting the area.*

Land a fish when it is tired!

That just about says it all. If you need to rush a fish out, make sure that you are aware of the price to be paid for this. You know that a fish has tired adequately to be landed when it is swimming on its side. But take heed – if the fish is spooked by a gaff / landing net / attempt at 'tailing'…. It will get a second wind and attempt an escape – this attempt at escaping is generally successful, so take heed. Make sure that the fish is tired enough to be landed.

Sometimes you have to rush a fish out, especially when there are large shapes lurking below the boat – shark will attack a hooked fish!

Cigarette burns line [also burns fisherman]:

Ask yourself why, equally skilled, non – smokers catch more than smokers? Come on!

Wading – pushing your luck:

Wading is wonderful – I have caught hundreds of fish whilst doing this. Don't take chances when wearing waders – you could lose more than the fish! It is sometimes difficult to judge depth when wading so make sure that your cellular phone and other accessories are protected from exposure to water. You never know what obstacles are in your path so tread carefully – you could trip at any moment. Wear footwear that will protect you from cuts and pokes and stinging and biting creatures, and, of course, leeches. When wading near drop-offs, keep away from the edge because it is so easy to slide into the drop-off. It pays to survey before you wade. Even if you are familiar with the waters, things could change drastically the next time you visit, so take nothing for granted. Slow but sure wins the race.

You also need to be aware of the possible presence of crocodiles and hippopotami. You may surprise an iguana or snake whilst wading. Don't allow panic to take over. An escaping iguana makes quite a splash and this can give you quite a shock. Snakes will generally try to escape so let them do this.

It helps to carry a stick that you can lean on whilst wading, the stick should be attached to your belt / person so that it can be released when you need two hands.

Sleeping on the job:

Some people manage to do this with their eyes open. Let me think about what advice to give you….zzzz… **WAKE UP!!!!** It is always a good idea to use a bite alarm when waiting for a bite. Make sure that rods are lashed so that they do not make regrettable one-way trips into the water.

Trying to walk on slimy rocks:

You know how a slug manages it? Slowly. Avoid this whilst you have a fish on. What the hell! Avoid it. Period.

Diving into murky water to catch a rod or for any other reason:

Unless you have super powers, equipped with x-ray vision, please promise you'll never do anything this stupid. You never know what is hidden in murky water. Aside from crocodiles and shark, there is always the possibility that you may get your head bashed in; you may even be serious injured by hidden rocks / trees / obstacles. And don't complain about the dangers – be aware of them!

Fishing into deep water over a sandy ridge / sandbank:

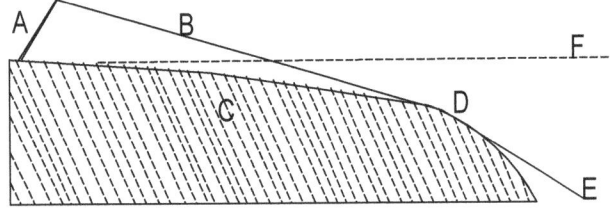

Legend: A: Rod; B: line from rod and before drop-off; C: Sandbank – could well have rocks as well; D: Drop-off; E: line after drop-off – note change in angle – line will bite into the drop-off at D. If there are rocks at "D", you stand a higher risk of experiencing line fray. The line extends from point "A" to the end of the cast at "E".

F=water level.

Always productive, but when you have a fish on, the line can cut into the sand "D", and when the fish turns…the line is dragged through sand – the result? Weakened line and/or increased strain. Go on, spend the money on line with high-abrasion resistance.

Wearing inappropriate footwear:

I have seen fish lost because an angler was injured due to fishing barefoot, hooking a nice fish and then having to walk barnacle-covered rocks to land the fish. *Make sure that your choice of footwear is practical.*

Must not slip and when cold, must keep your feet warm when required. Slops / beach tongs are widely used but these are inadequate for fishing on and around rocks.

When fishing saltwater, do not wear shoes without socks. Sand and stone can become stuck to the inside of shoes and literally 'sandpaper' your skin off – if this is not bad enough, there is an especially high risk of infection once the skin has been compromised. Wear socks with your sandals or fishing shoes. Better still, get the neoprene booties. 'Nuff sed.

Watch your back cast!

For conventional fishing, there are casting techniques for when the space behind you is inadequate for a full back cast. If these techniques are practiced beforehand, you will have adequate reach to your cast. Watch out for people and animals and obstacles behind you. A swinging sinker / fly line can do severe damage.

When you are fly fishing, you will generally need as much space behind you for as far as you can cast. It is not only the clearance that is important… you have to be aware of other people, especially those trying to pass you by. I generally carry a slasher for long grass but please do not damage our beautiful indigenous vegetation. If you are fishing private property, get the owner's permission to cut grass / remove vegetation. Wear a cap and glasses so that your head and eyes are protected for if and when your false casts go wrong.

Pollution caused me to lose my fish!

Ever hooked into a plastic packet whilst reeling in? It's not funny. Rusting cans can cut through line as easily as broken glass can. Discarded fishing line – hooked fish can swim through loops of this and …. Plastic bags – you have a fish on, it's a good one, you're fishing two hooks and the other hook snags onto the plastic bag / tyre / other refuse! You step on the remains of a fire only to find out that the fire was built over a hole, and the coals at the bottom are hot! Cigarette buds and packets, bait boxes and packaging…. This *can* cause you to lose a fish. If each one of us takes away just what we came with… We can make a difference. The next time we arrive, the response won't be one of disgust!

Landed fish can't be subdued to allow extraction of the hook:

I am sure that you have also seen many fish escape like this! If you are going to bag the fish, administer the last rites using a priest before attempting to unhook. If not, turn the fish upside down and hold it with a damp rag over the eyes – this generally calms the fish enough to allow you to dislodge the hook. If the fish has teeth, respect them, use a condom [oops – I mean protection!]. Seriously - fish like shark and barracuda.com – don't try to take out the hook – those teeth are wicked.

"Can't cast far enough":

I remember many times, fishing *Sandspit* in Port Shepstone where I cast my 6ounce sinker way out, then when I wasn't watched, reeled my line to within 50metres of the steep beach because I could see the Garrick milling about there or because that's where the 'hole' was. And the fishermen were asking me to cast for them and "Hey, how you cast so far?" Do you really need to cast far out? I suppose if you are targeting a reef that is far out, then read the next paragraph carefully. And use a shock leader if you are going to subject your tackle to extra strain.

If you really do, then only one thing can help you – practice, practice, practice. But don't practice when you are actually fishing. Go to the nearest sports field / open area. Make sure that no people / animals are in the target zone. Be aware that whilst you are practice-casting, there is the risk that your sinker may break free – make sure nothing that can be injured / damaged is within the cast area.

And sometimes, you really don't need to cast far enough. Fish are naturally found close to reefs and are seldom found in open waters where they have no protection – you will only find well camouflaged fish in open waters. Understand the creatures you are hunting, know their feeding habits – game fish are found in the outer limits of the reef, reef fish hug the reef because that is where they get their protection from. Besides, the reef supplies them with food as well.

Learn to look for close gullies and deep water 'holes'. These will hold fish. And if you hook something, put on pressure to get it away from the reef / structure or you stand a greater chance of losing it.

Failure to spot fish when sight-fishing.

It is crucial that you wear close-fitting glasses that prevent overhead glare, reflected glare and side-glare. This should be coupled with a decent peaked cap that provides shade over the glasses. This will empower you to spot fish with comparative ease.

RELATED TO LANDING FISH:

Gaffed fish pulls you overboard.

What? You didn't think the fish was big enough to do that? Have you ever seen a rod take off like a javelin, and if retrieved, you find that it was a 350g fish? Make sure that you are balanced when gaffing. Leaning over the side off the boat means that the gaff is too short. You could wind up losing the gaff, the fish, and possibly the gaffer too. Big fish that need to be gaffed require the use of a flying gaff and this type of gaffing should only be performed by suitably skilled / trained / experienced persons.

Gaffed fish swims away.

That's why a gaff has a non-slip handle. And it doesn't help if your hands are slippery. The gaffer should keep a firm grip on the gaff. The gaffing stroke must be synchronized with simultaneously lifting the fish on board. Provision should have been made in advance for space for the fish [in other words, for example, if you are on a boat, do not attempt to bring a fish on deck without making sure that there is space for a flapping fish], someone should be standing by with a priest / club to administer the *last rites*.

Missing with a gaff:

Inept gaffing loses many a decent fish. Sometimes, though, even the most experienced gaffer will miss-gaff a fish. When this happens, it becomes doubly difficult for the fish to be brought to the boat [the fish literally becomes boat-shy]. Inept gaffing can result in the line / or hook being struck by the gaff – you can figure out the outcome… If it's your first time, a solid strike with the gaff, accompanied by a continuous lifting just behind the head should do it. You should never attempt to gaff in the belly area as the gaff tears out easily.

Premature gaffing:

Even if the fisherman is exhausted and the fish is not, do not attempt to gaff a fish prematurely [I have seen experienced fishermen lose fish this way, even when they were assisted by experienced gaffers]. It is always advisable to wait until the fish has been suitably tired. The same applies to premature netting. Be patient. On the other hand, and where there are several lines out, fish like barracuda are powered to the boat and gaffed as soon as possible, mostly prematurely, and mostly because there are sharks around. In situations like this, an experienced gaffer is essential.

Gaff not sharp enough:

You want I should say something here that is not printable? Well I did.

Gaff jaw too big / small:

An experienced gaffer can overcome this. Just be careful and deliberate in the act of gaffing and you will be okay.

Landing net too small:

Don't try to force the fish into the net – try tailing the fish – this involves getting a firm grip on the tail between the fin and the body, and dragging the fish out the water [I wouldn't recommend this for eel and sea-snakes!]. Note that this should really only be attempted with a protective glove on. You can lip-land if the teeth are not considerable. Please remember that it is only possible to 'tail' certain fish where you can get a good grip on the meat just before the tail. It is almost impossible to 'tail' most freshwater fish.

Landing net hits fish:

*This should **never** happen. The fish is always brought to the net. The net is never brought to the fish.* Unless, of course, you are doing something illegal in which case I hope you get caught. If the landing net is in the water and the fish hits it, it is not the same as the net hitting the fish.

Tear (*as in torn*) [hole] in net.

Make sure that the landing net does not have a hole in it that the fish can fall / swim through – you could end up looking pretty stupid! It can be very hectic if the fish passes through a hole in the net with your line still attached! Patch up the net or attempt to beach the fish.

If you're fishing multiple hooks, the other hooks will snag in the net

– or somewhere else.

Fish using one hook

– what? You would like to catch two trophies at once? This is alays the chance you take with more than one hook...

Cast net stuck on the rocks:

Serves you right! There is risk to everything you do – a proper risk assessment must be carried out. A cast net is designed to trap fish by closing around the target – if you are going to attempt casting a net where there are rocks, you will need to pull the net in before it bottoms out.

Collapsing landing net:

I hate this design. I have yet to see one that does not decide to become floppy when a decent fish is on. If you insist on using this design, make sure the net is the right way up.

RELATED TO ACTS OF NATURE / GOD:

Stuck in mud!

Ya, right! Act of nature, right? Seriously, fighting a fish and being stuck in the mud is a dangerously bad combo. You have to decide what to do. Messy choices. Avoid walking / wading through mud – you never know what is embedded in it or how deep you will sink. The best way out of mud is to work your way out, backwards. If you are still sinking, then on your face boy! Bigger surface area means less sink. Think about it.

When driving your vehicle and you suspect that the terrain may be too soft and that you may just get bogged down, get someone to walk in front with a steel rod of say 12mm diameter. They can test the soil by pushing the rod into the ground. If the rod goes in easily, you are at risk of getting bogged. You may find that you can drive on suspect soil, but if you park the vehicle, it may sink slowly into the ground – and you may only find out about this when you pack up.

And talking about parking, be considerate – don't park where you end up blocking other traffic – your vehicle may be damaged when other vehicles attempt to pass you. You must always park parallel to the water so if your handbrake fails, it cannot roll into the water.

Make sure that your vehicle is roadworthy. Breakdowns can seriously put you at risk and compromise your fishing time. Jacks, tools and spare wheels must be in good condition.

Lightning

Graphite. Can you smell the meat roasting? And it's not a braai. Its electric!

Storm:

If you have a fish on and a storm is about to hit – what do you do? If you're fighting a kingie and have been for the past hour and the kingie is like bigger than 100 cm, you've still got a minimum of two hours to go. There's a lot to consider, starting with your life, how the weather will affect the water, lightning, storm debris and raised water levels - if you are near a river mouth…. Personally, I'd increase the pressure on the fish whilst monitoring the approaching storm. All I can add is that you should consider the combined effect of all the possible hazards and make a decision based on that. It is all about the risk you are taking, and remember: you are gambling with your life…

Hail:

Here's the thing: the closer you are to built-up areas, the smaller the hail stones. This means that most hail falling in rural areas is large. Find shelter, protect your equipment and wait out the storm. Hail can do serious damage. When you do find shelter, be aware that other creatures will also be looking for shelter too. So be on the lookout. Avoid tall trees.

Tide:

This generally occurs when the tide is coming in. You are on a sandbank / rock only accessible at low tide, and, just after the tide turns, You're into something decent. What do you do? I wouldn't stay out there if there was a stout rope anchoring me to the mainland. Keep the pressure on - quickly work your way back to higher ground. It *ain't* worth it.

Seagull takes fish:

I have seen many live baiters leave their bait swimming in a shallow pool, only to return later to find them gone.

What happened? Crab? Gull? Live bait should be kept under decent living conditions, an aerated container with protection from the sun – yes, that means a lid! You do want the bait to be alive, don't you?

Rats:

'Gives me the *ceebee-jeebeez* just thinking of them. I watched a fight break out between two groups of guys fishing for carp at *Midmar* mouth. I was sitting in my kick boat, busy looking for scalies when I spotted movement between two rocks. I watched as a rat took a packet of carp bait. It dragged the bait into a hole between the rocks.

Watch where you keep your supplies – if there are rats about – and there generally are - they will take away what they can and may very well contaminate anything else.

Mozzies [mosquitoes]:

The end of the day begins with swarms of these – don't suck in air through your mouth, use a repellent. It's a good time to be fishing, though.

RELATED TO HOOKS

Hook strength.

Always test hook strength by grasping the shank in one hand and the bend in the other - try and 'break' the hook by hand and if it bends / breaks, toss the sucker/s out]. If you have a batch of faulty hooks, return them to the supplier.

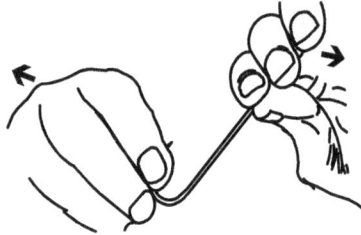

Test the strength of the hook by feeling the extent of "give" in the degree of flexion [ability to bend without losing shape] you experience [hold the shank just at the eye with one hand and the tip just below the sharpened point with the other hand. Pull and release. Refer to the sketch alongside] – if this changes the shape of the hook, it is not suitably hardened, if it does not flex at all, indications are that the hook is possibly too hard [possibly 'brittle']. There should just be a little 'give' and the hook returns to its original shape.

Remember that one end of the hook is sharp and is designed not just to penetrate, but to penetrate deeply. So, when you perform this relatively simple task, always be wary of the sharp end when you test a hook.

When disposing of hooks, force them into the ground, shank-first, and without line attached to them. Yes, be careful of the sharp end.

It cannot discriminate between fish flesh and your own.

The hook tears / breaks free:

Oh – bummer! This will even happen from time to time on a perfectly well-timed strike. It generally is a result of poor timing when striking. I have had this happen to me and I have to say that once a fish has been hooked and provided you are not putting excessive pressure on the fish, this would be the one valid reason for losing a fish. However, should you try and lift a fish out of the water and the hook tears free at this stage, you only have yourself to blame. Use a gaff or landing net.

Causes:

Know enough about the species you are after.

What sort of mouth do they have? [hard / soft] You have to know something about the fish you are targeting and this will automatically tell you whether you can strike hard or just lift the rod to strike.

Is your rod action too stiff? Is your tackle too heavy? *Lucky devil!* ☺

Seriously now – some people are convinced they need to use extra heavy rods and reels and line – just-in-case. Don't be a cowboy. Heavy action rods are for just that. They can exert tremendous force on a soft-mouthed fish or on light hooks causing you to lose fish. If this is you, go on, say it: "I'm a cowboy". Check Chapter 10 for balancing your tackle.

Extended fight.

Always try to cut down on the duration of a fight without putting too much pressure on the fish. However, if you are fishing for bass and fish like musselcracker, for example, in heavy structure, you are forced to put just that little extra pressure on the fish, whilst at the same time, never allowing it to relax. Just remember whilst fighting a fish – your rod should always be held upright. Your rod only goes down when you are applying side-strain to turn a fish. Never allow the fish to relax – ever.

Too much pressure?

The only time you could maybe be justified losing a fish through too much of pressure would be in trying to turn it away from a positively lethal snag hazard or you are running out of line. Too much pressure puts too much of strain on the tackle and the hooked fish. *Relax – you're supposed to de-stress when you're fishing – you're a little mixed up, aren't you?*

Did you strike too hard?

"No, not me?" "Then what is this fish jaw bone attached to your line?"

Hook not sharp enough:

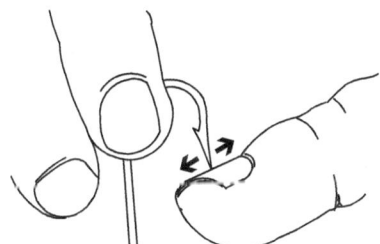

*To test the sharpness, carefully and **LIGHTLY** drag the point across your thumbnail. If it is adequately sharp, it will try to dig in and **not** slide – if not sharp enough, it will slide across the nail. If the hook slides across your nail, you will need to sharpen it or select another hook.* ***PLEASE BE CAREFUL!!!!***

How many of you out there are guilty of this? A hook is only sharp enough to fish with if the point does not slide when the sharp point is dragged across your thumbnail. A fish can easily throw a hook that is not sharp enough.

Carry a polishing stone for dressing the points of hooks as you are fishing. These can be bought from any hardware / engineering supply store.

When sharpening, drag the hook at the appropriate angle on the stone, point – first. Always sharpen into the point, not away from it.

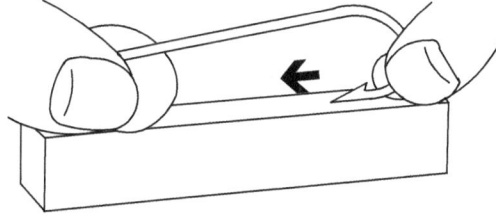

*Holding the shank of the hook, **drag** the point on the stone repetitively until adequately sharp. Always drag the hook into the stone [in the direction of the arrow, then lift and repeat until point is sharp], do not drag the hook in the opposite direction! And remember a coarse stone will never sharpen a small surface area effectively – get the polishing stone from industrial hardware supplier!*

Remember, sharpness is critical for penetration. Poor quality steels lose edge very easily. Check hooks regularly, especially after a snag or when re-using hooks. When you're fishing for tiger fish, sharpness is everything. But then when you're not fishing for Tobies, you are guaranteed to catch them, even with a blunt hook. And no bait.

And don't take it for granted that just - bought hooks are sharp enough to fish with. *Test everything before tying up traces.*

I have to tell you: I am partial to chemically- and laser-sharpened hooks. Try them. Remember that smaller hooks are made of thinner wire and are therefore naturally sharp…

Hook straightened:

You didn't test the hook before you used it, did you? Test every hook before you tie it on. If the hook bends, it has not been suitably hardened. When you experience this, you will probably find that the entire batch is faulty. Don't use too much pressure when fighting a fish. This is why your setup should be balanced against what you're targeting. I cringe when I see surf-sticks being used for carp. 30pound line!

Hook broke:

Congratulations Peter Pan! You broke Hook! When you test a hook for strength, you should feel the extent of "give" in the degree of flexion you experience [hold the shank just at the eye with one hand and the tip, just below the sharpened point with the other hand. Pull and release.] – if it flexes too much and deforms [straightens] it is not suitably hardened, if it does not flex at all, indications are that the hook is possibly too hard [approaching 'brittle']. There should just be a little 'give' and the hook returns to its original shape. I wouldn't try this with 10/0 and bigger hooks or hooks smaller than size 10.

Don't use the same trace over and over again. The more you subject a hook to strain, the more you are weakening it. Knots get tighter and tighter and monofilament line can become weaker when this happens. Tie new traces using new components. Prolonged exposure to the elements causes corrosion. Don't be a cheapskate – throw rusted hooks away, especially if they are pitted. Rust is the result of corrosion. Corrosion *embrittles* [hardens] steel, weakening it and leading to premature failure. Don't be using sandpaper to strip the rust off now!

Too many hooks:

Unless you are fishing with live bait for something like barracuda or wahoo, you only need one hook. There were times when I saw people deep-sea bottom-fishing and I cringed because they were using rigs with 8 to 10 hooks.

Just remember that wherever you're fishing, if you hook into something sizeable, the remaining hooks leave you with a serious snagging hazard. I once saw a trophy size bass lost because the person was using two hooks. One hook was in the mouth and the other got lodged in the tail! The result was the loss of a fish well over 5kg when the record at the time was around 4kg. Just use one hook. Please.

Barb too big:

There's a thing! How many of you are aware that the size of the barb can either make it easy for the hook to penetrate, or make it damn nearly impossible for penetration. If you ever watch someone being sutured, you will realize just how much effort is required to penetrate human skin with a needle. The purpose of the barb is to **retard** extraction of the hook – for this to actually work, the barb needs to penetrate **fully** into the flesh. You need to understand that although you might strike like a cowboy, the effect at the other end of the line might be much, much smaller, due to line stretch and the resultant loss of energy. Therefore, the degree of sharpness as well as the size of the barb is of critical importance. The smaller the barb, the better. I tell you what – the hell with the barb! You don't even need it! All you have to ensure when you hook a fish, is that all through the fight, you maintain tight line [no slack line]. Go on, try it – you will be amazed!

All you have to do is use a pair of pliers to squeeze the barb away [in most cases – for larger hooks you may need to file away the barb].

Hook rusted / pitted.

Why even bother going fishing if your hooks are corroded? Corrosion on a hook is almost always an invitation to "*break here*", at the site of corrosion. Toss out corroded hooks. Don't try to reclaim them. Oil hooks if you live in a corrosive environment. But – hey! Fishing is a corrosive environment! Get hold of sachets of desiccant [called silica gel – normally in pill-bottles] from your local pharmacy and put them with your tackle to keep hooks dry. *Keep silica gel away from kidz.com.*

Hook on lure / fly defective:

I don't know what it is with manufacturers of some flies and lures [mostly lures]. They come up with a lure that works well and compromise on the hook quality. How many times have you fished with a lure and found that hooks break or straighten? Inspect and test hooks on lures. Buy good quality trebles / hooks and replace the inferior quality ones. When you buy your flies / lures, insist on testing the hooks.

Lost fish on spoon:

When you buy a spoon, it generally comes with good quality trebles. The problem is that there is no leading hook at the front [line – end] of the spoon. So, add in a single "J" hook, curve just smaller than the widest part of the spoon. ***The hook must be free-swinging.***

Hook stuck in finger / part of body:

That's right, this is another way to lose fish – you cannot catch fish if you have a hook stuck in yourself.

If it's a treble, first cut the existing points off so that they too do not become lodged in you or something else, thereby creating a tug-of-war. Believe me, I have seen that happen.

Now I'm no Doctor, though I've performed much doctoring in my time. Whenever possible, get the person to professional help. If you're fishing a remote area with professional help too far away for immediate attention, you can't just tug the hook out – it may be curled around a nerve or blood vessel. Whatever it is that you do, remember that there is a barb at one end and an eye at the other. Address the problem according to the degree of urgency - I'm sure that there is no way in hell that you will attempt to take a hook out of an eye! But then…consider what you would have done if you were fishing barbless….

Causes:

Yeah, that's right – **you should be fishing barbless**.

Fishing too close together:

I hate graphite and glass jungles. Avoid them.

If people learn the first rule of fishing courtesy and give right of way to the first person on the spot, hey – nah, it'll never happen. People are too greedy.

But then maybe I can start a movement here or do I have more hope with castor oil instead?

Fly fishing in a stiff breeze / windy conditions:

Fishing is generally good when the wind starts picking up. Just be careful – wind can and will compromise your casting. Don't fly fish if the wind gets too strong.

Make sure that your false casts are downwind [fly fishing]:

And if you're trying this without a shooting head, you sure are looking for trouble. You should always wear glasses and a hat whilst fly fishing anyway.

Hooks lying loosely in a tackle box:

Never ever do this! Use a magnet or a container with a securely fitting lid. Not the plastic bag you bought the hooks in! How many times have you had to grope in your tackle box for something whilst focusing attentively on your line? Sharp things should be in containers or sheathes and only handled intentionally.

Striking with a float / lure:

Always strike so that the float / lure is not propelled towards your body. If you strike vertically upwards, the line naturally comes straight for you. Make sure no-one is alongside, and strike to one side.

Lifting a lure / line out of the water whilst reeling in:

There are many times when you need to do this. Just remember to do it whilst swinging your rod away from your body, preferably away from the windward side as well.

What to do? Ideally you want medical attention. Sometimes this is not possible for whatever reason. It all depends on where the person is hooked. In a fleshy area, the hook can be pushed until it comes out of the flesh, the barb is then cut off and the hook removed. It is best to have someone suitably qualified to do this.

CAN'T HOOK THE FISH!

This one is da bomb! How often do you just shake your head in disbelief, sometimes using the colourful *Cape* style of complementing the fish's mothers and grandmothers! ["*Jou ma se dingdong!*"]

Ya boet! Relax. Maybe this will be of help:

Causes:

Fly-fishing

– strike the moment you have the take, whilst the fish is pulling. Too much slack line and you probably won't even know that a fish has had a go at your fly. The secret is to try and keep the line between fly and rod-tip as straight as possible [difficult in rivers, but possible within reason]. All you have to do is develop a knee-jerk response with your arm and the 'take'. Don't strike hard [unless you're fishing for tigers]. Just a firm raising of the rod should do it – even for bass and shad. If you're in the surf zone with a fast, two-handed retrieve, the take itself sets the hook. So what if you're so impaired that you need to use a bite detector – why don't you go the whole hog and get an automatic hook setting device as well? Whatever turns you on, I guess. Oh yeah, and fishing barbless helps! If you are using a fly with a circle hook – just tighten up, retrieve rapidly until you feel the fish and keep tight line.

Deep sea – bottom fishing:

Try and limit your rig to 3 hooks – it would be a shame to lose a trophy because you were too greedy – but more to the point – you miss bottom fish because your strike is wasted. You have to lower the tip a fraction, whilst the fish is biting, reel in rapidly and then strike. Your hookup ratio will certainly rise.

When bottom fishing from a boat, your line should be on the bottom [Hello – that's why it is called 'bottom' fishing!]. You do this by allowing your reel to *freespool* [taming occasionally with your palm] until the line is felt to bottom out [you will feel the impact, followed by slack line. You are now on the bottom. But the boat will be drifting, sometimes imperceptibly, sometimes fast. So, to keep your bait on the bottom, you need to give line at the rate of the drift. And you will catch.

With normal fishing, you sometimes get a firm pull – the fish should be struck during this pull. It's the other types of bites you are concerned about – right? Well, here are some guidelines:

Surf zone fish – If you don't maintain reasonable tension between rod-tip and sinker, you are not going to get a good telegraph signal from the fish. Once you feel the bite, it depends on what you're fishing for. Small baits, small hooks, start reeling rapidly as you feel the machine gun telegraph signal. This should be enough to set the hook.

Garrick. (from the *Carangadae* family of fish) aka Leervis. Nothing more I can say for this species – except maybe to read the paragraph on live bait below. You should not lose it once hooked. This is one fish that generally stays in open water and does not head for the reef once hooked. It fights clean.

Musselcracker. (two types, the black musselcracker is from the *Sparidae* family of fish) aka "poenskop", "black Steenbras" the white musselcracker, *Sparodon Durbanensis*, aka "*brusher*", "*biskop*"

Threatened species. *Use extra strong hooks*. If he takes, you will hook him. But be prepared for a fight. Just also remember – this species is fond of swimming towards you after taking the bait. You have to reel like a demon to catch up with him, dropping the tip as you do so, then, once you feel the fish, pump your rod and reel rapidly for the first few meters! The natural instinct of this fish and other bottom-feeding predators is to head for a ledge or underwater 'cave'. Reeling in rapidly generally means that it is away from the bottom, reducing the possibility of the fish finding shelter. And if it gets to the reef, you have almost certainly lost the fish. Remember that this species is quite capable of crushing / mangling the hook so don't delay with the strike.

Stumpnose. (from the *sparidae* family of fish) there are two main species of stumpnose bream, the Natal Stumpnose and the Cape Stumpnose.

A repeated steady pulling [the tug lasts about half a second]. Mostly, this is a shy fish. Make sure that the rod you are using has a soft to medium action and you will feel the weight of the fish as it mouths the bait. Lower the tip, reel and strike man!

Steenbras. (from the *sparidae* family of fish)

Second to our national fish, the Galjoen, this fish has been singularly responsible for most salt-water fishing frustrations. You reel in and look at your naked hook amazed, saying: "I didn't even feel the bite!" It is capable of making your rod do the javelin thing as well. And when the fish thunders off and your rod flies through the air, and you strike, still no fish. I am convinced that this fish has hands, and that it uses them to tease us by viciously pulling the bait. If you persevere – you will be rewarded. *It do fight.*

Stonebream: Generally a positive take – you will hook into it. Fights well. Don't like the flesh much though.

'Simon'. [Salmon, Kob] Irrespective of the type of bait you are using, do not strike hard. Merely tighten your line and strike or you will snap your line. And don't look to steel wire for protection – they know when you use it - They won't bite if they feel wire!

Grunter, pompano – you had better be close to your rod! Be prepared to fight this fish to the end before it can be beached / boated.

Mullet. A very shy fish. Small hooks and perseverance. Good fighter too. You need a light action rod – this fish is soft mouthed. You use too much of pressure and you will almost certainly lose the fish. And don't cast into the shoal. Cast just ahead of the fish without a sinker. Use a float.

Karanteen, Pinkies - strike lightly when you feel the 'tak tak tak". Fish light, size 14 – 8 hooks.

Toby [puffer fish]– I've seen them jump out the water and walk up the beach and then take the hook. Don't believe me? Why would you even *WANT* to hook one?

Bronzies [bronze bream]. These beasties generally toy around with the bait. You can feel when they're there – striking on time comes with experience. Use a float.

Shad – hit when you feel the first "*shukkah shukkah*" don't wait for the third – your bait will already be gone. This outjie likes to grab the bait and swim towards you. I enjoy watching first-timers [some of them on their thirty-seventh trip] shake their heads in disbelief as they reel our and see that the bait has been and will never be again. Even experienced fishermen are not aware of this. When you feel slack line, slowly drop your tip and reel in and strike. You will see the difference. [if your sinker and trace lands behind you when you strike, you might be striking too hard or perhaps you forgot to cast]. Oh yes, if this happens, use your cellar phone to call an ambulance for the guy standing next to you – the one with a sinker in his head!

Kingies [kingfish]. This is a huge family of fish. The bite is simple, fly or bait or artificial lure: you are holding the rod in your hand, reel locked with a 'shifting spanner, and you watch dazed as the rod speeds away over the breakers. Seriously – make sure you have fighting experience before you target the bigger species. If it's a fight you want, it's a fight you'll get!

Yellowtail. When he takes, you'll know, spoon, spinner, bait or fly. You will know, and then you'll be a man my son. Even if you are a girl, you'll be a man, my son!

Cape snoek and walla walla. If they don't take the bait aggressively, they tend to just take it in the mouth and all you feel is a steadily increasing weight [you do know that you *are* fishing mid-water! – these fish are seldom caught on the bottom.] Wait for at least two seconds and then pump! Be ready for a fight although, more than often, I have been disappointed with the fight put up by snoek. *Watch out for the teeth!*

Dorado. Yup! If you can't hook this fish when it bites, shame! You must be unconscious – comatose or the seventh dwarf: "Dozey". Be vigilant when you are on the boat. You will learn to spot the electric blue, yellow and green of the dorado. This fish will circle anything that floats. Spotting it is catching it – all you then have to do is put a fly / bait in its path. Positive take. Careful – this fish is often accompanied by sailfish!

Sharks, rays, skates. Although I have caught many species from this huge family of fish, I have never focused on this group as a target – My hobby and my life has made me target the edibles – I seldom fish for sport although I often practice catch and release. But, nonetheless, should one of these steam trains take your bait, I have a hunch you'll know – there is nothing subtle about how they take a bait. They will put you and your tackle to the '*extremest*' of tests. Get ready for pain! Have a masseuse handy and water to cool the reel down.

Other salt-water fish. They generally pull hard enough to get your attention – if you strike whilst they are pulling, you should be a-okay.

Live bait: Remember that there will almost always be a frenzy of activity from your live bait as it is approached by a game fish. This is your early bite warning. When a predator takes live bait, it does not swallow on the spot. If you are missing a take on live bait, chances are that you are striking too early. The other reason is hook size. Generally, the hook bend should be 30 – 50% of the girth of the live bait. My general rule is 8 seconds before I strike. Allow the fish to run for at least 8 seconds before you switch from freewheel ratchet to strike mode. As you prepare to strike, turn off freewheel, lower the rod whilst reeling in, take a step back [not if you're balancing on a rock!] and pump. Leave all else to the power of learning and adrenalin. And when you strike, try and remember the breaking strain of the line you're using.

Pinkies and other smaller reef fish.com. Light rod, small hooks, small bait, light sinker or small sinker on the drift. Tip down when you feel the bite, raising the rod sharply whilst reeling at the same time should result in the hook being fished [you mean what I know].

Galjoen. The South African national fish. aka 'damba', 'black bream'.

Hey – you're normal! Only a select few are proficient at hooking these! A hookup rate of 1 in 10 is pretty good odds for these fish. I don't know many spearos who are successful at hunting galjoen either. This fish likes toying around with the bait. A longer snoot [my word for the length of the hook-line] helps as the bait drifts around and becomes more attractive in the process. When you feel the fish, slacken your line and strike on the pull [it's not the striking it's the re-baiting and waiting for the pull!] Nothing much more that I can tell you here – only that experience counts!

Dolphins – If you're missing them, you're doing just fine, mate. *Keep it up!*

Barracuda, Natal Snoek – Well if you can't hook one of these after that solid take, something's wrong with you – try golf – it will be less stressful. Both will give you a truly delicious, orgasmic fight. To make up for it, you'll have one helluva time getting the hook out its mouth if you fish catch and return. That's one frisky fish! General rule – the lighter the tackle – the more successful you will be in getting strikes. But be considerate if there are other boats around you as light tackle necessitates long runs, so other boats in the area will become a problem!

Seals – Yeah, I know I just want to *donder* them when I fish Cape waters, but I learnt how to Breathe! Breathe! Breathe! Anger management sucks – but it works. OH yes, and a black label.

Mudsuckers – if you can feel the take, you'll hook them. These guys fight well but are truly difficult to hook. Trout are easier to catch on fly.

Tilapia – like Bluegills and small bass, if you're missing the bite, …. Okay – maybe I shouldn't give advice like that. But Tilapia is one of the easiest fish to catch. If you're using the right bait then your problem has to be hook size. You are using a hook, aren't you?

Rainbow trout: Nothing to say here – make sure the worms are fresh – Oh! Wrong advice [that's for when you are alone in the boat]. These fish generally take a fly boldly. You have to strike on the take. So many bites are missed because of slack line or because the angler hasn't a clue. This fish is capable of mouthing the fly and spitting it out. If you didn't have slack line and wasn't wearing gloves, you might have felt those subtle takes. Stretch and warm those fingers regularly – numb fingers won't feel those subtle takes. Mark your line so it will act more readily as a bite indicator.

Brown trout: Very shy, very skittish. You have to practice [and maybe own] Stealth to catch these. Oh yes, and the lighter the leader – tippet combination, the better.

Use flies with small hooks [size 12 – 16]. Oh – and keep out of sight.

Bass and other game fish – artificial lures: You are probably striking too soon. I have found that a 1 to 2 second pause as soon as you feel the lure "stopped" - then strike.

Carp – when you get false bites – the *policeman* [bite indicator] is nodding up and down and there are no takes, I have found that reeling in a couple of turns does it. Although I disapprove of the use of a bomb, it's your choice. The normal bite with a *policeman* should involve a movement of at least six inches before you strike [the *policeman* should be located not closer than 30 cm to the rod tip].

RELATED TO SINKERS:

Wherever you are fishing, if you cast and land in a mudbank – chances are that you have lost your sinker. Unless you can literally stand over the spot where the sinker landed and apply steady hand pressure, you will never pull that sinker out. And in the odd occasion, if you do pull it out, it becomes a projectile. This condition is predominant after floods and when water levels drop, exposing mudbanks.

Sinker stuck, fish on:

If you are using one a grapnel sinker – you are really putting your knot tying skills and your tackle to extreme pressure. Leader knots must be touched with superglue. Allow slack line and the fish has a good chance of releasing the sinker for you.

Can't feel the bite

Snoot too long and the bite is not 'telegraphing' back to you.

High-risk of sinker getting stuck

Use a snapper swivel connecting your main line to the sinker. If you get stuck, the swivel will release under pressure.

Keep missing bites that I get only while reeling in:

Causes:

Change over to a suitable sized lure – something is striking your sinker.

RELATED TO FLOATS:

I can see the bites, but I keep on missing when I strike:

You have to realize that it is extremely difficult to strike and hook a fish if you're using a float, and the line between the rod tip and the float is not reasonably straight. Slack line again, guys. Remember –**any** slack line, and when you strike, all you are doing is pulling the slack line before any force is exerted on the hook and you are almost certain to lose the fish.

Simple rule – if you cannot control the degree of straightness between the rod tip and the float, don't use the float – or if you have a longer rod that will help achieve this, there you go!

No movement on the float, yet my bait is stripped from the hook:

- You are fishing too deep [your bait is lying on the bottom and the bite is not being transmitted to your float]
- You are swinging too violently when you cast and your bait is thrown clear off the hook before it lands in the water.
- Is there *chokka* [squid] where you are fishing? Also prawns. These critters don't bite as you would expect fish to normally bite. They strip your bait slowly and imperceptibly – normally in lagoons or in the bay.
- Float is too buoyant – use a smaller flat.

RELATED TO THE USE OF WADERS:

If you fall into the water wearing waders, you won't drown as long as you don't panic. Waders will not drag you down. Can you swim? If you can swim, you should be able to get to the bank wearing waders. Just ensure that the waders are fastened around the chest / thigh [whatever] so that they don't balloon when you propel yourself forward through the water and act as a drogue [brake]. When you get to the bank, don't try to stand up. Roll onto your back and raise your legs, emptying water from the waders first. Then you can get up. If you can't swim, the waders will not have anything to do with you playing the harp in heaven.

Funny thing – why do people always test the limits to which they can wade?

Watch it when you're wading in a river. Current has this nasty habit of increasing as the volume of water increases. Watch water levels carefully.

Playing a fish and wading:

[This may, at times, have nothing to do with waders] Remember one thing – there is no way that a section of water remains exactly the same. With time, everything changes, so don't rely too heavily on past knowledge of a fishing spot, especially when it involves going into the water. When wading and fighting a fish, you may easily be sucked into the current in a river, or slip into a hole, or step on broken glass / rusting metal. Be vigilant.

RELATED TO BOATING:

Kick-boating in rivers:

- Avoid using a float-tube in rivers. Too much of your body is in the water. Even if you are familiar with the waters – things change and can change drastically. The parts of your body that are submerged are exposed to a high injury risk.
- Use a life jacket on large waters – you may be a good swimmer, but so many things can compromise your ability to swim.

- If you have a fish on and you get caught in the current, what do you do? Chances are it's a yellow and it will go thundering upstream, trying to shake the hook. Whenever I go fishing with my kick boat, I always carry a stout length of soft rope. I use this to anchor myself to rocks and trees.com, and to keep myself out of the current or to hold myself in the current.
- When you are in rapids, enter feet-first even if you have a fish on. You can see and take evasive action as and when necessary. If the water is really wild, use your rope and flippers to paddle like mad to the side. Never waste time and energy paddling against the current [unless you're approaching water falls!]. Your attempt is always more productive oblique to the current. If you have a fish on, go with the flow – watch you don't make the mistake of giving too much of line!
- Remember if you are floating in a kick boat – you look like an island to creatures in the water. They may try and take refuge on you. Otters and snakes may try to climb onto you. If it is a snake, try and push it away with your rod.

Panic is a killer. **Don't**.

Remember that you are facing forwards – what if you are approached from behind?

I am in the current and there is a tree trunk lying / floating in the water, the river flows under the tree trunk / obstacle: Whatever you do, avoid the tree trunk. The current will try and drag you and your kick boat under, and you could end up being pinned to the trunk or below the trunk.

Make sure that just about everything is fastened to the kick boat with a lifeline or securely organized. Pockets should have zippers / Velcro, containers must be able to float, net and fish bag attached to the boat. You should always have a quickly-detachable lifeline to the boat. Your rod should be lashed in as well. You know what a life jacket is for? Carry a pool noodle if you don't want to wear a life jacket.

A boat with a motor should also have oars in case of emergency. If you are caught out without oars, wrap your shirt or some other cloth around your landing net and use it as an oar.

If you are going to leave the boat, make sure that it is secured and will not be blown away by the wind / current.

Never step onto the side of a boat, or on the seat: Stepping onto the side of the boat will almost certainly result in the boat taking water, or you taking water, or both. If you are getting into a boat from the water, get in over the back end [stern]. Never stand or move without warning others on board.

Punctured kick boat.

Don't panic. If your kick boat has just one inflatable chamber, you will appreciate that you might have made a fatal mistake. I have a block of polystyrene that I sit on when I am in my kick boat – it doubles up as a lifebuoy. You know those pool 'noodles'? Maybe you should carry one with your kick boat. A life-jacket is also an option – avoid the inflatable types as hooks love them.

Losing fish on anchor line:

How could you? Use side strain to keep the fish away, and when you feel the anchor rope rubbing against your line, you need to pass your rod over / under the anchor rope – safely and quickly without swamping the boat. It always pays to use a one hook trace as the second [or other hooks] always tends to find whatever snag is present.

If a boat has floorboards, use them.

They are there to prevent you from putting weight directly on the outer wall.

Standing in a boat and fishing, no stripping basket

I was fishing my friend *Garreth* Olivier's dam at his old farm in Thornville. Standing in his two-man rowing boat, alone, fly-fishing. I didn't see the grass carp. The grass carp didn't see me. I watched as the dry fly vanished in a tiny swirl about 5metres from me. Fish sees me, me sees fish. Fish takes off with a tremendous swirl, line shooting through rod guides, and loop gets stuck around row-lock. Result: Broken rod, no fish. The fish was more than a meter long! *Use a stripping basket.*

Leaning over side of boat to land / whilst fighting fish:

If you wanted to go for a swim, why didn't you wait until after you landed the fish?

Seriously now… A boat is designed to float and if you lean over the side, it will try and compensate. Avoid leaning over the side. Avoid standing near the side, particularly on small boats.

Fishing at night from a boat, light on:

Mainly in lagoons and often out at sea, a light shining into the water will attract fish that will sometimes try and jump into the boat – as much as this sounds like a good thing, it is not – you could be hurt by certain fish – they come in at speed. Avoid shining lights into the water at night.

Anchor stuck:

Keep a sharp knife handy if the anchor holds fast or the current is threatening to swamp the boat. You might need to cut the anchor rope. You might have a problem releasing or breaking an anchor with a chain. Use the quick-release mechanism if your life is under threat – better to lose just an anchor…

RELATED TO BEING CHASED/POISONED/STUNG/BITTEN

[Yes, this will prevent you from fishing, thereby causing you not to catch fish]. A knowledge of the first aid that may be necessary for the area you are fishing in is essential. Being poisoned means that you have actively eaten or touched something you shouldn't have – venomous means the poison/toxin is actively introduced into you by biting / stinging / stepping on / spitting.

Chased:

Many wild creatures will give chase if you approach them too closely or if you infringe on their territory. The most common stories are about Rhinos and Hippos [we don't hear about lions chasing people because the lions generally catch those people!].

You really have no reason to be on foot in areas supporting these creatures or other creatures that can and will chase you / attack you. Rhinos do not have good eyesight but will charge at you if they hear or see you. Hippos, buffalo and donkeys probably cause more human fatalities than all the other animals combined so don't take this lightly. Hippos are fiercely territorial will also charge a campfire at night and try to trample it out, and if you are in the way… Hippos seem ungainly but can run faster than you and they can swim much faster than you can.

And animals with young must be avoided – the parents will perceive you as a threat if there are babies around.

Hippo/croc. This would be a good time to walk on water! Run! Leave the fish. Leave the rod. Pray. In your will, leave your valuables to me.

Snakes. Remember that snakes will attempt an attack if you are blocking off their escape route, particularly if you are between them and their homes. If they rise with the upper body off the ground, *they are not posing for a photograph*. Back away and get out of there.

Puff adders are muscular short snakes with pattern on the back, resembling arrows pointing towards the tail. People are bitten by this snake mainly because they step on it – keep your eyes open in the bush! Widespread and arguably the biggest cause of snakebite deaths.

The **Rinkhals** is a black brown hooded snake with light creamy marks below the head. Make sure you have glasses on. It spits. Accurately. That's why its other name is the spitting cobra. Just back away from the snake a safe distance, allowing it to escape.

The **black mamba** is an olive greeny brown – blackish colour. The underside is an off-white to khaki in colour. It has a small hood which is spread if it intends to bite. It is called a black mamba because the inside of the mouth is black. If you are blocking a mamba's escape route, you are in trouble…

The **Cape Cobra** is a browny-gold hooded snake. It does not like to be disturbed and can be very vicious.
The **boomslang** and green mamba are safe as long as you leave them alone.

Stung:

Be wary of **bees**. Some people are allergic to bee stings and some people have never been stung. If you are in the last category, treat yourself as allergic and stay away. If a bee settles on you, brush it off lightly. Any aggressive behavior by you will result in an aggressive response from the bee. The bee will sting you if threatened. Remember it is prepared to die. If someone has been stung, the sting has to be removed. This has to be done carefully, preferably using a tweezer whilst not squeezing the sting too tightly or you will inject more venom into the site. Also, whether using a tweezer, needle or knife that the best practice is to sterilize the implement. You do not want to complicate things by introducing bacteria to the broken skin. If there are more bees around, beware!

Don't take bee stings lightly – many people die each year from bee stings. Remember that when you are stung, the bee releases a pheromone that literally instructs all bees in the vicinity to go into attack mode.

Wasps and hornets on the other hand can sting repetitively so the best policy is avoidance and also non-aggressive behavior. Avoid killing the creatures if you can.

You generally will look for shade when choosing a spot. Scout the area for **beehives** or **wasp / hornet nests**. If you see these, remember avoidance is the best policy. I sometimes find that with bees, I take a paper plate and pour some cool drink in it and leave it about 5m from the fishing spot. The creatures will be attracted to this more readily.

Be especially wary if you are drinking from a can / bottle. Bees may enter and you may inadvertently take a bee into your mouth… *This can kill you whether you are allergic or not*. How? Well the tissue in your mouth can swell to such an extent that it could block your breathing. Time for a tracheostomy.

Certain insects can also sting you. Scout the vegetation for hairy worms, **fire ants** and red ants. Each hair on a hairy worm has stinging cells. Avoidance, avoidance, avoidance.

When on the beach, look out for a bluish, semitransparent egg-shaped object floating on the water [on average 2-4cm long] – this is the Portuguese man-of-war, the **bluebottle**. It has meters of tendrils on which are mounted 100's of stinging cells [nematoblasts]. Stinging cells are triggered by touch, like a landmine is triggered to explode by pressure.

If stung, get the person out of the water. Remove the tendril – you actually can use your fingers – if squeamish or scared, use something to lift it off the skin or it will continue triggering stinging cells. The stories about vinegar and urine are not true – you have broken skin – why would you want to bathe it in acid? Some people are of the opinion that vinegar stops the nematoblasts from 'firing' and does not relieve your symptoms.

Hot water breaks down the toxin – bathe the area with water as hot as the person can handle for 10-20 minutes until the pain abates. An anti-inflammatory ointment will help. Ice can relieve the pain by numbing and reducing inflammation. If the person has chest pains or starts going into anaphylactic shock, get them away for treatment.

You see, it pays to be vigilant – prevention is better than cure.

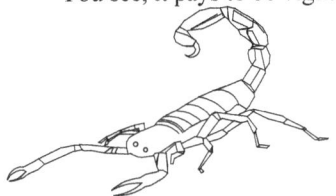

You should also be aware if there are **scorpions** in the area you are fishing. If there are, you do not want to be picking up / moving rocks where you will disturb these creatures. If you are unfortunate enough to be stung, and if the creature has thin pincers and a *thickish* tail, seek professional help, taking the creature along with you.

I am no doctor, but I carry dressings, antihistamine, antibacterial creams / tablets and simple drugs like aspirin and paracetamol. Clear the drugs you carry with your medical practitioner beforehand. And check expiry dates. Keep them in your **first aid kit**.

Bitten:

And then there are spiders.

These make great bait but you risk getting bitten. Button spider bites will require medical help. Some of the more dangerous spiders are the Black Widow, The poison Sac Spider and the Violin Spider. But treat all spiders as dangerous. So – these occur throughout Southern Africa. It means that your fishing trip is over and you can't catch fish. So just look out for webs and careful when reaching under rocks and into crevices.

Sac Spider *– this honey brown arachnid is very aggressive and will bite you. Bites aren't noticed until too late. Cytotoxic venom – designed to destroy living tissue.*

Violin spider *A brown spider, much smaller than the sketch alongside – nocturnal – therefore most spider bites are not noticed until the skin* *starts rotting away – the only way to deal with this is to have the dead skin excised. There is the shape of a violin on the cephalothorax [head].*

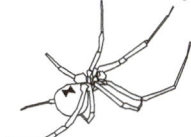 **Black Widow.** *The venom has a neurotoxin and you will need hospitalization and anti-venom. Black or brown and small, it is generally the female whose fangs are large enough to inflict a bite. Identifiable by a* **red** *'hourglass] symbol on the underside of the abdomen.*

And of course, there are **ticks** [not a true insect].

 If you are in an area where there are cattle / wild animals, be on the lookout for ticks. These buggers generally climb up grass blades and stalks waiting for something to walk on by, latching themselves to your clothing and crawling until they find flesh. They generally look for areas like the back of the thigh, behind your knees and in your groin. After walking through long grass, examine your clothing. If one has latched itself onto you, use a heated needle or cigarette to get it to retract its head from your flesh. If you pull it out, you risk breaking off the head and leaving it embedded in your flesh. I have had tick bite fever three times – well I'm an ox and didn't know that I had it each time until the embedded tick heads were found…. You do not want to go there.

 **Mosquitoes.** If you are in a malaria belt, you should be taking the necessary meds. This works well if you start taking it a week before you embark on your trip. Use the repellants, most of them work well enough if applied correctly. *Mozzies* are carriers of Malaria [blood borne disease] and have recently been found to carry other vile viruses & bacteria. You can't fish if you're sick – besides, Malaria can kill you if misdiagnosed.

 The **tsetse fly** This little bugger is responsible for thousands of deaths annually. Check those exotic areas you plan on visiting and be aware of this fly which transmits the dreaded 'sleeping sickness' by sucking your blood.

Horseflies. They will suck your blood.

Rats, bats, dogs and other biting animals. Treat all bites as potentially rabid and seek medical attention.

Treat most freshwaters as having **bilharzia**. Do not enter the water if you have broken skin. Aquatic snails are carriers of bilharzia – you want to use them a bait sometimes. Handle with care.

Lionfish and **stonefish** feed off the bottom in shallow gullies and pools on the coastline. They catch their prey by ambushing them and lie still in the water. Should you step on them, certain of their spines can inject you with a world of pain… and possibly death if no medical attention is received.

Can you believe that a fish like the **puffer fish** is amongst the most poisonous in the world? The skin and certain organs contain a deadly toxin that can and will neutralize you by attacking your nervous system. It is considered a delicacy in Japan = hell – I'm pretty adventurous but… People die every year from consuming the flesh from these creatures! Don't try it!

The **saltwater barbel [catfish]** has spines that will inject venom into you. The meat of this fish makes for delicious eating but before you get to eat it, handle them with care! The pectoral fins and the dorsal fins each have a spine that is sharp and can dig into you injecting you with venom. Most people use a side cutting pliers to snip off these fins before the fish is handled.

Sea urchins can inject you with venom if you step on them, but mostly, you are in trouble if you step on the spines – these break off inside your flesh upon penetration…

Stingrays have a spine on their tail capable of delivering a toxin that is capable of stopping your heart – so handle them carefully.

And then there's **man** [effluent generated by man's processes]. I read recently that a preliminary study was conducted on mercury levels in fish and indications were that fish have accumulated dangerous levels. I know that the study is ongoing, but I wouldn't regularly consume fish caught in any of our busy ports!

Almost all freshwaters have **leeches** - these critters latch onto your skin and suck blood out like vampires. Most of them are very small and become engorged quite quickly [yup – your blood!] They should not be pulled out but should be forced to release using a cigarette end or heated knife tip [please don't burn yourself!]. You will need to apply pressure to the bite site as they introduce anti-coagulants into the bite site to stop your blood from clotting so that they can suck you dry.

Simply being alert and making sure you do not walk into spider webs, looking out for hives and nests and hairy worms and ant colonies will make a difference. Avoid putting your hands / feet where you cannot see them. Before you put on shoes / boots, turn them upside down and tap them vigorously, making sure no surprises are waiting for your *'toesies'*. Shake out clothing before you put them on, shake and dust sleeping bags.

Preventive action, not corrective action.

POISONOUS PLANTS:

You may find edibles that have been contaminated with insecticide or worse. Make sure that any edibles you pick are thoroughly washed [fruit, spinach, mushrooms…]. But there are some plants you must be aware of and familiar with. You will be surprised to note that of the 10 most poisonous plants, most of them aren't very far from your home – as a matter of fact, some of them are in your homes!

You may well wonder how poisonous plants can prevent you from catching fish. Well, second to fishing, our national pastimes involve braaing [barbeques], and there are many toxic plants that may be used for kindling when starting a fire…. And there are many fruit and berries, too many to mention that are poisonous in one way or another…. Make sure children are aware of poisonous plants, fruit and berries and creatures.

So just from an innocent act of gathering firewood, you can get poisoned.

Simple contact is enough with some plants, and with others, burning releases noxious vapours, water intensifies acidic / alkaline properties… Some of the more common ones are:

Oleander – This is a flowering shrub with pink / white / purple / reddish flowers, 5 petals, each petal ending in a flat tip. The leaves are elongated with a central main vein. The branches are hardy and tough. Makes nice kindling…. Don't use it. The fumes are toxic and will poison food it comes into contact with.

Syringa. The leaves of this tree are mostly used for decorating Hindu temples. The plant has green berries which form in bunches and turn a shade of khaki when dry. Both the fruit and leaves are poisonous and I wouldn't recommend using the wood for fires.

Tamboti. This is a widespread ordinary-looking indigenous tree. ***No parts may be used in starting or sustaining fire. Will render meat poisonous and can kill you.*** Small oval pointed leaves. The fruit look like apples with three clear spherical bulges, Fruit are a pale green in colour with red brown tinges in places. The tree also has branches that have smaller fruit in clusters – each fruit resembles a cone from a gum [eucalyptus] tree. The larger fruit resembles an apple.

Castor oil plant. ['*Jamal*' tree] Used as a decorative bush in some gardens. One seed can kill a fully-grown man! The plant has leaves in various shades of reds, purples, violets and pinks with a greenish colour on the back of the leaf. The leaves are star-shaped and *knobbly* and the stems are fleshy and hairy. Flowers are hairy pink beauties growing in clusters. The seeds resemble beans. I have not encountered this plant in the wild.

The Devil's trumpet No doubt you have seen this shrub at construction sites and in fields. It is toxic. Seeds sometimes are harvested with maize or other grain and introduced into our systems after milling.

Bushman's poison apples. These look like miniature apples. Ingestion of the fruit can kill you. These plants were used by *san bushmen* to taint arrow tips with poison. The fruit resembles an elongated miniature apple and grows in clusters on a shrub. Will poison meat if used in a fire.

Take care, and see you on the water!
I do hope that you enjoy reading and using this book as much as I enjoyed writing it!
Good luck out there and be safe!!!

Annexures

	PRE-TRIP LIST
1.	☐ A copy of my book [essential] ☺
2.	☐ Fishing license, ID book, passport, cash, proof of booking if you are going to a resort. Border documents – always check for compliance requirements if you are leaving the country
3.	☐ Hat/cap and polarised glasses, reading glasses, magnifying glass
4.	☐ Rags to wipe hands
5.	☐ Spare line for emergency topping up of a reel, tracing up, leaders and shock-leaders
6.	☐ Wire for steel traces. Ferrules for the steel wire, crimping tool
7.	☐ A selection of hooks for the species you are targeting. Treble hooks for live baiting and lures
8.	☐ A selection of swivels and snapper swivels
9.	☐ Split rings and clips to attach lures, hooks and traces
10.	☐ A selection of floats
11.	☐ Fishing lures and flies
12.	☐ Pre-tied traces
13.	☐ Superglue for knots [buy the long-life type]
14.	☐ Bite indicator / policeman / fluorescent / other
15.	☐ A selection of weights ['sinkers'] including split shot and strip lead
16.	☐ Landing net / gaff. Will the handle be long enough to permit you to safely land your fish?
17.	☐ Is there need for a 'drop net'? refer to Chapter 8 for this item
18.	☐ Hook disgorger. See my design above. Make your own
19.	☐ Lip landing device [if you must use one]
20.	☐ Spring / electronic balance
21.	☐ Keep net
22.	☐ Cast net
23.	☐ Rod bucket [the kind you buckle around your waist to protect your midsection when fighting fish]. This will protect you from injury.
24.	☐ Bucket / container for live bait, aerator [battery operated / 12volt] and/or oxygen tablets for aerating water
25.	☐ Priest [a club used to administer the 'coup de grace' knock a fish senseless = is there any other way to describe it?]
26.	☐ Kick boat, flippers, hand pump / electric pump
27.	☐ Net for catching bait / checking life forms prevalent in the area
28.	☐ Prawn / worm pump and floating sieve
29.	☐ Rod stands and a spare rod stand for the baiting area so you do not have to set your rod on the ground or against rocks or other structures
30.	☐ Fine cotton for whipping + sewing and bait needle
31.	☐ Bait cotton [latex]
32.	☐ Spare reel and other reels
33.	☐ Rods and spare fishing rod
34.	☐ Gaff
35.	☐ Maps [the area you access may not have reception for your phone
36.	☐ Bomb mixture for carp ground baiting
37.	☐ Dips, *'boilees'* and pips
38.	☐ Bait knife and scissors and bait cutting boards. Sharpener / whetstone/sandpaper
39.	☐ Towel and spare clothes
40.	☐ Warm hooded top
41.	☐ Gloves

42.	☐ Raincoat, gumboots, umbrella
43.	☐ Waders. Wetsuit
44.	☐ Life jacket, pool noodle to make bungs and floats for bait
45.	☐ Tent and groundsheet. Don't forget the anchoring spikes for the tent
46.	☐ Sleeping bag
47.	☐ Gas lamp / lantern and stove. Candles, two litre bottles to render candles wind-proof
48.	☐ Gas lamp mantle
49.	☐ Spare batteries
50.	☐ Ski rope coz you never know what you will need to tie down
51.	☐ Refuse bags and plastic packets. Ground sheets to protect upholstery.
52.	☐ A roll of insulation tape. This is great for taping on floats without having to tie them in. many other uses
53.	☐ Headlight & / or torch [flashlight]
54.	☐ Matches / lighter + [emergency matches or a lighter kept in a waterproof bag along with your licence and other important documentation]
55.	☐ Toilet paper, paper towel
56.	☐ Toilet spade [shovel]
57.	☐ A bottle of water as emergency water
58.	☐ Cooler boxes for food and bait, spare containers
59.	☐ Pegs. Great for keeping plastic or other bags closed. Can also be taped to a stick and making a makeshift rod stand
60.	☐ Spices
61.	☐ Food and fruit [plan daily menus so you can buy only what you need to carry and generate shopping lists]
62.	☐ Knife and spoons for cooking, can and bottle openers
63.	☐ Cutlery
64.	☐ Pots, pans, three-legged / cast iron pot, stand for pot
65.	☐ Salt tablets for electrolyte replacement / isotonic
66.	☐ Aluminium foil
67.	☐ Firewood, charcoal, firelighters
68.	☐ Axe / bush knife / machete
69.	☐ Generator / inverter and fuel in proper containers, 2-stroke oil if required, necessary cables and extensions, spare globes and fittings, stands for lights
70.	☐ Phone charger, phone, spare sim if you are going out of the country
71.	☐ Tools including screwdrivers, long-nosed pliers
72.	☐ Small first aid kit [*panado*, gauze, antibacterial crème, anti-diarrhoea meds, malaria meds, deep heat, insect repellent, *allergex* …]
73.	☐ if any member of your group is on medication, make sure that they carry what is needed for the duration of the trip
74.	☐ Ice
75.	☐ milk powder/long life milk
76.	☐ juice concentrate
77.	☐ alcoholic beverages
78.	☐ water
79.	☐ Cool drinks
80.	☐ 12volt air pump / manual pump
81.	☐ And … Don't forget the bait! Check what you will need to take with and what can be obtained at the spot.
82.	☐ Soap, toothpaste and toiletries. Carry unscented soap for when you are fishing.
83.	☐ If you are going to watch TV, carry your satellite card and DVD's
84.	☐ playing cards and games

85.	☐ Tow-rope, spade [shovel]
86.	☐ a list of all persons coming on the trip and an account of monies paid
87.	☐
88.	☐
89.	☐
90.	☐
91.	☐
92.	☐
93.	☐
94.	☐
95.	☐
96.	☐
97.	☐
98.	☐
99.	☐
100.	☐

Index

'bullet' sinkers, 24
abalone, 99
Abalone, 72
Acknowledgements, xiii
action of the rod, 3
ACTS OF NATURE / GOD, 200
adjustable drag systems, 7
African pike, 169
After dark bite indicators, 53
Alikreukel, 66, 89
Angelfish, 104, 129, 141
ANTS, 159
Armadillo, 67, 89
Artificial baits, 54
artificial lures in salt water, 119
audible alarm, 53
Baardman, 104, 129, 141
back cast, 198
backing, 9
bait caster, 9
Baiting up for pan fries, 93
Balancing your tackle, 39
Balsa-wood floats, 27
banana-bunch trace, 46
Barb too big, 204
Barbel, 85
Barbels [catfish], 180
barbless, 22
barracuda, 95
Barracuda, 104, 129, 138, 207
Barrel sinkers, 25
bass, 88
Bass, 208
bats, 213
Beaching, 31
bees, 211
BEETLES, 159
bilharzia, 213
Bite indicators, 52
biting animals, 213
Bitten, 212
black mamba, 211
Black Musselcracker, 106, 133, 143
Black mussels, 71, 98
Black Tip Shark, 108, 135, 140
Black Widow, 213
Blacktail, 104, 129, 141
Blood Snapper, 108, 136, 145
Blood worm, 70
BLOODWORM, 159
bloodworm', 167
bluebottle, 212
Boat fishing, 174
BOATING, 209
Bonefish, 104, 129, 141
Bonito, 129, 138
boomslang, 211
braid, 188
Braid, 15
Bread, 59
bread crust, 82
breed earthworms, 66
bronze bream, 206
Bronze bream, 104, 129, 141
Brown trout, 208
Bullet sinkers, 24
Bung floats, 28
bung', 96

Bushman's poison apples, 214
butterflies, 167
BUTTERFLIES, 159
Buzzer, 167
BUZZER, 160
BUZZER LARVAE, 159
caddis, 167
CADDIS FLY, 160
CADDIS LARVA, 160
CADDIS NYMPH, 160
CADDIS PUPA, 160
Can't cast far enough, 199
CAN'T HOOK THE FISH, 205
Cape Cobra, 211
Cape salmon, 97
Cape snoek, 108, 140, 207
cape stumpnose, 109
Captain Fine, 107
Carp, 208
Carp rig, 81
Cast net, 200
Casting, 75
casting clip, 79
casting devices, 80
Castor oil plant, 214
catching pan-fries, 46
catfish, 180, 213
centre pin reel, 75
Centre Pin Reel, 7
Chased, 211
CHASED/POISONED/STUNG/BITT
    EN, 211
Cheap and nasty, 196
Cheese, 67, 89
Chiton, 89
chokka, 74, 102
Circle hooks, 20
clams, 73, 98
Cleaning prawns, 182
Cleaning the crab, 178
Cleaning your catch, 180
Cobia, 104, 129, 138
Collapsing landing net, 200
Cork floats, 27
Corroded / damaged / grooved line
    guides, 185
Corrosion, 6
CORYXID, 161
Coryxids, 169
Couta, 106, 133, 138
Crab, 67, 84
CRAB, 90
Crab bait, 60
Crabbing, 178
Crabs, 169
CRABS, 161
Cracker shrimp, 68, 91
Crankbaits, 57, 114, 125
Crayfish, 69, 92
Crayfish jig, 69
Crayfish trap, 69
CRICKETS, 161
crimping, 45
crocodile, 72
cross-sectional strength, 5
Cuttlefish, 170
damaged / grooved line guides, 185
Damaged reel / guides, 189

DAMSELFLIES, 161
Damselfly, 60
Deep runs and deep pools, 50
Deep sea – bottom fishing, 205
Devil's trumpet, 214
disk braking system, 7
Disposal of line, 16
diving lures, 57, 116, 126
dogs, 213
Dolphins, 207
Dorado, 130, 139, 207
Double taper, 153
Drag mechanisms, 8
drag nut, 7
Drag on too tight / too loose, 187
drag washers, 7
DRAGONFLIES, 161
Dragonfly, 60
Drop nets, 31
Drop shot hook, 112, 121
drop shot hooks, 56, 114
Drop shot hooks, 22
drop-off, 189
Dry fly, 58
Eel catfish, 105, 130, 141
Eels, 180, 195
eezi-cast' device, 78
Elf, 135
Englishman, 130, 142
Estuary Perch, 133, 143
exposure to salt water, 192
Extended fight, 202
extreme changes in weather, 48
eye of the hook, 18
Eye offset, 18
Failure to give line, 197
Fallen trees, 50
Fatigue, 19
FAV knot, 12, 41
Filleting, 182
Filling line, 10
fire ants, 212
FISH, 162, 194
Fish & Fry imitations, 170
Fish bait, 69, 85, 93
Fish baits, 61
Fish breaks free, 194
FISH EGGS, 163
Fish entangled, 190
Fish escapes, 196
Fish escapes down / up-stream, 195
FISHERFOLK, 195
Fishing for Carp, 81
Fishing from a float tube, 172
Fishing into deep water over a sandy
    ridge, 198
FISHING LINE, 187
FISHING ROD, 184
Fishing too light, 188
Fishing with a top bung, 97
Five fingers, 109, 137, 146
fixed spool reel, 79
fixed spool reels, 187
flatfish, 135, 145
Flies, 118
FLIES [TWO-WINGED], 163
float' on spool, 187
floating, 153

216

Floats, 26
FLOATS, 208
flounder', 145
Flour dough, 60
Fluorocarbon line, 15
Fly fishing, 150
Flying ants, 63
FLYING ANTS, 164
Flying gaff, 33
FORGOT SOMETHING, 184
frayed line, 189
freespool, 11
Freshwater shrimp, 65
FROGS, 164
Fruit, 62, 86
Gaffed fish, 199
Gaffing, 33
Galjoen, 105, 130, 142, 207
game fish, 138
gamefish trace, 45
Gap between reel and reel frame., 193
Gape, 17
garland', 92
Garrick, 105, 130, 139, 206
Garrick plugs, 124
geelbek, 95, 97
Geelbek, 105, 130, 142
General attractor patterns, 170
General Attractor patterns, 159
GENERAL ATTRACTOR PATTERNS, 164
glassies, 70
graphite composite rods, 5
Graphite rods, 5
Grapnel sinkers, 23
GRASSHOPPERS, 165
groundbait, 83
grunter, 91, 122
Grunter, 105, 130, 142, 206
GT, 105
Hail, 201
hairy worms, 212
Hake, 131, 142
*Hammerhead **Shark***, 108, 135, 140
Hand line, 177
High strain fight, 193
high water line, 50
Hippo, 211
Hook broke, 203
hook design, 17
Hook disgorger, 35
Hook eyelet, 4
Hook not sharp enough, 203
Hook rusted / pitted, 204
Hook straightened, 203
Hook strength, 202
Hook stuck in finger, 204
hook tears / breaks free, 202
HOOKS, 202
Hooks lying loosely, 205
HOPPER, 165
hornets, 212
Horseflies, 213
How to cast…. My way, 154
inappropriate footwear, 198
Inlets, 50
Insects and spiders, 63, 86
intermediate, 153
jig head, 55
jig head', 112
Joining lines, 41
Karanteen, 105, 132, 142, 206
Kariba worm, 88

Keys, 184
Kick-boating in rivers, 209
*king **mackerel***, 106, 133, 138
kingfish, 207
Kingfish, 105, 132, 139
Kingklip, 132, 142
kob, 95
Kob, 106, 132, 142, 206
kob spoon, 124
Landed fish can't be subdued, 198
Landing aids, 31
LANDING FISH, 199
langoustines, 93
large spot ***pompano***, 107, 134
lead metal, 25
leader and tippet size, 153
Leader knot jams, 191
Leader materials, 16
leech imitations, 113
leeches, 213
LEECHES, 165
less line on the reel, 10
Lightning, 201
Line breaks when casting, 190
line breaks without warning, 191
Line caught in tree / telephone & power lines, 194
Line caught on rod tip, 193
Line degraded, 191
Line guide missing, 184
line guides, 189
Line guides, 6
Line not threaded through guides properly, 185
line on reel, 187
Line tangled on reel, 192
Line too loose on reel spool, 193
Line too old, 191
Line twisted, 192
Lionfish, 213
Lip-landing, 33
Live bait, 95, 207
lizard, 113
LIZARDS, 165
Lobotus, 106, 132, 138, 143
Loose binding, 184
Losing fish on anchor line, 210
Mackerel, 70, 97, 106, 132, 143
Maggots, 63, 87
Marine worms, 70, 97
Marker buoys, 66
Marlin, 139
MAYFLIES, 165
Mayfly, 60
Mealie Meal [corn flour] dough, 64
midge, 160
MIDGE LARVA, 167
MIDGE PUPA, 167
mirrorfish, 105, 132, 139
Miss-casts, 191
mole crab, 74
mole crabs, 101
Molluscs, 170
MOLLUSCS, 167, 168
Moray, 104, 130, 141
mosquitoes, 201
Mosquitoes, 213
MOTHS, 159, 167
MOUSE, 167
Mouse imitation lure, 115
mud prawns, 68, 91
Mudsuckers, 208

Mullet, 106, 133, 143, 206
multiple hooks, 200
multiplier reel, 77
multiplier reels, 187
murky water, 197
Mussel worm, 70
musselcracker, 143
Musselcracker, 106, 133, 206
Mussels, 71
Natal snoek, 107, 134, 139
Natal Snoek, 207
*Natal **stumpnose***, 109, 136, 145
Natural baits, 59
needle hooks, 18
non-return' running trace, 96
Normal gaff, 33
not balanced, 188
Nymphs, 84
NYMPHS, 162, 166
Octopus, 71, 99
Offshore fishing, 138
Old knots, 191
Oleander, 214
Ordinary monofilament line, 14
Outlets, 50
overhanging branches, 80
Overwind, 193
*Oxeye **tarpon***, 109, 136, 145
paddletail, 142
Pear-shaped sinkers, 24
pencil bait, 72, 100
pencil-shaped float, 27
Perch, 106, 133, 143
periwinkle, 66, 89
Perlemoen, 72, 99
pickhandles', 129
Pinkie, 106, 133, 143
Pinkies, 206, 207
Plastic fish and creature imitations, 116, 126
Plastic floats, 27
plastic frog, 116
platanas, 86
Playing a fish and wading, 209
Plugs, 56
POISONOUS PLANTS, 214
policeman', 52
Pollution, 198
pompano, 122, 206
Pompano, 107, 133, 143
Poor knots / poor knotting technique, 191
popper', 115
Popper-type lure, 57
Porcupine quills, 26
Power lines, 186
power rating, 3
Prawn, 72, 99, 170
Press button reel, 79
PRE-TRIP LIST, 36
Prodigal son, 104, 129, 138
propellers', 115
Puff adder, 211
puffer fish, 213
Puffer fish, 107, 134, 143
Punctured kick boat, 210
Pushbutton, 13
Pushbutton reels, 187
Pyramid sinkers, 24
Queenfish, 107, 134, 139
Rainbow trout, 208
ratchet mechanism, 8
Rats, 201, 213

Ray, 135, 145
rays, 207
Rays, 108
Razor clams, 72, 100
razortooth, 32
red ants, 212
red bait, 100
Red bait, 73
Red **Steenbras**, 108, 136, 145
Redfish, 134, 144
Reel broke, 186
Reel jammed, 186
reel seat, 4
Removing the fins, 181
ribbonfish, 109
Rinkhals, 211
rock bait, 73
Rock bait, 100
Rock cod, 107, 134, 144
rock lobster, 69, 92
rod action too stiff, 202
Rod broke, 185
rod butt, 4
rod care, 5
rod comes apart, 186
Rod gone, 185
Rod too stiff / whippy, 185
Roll-casting, 157
rough stuff, 189
Sac Spider, 212
sailfish, 139
Sailfish, 140
salmon, 95
Salmon, 206
salt your bait, 66
saltwater barbel, 213
SALTWATER FLY FISHING, 169
SALTWATER NATURAL BAITS, 66
Saltwater shrimp, 73
Sand mussels, 73
sand prawns, 68, 91
sand shark, 108
Sand soldier, 107, 134, 144
sardine, 96
Sardine, 134, 144
Sardines, 70
S-bend spoon, 56, 123
Scaled species, 180
Scarborough reel, 8, 77
Schematic of a hook, 17
Scottsman, 107, 135, 144
Sea barbel, 107, 134, 144
sea catfish, 107, 134, 144
Sea Cucumber, 73, 101
Sea lice, 74, 101
sea urchins, 73
Sea urchins, 213
Seagull, 201
Seals, 207
SEDGE, 167
Seeds, 65
Seventy-four, 135, 144
shad, 97
Shad, 107, 135, 144, 206
Sharks, 207
Sharpness, 20
Shooting head, 153
Shrimp, 87
SHRIMP, 167
side-cast facility, 76
side-strain, 195

sight-fishing, 199
Sinker stuck, fish on, 208
SINKERS, 208
sinking lines, 153
Skate, 108, 135, 145
skates, 207
skipjack, 108, 136, 140
slack line, 194
Slack line:, 194
Sleeping, 197
slime, 50
slimy rocks, 197
slow action rod, 4
small black tadpoles, 61
Small creatures, 188
SNAILS, 168
Snails, slugs, 65
snake" line guides using monofilament line, 186
Snakes, 196, 211
Snapper, 108, 136, 144
Snoek, 108, 136, 140
Sole, 108, 135, 145
spare line for tying traces, 39
Speciality hooks, 21
spiders, 212
SPIDERS, 168
spin caster, 9
Spinner baits, 55, 112, 121
Spinner blades, 54, 111, 120
Spinners, 55, 112, 121
split shanks, 17, 43
split shot, 23
spool over-filled, 10
spool tension nut, 10
Spoon sinker, 25
Spoons, 56, 114, 123
spotted grunter, 130
Springer, 108, 136, 140
Squaretail Kob, 106, 132, 142
Squid, 74, 102, 170
stainless steel hooks, 17
Star drag, 9
star nut, 7
steel trace, 188
Steenbras, 206
stiff breeze, 205
Stingrays, 213
Stonebream, 206
stonefish, 213
Stonefly, 60
STONEFLY NYMPHS, 168
Storm, 201
storm starts, 186
strepie', 132
Strike Indicators, 154
strike too hard, 203
Strike too weak, 196
Striking too early, 196
Striking too hard, 196
Striking with a float / lure, 205
Striped frogs, 86
Stuck in mud, 200
stumpnose, 109, 122, 145
Stumpnose, 206
Stung, 211
Styrofoam strips, 27
sunscreen, 195
super-fast" action rod, 3
<u>**SUPERGLUE ON KNOTS**</u>, 40
Surf zone fish, 206

Surface Creature imitation lures, 57, 115, 125
Surface fish imitation lures, 57, 115, 125
surface fly, 58
Swimming prawn, 72
Syringa, 214
Tackle 'Box', 150
Tadpoles, 84
TADPOLES, 168
Tadpoles and frogs, 61
Tailing, 32
Tailing device, 32
Tamboti, 214
Tandem hook trace, 44
Tandem plastic bait fishing rig, 117
Tangles, 194
Tapeworm, 71
tarpon, 109, 136
Tear drop sinker, 25
test-cast, 191
Testing hooks, 19
the 'bowline' knot, 46
The 'clip-on' swivel, 30
The 'coffee grinder', 11
The barb, 20
The fight, 147
The gecko, 62
the haywire loop, 45
The landing net, 32
The multiplier reel, 9
The nail knot, 43
The platana, 61
The power swivel, 29
The reel, 152
The rod, 151
The striped frog, 61
The tackle box, 35
The three-way swivel, 29
Threadfin trevally, 105, 132, 139
ticks, 213
Tide, 201
tied on bite indicators, 53
tiger fish., 114
Tigerfish, 169
tilapia, 88
Tilapia, 208
Too much pressure, 202
Too much pressure:, 185
Top and mid-water fishing, 138
toxic substance, 23
Treble hooks, 22
Triple tail bream, 106, 132, 138, 143
trout, 208
tsetse fly, 213
Tuna, 140
twisted, 193
two-piece, 6
two-way swivel, 29
ultra-strong hooks, 18
Using your fingers, 52
Venus ears, 103
Venus Ears, 74
Violin spider, 213
Vundu, 85
WADERS, 209
Wading, 197
Wahoo, 137, 140
walla walla, 207
Walla walla, 109, 137, 140
Wasps, 212
Waste nylon, 188

218

Watching your line, 52
water boatman, 161
WATER BOATMAN, 169
water reeds, 50
Wave Garrick, 107, 134, 143
weedless, 22
weight forward, 153
Weight forward, 153

wet fly, 58
White **musselcracker**, 106, 133, 143
white mussels, 73
White mussels, 98
White **Steenbras**, 109, 136, 145
White stumpnose, 109
whole baby squid, 74
wildeperd, 109, 137, 146

winter, 50
Worm flies, 171
Worms, 65, 88
WORMS, 169
yellow belly, 107
yellowfish, 88

www.ingramcontent.com/pod-product-compliance
Lightning Source LLC
Chambersburg PA
CBHW082334180426
43198CB00039BA/2583